the dynamic company

C000170839

GUIDEBOOK TRADE DISTRIBUTORS   British Isles & General World

CORDEE
3a De Montfort Street, Leicester. LE1 3HD, Great Britain.
Tel: 0116 254 3579   Fax: 0116 247 1176
sales@cordee.co.uk   www.cordee.co.uk

David Atchison-Jones
Chief Editor

The Climbers Handbook to England & Wales
Jingo Wobbly – Euro Guides
First Published in April 2004
By Jingo Wobbly Climbing Books
(An imprint of Vision PC).
Holmwood House, 52 Roxborough Park,
Harrow-on-the-Hill, London. HA1 3AY

Copyright © David Atchison-Jones
Graphics by Botticelli
Image Scanning – Professional Film Company, London
Printing – Fratelli Spada SPA, Roma.

Photos:
Front top left: Golden Mile E5, 6b; Cheetor, Derbs.
(Chris Hamper)
Front top right: The Powerband V10, f 7c+
(Sean Myles)
Lower left: Birmingham World Cup competition
(Indoor wall now at the Rockface)
Lower right: Great White E7 6b; White Tower Pembroke
(Mick Lovatt)

Frontispiece: Pleasure Dome E3,6a Stennis Head,
Pembroke,
(Jason Porter)

Title page:
Windy Bouldering at Sheeps Tor, Dartmoor,
(Steve Glennie)

ISBN   1-873 665 41-5

The CLIMBERS HANDBOOK to ENGLAND & WALES

DAVID ATCHISON-JONES

JINGO WOBBLY CLIMBING BOOKS - LONDON

JINGO WOBBLY EURO-GUIDES

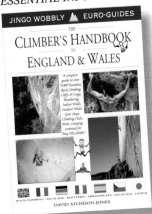

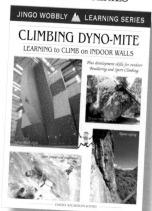

Acknowledgements: To include a full list of people who have helped with this book would run to another complete 16 page section of this book. I would therefore like to collectively thank everyone who has helped and continues to help with this huge project, and hope that the final production of the book acts in itself as a worthy acknowledgement.

JINGO WOBBLY ▲ LEARNING SERIES

CLIMBING DYNO-MITE

LEARNING to CLIMB on INDOOR WALLS

Plus development skills for outdoor Bouldering and Sport Climbing.

Bouldering technique

Alpine safety

Indoor Wall skills

Sport power and endurance

DAVID ATCHISON-JONES

Learning Indoors
This book is written in a clear and modern way that deals with all the aspects of learning to climb at your indoor wall. It will help before and after your early climbing lessons, and give you common sense thinking, before purchasing any climbing equipment. It is designed to be flexible, and allows all styles of beginners instruction at your local wall.

Learning how to climb
A massive 140 pages are given, in learning how to climb and perfect your bouldering moves and body flow. When you have to cope with complex climbing decisions on an outdoor cliff, you will have prepared properly, and be a confident, smooth climber in control.

Learning the ropes
It's always difficult to take in all the ropework and knots involved with climbing when you first begin. With the use of hundreds of photos, all the techniques are clearly and colourfully illustrated, both in the rock gym and outside.

A book that is written and designed for anyone new to climbing

'And oudoors too'

The book doesn't stop inside. It then deals with outdoor sport climbing - top roping and leading. Hazards of outdoor climbing are shown, along with different methods of belaying and climbing techniques. it graduates up to the giant 1000 metre gorges of Europe. All modern sport climbing multi-pitch techniques are illustrated, along with breathtaking photos.

VIA FERRATA SECTION
At the end of the book, there is a special section on Via Ferrata climbing and methods; to give you a fully comprehesive knowledge of European climbing.

CLIMBING DYNO-MITE 288 pages, colour,   **£ 18.95**
Flexibound,   210mm x 151mm (A5)   **ISBN: 1-873-665-71-7**

The title 'Climber's Handbook,' sums up the objective for me. This book has to be the ideal single volume, which includes all the handy information that any climber in England and Wales needs at an instant. If you ever need any address, phone number, or idea of where to go and climb; then you reach for your trusty handbook first. A proper climbers handbook must be something that can stay up to date, be easy to carry, and include a really wide variety of topics and information, and be easy to use. These four remits are critical to the design and concept of the handbook, and only time will tell where we have succeeded, or where we need to improve.

Gathering all the information to include in the handbook has taken a good many years, and started with my Crag Guide to England and Wales that began in the mid 1980's and listed over 1400 cliffs. During that period there was far less information and the www didn't exisit in any significance. The emphasis then was to include absolutely everything and bring to climbers awareness all there was out there. Life has gone full circle and today our biggest problem is information overload. Climbing guidebooks are encylopedic, routes are everywhere, shops sell everything, and every town in the country has a climbing wall - or does it? It became pretty obvious that the task in hand, was to intelligently edit from experince, the right level of information that would always be current and useful, to just about every level of climber.

A handbook is also something that you want to find things in, quickly. We have split up the information into 3 distinct sections. The first part is a series of 21 maps that entirely cover England and Wales, and show the commercial activities associated with climbing, primarily indoor walls and specicalist climbing hardwear and book shops. The second part is a series of maps that cover just about all the climbing areas, with cliffs, campsites, pubs and cafes all shown. The final part is at the back of the book, and is a basic list of names, addresses and phone numbers that could be of general use and save having to go onto the web.

Editing what goes in and what doesn't, is the trickiest part of compiling the handbook. We started with enough information for about 22 volumes! There has been no ultimate strict reason for our choices, other than simply, what would be handy for your average climber who has a job, likes to go climbing at an indoor wall once or twice a month, and likes to get out climbing for the odd weekend. This prime candidate is someone who doesn't have every climbing guidebook to the entire country, doesn't spend 3 hours everyday surfing rockchat websites, and doesn't have time to study and remember every climbing magazine article ever published. This handbook in a way is the answer to - get me highly knowledgeable quick, and also not having to remember a thing since you can always flip open the book for reference anyway.

We could have just compiled a massive directory for climbing but felt it would be a wasted opportunity. An integral part of climbing is inspiration, seeing something that looks like a challenge to climb, and then enjoying the weeks of anticipation before going to try it. It's also something quite instinctive too, if you like the look of somewhere to climb, then you follow a good hunch and have a good time. Nothing is more infuriating than being sold a duff climbing wall over the telephone, only to turn up with the wrong preparation, or with friends that won't even be able to leave the ground.

Our final part was to have as opinion, something which would be impossible for an organisation or club to ever achieve, the members could never agree on anything other than a squishy watered down comprimise. Yes, we have a pretty firm opinion on most climbing issues, it's fun because it often gives the reader something quite juicy to read. We might not get it right every time, and will have those that disagree with our standpoint. But in fairness, we do visit and climb at every wall in the country, take virtually all the photographs ourselves, and do a massive amount of climbing in the UK and all over Europe. Our editorial decision's are based on fact, experience, and maybe an incy wincy bit of wisdom, - and not simply bogus web chitter chattle.

By turning to the inside front cover, you will see a map of England and Wales that shows how we have split up the whole country and what page the index map is on for each area. Down the side of the book are area markers to help you with this when you flip around the book. The maps are not intended to be cartographic wonders, but are to primarily show you the walls and shops in relationship to the main towns and roads. In nearly all of our books, we use a great many icons. They have lots of hidden uses and meanings, but should always work in the simplest of ways to indicate where something is. If you want to take the time to read up on what each icon stands for, then you can extract a lot more information out of the handbook, if you can't be bothered - then it still should work fine for you. If anything has a colour, then the chances are that the colour will give you extra information.

Grotto

3 We mark each climbing wall with a round dot, and a little leader to it's rough location. Yellow for an indoor wall and green for an outdoor wall. In this way you can look at an area quickly, and easily identify all the walls. Opposite the map is a tabular chart that corresponds with the markers. We have done this so you can simply compare all the walls in an area quickly, and decide which wall is best for you. We order the walls only by size from the largest at the top. If it all looks a bit too confusing, then turn over the page and you will find a photo and written description to every wall in the sector, simply make your choice. For those folk with a degree in iconography, the tabular chart will reveal a huge amount of information about each wall, and can save you a wasted journey, or really finding the best place to get pumped solid. When we visit each wall, we chart it out to categorise every piece of climbing surface (we don't accept figures sent to us). We split the wall into bouldering and roped areas, and have 7 whole different categories for bouldering alone. Climbers who are experienced will know the jargon, but for novices - look at the photos to the right. At every wall you can see exactly how much bouldering sqm there is in each category.

Freeform Rock

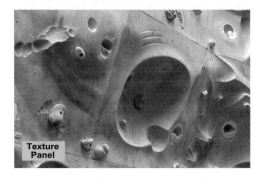

Texture Panel

We split the roped climbing into a maximum of 6 general types, governed by height and angle usually. This is to illustrate how much climbing there is of

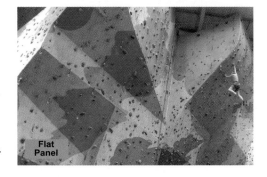

Flat Panel

a particular height, and how hard it is going to be. You may even need a magnifying glass, but you can see how high each sector it, how many individual climbing lines there are (number of people that can climb at the same time), and the set number of routes. We also show the surface texture and rough angle for each sector. This will enable you to choose a wall that has an ideal amount of top roping, or long leading at just vertical, or short cap overhangs. Group leaders will see at an instant if there is a good and extensive instructional area. When you have chosen your wall, they you can turn to find it and see all the relevant useful details such as opening times, phone and address, directions of how to find the wall & parking info. Little icons illustrate the level of facilities on offer. Prices will change, but usually stay pretty consistent.

Brick

Black squares on the maps will show you the climbing shops. If you are climbing in an area and it is a wet day, then knowing all the shops in the area will be of great use and should occupy some time. If you are on the way to a wall or somewhere, just remember to look up the handbook to see if you are passing any climbing shops. We ask shops to illustrate what they permanently stock on the premises, and would make a detour worthwhile in emergency for some gear. We have found shops to underestimate the levels so not to disappoint customers. A lot of shops will do special orders but we don't cover this. We also don't cover camping and walking gear. We use coloured markers to illustrate the rough levels of equipment that the shops keep on stock; Green for beginners, blue for UK climbing, red for European, and purple for world class. If you want something in particular, always ring first.

Woody

Campus Board

SHOES	1-5 different models of rock shoes	GEAR	Screwgate krabs & slings	BOOKS	Local climbing guidebooks
SHOES	6-10 different models of rock shoes	GEAR	Basic harness	BOOKS	Good national collection of guides
SHOES	11-16 different models of rock shoes	GEAR	Nuts on wire, tube belay	BOOKS	European sport climbing books (15)
SHOES	16+ different models of rock shoes	GEAR	Gri Gri	BOOKS	World climbing guides (20 ish)
ROPES	Rope off a reel	GEAR	Via ferrata lanyards	ICE	Basic walking ice axe
ROPES	50 m packeted single 10-11mm ropes	GEAR	10 styles of harness	ICE	Front point crampons
ROPES	50 m packeted double 9mm ropes	ROPES	15 styles of harness & comp harness	ICE	Technical ice climbing gear
ROPES	60 m packeted single 10-11mm ropes	CAMS	Basic Cams	ICE	Avalanche transceivers
ROPES	70 m packeted single 9.7 mm ropes	CAMS	Flexiwire cams		
ROPES	70 m packeted single 9.3mm ropes	CAMS	Tri cams		
ROPES	80 m packeted single ropes	CAMS	Quadcams with fast action		
ROPES	100 m packeted bi-colour ropes	CAMS	Microcams		

The handbook is also intended to be used with web search engines. We are aware of most climbing clubs and list each town if it has a climbing club or a mountaineering club. If you then put these into any good search engine you should be able to find their website and contact them. Club secretaries change, as do web addresses, so we felt this to be the simplest approach. All shops, walls, clubs, cliffs and information supplied in the book is at no charge. Our intention is to have everyone listed.

The second part of the book is easily navigated from the inside back cover. There is a map that shows all the climbing areas in England and Wales, with the page numbers indicated. There are also edge markers on the pages to help too. It is not our intention to list all the cliffs that there are. We have over 2500 on our database, and that is less than half of what there moderately is. Our intention is to show you a good selection of cliffs for anyone new to an area, just so you can easily start in the right direction.

We have plotted most of the usual campsites on every map, and give you a rough indication to the level of toilets and showers, plus opening dates and contact numbers. We list the postcode of every campsite to enable global tracking or internet search accuracy. Out of pure inspiration and necessity, we have included all the good pubs that we visit during our trips each year, and we would be delighted to receive feedback on any good taverns that we have failed to spot or include. At least when we are too old to climb (never), we can spend the summers just checking out the good drinking spots.

How much information to put on the maps has been difficult to decide, and you will notice variations in style. We are interested in feedback on this since it is always a compromise between having stacks of information - versus instant clarity. Our basic system is to use colour to designate the style of climbing to be found at a cliff; blue for trad, red for bouldering, yellow for sport climbing, and a few others - just look at black and some of the radical cliffs! In the central Peak District we have also added ears to this to show the best level of climbing at a cliff - an experiment! All of the general icons are explained on the page marker flaps at either end of the book.

Most cliffs will be included as a simple entry in text, and included for basic awareness. We do not list details of how to find the cliff, but do list the grid reference to every one (virtually) of the 600 cliffs in the handbook. With a good road map and a reasonable GPS tracking system, you should find any cliff and we don't have to print twice the number of pages. Hopefully though, you will be enticed by the description, or photo, or any other details, and be interested in buying a guidebook to the cliff, not that all of the descriptions of how to actually find cliffs are that inspiring. We try to list the guidebooks that each cliff features in and give a little appraisal, and sometimes a jibe at each. All climbing guidebooks are immense pieces of work and deserve tremendous accolade. However, we do feel that a newcomer to an area does need to know what they are getting into, especially when they may be ill prepared i.e. coming from a very low risk climbing wall environment.

Some of the cliffs get a wholly myriad of techno icons that give you rock type, walk in times, cliff height, etc. Our little coloured boxes may need explaining. The colour represents routes of the grade, and a full column means a minimum of 10 routes in that grade. Half means only five, etc. This illustration will show you if there are enough routes to occupy you in a particular grade for an hour or a full day. If there were 3 cliffs in an area with 3 full columns, then you might think about a weekend there and buy the guidebook. If they were all purple (8a) then you might choose somewhere else. Note also that this box is surrounded by a thick black line to illustrate direction of cliff. The more you look, the more you find. Our final piece of innovation is out rock stability scale. In our learning books we have an insanity scale from 1-12, with bouldering being low, and trad starting at grade 7. We have therefore subdivided the numbers 7 and 8 into rock stability around England and Wales. Overleaf are some examples and should prove amusement discussion in the pubs. At least when you see a cliff now with a high rating, you know it is going to be dodgy and that you have to be extra careful. The scale is completely personal and only an overall judgement, rock can always snap on a 7.0 rated cliff. Have a good exploration of the great climbing out there.

CLIMBER'S INSANITY SCALE

	CLIMBING ACTIVITY	RISK INVOLVEMENT	COMPARISON
1	Induction day at an indoor climbing wall	Instructor supervised climbing at a well organised wall	1st lesson in gymnastics
2	Indoor bouldering	A climbing wall with deep and soft crash pads	Judo
3	Indoor Sport climbing Outdoor top rope climbing	Climbing to a controlled height with reliable safety facilities	Sailing
4	Outdoor bouldering	Climbing and assessing as you go on unknown rock	Horse riding
5	Outdoor single pitch sport routes - Via Ferrata	Bolt equipped climbing, with in-situ climbing equipment	Horse jumping
6	Outdoor multi pitch sport routes	Big routes in European river gorges - bolt equipped	Round the world Yachting
7	Traditional - classic style climbing with protection	Free climbing but placing your own protection on lead	Motorbike racing
8	Traditional climbing on loose rock	Climbing where even the protection you place can fail	Isle of Man TT racing
9	Alpine rock climbing	Trad-climbing, at high altitude and 7 hours plus on a route	Cave diving
10	Alpine North Faces	Very steep and committing rock and ice climbing	Solo round the world yachting
11	Himalayan glaciers and remote mountain rangers	Navigating giant glaciers and seracs, severe storms, altitude	Rowing the Atlantic
12	8000 metre peaks	Entering the oxygen free - death zone	Swimming outside the shark netting
13	8000 metre peaks with no experience!!!!!	Killing other climbers in rescue attempts	Trying to outswim a shark

This Jingo Wobbly scale of climbing Insanity, is intended to illustrate the level of objective danger that is associated with each different discipline of climbing. Inexperience or foolhardiness at any level - is the equivalent of grade 13; it is intended to show how much more serious climbing gets when you leave the relatively safe environment of the indoor climbing wall.

7.0 *Very solid, fine grain with no crumbling surface* — **Stanage, Froggatt, Roaches, Black Rocks**

7.1 *Solid but bigger grain with a slight crumbling crust* — **Sennen Cove, Hay Tor, Bridestones, Cratcliffe Tor**

7.2 *Solid and hard, some loose blocks and big flakes* — **Bwlch-Y-Moch, Dow Crag, Shepherds Crag, Milestone Buttress**

7.3 *Solid in general but crumbly areas* — **Dinas Cromlech, Huntsman's Leap Craig Yr Wrysgan, Conger Cove**

7.4 *Solid but snapping flakes and bits* — **Stennis Head, Saddle Head, Unknown Upper (Avon), North Stack**

7.5 *Areas of unstable rock on a generally sound cliff* — **Black Crag, Cloggy Pinnacle, High Tor Raven Crag-Langdale, Gogarth Main**

7.6 *Fragmented areas of chunks* — **Chee Tor, Esk Buttress, Mother Carey's**

7.7 *Loose flakes constantly* — **Gogarth Upper Tier, Rubicon Wall Carreg-Y-Barcud, Suspension Buttress**

7.8 *Loose blocks and flakes* — **Carreg Wasted, Stackpole, Go Wall, Ogmore**

7.9 *Detached larger blocks and loose in general* — **Ravensdale, Wildcat, Trowbarrow, Boulder Ruckle**

8.0 *Soft rock - but generally hard* — **Sharpnose, Bowden Doors, Lands End,**

8.1 *Soft rock with inconsistency* — **Bowles Rocks, Harrisons,**

8.2 *Soft rock with flakes that won't hold gear* — **Baggy slabs, Helsby**

8.3 *Soft and crumbly surface texture* — **Bulls Hollow**

8.4 *Big soft areas but still solid in general* — **Mousetrap Zawn**

8.5 *Soft now, and not holding much gear* — **Compass Point**

8.6 *Highly soft and holding imaginary gear* — **Beachy Head, Upper Homs Crag (Lleyn)**

8.7 *Very soft and holding no gear* — **Saltdean**

8.8 *Soft and loose in make up* — **Dover Cliffs**

8.9 *Soft, loose with mud and grit* — **Hastings**

9.0 *Truly fully radical* — **Exmansworthy**

★★★★
Awesome Walls
WICC
Edge - Sheffield
Westway-Indoor
Leeds
Hull

★★★★
The Castle
Foundry
Gloucester
Kendal
Rope Race

★★★
Rock Face
Warrington
Bear Rock
Sunderland
Beacon
Bristol
Ingleton
Huddersfield
Newton Aycliffe
Nottingham

★★★
Mile End
Leicester
Rochdale
Newcastle
BBurn-BolUK
Arethusa
Preston
Amersham
Bude
West-Out
Norwich-UEA
Evolution
Swindon
Calshot
Wimborne

★★
Brunel
Broughton
High Sport
Oxford
Llangorse
Hatfield
Penrith
Hartlepool
Sobell-London
Wymondham
Guildford
Chester
Bognor
Keswick

★★
Capel Curig
Stowmarket
Salford Uni
Wirksworth
Bournemouth
Car St. Aid
Matrix
Pontypridd
Oldham
Portsmouth
BBurn-Ymca
Martley
Peterborough
Bangor
Cramlington
Cleethorpes
Glossup
Clitheroe
Shoreham
Cockermouth

★
Burnley
Aberystwyth
Southport
Mepal Wall
Lanc Univ
Car-Sands
Stourbridge

East Ham
Lowestoft
Hebburn
Llanrwst
Balderstone
Prestatyn
Ackers
Stoke Damerel
The Mill
Stubbers
Ambleside

★
Cheshunt
Kitto YMCA
Crystal Palace
Sunbury
Green Park
Bourne End
Ashburton
Barrow
Lipsom
Harrow-Leisure
Ipswich
Whitchurch
Southampton
Taunton
Cambridge
Leeds Univ
Wells
Llandudno
Ivybridge
Aston Univ
Hendon
Godalming
Bexhill Coll
Billingham
Blackpool
Vernon
Guiseley
Scunthorpe
Carnegie
Basingstoke
Basildon
Hawkwell

We award stars for general climbing appeal that ranges from bouldering, to big lead wall climbing. The list is not in a critical order, since it is impossible for instance, to compare a beginners bouldering venue, with an experts 7b wall. There is however, a pretty fair order of descending merit, for those climbers seeking 'cutting edge' climbing.

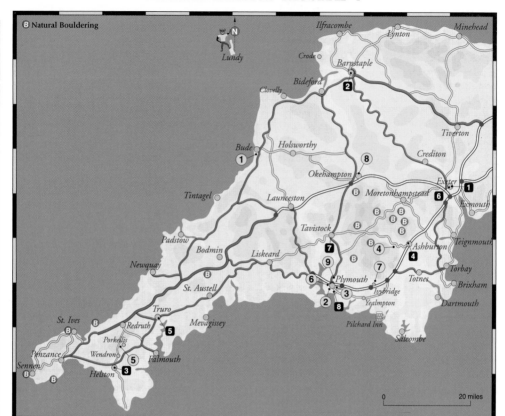

B Natural Bouldering

SPECIALIST CLIMBING SHOPS:

1 Taunton Leisure: SHOES ROPES GEAR CAMS BOOKS ICE
110 Fore Street, Exeter, Devon EX4 3JF
Tel: 01392 410 534   Open: M-Sat 9am - 5.30pm

2 No Sweat: SHOES ROPES GEAR CAMS BOOKS ICE
74 High Street, Barnstaple EX31 1MX
Tel: 01271 371 255   Open: M-Sat: 9-5.30pm

3 Outback Trading: SHOES ROPES GEAR CAMS BOOKS ICE
The Angel Centre, Tyacke Road, Helston, Cornwall TR13 8RR
Tel: 01326 569 569   Open: M-Sat 9.30-5.30pm

4 Trailventure: SHOES ROPES GEAR CAMS BOOKS ICE
7 North Street, Ashburton, Devon TQ13 7QJ   (Main junction in town)
Tel: 01364 652 522   Open: M-Sat 9-5.30pm Sun 11-4pm

5 Penrose Outdoors: SHOES ROPES GEAR CAMS BOOKS
Town Quay, Truro, Cornwall TR1 2HJ   (Between Tesco & Radio Cornwall)
Tel: 01872 270 213   Open: M-Sat 9-5.30pm

6 Moorland Rambler:
148-149 Fore Street, Exeter EX4 3AN
Tel: 01392 432 681

7 The Outdoor Shop:
22/23 West Street, Tavistock, Devon PL19 8AN
Tel: 01822 613 089

8 Kayaks & Paddles: SHOES ROPES GEAR CAMS BOOKS
Unit 319-320 Faraday Mill, Faraday Rd, Plymouth, PL4 0SP
Tel: 01752 600 722   Open: M-Fri 9.30-5.30pm Sat 10-5pm

CLIMBING CLUBS - WEBSITE KEYWORDS
STOKE DAMEREL-CC (Plymouth)
SOUTH DEVON-MC

STOKE DAMEREL WALL

Basic gear / local books   Good UK gear / UK books   Big range / Europe books   Expert range / Worldwide

1 - PLYMOUTH

2 - BRISTOL/YEOVIL

3 - GUILDFORD

4 - MAIDSTONE

5 - LONDON

6 - IPSWICH

7 - OXFORD

8 - GLOUCESTER

9 - SOUTH WALES

10 - NORTH WALES

11 - BIRMINGHAM

Dedicated Bouldering (Square metres)

Grotto	Freeform Rock	Texture Panel	Flat Panel	Brick	Woody	Campus Board
66	0	0	54	0	0	9
0	0	0	0	0	0	0
12	0	0	0	0	0	0
62	48	0	40	0	0	0
28	0	0	0	0	12	3
0	0	0	0	0	14	0
0	0	0	0	0	0	0
0	0	0	0	0	0	0
0	0	0	0	0	0	0

Climbing wall - Sector by sector analysis

Bouldering Sqm. · Climbing Total Sqm.

Instructional · Top Rope-insitu · Lead-Tilting — Sector Sq.m

T/R Bouldering · Leading · Competition

(Sector Height - Individual lines - Total routes in sector)

Climbing Walls

① Bude - Barn C.C. — B 129, C 327
FP 6m-2-8 (24) · FP 5-2-10 (15) · FP 13-1-3 (39) · FP 13-1-3 (39) · FP 13-1-3 (39) · FP 14-1-3 (42)

② Stoke Damerel-PL — B 0, C 201
B 7m-7-14 (70) · B 7-6-12 (63) · B 8m-2-4 (16) · FP 7m-2-7 (16) · FP 8m-5-18 (36)

③ Lipsom-PL — B 12, C 173
FP 7-7-10 (119) · FP 6m-2-30 (18) · FP 6m-3-18 (24)

④ Ashburton — B 150, C 164
FR 3m-4-8 (14)

⑤ The Mill — B 43, C 141
FP 6m-4-24 (42) · FP 6m-1-15 (18) · FP 7m-1-12 (14) · FP 8m-2-16 (24)

⑥ Kitto YMCA-PL — B 14, C 141
TP 5m-1-2 (5) · TP 7m-1-7 (19) · TP 7m-6-16 (50) · TP 7m-1-2 (9) · FR 7m-1-4 (20) · TP 8m-2-5 (24)

⑦ Ivybridge — B 00, C 108
B 6-10-22 (108)

⑧ Okehampton — B 00, C 73
B 9m-5-10 (73)

⑨ Marjon Wall-PL — B 00, C 71
B 5m-3-15 (35) · B 6m-7-35 (36)

BARN CLIMBING CENTRE, BUDE

1 - PLYMOUTH · 2 - BRISTOL/YEOVIL · 3 - GUILDFORD · 4 - MAIDSTONE · 5 - LONDON · 6 - IPSWICH · 7 - OXFORD · 8 - GLOUCESTER · 9 - SOUTH WALES · 10 - NORTH WALES · 11 - BIRMINGHAM

1 - PLYMOUTH 2 - BRISTOL/YEOVIL 3 - GUILDFORD 4 - MAIDSTONE 5 - LONDON 6 - IPSWICH 7 - OXFORD 8 - GLOUCESTER 9 - SOUTH WALES 10 - NORTH WALES 11 - BIRMINGHAM

BUDE ***

① The Barn Climbing Centre
Walesborough Farm, Marhamchurch,
Bude, Cornwall EX23 0JD
www.barn-climbing.co.uk
Tel: 07944 00 25 63
Access: 1.4 miles S of Bude T/centre.
Take the main A39 going S from the
southern junction of A3073 to town
centre. After 0.7mile turn R onto Farm
track (opposite road to Marhamchurch).
Take this track for 300 yds, and is then
on the L, & is located next to a big green
grain silo.
P Park with consideration, free.
Ad; £4.50 ~ Kid; £3.00 ~ no 1st time fee.
Mon / 2pm -10pm;
Tues - Closed
Wed-Sun / 2pm -10pm
Kids night - Thurs, 6-8.30pm

*A great facility for the South West, with a
good farm earthy feeling of cows from a
bygone era. A conversion of a giant barn
gives a wonderful bouldering facility. Run
by Simon Young, the problems set are
superb, and of continual interest; making
a trip to this wall - well worth the effort.
Also check out for regular boulder comps.
Now with the addition of the tall grain silo-
lead area, weird but pumpy.*

Insitu 6 Hire Hire DEEP-MATS
kids club INTRO ADV T GLOOMY
FUN INTENSE EARTHY FRIENDLY BRIGHT

PLYMOUTH (C-WNW) *

② Stoke Damerel
Stoke Damerel Community College,
Somerset Place, Plymouth, Devon PL3 4BD
Tel: 01752 609 128
Access: 0.5 mile SW of Plymouth Argyle
Footy ground. From Main A38, go S on
the A386 for 2 miles to Jtn with A3064.
Carry straight on up Milehouse Rd, after
0.5m t-L onto Molesworth Rd, then soon
L again onto Somerset Place
P Free parking
Ad; £? ~ Kid; £?
no 1st time fee.
Thurs / 8pm -10pm;
Fri / 7pm -10pm;
Sun / 10am -10pm
Details: John Axworthy 01752 661 387
*A good wall that has been supported by
the local Stoke Damerel climbing club. A
good variety of climbing in a big sports
hall.*

Insitu INTRO CASUAL FRIENDLY BRIGHT

PLYMOUTH (C-ENE) *

③ *Lipsom College*

Lipsom Community College, Bernice
Terrace, Plymouth, Devon PL4 7PG
Tel: 01752 662 997
Access: 1.5 mile SW of A38 over R.Plym.
From the A38 take the A374 for 0.6
mi, then turn R onto B3214 (Old Laura
Rd-Alexandra Rd). After passing under
railway bridge, turn L onto BerniceTerrace
and continue all the way to the end. The
wall is located in the College sports hall.

P Free parking
Ad; £3.00 ~ Kid; £3.00
no 1st time fee.
Thurs night / 7pm -10pm
Friday night / 7pm -10pm
*A good small wall in the main sports hall
of the College. A paint job has certainly
give the brick wall a bit of life, and most of
the routes are bolt ons.*

 INTRO FUN CASUAL QUIET

LIPSOM WALL

ASHBURTON *

④ *Dart Wall*

River Dart Adventures, Holne Park, Ashburton, Devon. TQ13 7NP
Tel: 01364 652 511
Access: 2 mile W of Ashburton t-ctr. From the A38 take the Ashburton S exit. Turn immediately L and follow
tourist signs to Adventure centre, say at the entrance that you only want the climbing wall. Free parking **P**
Ad; £3.00 ~ Kid; £3.00 no 1st time fee.
Mon-Sun / 11.30am -10pm
*A very good bouldering venue that is fully matted out. A good use made of available space, well lit even into
the deepest and darkest corners. A very good combination of a fun kids facility, plus steep flat wood panels.
No heating and chilly. Situated on an outdoor theme park in beautiful landscape.*

DART WALL

DEEP-MATS

 INTRO

LEISURE

FUN
QUIET
EARTHY

1 - PLYMOUTH
2 - BRISTOL/YEOVIL
3 - GUILDFORD
4 - MAIDSTONE
5 - LONDON
6 - IPSWICH
7 - OXFORD
8 - GLOUCESTER
9 - SOUTH WALES
10 - NORTH WALES
11 - BIRMINGHAM

1 - PLYMOUTH

2 - BRISTOL/YEOVIL

3 - GUILDFORD

4 - MAIDSTONE

5 - LONDON

6 - IPSWICH

7 - OXFORD

8 - GLOUCESTER

9 - SOUTH WALES

10 - NORTH WALES

11 - BIRMINGHAM

HELSTON *
⑤ The Mill

Tocarne, Wartha Mill, Porkellis, Helston,
Cornwall TR13 0HX
Tel: 01209 860 822
Access: 4 miles NNW of Helston. (200
yds W of Porkellis hamlet). Take the
B3297 Helston to Redruth, after 2 miles
at Trenear continue for another mile (1m
before Burras), turn R down small lane.
After 1mile and a few twists, the mill is on
the left at the bottom of the hill. Wall is in
the tall building to the right of the house.
🅿 Free parking, and think first please.
Ad; Please donate for the up keep.
no 1st time fee.
Mon - Sun / 9am -11pm
This wall is a private top level bouldering
and climbing facility, and climbers are
welcome to share it. No under 18's are
allowed - strictly.
*A wonderful bouldering facility built by a
complete climbaholic. We are grateful for
the opportunity to be allowed to use this
facility. Only visit if you can respect other
peoples property and remember to turn off
the lights when you leave. Superb training
holds in all the right places, good technical
moves.*

5 CALM EARTHY SERIOUS

PLYMOUTH (C-NW) *
⑥ Kitto Centre Wall

YMCA Kitto Centre, Honicknowle Lane,
Honicknowle, Plymouth, PL5 3NG
Tel: 01752 201 918
Access: 2m NW city centre. From the
main A38, turn S onto the A386. After
0.5m turn R at traffic-lts onto Ham
Drive, soon after 0.25m, turn R onto
Honicknowle Lane, centre is on the R in
about 1 mile.
    Free parking
Ad; £3.20 ~ Kid; £2.50
no 1st time fee.
Mon & Tues / 6pm -9.30pm
Mon - 6-7.30pm Kids club
Wed-Sun / Groups by arrangement
*A very nice small wall that is steep in
parts, but not intimidating at the same
time. Good texture on the panels allowing
a good possible variety of routes. Gets
noisy at times with sports hall in general
use.*

  DEEP-MATS

THE MILL

KITTO WALL

IVYBRIDGE

HAYTOR ROCK'S WALL

⑧ *Haytor Rocks Climbing Wall*

Ivybridge Community College, Harford Road, Ivybridge, PL21 0JA

Tel: 01752 698 315

Access: 500 yds NE of town centre. Turn off A38 and follow the road into Ivybridge and around town centre to the East. From here a road leads up the big hill and to the College.

🅿 Free parking.

Ad; £2.50 ~ Kid; £1.50
no 1st time fee.

Wed / 7pm - 9.30pm
8.30-9.30 adults only.

The end to a sports hall is covered in bolt on holds, and is painted in a Dartmoor vista. Great fun for beginners and those wanting to learn to climb. Nice sized holds for those without proper rock shoes; lots of nice vertical hard problems too.

OKEHAMPTON

⑧ *Okehampton Wall*

Okehampton Community College, Mill Road, Okehampton. EX20 1PW

Tel: 01837 54546

Access: 500 yds N of town centre.

🅿 Free parking.

Ad; £3.00
Group rate too.
no 1st time fee.

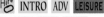

Mon - Sun / ring for availability

On the inside wall of a sports hall, which has been developed with bolt on holds for climbing use and introductory ropework. With a new sports centre being built nearby, the wall should be more available now for use. Enquire for latest developments.

WOODIE AT THE MILL

MARJON WALL

PLYMOUTH (N)

⑨ *Marjon Wall*

College of St. Mark & St. John, Derriford Road, Plymouth.

Tel: 01752 636 876

Access: 3.4m NNW city centre near airport. From the main A38, turn N onto the A386. After 2m at main Derriford roundabout, turn R and follow signs to College. Wall is just past the main centre entrance

🅿 Parking needs £ coins (3) refundable for wall users.

Ad; Groups enquire. no 1st time fee.

Wall is suitable for group instruction use and can be booked by prior arrangement with an instructor.

Wed-Sun / Groups by arrangement

A small wall, but useful for teaching beginners ropework and climbing techniques. The centre has contacts with instructors, ring for details.

1 - PLYMOUTH
2 - BRISTOL/YEOVIL
3 - GUILDFORD
4 - MAIDSTONE
5 - LONDON
6 - IPSWICH
7 - OXFORD
8 - GLOUCESTER
9 - SOUTH WALES
10 - NORTH WALES
11 - BIRMINGHAM

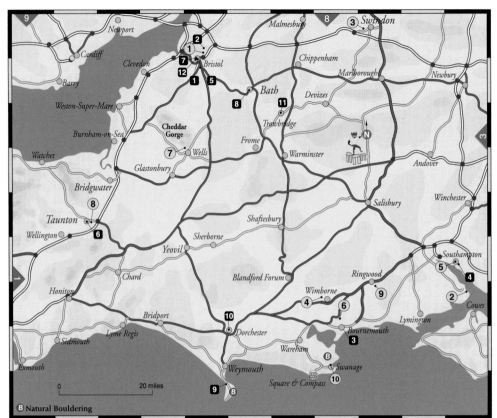

B Natural Bouldering

SPECIALIST CLIMBING SHOPS:

1 Quip-u-for-Leisure: SHOES ROPES GEAR CAMS BOOKS ICE
60 West Street, Old Market, Bristol, BS2 0BL
Tel: 0117 955 8054 Open: Tues-Fri 9am - 4.30pm, Sat 9-5pm

2 Snow & Rock: SHOES ROPES GEAR CAMS BOOKS ICE
1-3 Shield Retail Centre, Gloucester Rd. North, Filton, Bristol BS34 7BQ
Tel: 0117 914 3000 Open: M-Fri 10am - 6.00pm Sat 9-6pm Sun 11-5pm

3 Cotswold: SHOES ROPES GEAR CAMS BOOKS ICE
Unit 1, Castle Lane West, Bournemouth BH9 3LJ (Next - Laura Ashley & Pizza Hut)
Tel: 01202 529 123 Open:M-W-F:9.30-6.30pm;Tu-10am,Th-8pm,Sat 9-6,Sun10-4.

4 Cotswold: SHOES ROPES GEAR CAMS BOOKS ICE
13 Lower Northam Rd, Hedge End, Southampton SO30 4FN Sun10.30-4.30
Tel: 01489 799 555 Open:M-Sat:9.30-6.00pm;Mo-9am,Tu-10am,Th-8pm,Sat 9-6,

5 Taunton Leisure: SHOES ROPES GEAR CAMS BOOKS ICE
38-42 Bedminster Parade, Bristol, BS3 4HS
Tel: 0117 963 7640 Open: M-Sat 9am-5.30pm

6 Taunton Leisure: SHOES ROPES GEAR CAMS BOOKS ICE
40 East Reach, Taunton, Somerset, TA1 3ES
Tel: 01823 332 987 Open: M-Sat 9am-5.30pm

7 Ellis Brigham: SHOES ROPES GEAR CAMS BOOKS ICE
160 Whiteladies Road, Bristol, BS8 2XZ
Tel: 0117 974 1157 Open: M-Sat 9.30-6.00pm; Winter Sundays 11-5pm

8 BCH Camping & Leisure:
30 South Gate, Bath, BA1 1TP
Tel: 01225 460200

9 Scuba Centre Portland:
Victoria Square (End of causeway on the right), Fortuneswell, DT5 1AL
Tel: 01305 826666

10 Great Western Camping Ltd:
28 High East Street, Dorchester, DT1 1HF
Tel: 01305 266800

11 BCH Camping & Leisure:
8-12 Islington, Trowbridge, BA14 8QE
Tel: 01225 764977

12 Stanfords Books and Maps: BOOKS
29 Corn Street, Bristol, BS1 1HT
Tel: 0117 929 9966

BOREAL

CLIMBING CLUBS - WEBSITE KEYWORDS
WESSEX-MC (Dorset-Hants-Wilts), SWINDON-MC
SOUTHAMPTON RATS-CC, NEWBURY-MC

Basic gear / local books Good UK gear / UK books Big range / Europe books Expert range / Worldwide

1 - PLYMOUTH

2 - BRISTOL/YEOVIL

3 - GUILDFORD

4 - MAIDSTONE

5 - LONDON

6 - IPSWICH

7 - OXFORD

8 - GLOUCESTER

9 - SOUTH WALES

10 - NORTH WALES

11 - BIRMINGHAM

Dedicated Bouldering (Square metres)   **Climbing wall - Sector by sector analysis**

Grotto	Freeform Rock	Texture Panel	Flat Panel	Brick	Woody	Campus Board	Climbing Walls	Bouldering Sqm (B)	Climbing Total Sqm (C)	Instructional / T/R Bouldering	Top Rope-insitu / Leading	Lead-Tilting / Competition	Sector Sq.m (M)
52	0	40	72	0	0	7	① Bristol C.C.	171	941	FP 6m-6-20 · 68 / FP 10m-3-7 · 35	FP 7-21-53 · 231 / FP 12-9-23 · 96	FP 10-6-14 · 60 / FP 10-23-46 · 280	
22	36	0	28	0	0	0	② Calshot	86	390	TP 6m-5-16 · 42 / TP 6-5-17 · 42	FP 8m-3-10 · 26 / TP 8-18-41 · 176	FR 8m-7-28 · 56 / TP 12-3-11 · 48	
18	0	30	0	0	0	0	③ Swindon	48	354	FR 9-6-14 · 54 / FR 9m-6-20 · 54	FR 9m-3-14 · 45 / FP 9-5-15 · 54	FP 9m-9-20 · 63 / FP 9m-4-9 · 36	
30	0	0	30	0	0	2	④ Wimborne	62	226	FP 6m-4-10 · 26 / FP 7m-6-17 · 49	FP 5m-1-3 · 5 / TP 7-4-16 · 36	FR 7m-3-10 · 23 / FR 7m-3-10 · 25	
20	0	0	22	0	0	0	⑤ Southampton	42	159	FP 6m-3-5 · 8 / TP 6m-6-12 · 36	TP 6m-4-8 · 30 / TP 6m-6-12 · 33		
0	0	0	0	12	0	0	⑥ Bournemouth	12	138	FR 7m-1-6 · 14 / FR 7m-5-18 · 42	FR 7m-3-11 · 42 / FR 7m-3-7 · 28		
0	0	0	20	0	0	0	⑦ Wells	20	108	TP 5m-1-4 · 8 / TP 5-6-18 · 35	FP 5m-1-3 · 5 / TP 5-4-16 · 25	FR 6m-2-6 · 15	
28	40	3	0	0	0	0	⑧ Taunton	71	0				
0	0	0	0	0	0	0	⑨ Ringwood	00	71	B 7m-6-7 · 42			
0	0	0	33	33	0	0	⑩ Swanage	66	0				

(Sector Height - Individual lines - Total routes in sector)

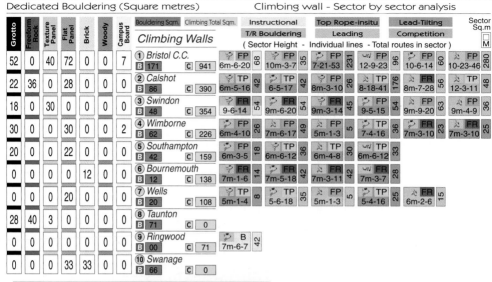

WIMBORNE PUMP ROOM & THE EDGE

1 - PLYMOUTH | 2 - BRISTOL/YEOVIL | 3 - GUILDFORD | 4 - MAIDSTONE | 5 - LONDON | 6 - IPSWICH | 7 - OXFORD | 8 - GLOUCESTER | 9 - SOUTH WALES | 10 - NORTH WALES | 11 - BIRMINGHAM

BRISTOL ***

(1) ***The Bristol Climbing Centre***
St. Werburghs Church, Mina Road,
St. Werburghs, Bristol, BS2 9YH
www.undercover-rock.com
Tel: 0117 941 3489 *Fx: 0117 954 2425*
Access: 2 miles NE of Bristol C.centre. Leave the M32 at junction 2. On the roundabout of this junction is a slip road that goes back onto the motorway heading N (M4); Mina road comes off this before it goes back onto the motorway. The church is 800 yds on the right.
P Park with consideration, free.
Ad; £6.00 ~ Kid; £3.20
1st time fee ~ £1
Mon - Fri / 10am -10pm;
Sat - Sun / 10am - 6pm;

A traditional earthy, and very busy climbing centre. A converted church offers an incredible amount of climbing for the size, with every nook and cranny exploited. Bouldering always seems to be changing itself around, but well catered for with keen problem setters.

Insitu Hire Hire kids club INTRO ADV
T
CASUAL EARTHY FUN SERIOUS INTENSE

CALSHOT ***

(2) ***Calshot Wall - Sunderland Hangar***
Calshot Activities Centre, Calshot Spit,
Fawley, Southampton, SO45 1BR
www.calshot.com
Tel: 023 8089 2077 *Fx: 023 8089 1267*
Access: 8 miles SSE of Soton C.centre. Find the main A326 that runs down the peninsular to the South of Southampton, follow this to Fawley but keep on going to the end. Carry on and say at the parking entrance you are climbing. A note in your window is also helpful.
P £4; but free for centre users.
Ad; £4.50 ~ Kid; £3.50
1st time fee ~ £2.50
Sat,pm-3hrs, one off; £5
Mon - Fri / 6.30pm -10pm;
Sat - Sun / 1pm - 5pm;

A giant old flying boat hangar is home to a variety of different climbing walls. Plenty of variety and so much scope there is little likely for any queing on routes. A good new bouldering area for everyone too.

Insitu Hire Hire DEEP-MATS
INTRO ADV kids club T
CASUAL FUN QUIET WEIRD

SWINDON* (See section 8)**

(3) ***The Link Centre Wall***

BRISTOL WALL

BRISTOL WALL

CALSHOT WALL

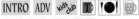

CALSHOT COMPETITION WALL

1 - PLYMOUTH

2 - BRISTOL/YEOVIL

3 - GUILDFORD

4 - MAIDSTONE

5 - LONDON

6 - IPSWICH

7 - OXFORD

8 - GLOUCESTER

9 - SOUTH WALES

10 - NORTH WALES

11 - BIRMINGHAM

1 - PLYMOUTH

2 - BRISTOL/YEOVIL

3 - GUILDFORD

4 - MAIDSTONE

5 - LONDON

6 - IPSWICH

7 - OXFORD

8 - GLOUCESTER

9 - SOUTH WALES

10 - NORTH WALES

11 - BIRMINGHAM

WIMBORNE MINSTER ***
④ *The Edge & The Pump Room*
Queen Elizabeth Leisure Center,
Blandford Rd, Wimborne, BH21 4DT
www.eastdorset.gov.uk
Tel: 01202 888 208
Access: 0.5 miles NW of Wimborne
ctr. Best to approach Wimborne
from W side (A31), then turn L onto
the B 3082 for Blandford. At the top
of the hill the centre is on the L. Go
around to reception first.
🅿 £4; but free for centre users.
Ad; £4.00 ~ Kid; £3.30
no 1st time fee
Mon - Fri / 5.30pm -10pm;
Sat - / 9am - 6.30pm;
Sun - / 9am - 7.30pm;
*A leisure centre that is used by the
school during the day, with public
use at other times. A nice and fresh
modern centre, with a friendly style
wall for beginners and intermediates.
Also a separate, full on pump room
for good boulder workouts.*

Insitu Hire DEEP-MATS

INTRO ADV kids club SWIM

CASUAL EARTHY

BOURNEMOUTH **
⑥ *Hot Rocks Climbing Wall*
Sports Hall, Talbot Campus, Bournemouth
University, Fern Barrow, Poole, BH12 5BB
www.bournemouth.ac.uk/sports
Tel: 01202 595 012   *Fax: 01202 595 720*
Access: 2.5 miles NW of Bournemouth
ctr. From Ringwood take A348 to B-mth,
and at the end turn SW onto A3049 to
B-mth (Wallisdown Road). After 1.6miles
at 2nd big roundabout, Talbot campus is
on Rt. Sports Hall is signposted.
🅿 £ Free at present, but P&D in the day
is planned. Easier to park after 4pm.
Ad; £4.00 ~ Kid; £4.00
no 1st time fee
Mon - Thurs / 8.00pm -10pm;
Fri / 8am - 6.00pm;
Sat - Sun / 9am - 6.00pm;
*A nice rock textured wall which is
separated from the end of the sports hall,
except for examination period (Daytime
mid May-mid June). Good featured rock
with plenty of bolt on climbs. Saving
scheme for multi-visit users.*

 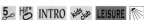

Hire INTRO kids club LEISURE

CASUAL FRIENDLY FUN HUMID

SOUTHAMPTON WALL

SOUTHAMPTON *
⑤ *Southampton Wall*
St. Marys Leisure Center, St. Marys Road, Southampton, SO14 0BL
Tel: 023 8022 7579   www.eastdorset.gov.uk
Access: 0.5 miles NW of Soton C.ctr. From the M27/M3 Jtn, take the A33 straight
down to the big roundabout at the city centre. St. Marys Road is the 4th exit
before the A335 Onslow Rd to Swathling. 🅿 £2-3 pay and display - dodgy area!
Ad; £3.35 ~ Kid; £2.80   no 1st time fee
Mon - Fri / 9.20am -10pm;   Tues 8-10pm Rats club. (Wed 8-10pm Institute only.)
Sat - Sun - / 10am - 6.00pm;
Ring to check for kids birthday parties using the entire climbing wall.
*A very good conversion of a squash court giving plenty of scope for beginners, but
still demanding enough for enthusiasts. All TR insitu.*

 INTRO LEISURE  FUN CASUAL EARTHY GLOOMY

BOURNEMOUTH WALL

WELLS *
⑦ *The Blue School Wall*

The Blue School, Kennion Road, Wells,
BA5 2NR
Tel: 01749 677 786
Access: 0.5 miles NW of Wells T ctr.
Not at the Leisure Centre! Approaching
from the N on the A39, the town centre
is reached and the playing fields are
seen on the R, take the road after these
for access to the main reception and
sports hall.

Ⓟ £ Free
Ad; £3.00 ~ Kid; £2.50
Sat - 3 hrs,pm. £3.50

School has priority 9am-3pm
Mon - Thurs / 9am -10pm;
Mon - 7-9pm Adults only,
Wed - 4-6pm Kids with instructor
Fri / 9am - 9.00pm;
Sat & Sun / 9am - 6.00pm;

*A very nice small wall situated in an airy
small sports hall, one end for climbing
and the other set up for caving. Very good
selection of slabs to a mini comp style
ohang. Natural features add hugely to this
small wall fortunately with some tricky
routes, very suitable for juniors.*

TAUNTON *
⑧ *'Clingers' Wall*

Blackbrook Pavilion, Blackbrook Way,
Taunton, TA1 2RW
Tel: 01823 333 435
Access: 1.7 miles E of Taunton ctr. Just
next to J35 of M5. From Mway, take
main road towards Taunton, after 0.5m
turn L into Bridgewater Rd, then L via
Wordsworth Drive into Blackbrook Way.

Ⓟ £ free.
Ad; £3.00 ~ Kid; £1.40
£2 ~ 1st time induction fee
Mon - Fri / 7.00am -10.30pm;
Wed / 5-8pm Courses only
Sat - / 8.30am - 6pm;
Sun - / 8.30am - 10pm;

*A purpose built small bouldering room. A
small fun slab plus 2 vertical walls with
natural rock features. A bit limited but
some interesting moves and technical
layaways. A good 60º steep part that is
4m high and leads to a 3m roof above
good crash pads. Fun bolt ons too. A good
wall for power building.*

BLUE SCHOOL WALL

RINGWOOD
⑨ *Ringwood Wall*

Ringwood Recreational Ctr. (Leisure Ctr),
Parsonage Barn Lane, Ringwood BH24 1PX
Tel: 01425 478 813
Access: 0.25 miles NW of Ringwood ctr.
From A31, turn South onto B3347, and
soon turn L, with signs to centre.

Ⓟ £ free.
Ad; Ring for details
Mon - Fri / 7am -11pm;
Sat - Sun / 8am - 6pm;
In sports hall which may be in use.
*A very old fashioned brick wall with a
couple missing. More of use as an abseil
facility for novices.*

SWANAGE
⑩ *Swanage Wall*

Swanage Youth & Community Ctr, Chapel
Lane off High St, Swanage, BH19 2PW
Tel: 01929 423 421
Access: 0.2 miles W of Swanage ctr.
From town Ctr, leave on one way system
to the S, just past the big church on Lt.

Ⓟ £ free but limited spaces
Ad; £1-2
Used for fun competition
in town carnival week.
*A small basket ball hall has a selection of
bolt on holds on 3 sides, basic and intro.*

TAUNTON WALL

1 - PLYMOUTH
2 - BRISTOL/YEOVIL
3 - GUILDFORD
4 - MAIDSTONE
5 - LONDON
6 - IPSWICH
7 - OXFORD
8 - GLOUCESTER
9 - SOUTH WALES
10 - NORTH WALES
11 - BIRMINGHAM

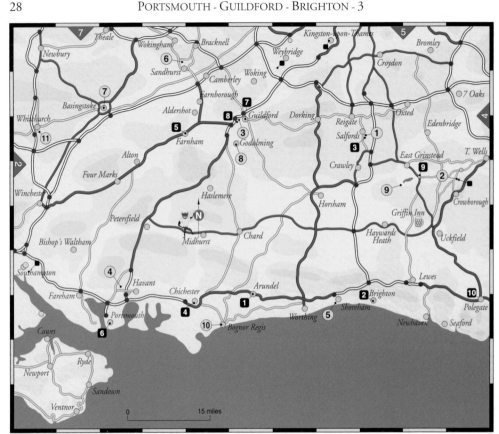

1 - PLYMOUTH
2 - BRISTOL/YEOVIL
3 - GUILDFORD
4 - MAIDSTONE
5 - LONDON
6 - IPSWICH
7 - OXFORD
8 - GLOUCESTER
9 - SOUTH WALES
10 - NORTH WALES
11 - BIRMINGHAM

SPECIALIST CLIMBING SHOPS:

1 Peglers: SHOES ROPES GEAR CAMS BOOKS ICE
70 Tarrant Street, Arundel, BN18 9DN
Tel: 01903 884686 Open: M-Sun 9am-6pm (except xmas day)

2 Open Spaces: SHOES ROPES GEAR CAMS BOOKS ICE
69 Trafalgar Street, Brighton BN1 4EB
Tel: 01273 600897 Open: M-Sat 10am-5.30pm

3 High Sports: SHOES ROPES GEAR CAMS BOOKS ICE
Orchard Business Centre, Bonehurst Road, Salfords, Surrey RH1 5EL
Tel: 01293 822 884 Open: M-Fri 12pm-10.00pm, Sat & Sun 9.30am-7.30pm

4 Cairnsmore: SHOES ROPES GEAR CAMS BOOKS ICE
51 West Street, Chichester, PO19 1RP
Tel: 01243 771321 Open:M-Fri 9.30pm-5.30pm, Sat 9am-5.30pm,Sun 10.30am-4pm

5 Breaking Free: SHOES ROPES GEAR CAMS BOOKS ICE
The Borough, Farnham, Surrey GU9 7ND (On the main high street at East end)
Tel: 01252 724347 Open: M-Sat 9am-5.30pm

6 Snow & Rock:
Port Solent, Portsmouth, PO6 4TP
Tel: 0845 100 1000

7 Field & Trek:
202 High Street, Guildford GU1 3HZ
Tel: 01483 573286

8 Unisport - Vertex: SHOES GEAR
University of Surrey, Bath, Guildford, GU2 5XH
Tel: 01483 259201

9 Global Adventure: SHOES ROPES GEAR BOOKS ICE
The Square, Forest Row, East Sussex, RH18 5ES
Tel: 01342 825069 Open: M-Sat 9am-5.30pm

10 Hike & Bike:
1 North Street, Polegate, BN26 5UG
Tel: 01323 871861

CLIMBING CLUBS - WEBSITE KEYWORDS
BASINGSTOKE-CC, BRIGHTON EXPLORERS CLUB,
EAST GRINSTEAD-CC, GUILDFORD-MC,
SOUTH DOWNS-CC (Brighton)

Basic gear / local books   Good UK gear / UK books   Big range / Europe books   Expert range / Worldwide

Dedicated Bouldering (Square metres) — Climbing wall - Sector by sector analysis

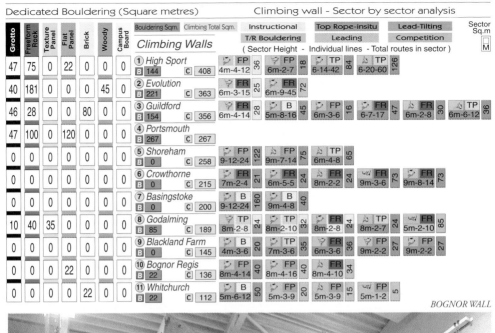

Bouldering Sqm | Climbing Total Sqm

Instructional · Top Rope-insitu · Lead-Tilting · T/R Bouldering · Leading · Competition

(Sector Height - Individual lines - Total routes in sector) — Sector Sq.m M

Grotto	Freeform Rock	Texture Panel	Flat Panel	Brick	Woody	Campus Board	Climbing Walls	B	C	Sectors
47	75	0	22	0	0	0	① High Sport	144	408	FP 4m-4-12 (36) · FP 6m-2-7 (18) · TP 6-14-42 (84) · TP 6-20-60 (126)
40	181	0	0	0	45	0	② Evolution	221	363	FR 6m-3-15 (25) · FR 6m-9-45 (72)
46	28	0	0	80	0	0	③ Guildford	154	356	FR 6m-4-14 (28) · B 5m-8-16 (45) · FP 6m-3-6 (16) · FR 6-7-17 (47) · FR 6m-2-8 (30) · TP 6m-6-12 (36)
47	100	0	120	0	0	0	④ Portsmouth	267	267	
0	0	0	0	0	0	0	⑤ Shoreham	0	258	FP 9-12-24 (122) · FP 9m-7-14 (75) · TP 6m-4-8 (65)
0	0	0	0	0	0	0	⑥ Crowthorne	0	215	FR 7m-2-4 (21) · FR 6m-5-5 (24) · FR 8m-2-2 (24) · FR 9m-3-6 (73) · FR 9m-8-14 (73)
0	0	0	0	0	0	0	⑦ Basingstoke	0	200	B 9-12-24 (160) · FR 9m-4-8 (40)
10	40	35	0	0	0	0	⑧ Godalming	85	189	TP 8m-2-8 (24) · TP 8m-2-10 (32) · FR 8m-2-8 (24) · TP 8m-2-7 (24) · FR 5m-2-10 (85)
0	0	0	0	0	0	0	⑨ Blackland Farm	0	145	B 4m-3-6 (20) · TP 7m-3-6 (35) · FR 6m-3-6 (36) · FP 9m-2-2 (27) · FP 9m-2-2 (27)
0	0	0	22	0	0	0	⑩ Bognor Regis	22	136	FP 8m-4-14 (40) · FP 8m-4-16 (40) · FR 8m-4-10 (34)
0	0	0	0	22	0	0	⑪ Whitchurch	22	112	B 5m-6-12 (50) · FP 5m-3-9 (20) · FP 5m-3-9 (15) · FP 5m-1-2 (5)

BOGNOR WALL

1 - PLYMOUTH · 2 - BRISTOL/YEOVIL · 3 - GUILDFORD · 4 - MAIDSTONE · 5 - LONDON · 6 - IPSWICH · 7 - OXFORD · 8 - GLOUCESTER · 9 - SOUTH WALES · 10 - NORTH WALES · 11 - BIRMINGHAM

1 - PLYMOUTH

2 - BRISTOL/YEOVIL

3 - GUILDFORD

4 - MAIDSTONE

5 - LONDON

6 - IPSWICH

7 - OXFORD

8 - GLOUCESTER

9 - SOUTH WALES

10 - NORTH WALES

11 - BIRMINGHAM

SALFORDS - REDHILL **
(1) High Sports
Unit 6, Orchard Business Centre,
Bonehurst Lane, Salfords, RH1 5EL
www.high-sports.co.uk
Tel: 01293 822 884
Access: 2.7 miles NNE of Gatwick
airport., between Salfords and Horley on
the E side of the A23. Just S of Salfords
the Business centre is signposted.
P £ free
Ad; £6.50 ~ Kid; £5.00
£15 joining fee
£ 8.50 for a 3 hr-sat pm 1-visit.
Mon - Fri / 12.00pm -10pm;
Sat - Sun / 9.30am - 7.30pm;
*A purpose built climbing centre, with a
big number of short routes. Plenty of fun
bouldering too in the centre grotto area,
plus a small matted grotto room.*

CROWBOROUGH ***
(2) Evolution Wall
See section 4.

GUILDFORD **
(3) The Vertex
Sports Centre, Unisport, University of
Surrey, Guildford, GU2 7XH
www.high-sports.co.uk
Tel: 01483 689 201   Fx: 01483 300 245
Access: 1mile NW of Guildford Ctr. From
the junction of the A3/A31, carry on up
the A3 for another jtn, and follow signs
to Univ. At the entrance to the Univ, use
the 1st car park on Lt, Sports hall is
opposite.
P P £ free at W/E and after 5pm in
evenings; £4 otherwise - check 1st.
Ad; £3.50 ~ Kid; £3.50
£1 registration fee
£ 4.50 for a 3 hr-sat pm 1-visit.
Mon - Fri / 08.30pm -10.30pm;
Wed / 2-5pm kids only
Sat / 9am-12pm kids only
Sat / 9.00am - 4.30pm;
Sun / 08.30am - 10.30pm
*A wall in many parts and of different
development. A converted squash court
gives short roped climbs, with a grotto
bouldering area just outside. Additional
two part wall of a long traverse around
the mezzanine of a sports hall (brick),
plus some good freeform bits.*

HIGH SPORTS WALL

PORTSMOUTH **
(4) The Cellar - Fort Purbrook
Fort Purbrook, Portsdown Hill Road,
Cosham, Portsmouth PO6 1BJ
Tel: 023 9232 1223
Access: 2 miles S of Waterlooville.
Exit the A3(M) at Jtn 5 onto the big
roundabout. Exit at 1 o'clock on the
Havant turn, then very soon turn L onto
the B 2177 that goes over the A3(M).
Fort Purbrook is about 1 mile on the
R. Go through Main arch to locate
reception.
P £ Free, park outside main entrance
to fort.

Ad; £3.50 ~ Kid; £2.50
Mon - Fri / 9am -9pm;
Sat & Sun / 9am - 1.00pm;
*A classically bizzare use of some
underground amunition chambers. Two
bouldering rooms; one with lots of big
bolt-ons for kids and playing around, and
the other as a freeform area with hard
problems. Good for fingertip training. All
areas have a rail at 4m so you can top
rope any of the problems.*

GUILDFORD WALL

PORTSMOUTH WALL (Sophie Hoyle climbing)

PORTSMOUTH WALL

GUILDFORD WALL

1 - PLYMOUTH
2 - BRISTOL/YEOVIL
3 - GUILDFORD
4 - MAIDSTONE
5 - LONDON
6 - IPSWICH
7 - OXFORD
8 - GLOUCESTER
9 - SOUTH WALES
10 - NORTH WALES
11 - BIRMINGHAM

1 - PLYMOUTH
2 - BRISTOL/YEOVIL
3 - GUILDFORD
4 - MAIDSTONE
5 - LONDON
6 - IPSWICH
7 - OXFORD
8 - GLOUCESTER
9 - SOUTH WALES
10 - NORTH WALES
11 - BIRMINGHAM

SHOREHAM **
⑤ The Adur Climbing Wall
Adur Activities Centre,
Brighton Road, Shoreham-by-
Sea, BN43 5LT
Tel: 01273 462 928
www.aoac.org.uk
Access: 0.3 miles WSW
of Shoreham High St.
Fron A27/A283 Jtn,
follow A283 main road S
towards Shoreham. At the
Ⓟundabout in Shoreham,
turn R over the bridge and
the centre is on the R - a big
white building.
£ Free
Ad; £5.50 ~ Kid; £4.25
Sat - 3 hrs,pm. £5.50
Mon - Fri / 9am -10pm;
Sat & Sun / 9am - 7.00pm;
*A brand new and purpose
built climbing wall. A good
little centre that is an
impressive 9.4 metres high,
and with this scope, should
attract some good route
setters. A bouldering area is
in the pipeline but not built
as yet.*

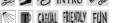

BASINGSTOKE WALL

CROWTHORNE
⑥ Harrison Rock Room
Wellington College Sports Club, Dukes Ride, Crowthorne, Berks, RG45 7PT
Tel: 01344 444 244
Access: 1mile WSW of Crowthorne. From Approach from A 321 and turn onto the B 3348. The
Sports Centre is 1st on the R before the main college. £ Free Ⓟ
Ad; £6.00 ~ Kid; £5.50   Mon - Sun / by appointment only.
Mainly a teaching facility for groups with a leader who posesses a SPA certificate.
*A small, but tall room ,has been built as a climbing wall with simple climbs for beginners. There may
be courses run, ring for latest.*

BASINGSTOKE *
⑦ Basingstoke Climbing Wall
Sports Centre, Festival Place,
Basingstoke, Hants, RG21 7LE
Tel: 01256 326 331
Access: In middle of shopping town
ctr, Porchester Sq. No car access.
Ⓟ £ Pay & Display; Park in Festival
place car park, £1 per hour ish.
Ad; Club use only
Tues / 8.20pm -10.20pm;
Thurs / 8.20pm -10.20pm;
Climbing club noticeboard at wall
for club information.
*An old brick wall with natural
rock inserts that are spaced to
make quite difficult and sustained
climbing. Now with lots of bolt-ons
too, making a good selection of
routes. Limited by pure vertical wall,
but still very good technical climbing.
Platforms for teaching belay
techniques.*

GODALMING *
⑧ Charterhouse Wall
Charterhouse Club, Queens Sport
Ctr, Dukes Drive, Godalming, GU7
2RS
Tel: 01483 239 600
www.aoac.org.uk
Access: Godalming
Ⓟ £ Free
Ad; £3 ~ Guest; £5
Mon, W,T,S,S / 9am -10pm;
Tues / 9am - 9.00pm;
Fri / 9am - 6.00pm;
Mon / 6-10pm, Kids only
Sat / 09.30am - 12.30pm Kids only
School has use during day and may
close at 8pm during holidays
*A small friendly private members
club. Good variety of routes up to
6c, bring your own equipment for
leading. Guests need to be signed
in by climbing members, phone to
check.*

EAST GRINSTEAD

⑨ Blackland Farm
Blackland Farm Activities Centre,
Grinstead lane, East Grinstead RH19 4HP
Tel: 01342 810 493
Access: 3.2 miles SSW of E. Grinstead.
From town Ctr, take the B2110 going
SW. After a mile turn L onto road to Saint
Hill, continue down and past the end of
a resevoir, carry on up hill and Farm is
on the R.
P £ Free
Ad; £ring to check

*An activities centre with an indoor wall
and outdoor climbing and abseiling tower.
May be of use to groups with a qualified
instructor. Is used by the centre for its own
groups so check first.*

BOGNOR REGIS **

⑩ The Bognor Climbing Wall
Arena Sports Centre, Westloats Lane,
Bognor Regis, W. Sussex PO21 5JD
Tel: 01243 870 000
Access: 1 mile NW of Bognor Stn. & town
ctr. Approach from the A29 coming into
Bognor, turn R onto the A259 at town Ctr
roundabout. After 0.5m Westloats Lane is
on the L, follow signs to sports ctr.
P £ Free
Ad; £4.50 ~ Kid; £3.50
Sat - 3 hrs,pm. £4.50
Mon - Fri / 5pm -10.30pm;
Sat & Sun / 9am - 6.00pm;
*A small wall but of very high quality and
a great reputation for good route setting.
Popular and has a good following. The
wall can be easily filled by a group-party
booking so ring to check in advance.*

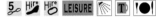
  LEISURE 🔲 T 🍽
INTRO ADV kids club 🍺
FUN BRIGHT CASUAL FRIENDLY

WHITCHURCH *

⑪ The Testbourne Wild Wall
Testbourne School, Micheldever Road,
Whitchurch, Hants, RG28 7JF
Tel: 01256 892 261
Access: 0.4 miles SSE of Whitchurch
Ctr. From the staggered cross roads at
the village centre, take the Winchester
Rd, going S. After 500 yds, Micheldever
Road is taken on your L. The School is
then on the R, and the Sports hall is at
the lower end.
P £ Free
Ad; Wall is for school and climbing club
use, ring for details.
Mon / 8.30pm -10.00pm;
Wed / 6.30pm - 10.00pm;
*A small wall at the end of a sports
hall which is nice and fun for kids. Old
brickwork gives very simple climbing too,
but also some superb fingertip routes on
brick edges. Bouldering is pure traversing
on fine brick edges, fun on a winters
evening.*

INTRO kids club LEISURE T 🔲
CALM CASUAL

BLACKLAND FARM

WHITCHURCH WALL

1 - PLYMOUTH | 2 - BRISTOL/YEOVIL | 3 - GUILDFORD | 4 - MAIDSTONE | 5 - LONDON | 6 - IPSWICH | 7 - OXFORD | 8 - GLOUCESTER | 9 - SOUTH WALES | 10 - NORTH WALES | 11 - BIRMINGHAM

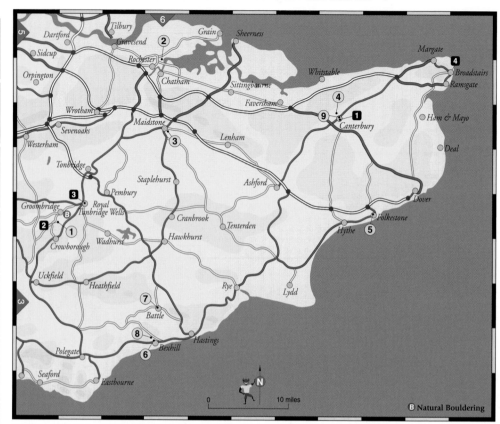

SPECIALIST CLIMBING SHOPS:

1 Field & Trek: SHOES   ROPES   GEAR   CAMS   BOOKS   ICE

3 Palace Street, Canterbury, CT1 2DY
Tel: 01227 470 023   Open: M-Sat 9am-5.30pm, Thurs - 8, Sat -6, Sun 10-4pm

2 Evolution Wall: SHOES   ROPES   GEAR   CAMS   BOOKS

Plumyfeather Farm, Lye Green, Crowborough, TN6 1UX (5 mins from Harrisons)
Tel: 01892 862 924   Open: M-Fri 2pm-10pm, W/E 10am-6pm, 10-10 in hols.

3 Country Trails: SHOES   ROPES   GEAR   CAMS   BOOKS

39 Mount Pleasant, Tunbridge Wells, TN1 1PN (100m up from Station)
Tel: 01892 539002   Open: M-Sat 9am-5.30pm

4 Revolution: SHOES   ROPES   GEAR   CAMS   BOOKS

Revolution Skatepark Ltd, Dane Valley, RoadBroadstairs, Kent
Tel: 01843 866707   Open: Tue, Wed, Fri, Sat, 10am-10pm, Sun 10am-8pm

CLIMBING CLUBS - WEBSITE KEYWORDS

TUNBRIDGE WELLS-MC
MAIDSTONE-CC

Basic gear / local books   Good UK gear / UK books   Big range / Europe books   Expert range / Worldwide

Dedicated Bouldering (Square metres) — Climbing wall - Sector by sector analysis

Legend: Bouldering Sqm. | Climbing Total Sqm. | Instructional | Top Rope-insitu | Lead-Tilting | Exterior | T/R Bouldering | Leading | Competition | Sector Sq.m M
(Sector Height - Individual lines - Total routes in sector)

Grotto	Freeform Rock	Texture Panel	Flat Panel	Brick	Woody	Campus Board	Climbing Walls	B	C	Sectors
40	181	0	0	0	45	0	① Evolution	221	363	FR 6m-3-15 [25] · FR 6m-9-45 [72]
30	90	0	0	0	12	4	② Arethusa	120	363	FP 10m-3-8 [40] · TP 10-4-12 [50] · TP 10-2-6 [20] · FR 13-1-10 [26]
0	0	0	0	0	0	0	③ Maidstone	0	140	B 7-14-28 [140]
0	0	0	0	14	0	0	④ Canterbury Univ.	14	74	B 6-5-20 [60]
0	0	0	0	0	0	0	⑤ Folkestone	0	64	B 8-2-2 [40] · B 8m-2-2 [24]
0	0	0	30	0	0	0	⑥ Bexhill Leisure C.	30	63	B 7m-4-16 [33]
0	0	0	0	0	0	0	⑦ Battle Wall	0	55	TP 5m-1-2 [5] · FP 5m-2-4 [10] · FP 5m-2-6 [10] · FP 5m-2-4 [10] · FP 5m-4-8 [20]
0	0	0	0	0	0	0	⑧ Bexhill College	0	46	TP 8-1-5 [16] · FP 8m-1-3 [10] · FP 8m-2-2 [20]
0	0	0	0	0	0	0	⑨ Canterbury-Kings	0	45	B 6m-4-40 [45]

EVOLUTION CLIMBING CENTRE

1 - PLYMOUTH
2 - BRISTOL/YEOVIL
3 - GUILDFORD
4 - MAIDSTONE
5 - LONDON
6 - IPSWICH
7 - OXFORD
8 - GLOUCESTER
9 - SOUTH WALES
10 - NORTH WALES
11 - BIRMINGHAM

1 - PLYMOUTH

2 - BRISTOL/YEOVIL

3 - GUILDFORD

4 - MAIDSTONE

5 - LONDON

6 - IPSWICH

7 - OXFORD

8 - GLOUCESTER

9 - SOUTH WALES

10 - NORTH WALES

11 - BIRMINGHAM

CROWBOROUGH ***

① Evolution Climbing Centre
Plumyfeather Farm, Lye Green,
Crowborough, East Sussex TN6 1UX
www.evolutionclimbingwall.co.uk
Tel: 01892 862 924
Access: 2.3 miles N of Crowborough town
Ctr, (1.2m SW of Harrisons Rocks). From
Groombridge village, take the B 2188
towards Crowborough. After 1.3 mile
continue past a small road on the L to
Motts Mill, the Farm is 100 yds on the L.
🅿 Park free.
Ad; £8.00 ~ Kid; £6.00 ~ no 1st time fee.
Mon - Fri / 2pm -10pm;
Sat - Sun / 10am -10pm
Sometimes, wall is open extra if climbing
courses are being held at the centre.
*A superb new bouldering facility that has
been built with a handy sport England
grant and a lot of hard work from local
climbers. Excellent overhang and grotto
area. Suitable for beginners to experts,
now with a new steep plastic-woodie
added. Fully equipped for disabled people
wanting to climb.*

CASUAL FUN FRIENDLY MUSICAL

ROCHESTER ***

② Arethusa Wall
Lower Upnor, Rochester, Kent, ME2 4XB
Tel: 01634 296 358
Access: 2.9 miles NE of Rochester town
Ctr. From the main A2 leaving London,
take the A289 ring road to the N (Grain).
After 4 miles reach a giant roundabout
and take the A 228 back towards
Rochester. After 0.5m turn L at the next
roundabout (Gillingham) and in 100 yds
is a small turning to Lower Upnor. Keep
on the small road going straight, all the
way through the village and eventually
the sailing centre, the wall is right at the
very end on the L.
🅿 Free parking
Ad; £4.50 ~ Kid; £3.50
£4.50 annual fee,
Sat - 3 hrs,pm-one off visit. £9
Tues & Thurs / 5pm -10pm;
Wed / 2pm -10pm;
Sat & Sun / 10am -5.30pm
*A good climbing centre that has a very
keen local following with both beginners
and the very best climbers in the SE of
England, Font 8a - no problem. There
are several walls, and indoor converted
squash court, very well done and matted
out for top level bouldering. A big leading
room, and an outdoor wall - floodlit for
good evening romping.*

MAIDSTONE

③ Maidstone Wall
Maidstone Leisure Centre, Mote Park,
Madidstone, Kent ME15 7RN
Tel: 01622 761 111
Access: 1 mile SE of Maidstone town
Ctr. Town centre 1 way is clockwise,
enter on the A 249 for ease. Mote Park
is signposted in brown to the SE of town.
Leisure center has its own entrance.
🅿 Free parking
Ad; £ enquire at the visit
Mon-Fri / 9pm -11pm;
Sat & Sun / ring for availability
Wall is situated in an aerobics room that
is used quite a lot.
*An old fashioned wall with natural rock
inserts in a brick wall. There is good
climbing on it though, so it is a pity about
the lack of easy access. Suitable for group
instruction with qualified leader.*

QUIET

INTRO ADV kids club OPEN FEEL MUSICAL NOISY
FRIENDLY FUN INTENSE SERIOUS BRIGHT

Arethusa bouldering room, bouncy and fun.

ARETHUSA WALL

CANTERBURY

④ *University of Kent Wall*

Sports Centre, University of Kent, Canterbury, CT2 7NL

Tel: 01227 823 623

Access: 1.3 miles NNW of Canterbury village Ctr. Follow signs for the Uni from West side of inner ring road.

P Find a space! Pay and display but may be refundable for sports users. Park in main visitors car park on the right as you zoom down Giles lane.

Ad; Enquire at time

Mon - Fri / 9am -10.30pm

Sat / 9.30am - 6pm

Sun / 10.30am - 6pm

The wall is in the corner of a multi purpose sports hall so ring and check before making a journey. Best in morning and afternoons, & club night.

A classic old fashioned wall that looks a bit bland you may think. Lots of chipped incuts and holds, pockets to give very good bouldering moves. A creative approach is needed, but is rewarded also. Good for foot technique. Planned development is big, but still needs to find some funding.

SWIM LEISURE   CASUAL

FOLKESTONE

⑤ *Folkestone Wall*

Folkestone Leisure Centre, Radnor Park Ave, Folkestone CT19 5HX

Tel: 01303 850 222

Access: 0.3m NW from central train station. The main road in from J12 of the M20 leads to the Central station on the R, turn L into Radnor Park West, and then L again into R-P Ave. Leisure centre is at the end on the R.

P Free parking

Ad; £3.30 ~ Kid; £2.90 no 1st time fee.

Mon -Fri / 9am -10pm

Sat & Sun / 9am -8pm

In a sports hall used by many other activities, ring for availability.

A very nice looking and colourful wall, but very old fashioned and needs complete refurbishment. Uses: for instruction of abseil technique, beginners climbing.

SWIM LEISURE   QUIET

FOLKESTONE WALL

UNIVERSITY OF KENT WALL

1 - PLYMOUTH
2 - BRISTOL/YEOVIL
3 - GUILDFORD
4 - MAIDSTONE
5 - LONDON
6 - IPSWICH
7 - OXFORD
8 - GLOUCESTER
9 - SOUTH WALES
10 - NORTH WALES
11 - BIRMINGHAM

BEXHILL*

⑥ *Leisure Centre Climbing Wall*
Bexhill Leisure Centre, Down Road, Bexhill on Sea, East
Sussex. TN39 4HS
Tel: 01424 731 171
Access: 0.5 mile NW of Bexhill Stn. Centre is 100 yds NW
of the jtn of A259 and A 269 (London Road).
🅿 Free parking.
Ad; £7 per hour for the whole room.   no 1st time fee.
Mon - Fri / 06.45am - 11.30pm
Sat / 8am - 10pm Sun / 8am - 11pm
*There is a special room, like a shaft which is purpose built
for climbing. This is self contained and good for group
use. The room is breeze block with natural rock inserts
and plenty of beginners holds. There is scope for harder
problems, and especilly on the textured panel, traverse wall
in an adjacent aerobics room, subject to availability - but is
often available. Good intro facility.*

 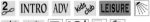   

BATTLE

⑦ *Battle Climbing Wall*
Claverham Community College, North Trade Road,
Battle, East Sussex, TN33 0HT
Tel: 01424 774 772
Access: ?
🅿 Free parking.
Ad; £3.30 ~ Kid; £2.75
Mon / 7pm - 9pm
Sat - Sun / 10am - 6pm
*Used by pupils in the day, please ring for availability.
A small wall that is generally quiet and little used,
situated in the gym of a school. A few routes that
would keep the casual visitor interested for a few visits.
Bouldering can be worked out using the crash pads.
Rumour has it that the local club may update the wall
soon with new routes and problems.*

BEXHILL*

⑧ *Bexhill College Wall*
Bexhill College, Penland Road,
Bexhill on Sea, East Sussex
TN39
Tel: 01424 214 545
Access: N of town ctr.
🅿 Free parking.
Ad; £??
Mon - Sun / ring for
availability
*The college has just moved
to a new building and a new
purpose built wall is in the
plans around the same size
as the old one, 8m high
and about 4 lines. Should
be available for public use
outside school hours.*

CANTERBURY

⑨ *Kings School Wall - Outdoors.*
Kings School Recreation Centre, 1 St.
Stephen's Road, Canterbury CT2 7HU
Tel: 01227 595 602
Access: 800 yds NE of North gate in town
centre.
🅿 Free parking.
Ad; £3.50 ~ Kid; £3.50
Daily memb £2.60. 3 hrs Sat £6.10
Mon - Fri / 7am - 10pm
Sat - Sun / 7am - 7pm
*Used by pupils in the day, please ring for
availability.
A small brick wall with a superb selection of
natural inset pieces of rock. A good array of
beginners bolt ons. Good fun for a summer
evening.*

   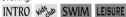   

BEXHILL LEISURE CENTRE WALL

KINGS SCHOOL WALL

1 - PLYMOUTH

2 - BRISTOL/YEOVIL

3 - GUILDFORD

4 - MAIDSTONE

5 - LONDON

6 - IPSWICH

7 - OXFORD

8 - GLOUCESTER

9 - SOUTH WALES

10 - NORTH WALES

11 - BIRMINGHAM

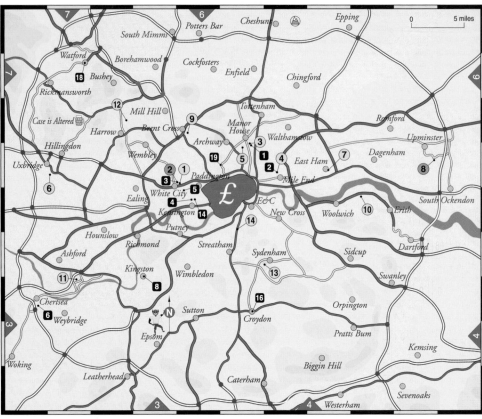

SPECIALIST CLIMBING SHOPS:

1 Urban Rock: `SHOES` `ROPES` `GEAR` `CAMS` `BOOKS` `ICE`
Castle Climbing Ctr, Green Lanes, London N4 2HA (5mins Manor Park tube)
Tel: 020 8211 0475 Open: M-Fri 2pm - 10.00pm Sat & Sun 10am-7pm

2 Rock On: `SHOES` `ROPES` `GEAR` `CAMS` `BOOKS` `ICE`
Mile End Climbing Ctr, Haverfield Rd, London E3 5BE
Tel: 020 8981 5066 Open: M-Fri 12pm-9pm, Sat & Sun 10am-6pm

3 Urban Rock: `SHOES` `ROPES` `GEAR` `CAMS` `BOOKS` `ICE`
Westway Climbing Ctr, 1 Crowthorne Rd, London W10 6RP
Tel: 020 8964 0185 Open: M-Fri 12pm - 10.00pm Sat & Sun 10am-8pm

4 Snow & Rock: `SHOES` `ROPES` `GEAR` `CAMS` `BOOKS` `ICE`
188 Kensington High St, London W8 7RG
Tel: 020 7937 0872 Open:M-Fri 10am-7pm, Sat 9am-6pm, Sun 11.30am-5.30pm

5 Cotswold: `SHOES` `ROPES` `GEAR` `CAMS` `BOOKS` `ICE`
42-46 Shepherds Bush, London W12 8ND (Next to S-Bush tube-Central line)
Tel: 020 8743 2976 Open: M,W,F,Sa, 9.30-6.00pm;Tu 10-6pm,Th 9.3-8,Su 11-4.30

6 Snow & Rock: `SHOES` `ROPES` `GEAR` `CAMS` `BOOKS` `ICE`
99 Fordwater Road, Chertsey, Surrey KT16 8HH (J11- M25)
Tel: 01932 566 886

7 Cotswold: `SHOES` `ROPES` `GEAR` `CAMS` `BOOKS` `ICE`
St. Clements Ho, Leyden St, London E1 7LL
Tel: 020 7655 4660 Open: M-Fri 8.30am-6pm, Th-7pm, Sat 10-5, Sun 10-4pm

8 Cotswold: `SHOES` `ROPES` `GEAR` `CAMS` `BOOKS` `ICE`
72-76 Clarence St, Kingston upon Thames, Surrey, KT1 1NW
Tel: 020 8549 9500 Open: M,W,F,Sa, 9.30am-6pm, Tu 10-6, Th 10-8, Su 11-5

9 Snow & Rock:
150 Holborn, London, EC1N 2LC (Opp Chancery Lane tube)
Tel: 020 7831 6900

10 Ellis Brigham:
3-11 Southampton Street, Covent Garden, WC2E 7HE
Tel: 020 7395 1010

11 Snow & Rock: `SHOES` `ROPES` `GEAR` `CAMS` `BOOKS` `ICE`
4 Mercer Street, Covent Garden, WC2H 9QA
020 7420 1444

12 Tiso-Selfridges:
400 Oxford Street, London, W1A 1AB
020 7629 1234

13 Field & Trek:
105 Baker Street, London, W1M 1FE
Tel: 020 7224 0049

14 Ellis Brigham: `SHOES` `ROPES` `GEAR` `CAMS` `BOOKS` `ICE`
178 Kensington High Street, W8 7RG
020 7937 6889

15 Field & Trek:
64 Long Acre, Covent Garden, WC2E 7LJ
020 7379 8167

16 Field & Trek:
32 Church Street, Croydon, CR0 1RB
020 86808798

`Basic gear / local books` `Good UK gear / UK books` `Big range / Europe books` `Expert range / Worldwide`

Dedicated Bouldering (Square metres)

Climbing Wall	Grotto	Freeform Rock	Texture Panel	Flat Panel	Brick	Woody	Campus Board	Bouldering Sqm (B)	Climbing Total Sqm (C)
① Westway C.C.	52	130	0	16	0	0	6	204	1460
② Westway Outdoor	0	0	0	0	0	0	0	0	298
③ Castle C.C.	178	44	0	95	0	0	3	320	941
④ Mile End C.C.	64	65	338	70	64	24	8	633	812
⑤ Sobell Leisure	12	30	40	0	224	0	0	306	422
⑥ Brunel University	18	0	70	0	0	0	0	88	302
⑦ East Ham Leisure	20	0	24	0	0	0	0	44	246
⑧ Upminster	0	0	0	0	0	0	0	0	200
⑨ Hendon	46	0	68	0	0	0	0	112	195
⑩ Thamesmead	0	18	0	12	0	0	0	30	132
⑪ Sunbury Leisure	0	0	0	0	0	0	0	0	119
⑫ Harrow Leisure	0	0	0	0	0	0	1	1	114
⑬ Crystal Palace	25	18	15	50	0	0	0	108	108
⑭ Brixton	0	0	0	0	0	0	0	0	70

Climbing wall - Sector by sector analysis

(Sector Height - Individual lines - Total routes in sector)

Climbing Wall	Instructional	T/R Bouldering	Top Rope-insitu	Leading	Lead-Tilting	Competition	Exterior (Sector Sq.m M)
① Westway C.C.	TP 7-10-17 (67)	FP 9-20-68 (90)	TP 9-20-68 (189)	FR 11-16-48 (191)	FP 11-32-93 (385)		FR 12-26-75 (280)
② Westway Outdoor	FP 14-4-4 (140)	FP 6-2-6 (19)	FP 14-6-19 (140)				
③ Castle C.C.	FP 8m-8-26 (112)	FR 7-30-99 (273)	FR 7-11-44 (84)	8-2-6 (20)	FP 12-5-20 (72)		FP 12-5-20 (60)
④ Mile End C.C.	TP 7m-4-8 (28)	FR 7m-2-6 (21)	8m-6-18 (48)	FP 9m-2-6 (36)	TP 9m-1-4 (10)		TP 9m-3-10 (36)
⑤ Sobell Leisure	B 8m-2-8 (32)	FR 8m-4-12 (32)	TP 13m-2-3 (52)				
⑥ Brunel University	TP 5m-4-5 (25)	B 7m-3-5 (28)	FR 7m-3-8 (21)	FR 7-2-10 (70)	FR 7m-5-13 (49)		
⑦ East Ham Leisure	TP 5m-3-11 (20)	TP 7-2-7 (18)	FR 7m-8-24 (63)	TP 9-4-12 (44)	FP 8m-2-4 (22)		10-3-8 (35)
⑧ Upminster	FR 6m-2-4 (12)	FR 7-2-4 (21)	FP 9m-4-20 (40)	B 5-2-6 (20)	B 8m-4-12 (32)		B 10-5-20 (75)
⑨ Hendon	FP 7m-5-14 (42)	FR 6m-2-4 (12)	FR 9-2-6 (27)				
⑩ Thamesmead	FP 6m-3-6 (26)	FP 4m-3-6 (12)	FP 5m-5-9 (28)	FP 6-5-10 (36)			
⑪ Sunbury Leisure	FR 4m-9-16 (38)	TP 4-2-6 (13)	FR 7m-3-8 (21)	TP 5-1-5 (8)	FP 7m-3-10 (28)		FP 7-1-4 (11)
⑫ Harrow Leisure	FP 7m-1-4 (7)	FP 7-2-6 (14)	FR 6m-6-14 (50)	TP 7-5-15 (42)			
⑬ Crystal Palace							
⑭ Brixton							

CASTLE CLIMBING CENTRE - LOWER PART

17 Field & Trek:
42 Maiden Lane, Covent Garden, WC2E 7LJ
Tel: 020 7379 3793

18 Venturesport:
92 The Parade, Watford, WD17 1AW
Tel: 01923 244 100

19 Outdoor Emporium:
67 Camden Road, NW1 9EU
Tel: 020 7428 9533

20 Decathlon:
Surrey Quays, Canada Water, SE16 2XU
Tel: 020 7394 2000

21 Stanfords: *BOOKS*
12-14 Long Acre, Covent Garden, WC2E 9LP
Tel: 020 7836 1321 Open: M-Fri 90am-7.30pm, Sat 10-7, Sun 12-6pm

CLIMBING CLUBS - WEBSITE KEYWORDS
LONDON-MC, LONDON ROCKHOPPERS CLUB,
NORTH LONDON-MC, CROYDON-MC

Right margin tabs: 1 - PLYMOUTH | 2 - BRISTOL/YEOVIL | 3 - GUILDFORD | 4 - MAIDSTONE | 5 - LONDON | 6 - IPSWICH | 7 - OXFORD | 8 - GLOUCESTER | 9 - SOUTH WALES | 10 - NORTH WALES | 11 - BIRMINGHAM

42

climbing Walls
International

DR

☎ 0113 284 2369   💻 www.drclimbingwalls.com

LATIMER ROAD ★★★★

① ② *The Westway Climbing Centre*
1, Crowthorne Road, W10 6RP
Tel: 020 8969 0992   www.westwayclimbingcentre.com
Access: 0.8 miles N of Shepherds Bush roundabout. Arrive at
Latimer Road tube stn, turn R going out of entrance & go N
up Bramley Road. Go under the motorway and turn L down
Crowthorne Rd. Centre is at the end.
P Underground parking, car empty!
Ad; £7.00 ~ Kid; £4.20   Membership fee ~ £1.50
Mon - Fri / 10am -10pm;   Sat - Sun / 10am - 8pm;

*A super sized centre with a splendiferous amount of climbing.
Housed in a white hangar beneath the motorway, are stacks of
walls of every shape and variety. A complete centre with courses
and catering for all standards of climber. Outside is an all weather
wall of an awesome size, just a bit noisy from traffic. Bouldering is
planning to be extended! In search of that elusive 5th star.*

Insitu Hire Hire
DEEP-MATS
INTRO ADV
kids club LEISURE
[shower] T ♫
FUN CASUAL
BUSY INTENSE

1 - PLYMOUTH
2 - BRISTOL/YEOVIL
3 - GUILDFORD
4 - MAIDSTONE
5 - LONDON
6 - IPSWICH
7 - OXFORD
8 - GLOUCESTER
9 - SOUTH WALES
10 - NORTH WALES
11 - BIRMINGHAM

1 - PLYMOUTH
2 - BRISTOL/YEOVIL
3 - GUILDFORD
4 - MAIDSTONE
5 - LONDON
6 - IPSWICH
7 - OXFORD
8 - GLOUCESTER
9 - SOUTH WALES
10 - NORTH WALES
11 - BIRMINGHAM

STOKE NEWINGTON ★★★★
③ **The Castle Climbing Centre**
Green Lanes, London N4 2HA
www.castle-climbing.co.uk
Tel: 020 8211 7000
Access: 0.4 mile SSW of Manor
House tube stn. Exit stn, where
seven sisters road crosses Green
Lanes. Take the corner opposite
to Finsbury Park, go down Green
Lanes (numbers decreasing). Centre
is an old tall pumping station, 800
yds on the L.
P £ free, no valuables in car.
Ad; £8.50 ~ Kid; £4.50
£4 memb fee; £9.00 3hr sat-1st visit
Mon - Fri / 2pm -10pm;
Sat - Sun/ 10am - 7pm;
Bank hols / 10am - 10pm;
*A converted old water pumping
station, ideal for your own pump
out. A good labyrith of grottos and
bouldering areas to enthuse anybody,
plenty of top ropes in-situ and a really
trendy Gaggia expresso café. All
standards of courses run and a good
scene.*

CASTLE FREEFORM BOULDERING AREA

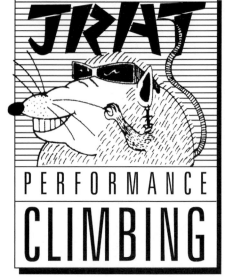

1 - PLYMOUTH
2 - BRISTOL/YEOVIL
3 - GUILDFORD
4 - MAIDSTONE
5 - LONDON
6 - IPSWICH
7 - OXFORD
8 - GLOUCESTER
9 - SOUTH WALES
10 - NORTH WALES
11 - BIRMINGHAM

CASTLE COMPETITION WALL

MILE END ***
④ *Mile End Climbing Centre*
Haverfield Road, London E3 5BE
www.mileendwall.org.uk
Tel: 020 8980 0289
Access: 0.35 mile NW Mile End tube stn.
Exit tube stn. onto Mile End Road. Cross
over onto N side, going L and go to
main lights in 50 yds. Turn R going N up
Grove Rd, after 300 yds pass under rail
bridge, continue for 100 yds and then
turn L down Haverfield Rd, centre is at
the end on the L.
🅿 £ free
Ad; £6.00 ~ Kid; £3.40
£4 joining fee
£ 10 for a 3 hr-sat pm 1-visit.
Mon-Fri/ 12pm-9.30pm; (Fri 9pm)
Sat - Sun / 100am - 6pm;

*A real classic earthy and raw climbing
centre that has developed over many
years thanks to a team of enthusiastic
climbers. A specialist bouldering venue
with a huge array of traversing, monkey
rooms, woodies etc. Also now an outdoor
bouldering freeform for summer days and
evenings. Limited leading but still very
good for beginners.*

FRIENDLY FUN EARTHY CASUAL INTENSE BUSY

FINSBURY PARK **
⑤ *Sobell Leisure Centre*
Hornsey Road, London N7 7NY
Tel: 020 7609 2166   www.aquaterra.org
Access: 0.45 mile SSW Finsbury Park tube stn. Exit tube stn.
onto 7 sisters Road. Cross over onto S side, going R, and go L
along 1 way system Isledon Rd. After 400 yds, the centre is on
the R. 🅿 £ 4 in customer car park.
Ad; £3.50 ~ Kid; £3.50
Mon-Fri/ 9am-10.30pm; Sat / 9am - 6pm; Sun / 9am - 10pm;

*A historic climbing venue that was the
most popular London climbing wall
during the 1980's. A brick traversing
corridor that gleams with polish, yet
still has some of the all time classic
problems. A new small bouldering
area that is very well matted out.
Leading is limited, but there are 2
huge competition routes that rarely
ever get changed.*

FUN GRIPPING QUIET LEISURE

UXBRIDGE **
⑥ *Brunel Wall*

Brunel University Sports Centre, Kingston Lane, Uxbridge, UB8 3PH
Tel: 01895 203 305
Access: 1 mile SSE of Uxbridge tube stn. From A 40 (M40) exit at the top of the hilll, take the B483 towards (S) Uxbridge and to a 2nd roundabout (1mile). Carry on keeping left at town onto the A4020 towards Hillingdon, afte 0.65 mile Kingston Lane is on the R, and Univ is signposted. Sports centre is the 1st set of big buildings.

P £ free
Ad; £3.00 ~ Kid; £2.50
Mon - Fri / 9.30pm -10.30pm;
Sat / 9.30am - 5.30pm;
Sun / 9.30am - 7.30pm;
An excellent wall for teaching and instructing. Lots of natural features which encourage good technique. Deep mats for very airy and high bouldering. A wall that has been continuously popular and has certainly stood the test of time. A big wall and a specialist bouldering grotto.

EAST HAM *
⑦ *East Ham Wall*

East Ham Leisure Centre, 324 Barking Road, East Ham, E6 2RT
Tel: 020 8548 5850
www.gll.org
Access: 100 yds SW of East Ham town ctr. From the A406 North circular road, exit on the A124 for East Ham. This is actually the Barking Road. The L/C is 0.6 mile from N/Circ, just before the town ctr traffic lights. Entrance is through the town hall on L.

P £ free, but extremely limited on site.
P £ pay and display locally.
Ad; £5.45 ~ Kid; £3.30
Mon - Fri / 8am -0.30pm;
Sat - Sun / 8am - 5pm;
A useful conversion of an old tram shed that gives a corridor style wall. A good array of walls that suit beginners to intermediates. A small bouldering area with cute inset lighting.

BRUNEL WALL (Alice in Wonderland climbing)

EAST HAM WALL (Mike George climbing)

1 - PLYMOUTH   2 - BRISTOL/YEOVIL   3 - GUILDFORD   4 - MAIDSTONE   5 - LONDON   6 - IPSWICH   7 - OXFORD   8 - GLOUCESTER   9 - SOUTH WALES   10 - NORTH WALES   11 - BIRMINGHAM

UPMINSTER *

⑧ Stubbers Wall

Stubbers Adventure Centre, Ockendon Road, Upminster, Essex, RM14 2TY
www.stubbers.co.uk
Tel: 01708 224 753

Access: 1.5miles SSW of Upminster Stn. Exit J29 of M25, head E on the A127 for 0.7m. Turn R (via L turn off) onto B186 (Warley St), after 1mile, dog leg R then L and continue for another 1 mile. Turn R onto B 1421 Ockendon Rd, centre is 1.2 miles on the L.

P £ free
Ad; £5 ~ Kid; £4.00

Mon - Sun / 9am - dusk
Subject to centre using the wall

Quite an old fashioned wall built of bricks, concrete with inset pieces of stone. Set in lovely countryside for the time being anyway. A nice place for introductory climbing and to learn the ropes etc.

INTRO   kids club   🚿   T   BRIGHT

CASUAL   QUIET   OPEN FEEL   GRIPPING

HENDON *

⑨ Hendon Leisure Centre Wall

Marble Drive, Brent Cross, NW2 1XQ
www.gll.org
Tel: 020 8455 0818

Access: 0.3 miles SE of Brent X shopping centre. 1st you need to get onto Tilling road that runs parallel with the NC road on the S side at Brent X. Easist to locate via roundabout at the bottom of the M1. A small turning off the roundabout locates this. Follow for 0.3m, then turn R onto Claremont Rd, then left into Marble Drive and the Centre is at the end.

P £ free
Ad; £4.25 ~ Kid; £3.25

Mon - Fri / 9am -10pm;
Sat / 9am - 6pm; Sun / 9am - 10pm;
Sat and Sun afternoons often have private parties so ring to check. Youth climbing clubs fully occupy the wall too.

A small wall with a small sporty leading sector, but best is the freeform bouldering with good matting. A good teaching area, and good for beginners - with plenty of big holds.

 INTRO ADV kids club LEISURE

CASUAL FRIENDLY 🚿 🍽

STUBBERS WALL

HENDON WALL

THAMESMEAD

⑩ Dynamic Experience

Arch 3, Harrow Manor Way, Thamesmead, London SE28   Tel: 07721 501 629

Access: 0.6 miles N of Abbey Wood Stn. From the Stn, go N on Harrow Manor Way and go directly over the 1st roundabout, then 100 yds later filter L before the flyover starts. The Wall is in the arch underneath the flyover. **P** £ free, but the area is a bit dodgy!
Ad; £5 ~ Kid; £3.50   £1 annual fee.   £6 for a 1st time visit.

Mon - Fri / 9am -9pm;
Sat -Sun/ 9am - 6pm;

A small wall making good use of an inner city arch. Development of the small centre is planned, watch this space.

INTRO QUIET

THAMESMEAD WALL

SUNBURY *
⑪ *Sunbury Leisure Centre*
Nursery Road, Sunbury on Thames,
TW16 6LG
Tel: 01932 772 287
Access: 0.3 miles SW of Sunbury Stn.
From the M3 Jtn1, take the exit before
the W/bound entry on the L, this is
Green St. After 200 yds turn R into
Nursery Road and the centre is 100 yds
on the R.
🅿 £ free
Ad; £3.20 ~ Kid; £2.50
Tue/ 5pm -10pm
Wed / 6pm - 10pm
Thur / 8pm - 10pm
Ring for availability at other times
*A wall on the end of a multi purpose
sports hall that is used by other activities.
A good quality wall at that, compact and
with very good bouldering texture. More
of this would be really good. A local
climbing club called 'The Heights,' check
it out.*

HARROW *
⑫ *Wealdstone Wall*
Harrow Leisure Centre, Christchurch
Avenue, Wealdstone, HA3 5BD
Tel: 020 8901 5980
Access: 1 miles NNE of Harrow Ctr.
Take the A 409 to Wealdstone, then turn
R onto Palmerston Road at the main
roundabout, this leads down to a mini
roundabout and follow signs to centre P.
🅿 £ free
Ad; £4.60 ~ Kid; £3.10
Mon - Sun / 7am -11pm;
*A converted squash court with bolt on
routes. End wall is bigger with some
textured panels. A pure introduction facility
and good for kids parties.*

CRYSTAL PALACE *
⑬ *National Sports Centre Wall*
Ledrington Road, Crystal Palace SE19 2BB
Tel: 020 8778 9876
Access: 0.3 miles NNE of Crystal Palace
Stn. Follow local signs to centre.
🅿 £ free
Ad; £4.60 ~ Kid; £3.10
Mon - Fri / 8am -10pm;
Sat / 9.30am -7pm;
Sun / 9.30am -5pm;
*A converted squash court with good
textured rock and well planned.*

BRIXTON
⑭ *Brixton Wall*
Brixton Recreation Centre, 27 Brixton
Station Road, SW9 8QQ
Tel: 020 7926 9779
Access: Centre of Brixton
Ad; £3 ~ Kid; £2.05
Mon & Wed evening courses 7-10pm.
Enquire at centre for other times.
*Details unknown but presumed small
but good.*

SUNBURY WALL   *HARROW & WEALDSTONE WALL*

1 - PLYMOUTH
2 - BRISTOL/YEOVIL
3 - GUILDFORD
4 - MAIDSTONE
5 - LONDON
6 - IPSWICH
7 - OXFORD
8 - GLOUCESTER
9 - SOUTH WALES
10 - NORTH WALES
11 - BIRMINGHAM

1 - PLYMOUTH
2 - BRISTOL/YEOVIL
3 - GUILDFORD
4 - MAIDSTONE
5 - LONDON
6 - IPSWICH
7 - OXFORD
8 - GLOUCESTER
9 - SOUTH WALES
10 - NORTH WALES
11 - BIRMINGHAM

SPECIALIST CLIMBING SHOPS:

1 Open Air: SHOES ROPES GEAR CAMS BOOKS ICE
Green Street, Cambridge, CB2 3JU
Tel: 01223 324666   Open: Mon-Sat 9am - 5.30pm

2 Field & Trek:
23-25 Kings Road, Brentwood, CM14 9DJ
Tel: 01277 222230

3 Field & Trek:
32 Fitzroy Street, Cambridge, CB1 1EW
Tel: 01223 307156

4 Field & Trek:
8-9 Grays Brewery Yard, Chelmsford, Essex, CM2 6QR
Tel: 01245 283999

5 Outdoor People:
Stowupland Road, Stowmarket, IP14 5AH
Tel: 01449 675511

6 Action Outdoors:
3 Great Colman Street, Ipswich, IP4 2AA
Tel: 01473 211647

7 Stepping Out:
55 St John's Street, Bury St Edmunds, IP33 1SN
Tel: 01284 763150

8 Decathlon:
St. Edwards Way, Romford, RM1 1JH
Tel: 01708 736 665

CLIMBING CLUBS - WEBSITE KEYWORDS
CHELMSFORD-MC
IPSWICH-MC

CAMBRIDGE WALL

Basic gear / local books   Good UK gear / UK books   Big range / Europe books   Expert range / Worldwide

Dedicated Bouldering (Square metres)   Climbing wall - Sector by sector analysis

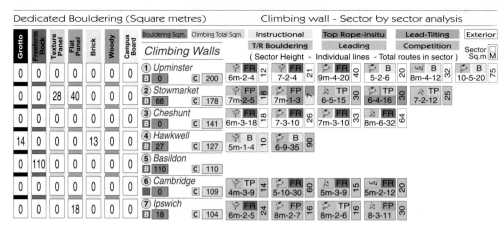

Grotto	Freeform Rock	Texture Panel	Flat Panel	Brick	Woody	Campus Board	Climbing Walls	Instructional / T/R Bouldering	Top Rope-insitu / Leading	Lead-Tilting / Competition	Exterior / Sector Sq.m [M]
0	0	0	0	0	0	0	① Upminster B 0 C 200	FR 6m-2-4 |12| FR 7-2-4 |21|	FR 9m-4-20 |40| B 5-2-6 |20|	B 8m-4-12 |32| B 10-5-20 |75|	
0	0	28	40	0	0	0	② Stowmarket B 68 C 178	FP 7m-2-5 |18| FP 7m-1-3 |7|	TP 6-5-15 |30| TP 6-4-16 |30|	TP 7-2-12 |25|	
0	0	0	0	0	0	0	③ Cheshunt B 0 C 141	FR 6m-3-18 |18| FR 7-3-10 |26|	FR 7m-3-10 |33| FR 8m-6-32 |64|		
14	0	0	0	13	0	0	④ Hawkwell B 27 C 127	B 5m-1-4 |10| B 6-9-35 |90|			
0	110	0	0	0	0	0	⑤ Basildon B 110 C 110				
0	0	0	0	0	0	0	⑥ Cambridge B 0 C 109	TP 4m-3-9 |14| FR 5-10-30 |60|	FR 5m-3-9 |15| FR 5m-2-12 |20|		
0	0	0	18	0	0	0	⑦ Ipswich B 18 C 104	FR 6m-2-5 |24| FP 8m-2-7 |16|	TP 8m-2-6 |16| FP 8-3-11 |30|		

(Sector Height - Individual lines - Total routes in sector)

CHESHUNT WALL

1 - PLYMOUTH · 2 - BRISTOL/YEOVIL · 3 - GUILDFORD · 4 - MAIDSTONE · 5 - LONDON · 6 - IPSWICH · 7 - OXFORD · 8 - GLOUCESTER · 9 - SOUTH WALES · 10 - NORTH WALES · 11 - BIRMINGHAM

Sidebar tabs:
1 - PLYMOUTH
2 - BRISTOL/YEOVIL
3 - GUILDFORD
4 - MAIDSTONE
5 - LONDON
6 - IPSWICH
7 - OXFORD
8 - GLOUCESTER
9 - SOUTH WALES
10 - NORTH WALES
11 - BIRMINGHAM

UPMINSTER *
① *Stubbers Adventure Centre*
See London-5 section.

STOWMARKET **
② *The Cragg*
Mid Suffolk Leisure Ctr, Gainsborough Road, Stowmarket, IP14 1LH
Tel: 01449 674 980
Access: 0.15 miles WWN of town stn. From the town centre take the B1175 going west (Bildeston). After 100 yds turn R onto Onehouse road, soon after Gainsborough Rd is on the R.
🅿 Free parking
Ad; £3.60 ~ Kid; £2.40
Mon - Fri / 7am - 11pm;
Sat & Sun / 8am - 11pm
Ring to check for casual climbing as the wall has limited space if a group is currently using the wall.
A lovely and diverse small wall with lots of highly textured panels to keep the boulderer happy for ages. Just high enough for a pump. A keen team of routesetters & problem co-ordinators.

CHESHUNT *
③ *Cheshunt Wall*
Herts Young Mariners Base, 231 Windmill Lane, Cheshunt, Herts, EN8 9AJ
Tel: 01992 628 403
Access: 0.5 mile NE of Cheshunt Stn. Ctr. Turn off A10 into the town centre where a turning Windmill Lane leads to the Stn. Go over the level crossing, and continue for 50 yds, then take the track on the L which leads to the activity centre buildings.
🅿 Free parking
Ad; £ 4.50   Kid; £3.50
Memb fee £10   1 off 3-hr visit £14.50
Mon-Fri / 9am - Dusk;
Sat & Sun / 9am - 5pm
All persons using the wall must be experienced climbers.
A watersport activities centre with a lovely climbing tower. Set in a beautiful outdoor setting and high enough for some really good climbing. Well orientated for lots of nice sunshine, good tufa's and arêtes. Lots of good chunky holds and ideal for group use. Some steep sections to really test beginners. Please contact centre first for group use.

STOWMARKET WALL

HAWKWELL WALL

HAWKWELL *
④ *Hawk Wall*
Clements Hall Leisure Ctr, Clements Hall
Way, Hawkwell, SS5 4LN
Tel: 01702 207 777
Access: 0.6 mile E of Rayleigh. Take
the A127 going E and past Rayleigh,
continue for 3.5 miles then turn L onto
the B1013 on the W side of Southend
Airport, goint towards Hockley. After 2
miles from the A127, take the turning on
the R - Rectory Road, then soon left to
the centre.
🅿 Free parking
Ad; £ 3.85 per Hour - Kid; £3.85
Memb fee £0.65   1 off 2-hr visit £7.05
M,T,W,F,S / 8am - 10pm
Closed Thurs & Sat.
Wed 5pm - 7pm kids only
The wall is in a quiet sports room which
generally doesn't clash with other uses.
*An old style block wall with inset pieces
of natural rock. - Classic 1980's. Good for
introductory sessions, plus really deep
mats for good and high bouldering.*

PITSEA - BASILDON *
⑤ *Eversley Wall*
Eversley Leisure Ctr, Crest Ave, Pitsea,
Basildon, Essex SS13 2EF
Tel: 01268 583 076
Access: 1 mile ENE of Pitsea town ctr
(Not the L/C in town ctr). Come off the
A13 Pitsea interchange and down onto
roundabout, continue going E on the
London Rd - B1464, for 800 yds then
turn L into Rectory Road. After 700 yds
turn R onto Crest Ave, as road bears
around to R after 400 yds go straight on
to centre and car park.
🅿 Free parking
Ad; £ 3.50 - Kid; £2.45
Mon - Sun / 10am - 10pm
A textured concrete wall with real rock
inserts. It offers very high standard 5b(t)
upwards bouldering and traversing. State
of the art in the 1980's. Excellent stamina
training but little for the beginner and
hopeless without good rockshoes.

CAMBRIDGE *
⑥ *Kelsey Kerridge Wall*
Queen Anne Terrace, Gonville Place,
Cambridge, CB1 1NA
Tel: 01223 462 226
Access: 0.5m SE of town Ctr. Navigate
somehow to the inner ring road - east
side - A603, and the big open space of
Parkside. Gonville Place runs into East
Rd to the N, and Lensfield R to the S.
Sports centre is marked with car park.
🅿 Pay and display multi storey.
Ad; £ 4.45 - Kid; £4.15
Mon & Wed - 6pm - 11pm
Tue & Thu - 8pm - 11pm
A small & compact bouldering facility
with some semi-deep mats. Good for
introductory beginners. Mixture of texture
and bolt ons, a bouldering route book is
available from reception.

IPSWICH *
⑦ *Copleston Wall*
Copleston Centre, Foxhall Rd, IP4 5HD
Tel: 01473 274 178
Access: 2 mile ESE of Ipswich Ctr. Two
main roads A1214 & A1156 run out of
town and are joined by A1189 (Bixley-
Heath Road). At the centre of this at
r-bout head back into town on the Foxhall
rd. After 0.5m turn R into Britannia Rd,
then 2nd Rt into Copleston Rd & High
School, wall is in the sports ctr.
🅿 Free parking
Ad; £ 3.20 - Kid; £2.00
Wed & Fri/ 6pm - 11pm
Thur / 8-11pm
Sat & Sun/ 1-5pm
A new wall that is pretty flat and relies on
the ingenuity of the route setters. More is
planned so watch this space. Has its own
junior climbing club;
www.coplestonclimbing.co.uk

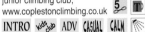

EVERSLEY WALL

COPLESTONE WALL

1 - PLYMOUTH
2 - BRISTOL/YEOVIL
3 - GUILDFORD
4 - MAIDSTONE
5 - LONDON
6 - IPSWICH
7 - OXFORD
8 - GLOUCESTER
9 - SOUTH WALES
10 - NORTH WALES
11 - BIRMINGHAM

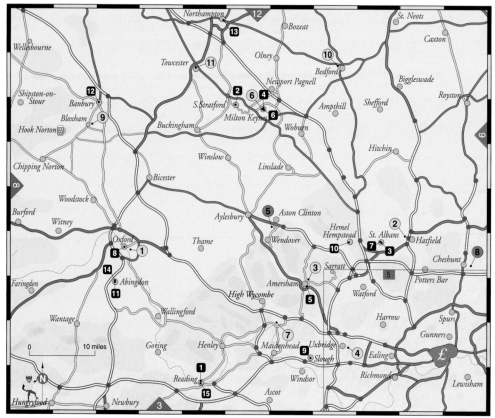

SPECIALIST CLIMBING SHOPS:

1 Cotswold: `SHOES` `ROPES` `GEAR` `CAMS` `BOOKS` `ICE`
271 Basingstoke Road, Reading, RG2 0HY
Tel: 0118 987 5177   Open: M,W,T,F, 9.30-6.00pm;Tu(10)&W,Th-8pm,Su 10.3-4.30

2 The Outdoor Shop: `SHOES` `ROPES` `GEAR` `CAMS` `BOOKS` `ICE`
27/31 High St, Stoney Stratford, Milton Keynes, MK11 1AA
Tel: 01908 568913 Open: M-Fri, 10-6.00pm; Thurs-7pm, Sat 9-6pm, Sun 11-4pm

3 Cotswold: `SHOES` `ROPES` `GEAR` `CAMS` `BOOKS` `ICE`
91 Victoria Street, St. Albans, AL1 3TJ
Tel: 01727 847 888   Open: M,W,T,F, 9.30-6.00pm;Tu(10),Th-8pm,Su 10.3-4.30

4 Silver Trek: `SHOES` `ROPES` `GEAR` `CAMS` `BOOKS` `ICE`
Unit 32 Xscape, Milton Keynes, MK9 3XS
Tel: 01908 200 388   Open: M-Sat 10am-8pm, Tue,W,T - 9pm.

5 Foxes: `SHOES` `ROPES` `GEAR` `CAMS` `BOOKS` `ICE`
1 London Road, Amersham, HP7 OHE (Opposite Tesco in old Town)
Tel: 01494 431431 Open:M-Sat 9am-5.30pm

6 Ellis Brigham: `SHOES` `ROPES` `GEAR` `CAMS` `ICE`
Unit 17 Xscape,602 Marlborough Gate, Milton Keynes, MK9 3DD
Tel: 01908 609122 Open:M-Sat 10am-7pm, 11-5 Sun

7 High Adventure: `SHOES` `ROPES` `GEAR` `CAMS` `ICE`
Breaking Away, 28 Holywell Hill, St. Albans, AL1 1BZ
Tel: 01727 833586 Open:M-Fri 10am-6pm; Sat 9.30-5.30

8 Touchwood Sports:
107 St Aldates, Oxford, OX11BU
Tel: 01865 725220

9 Field & Trek:
313 High Street, Slough, SL1 1BD
Tel: 01753 554252

10 The Complete Outdoors:
London Road, Hemel Hempstead, HP1 2RS
Tel: 01442 873133

11 Touchwood Sports:
4 High Street, Abingdon, OX14 5BA
01235 530008

12 Active Outdoor & Ski:
Castle Centre, Banbury, OX16 8UH
01295 273 700

13 White and Bishop Ltd:
13-17 Bridge Street, Northampton, NN1 1NL
Tel: 01604 230901

14 Walkabout:
3 East St Helens Street, Abingdon, OX14 5EG
01235 527704

15 Silver Trek Ltd:
29 Oxford Road, Reading, RG1 7QE
01189 582211

CLIMBING CLUBS - WEBSITE KEYWORDS
AYLESBURY-CC, BEDFORD-MC, HERTFORDSHIRE-MC, HILLINGDON-MC,
MILTONKEYNES-MC, OXFORD-MC, NEWBURY-MC

Basic gear / local books   Good UK gear / UK books   Big range / Europe books   Expert range / Worldwide

Dedicated Bouldering (Square metres) — Climbing wall - Sector by sector analysis

Grotto	Freeform Rock	Texture Panel	Flat Panel	Brick	Woody	Campus Board	Climbing Walls	Bouldering Sqm (B)	Climbing Total Sqm (C)
22	0	23	40	0	0	0	① Oxford Brooks	85	375
22	14	0	0	0	0	0	② Hatfield	35	332
30	40	0	22	0	0	0	③ Amersham	92	306
18	0	70	0	0	0	0	④ Brunel University	88	302
21	0	0	0	0	0	0	⑤ Green Park	0	188
0	18	0	0	0	0	0	⑥ Milton Keynes	18	174
20	0	0	35	0	0	0	⑦ Bourne End	55	143
0	0	0	0	0	0	0	⑧ Cheshunt	0	141
0	0	12	0	0	0	0	⑨ Bloxham	12	90
0	0	0	0	0	0	0	⑩ Bedford	0	84
0	0	0	0	0	0	0	⑪ Towcester	0	119

Instructional / Top Rope-insitu / Lead-Tilting / Exterior
(T/R Bouldering — Leading — Competition — Sector Sq.m M)
(Sector Height - Individual lines - Total routes in sector)

Climbing Walls	Instructional	T/R Bouldering	Top Rope-insitu	Leading	Lead-Tilting	Competition	Exterior
① Oxford Brooks	FR 5m-7-10 (50)	FP 10-2-10 (48)	TP 12-6-19 (66)	TP 11-3-8 (60)	TP 12-4-13 (66)		
② Hatfield	TP 12m-2-7 (24)	FR 9m-2-6 (27)	TP 12-4-12 (48)	TP 12-8-24 (84)	TP 12-6-12 (84)	FP 14-2-3 (29)	
③ Amersham	FR 5m-2-3 (10)	TP 5-6-10 (40)	TP 11-3-10 (40)	TP 11-4-7 (80)	TP 11-1-4 (22)	TP 11-1-6 (22)	
④ Brunel University	FR 5m-4-5 (25)	B 7m-3-5 (28)	FR 7m-3-8 (21)	FR 7m-8-32 (70)	FR 7-2-10 (21)	FR 7m-5-13 (49)	
⑤ Green Park	FR 6m-2-6 (30)	FR 9m-4-8 (30)	7-1-4 (20)	FR 9m-6-15 (65)	7-2-8 (30)	FR 9m-1-2 (12)	
⑥ Milton Keynes	FR 12-6-18 (72)	FR 14-6-18 (84)					
⑦ Bourne End	FR 6m-1-6 (30)	FP 5-5-15 (30)	FP 6m-5-15 (9)	FP 6-1-3 (9)	FP 5m-1-3 (5)	FP 6-1-3 (6)	
⑧ Cheshunt	FR 6m-3-18 (18)	FR 7-3-10 (26)	FR 7m-3-10 (33)	FR 8m-6-32 (64)			
⑨ Bloxham	B 6m-7-10 (66)	TP 6m-2-4 (12)					
⑩ Bedford	B 6-10-40 (84)						
⑪ Towcester	B 9m-7-14 (81)						

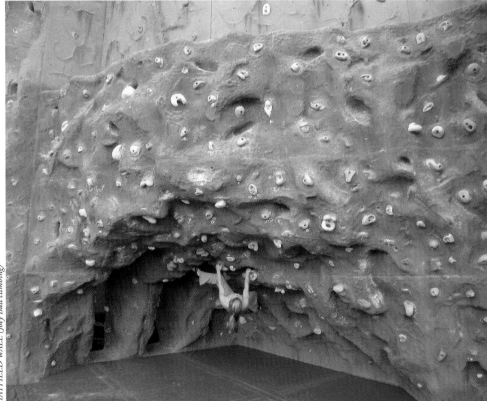

HATFIELD WALL (Joey Bull climbing)

1 - PLYMOUTH · 2 - BRISTOL/YEOVIL · 3 - GUILDFORD · 4 - MAIDSTONE · 5 - LONDON · 6 - IPSWICH · 7 - OXFORD · 8 - GLOUCESTER · 9 - SOUTH WALES · 10 - NORTH WALES · 11 - BIRMINGHAM

1 - PLYMOUTH

2 - BRISTOL/YEOVIL

3 - GUILDFORD

4 - MAIDSTONE

5 - LONDON

6 - IPSWICH

7 - OXFORD

8 - GLOUCESTER

9 - SOUTH WALES

10 - NORTH WALES

11 - BIRMINGHAM

OXFORD **
① Rock Solid Climbing Wall
Oxford Brooks University, Sports Centre, Cheney Lane, Headington, Oxford, OX3 0BD
Tel: 01865 484 373
Access: 1.4 mile E of City Ctr. From M40-A40 to ring road at Barton, go st over towards CC on A420 (London Rd), after 1.2 miles, turn L onto Gipsy Lane - 700 yds at T-lights, turn R into Warneford La, then very quickly R again into Cheney Lane. 400 yds down on the R is the entrance to the S-Centre.
P £ free but heavily used by students in the day.
Ad; £4 ~ Kid; £4
Mon - Fri / 7.30am -11pm;
Sat - Sun/ 9am - 10pm;
A two part wall in a thriving University sports centre. A good bouldering area that is suitable for easy and difficult bouldering, and welcoming for beginners. A tall leading shaft gives a very good variety of routes, angles and all levels of climbing. There is a shop at the sports centre which sells some basic climbing gear Mon-Fri, 1-5pm.

 DEEP-MATS
INTRO ADV LEISURE
FUN BRIGHT GLOOMY

HATFIELD **
② Hatfield Climbing Wall
Hertfordshire Sports Village, de Havilland Campus, Hatfield Business Park, Hatfield, Herts. AL10 9EU
www.hertsportsvillage.co.uk
Tel: 01707 284 466
Access: 0.5 mile W of Galeria Ctr. Exit the A1(M) at Jtn 3 and take the main road going N, parallel with the motorway. After 0.6m at the big r-bout, turn L away from Hatfield ctr, then immediately R into H.Bus.Ctr. The sports centre is signposted around to the L.
P £ free for centre, but pay and display may apply so check.
Ad; £5 ~ Kid; £5
Mon - Fri / 9am -10.30pm;
Tues / 2-4pm University only
Sat - Sun/ 8am - 8pm;
A very new wall in the entrance foyer to the sports centre. A nicely planned wall with a very good bouldering area and lots of possibilities. Leading is good and long, and is ideal for introducing beginners. High belay points for easy ropework and multi-pitch teaching.

 INTRO
SWIM LEISURE
FUN CALM QUIET BRIGHT

AMERSHAM ***
③ The Climb
Chiltern Pools, Bensheim Way, Chiltern Ave, Amersham, Bucks HP6 5AH
Tel: 01494 721 112
Access: 0.3 mile ENW of Station at (New)Amersham on the Hill. Approach Amersham from M25 (J18) on the A404. 1mile before Amersham ctr is a roundabout, go R and under railway bridge, then L up to New Amersham and the Pools are on the L in 900 yds. Turn L into Bensheim way and then L to park for the Climb.
P £ free but you need to pay £3 with coins, it is refunded if you use the Climb.
Ad; £5.95 ~ Kid; £3.40
Mon - Fri / 10.30am -10.30pm;
Sat - Sun/ 12.30pm - 9pm;
Sat & Sun - 8am-12.30 Kids club only
A very good and dedicated climbing centre with a whole range of instruction courses and keen climbers. A converted swimming pool offers a good height to make all the routes a good length. The texture of the wall is superb freeform, which allows for very technical routes. Two hydraulic walls give competition angle climbing and add good space alternatively for beginners. A good bouldering area too. Now with air-conditioning.

 DEEP-MATS INTRO ADV kids club
SWIM
FRIENDLY CASUAL BRIGHT MUSICAL

OXFORD WALL - Bouldering section.

AMERSHAM WALL (Malcolm the 'Wizzard,' climbing)

1 - PLYMOUTH
2 - BRISTOL/YEOVIL
3 - GUILDFORD
4 - MAIDSTONE
5 - LONDON
6 - IPSWICH
7 - OXFORD
8 - GLOUCESTER
9 - SOUTH WALES
10 - NORTH WALES
11 - BIRMINGHAM

1 - PLYMOUTH | 2 - BRISTOL/YEOVIL | 3 - GUILDFORD | 4 - MAIDSTONE | 5 - LONDON | 6 - IPSWICH | 7 - OXFORD | 8 - GLOUCESTER | 9 - SOUTH WALES | 10 - NORTH WALES | 11 - BIRMINGHAM

UXBRIDGE **

④ ***Brunel Wall***

See London section - 5.

AYLESBURY - ASTON CLINTON *

⑤ ***Green Park Climbing Wall***

Green Park Centre, Aston Clinton, Aylesbury, Bucks, HP22 5NE
Tel: 01296 633 800
Access: 4.5 mile ESE of Aylesbury. Leaving Aylesbury on the A41 towards Tring, after 1 mile, take the small road on the R into Aston Clinton, As you continue, pass the B489 (Ivinghoe), and 50 yds further on turn R (South) onto Stable Bridge Road. The entrance is 80 yds on the R before the canal hump bridge.
P £ free on site.
Ad; £ enquire
Mon - Sun / 9am -late

This Wall is private and is run by the Scout association. It is a facility for group use by prior booking, and arrangement with local climbing clubs, please contact local clubs or centre for further advice.

An outdoor wall set in lovely countryside. Two towers that provide plenty of fun for beginners and more experienced climbers. Popular in summer evenings but also is floodlit. Slabbly routes with good bolt placements, plenty of top belays for multi-rope use. (Instructor climber needed to set up any top ropes). Good centre facilities closeby, picnic tables and shelter.

6 CASUAL QUIET OPEN FEEL

MILTON KEYNES

⑥ ***Climbzone***

Silver Trek, Unit 32 Xscape, Milton Keynes, MK9 3XS
Tel: 01908 200 388
Access: 0.5 mile ESE of MK central Stn. Land on planet Milton Keynes in the Centre and find the giant white wedge shaped building - interior ski centre. Enter via shops and ask for climbzone.
P £ pay and display - ouch.
Ad; £7.00 Kid; 7.00
Mon, Fri, Sat / 10am - 8pm
Tue, W, T / 10am -1 0pm
Sun / 11am - 7pm

A shopping centre climbing wall which gives great fun to kids, and those that want to try out climbing. Very hot and thematic, viewing gallery for shoppers, trendy.

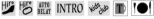

Hire Hire AUTO BELAY INTRO kids club T
FUN NOISY HUMID WEIRD BUSY

CHESHUNT **

⑧ ***Chesunt Wall***

See Ipswich section - 6.

GREEN PARK *Winter raiment*

CLIMBZONE *Milton Keynes*

BOURNE END *

(7) *The Wall*

Bourne End Junior Sports Club, New Road, Bourne End SL8 5BW

Tel: 01628 528 110

Access: 0.5 mile ENE of village centre and station. From village ctr, take the A4094 towards Beaconsfield, turn L at mini roundabout onto Corse End Rd. Take the 2nd L which is New Rd, and the sports hall is 400 yds up on the R; just past Wye Valley school.

P £ free & outside.

Ad; £4.00 Kid; 2.50

Mon, Tue, Thurs / 5pm - 10pm
Available fro group hire at other times, ring for details.

A very nice small facility with a good friendly feel. A whacky wonderful bouldering grotto, which is nice and brightly lit. Small leading area with top ropes in place, designed and suited for juniors, but adults don't get too embarrased, some of the routes will spit you off easily enough. A very enthusiastic atmosphere with photos and climbing interest, also a small gear shop with most things for beginners.

3 Hire DEEP-MATS LEISURE

INTRO kids club FRIENDLY FUN BRIGHT

BOURNE END - THE WALL

BOURNE END - THE LOUD GROTTO

1 - PLYMOUTH 2 - BRISTOL/YEOVIL 3 - GUILDFORD 4 - MAIDSTONE 5 - LONDON 6 - IPSWICH 7 - OXFORD 8 - GLOUCESTER 9 - SOUTH WALES 10 - NORTH WALES 11 - BIRMINGHAM

1 - PLYMOUTH

2 - BRISTOL/YEOVIL

3 - GUILDFORD

4 - MAIDSTONE

5 - LONDON

6 - IPSWICH

7 - OXFORD

8 - GLOUCESTER

9 - SOUTH WALES

10 - NORTH WALES

11 - BIRMINGHAM

BLOXHAM

⑨ *Dewey Climbing Wall*

Dewey Sports Centre, Bloxham School, Bloxham, OX15 4PE
Tel: 01295 720 072
Access: 0.25 mile NE of Bloxham. From the Centre of the Village, drive out on the A361 towards Banbury. At the N end of Bloxham is the School - carry on past for 100 yds then turn R down Strawberry Terrace, soon turn R down Brickle Lane and to the end. Then a quick left, right and left again leads you to the Dewey Sports Centre.

[P] £ free
Ad; £3.50
Mon - Fri / 6pm - 9pm;
Closed in school holidays.
A small wall that is good for instruction purposes and has a whole variety of problems. A limited facility but still good if you are prepared to search out good technical problems. Part of the Bloxham school. Usually there is a club night on tuesdays.

CASUAL QUIET

TOWCESTER

⑪ *Sponne Climbing Wall*

Sponne School, Brackley Road, Towcester, NN12 6DJ
Tel: 01327 350 284
Access: 0.25 mile SW of Towcester Shops. From the r-bout A5-A43, take the A43 for 1 mile south to another R-bout, here turn L, and follow this road to the centre of Towcester and you pass the school on your L.

[P] £ free outside sports hall.
Ad; £24 per hour for groups.
By arrangement during the following times;
Mon - Fri / 6pm - 9pm (Mon 5pm)
Sat - Sun / 9am - 9pm
Contact Nadine Eddy at School.
www.sponneschool.northants.sch.uk/climbingwall.html
A small wall that is suitable for instruction purposes. There are lines in place to quickly set up top ropes. With an insitu rope belay bar, clipping points and lower offs for learning lead climbing. Inset pieces of natural stone can give some very good and technical boulder problems. A useful local facility and ideal for youth and school groups.

CALM CASUAL

CASUAL QUIET

BEDFORD

⑩ *Ash Climbing Wall*

Alexander Sports Centre, De Montfort University, Sidney Road, Bedford MK40 2BQ
Tel: 01234 345 208   www.dmu.ac.uk
Access: 1 mile WNW of town ctr. Easiest approach is from A6 to the North. Arrive the the roundabout (end of dual carriageway). Turn R onto the A 5141 (Shakespeare Rd). Take the 2nd turning on the R, Cowper Rd, and follow this to the end and the sports center is on the R (as the road turns L into Sidney Rd.)
   £ free
Ad; £3.30 ~ Kid £1.60
Mon - Fri / 9am - 10pm;   Sat - Sun / 9am - 5pm;
Situated in a main sports hall and can conflict with other activities, ring for availability. *A side wall to a busy sports hall, vertical with lots of bolt on holds. At least a hold per block that allows a reasonable amount of climbing. Area and University would benefit with a more up to date facility.*

CASUAL QUIET LEISURE

SPONNE CLIMBING WALL

BEDFORD - ASH WALL

1 - PLYMOUTH

2 - BRISTOL/YEOVIL

3 - GUILDFORD

4 - MAIDSTONE

5 - LONDON

6 - IPSWICH

7 - OXFORD

8 - GLOUCESTER

9 - SOUTH WALES

10 - NORTH WALES

11 - BIRMINGHAM

1 - PLYMOUTH
2 - BRISTOL/YEOVIL
3 - GUILDFORD
4 - MAIDSTONE
5 - LONDON
6 - IPSWICH
7 - OXFORD
8 - GLOUCESTER
9 - SOUTH WALES
10 - NORTH WALES
11 - BIRMINGHAM

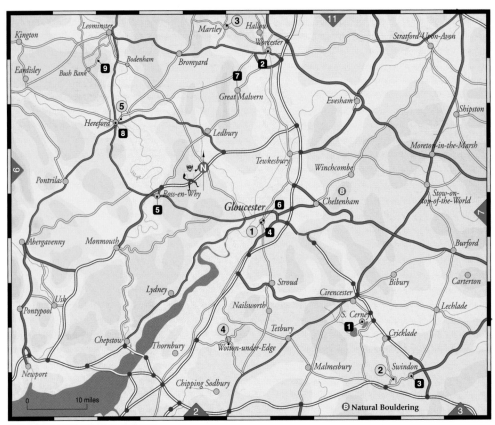

Natural Bouldering

SPECIALIST CLIMBING SHOPS:

1 Cotswold: SHOES ROPES GEAR CAMS BOOKS ICE
Gateway Visitor Ctr, Spine Rd, South Cerney, Cirencester, GL7 5TL
Tel: 01285 863 930 Open: M-F,9.30-6.00pm;We-10, Sa-9,Th-8pm,Sun 10.3-4.30

2 Mountain Shack: SHOES ROPES GEAR CAMS BOOKS ICE
22/24 New Street, Worcester, WR1 2DP
Tel: 01905 611115 Open: M-Sat 9am-5.30pm

3 Mountain Shack: SHOES ROPES GEAR CAMS BOOKS ICE
The Arcade, Brunel shopping ctr. Swindon, SN1 3NH
Tel: 01793 532 244 Open: M-Sun 9am-5.30pm

4 Vertical World: SHOES ROPES GEAR CAMS BOOKS
The Warehouse Climbing Wall, Parliament St, Gloucester, GL1 1HY
Tel: 01452 302351 Open:M-F 5pm-9pm, W/e 10am-8pm, also open by request.

5 Escape: SHOES ROPES GEAR CAMS BOOKS ICE
Crofts Lane, (off Broad St.) Ross on Wye, Herefordshire, HR9 7AB
Tel: 01989 565676 Open:M-Sat 9am-5.30pm

6 Field & Trek:
74 Westgate, Gloucester, GL1 2NZ
Tel: 01452 416549

7 Malvern Outdoors:
17 Church Street, Malvern, WR14 2AA
Tel: 01684 899144

8 Out & About:
10 Commercial Road, Hereford, HR1 2BB
Tel: 01432 274084

9 Sheppards Stores Ltd: SHOES ROPES GEAR CAMS ICE
Upperhill, nr Leominster, HR6 OJZ
Tel: 01568 720262 Open: M-Sat 8.30am-5pm, Sun 10.30am-4.30pm

CLIMBING CLUBS - WEBSITE KEYWORDS
GLOUCESTER-MC, WORCESTER-MC, SWINDON-MC, BEWDLEY-MC,
BROOMSGROVE & REDDITCH-MC

Basic gear / local books   Good UK gear / UK books   Big range / Europe books   Expert range / Worldwide

Dedicated Bouldering (Square metres)

Grotto	Freeform Rock	Texture Panel	Flat Panel	Brick	Woody	Campus Board
86	64	16	87	0	8	3
18	0	30	0	0	0	0
0	24	23	0	0	0	0
0	0	0	0	0	0	0
0	0	0	0	0	0	0

Climbing wall - Sector by sector analysis

Bouldering Sqm. — Climbing Total Sqm.

Instructional / T/R Bouldering — Top Rope-insitu / Leading — Lead-Tilting / Competition — Exterior

(Sector Height - Individual lines - Total routes in sector) — Sector Sq.m M

Climbing Walls	B	C	Instructional / T/R Bouldering		Top Rope-insitu / Leading		Lead-Tilting / Competition		Exterior	
1 *The Warehouse*	264	896	FR 5-10-23	70	TP 8-9-27	88	FP 11-8-24	99	FP 11-19-60	220
									TP 11-9-17	77
									TP 13-6-14	78
2 *The Ridge*	48	354	FR 9m-6-14	54	FR 9m-6-20	54	FP 9-3-14	45	FP 9-5-15	54
									FP 9-9-20	63
									FP 9-4-9	36
3 *Martley*	47	185	FR 8m-1-3	8	TP 8-4-10	38	TP 11-6-15	50	TP 8-5-11	42
4 *Wooton*	0	78	B 6m-8-12	78						
5 *Hereford*	0	56	B 6-7-12	56						

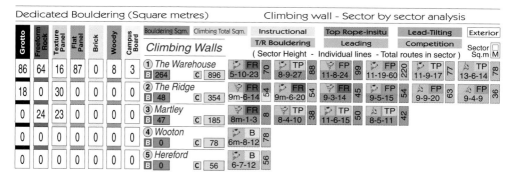

SWINDON - THE RIDGE, BOULDERING AREA

1 - PLYMOUTH

2 - BRISTOL/YEOVIL

3 - GUILDFORD

4 - MAIDSTONE

5 - LONDON

6 - IPSWICH

7 - OXFORD

8 - GLOUCESTER

9 - SOUTH WALES

10 - NORTH WALES

11 - BIRMINGHAM

1 - PLYMOUTH   2 - BRISTOL/YEOVIL   3 - GUILDFORD   4 - MAIDSTONE   5 - LONDON   6 - IPSWICH   7 - OXFORD   8 - GLOUCESTER   9 - SOUTH WALES   10 - NORTH WALES   11 - BIRMINGHAM

GLOUCESTER ★★★★

① *The Warehouse*
Parliament St, Gloucester,
GL1 1HY
www.the-warehouse.co.uk
Tel: 01452 302 351
Access: 100 yds SW of town ctr. You need to locate the Inner-Inner ring road around the town centre. Follow this to the South where the A430 (Bristol Road comes in). Then turn up Southgate St. towards the Centre (Docks on the L). This passes Spa Rd, then Albion St, and ends at a triangle with Parliament St on your R.
P £ local pay and display
Ad; £6 ~ Kid; £4.50
Memb: £1.50
1 off Sat 3 hrs; £7.50
Mon - Fri / 12pm - 10pm
Sat / 9am - 10pm
Sun / 10am - 9pm

STUBBERS WALL

A fully converted old warehouse to a warren of climbing habitats. The entrance is a café with a bar, games etc. and a trendy modern feel to it - groovy man. Behind this modern facade is a cascade of climbing rooms that offer big leading routes, medium fun beginners areas, and then a bouldering attic with a stone moulded elephant. Just about everything for the newcomer to the expert rock gorilla. It's a big wall and plenty of climbing area that still feels comfortable and friendly.

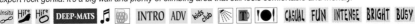

Insitu   Hire   Hire   **DEEP-MATS**   ♪   ⊕   **INTRO**   **ADV**   kids club   ☒   **TD**   **|●|**   **CASUAL**   **FUN**   **INTENSE**   **BRIGHT**   **BUSY**

WAREHOUSE ATTIC BOULDERING AREA

WAREHOUSE MAIN WALL

1 - PLYMOUTH

2 - BRISTOL/YEOVIL

3 - GUILDFORD

4 - MAIDSTONE

5 - LONDON

6 - IPSWICH

7 - OXFORD

8 - GLOUCESTER

9 - SOUTH WALES

10 - NORTH WALES

11 - BIRMINGHAM

SWINDON ***
② *The Ridge Climbing Wall*
The Link Centre, Whitehill Way,
Westlea, Swindon, SN5 7DL
www.swindon.gov.uk/link
Tel: 01793 445 566
Access: Exit M4 at J16 (Swindon
West). Follow big brown signs to the
Link Centre.
🅿 £ free and plenty of it.
Ad; £5.80 ~ Kid; £5.80
Bouldering only £3.30
Mon - Fri / 2pm - 10pm
Sat - Sun / 10am - 6pm

*A good facility, expecially for 1st time
climbers. Most of the areas are ideal
for grade 5 and 6 routes, apart from
the daunting and wow-steep centre
section. Textured panel bouldering
is well designed for all levels. The
whole wall and approach gets a high
level of commitment from a general
leisure centre - long may it continue.
Note: Café is closed on Mondays;
centre has ORANGE lighting - weird.*

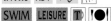
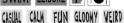

MARTLEY **
③ *Sport Martley Climbing Wall*
Sport Martley - Chantry High School,
Martley, Worcestershire, WR6 6QA
Tel: 01886 888 999
Access: 500 yds SW of village
ctr. As you enter the village from
Worcester (Worcester Rd), the
centre is on the R.
🅿 free on site.
Ad; £4.00 ~ Kid; £4.00
Memb fee £2.50
i off, sat 3 hrs; £6.50
Mon - Fri / 4pm - 10pm
Sat - Sun / 9am - 5pm

*A good small wall that is ideally
suitable for beginners, indeed
excellent. A very small bouldering
area with crash pads. Panels have
good texturing so the routes double
in quantity by using panel footholds
only. All routes can be lead, but bolts
are a bit farther apart than usual
- interesting!*

WOOTON UNDER EDGE

④ *Wooton Wall*

Katherine Lady Berkleys School, Sports Centre, Wooton Under Edge GL12 8RB
Tel: 01453 842 626
Access: 800 Yds S of Wooton under Edge. School and sports center is obvious by the playing fields.
🅿 £ free
Ad; £ enquire

School uses the facilities during the day and becomes the local sports center in the evenings and weekends, ring for details and availability.

An old style wall with brick holds. A vertical environment in which to teach ropework and basic climbing techniques. Somewhat limited.

CALM

WOOTON UNDER EDGE WALL

HEREFORD

⑤ *Hereford Climbing Wall*

Hereford 6th form College, Folly Lane, Hereford, HR1 1LU
Tel: 01432 355 166
Access: 1.3 miles WNW of city ctr. From the inner ring road on the N side of town, exit at 2 o'clock on the A465 towards A4103. Going up to the top of the hill, Folly lane is on the R and the College is on the L.
🅿 £ free.
Ad; £ by arrangement

Available generally in the evenings and at weekends when the college is not using the sports hall. For groups with their own qualified climbing instructor.

A very old fashioned brick wall with brick slots and concrete chimneys. Leading bolts in place. This style of wall allowing teaching of ropework techniques - limited scope.

  LEISURE   **QUIET**

HEREFORD WALL

1 - PLYMOUTH

2 - BRISTOL/YEOVIL

3 - GUILDFORD

4 - MAIDSTONE

5 - LONDON

6 - IPSWICH

7 - OXFORD

8 - GLOUCESTER

9 - SOUTH WALES

10 - NORTH WALES

11 - BIRMINGHAM

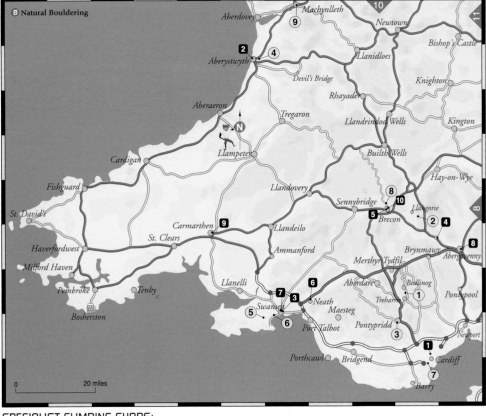

B Natural Bouldering

SPECIALIST CLIMBING SHOPS:

1 Up & Under: SHOES ROPES GEAR CAMS BOOKS ICE
490 Cowbridge Road East, Victoria Park, Cardiff, CF5 1BL
Tel: 02920 578 579 Open: M-Sat 9.30am-6pm

2 Badlands: SHOES ROPES GEAR CAMS BOOKS ICE
40c Great Darkgate Street, Aberystwyth, SY23 1DE
Tel: 01970 625 453 Open: M-Sat 9am-5.30pm; Some Sunday's in summer.

3 Out & About: SHOES ROPES GEAR CAMS BOOKS ICE
36 Castle Street, Swansea, SA1 1HZ
Tel: 01792 461 777   Open: M-Fri 9.30am-5.30pm, Sat 9-6pm, Sun 11-5pm

4 Crickhowell Adv: SHOES ROPES GEAR CAMS BOOKS ICE
1 High Street, Crickhowell, NP8 1BW
Tel: 01873 810 020 Open: M-Sat 9am-5.30pm, Sundays too

5 Crickhowell Adv: SHOES ROPES GEAR CAMS BOOKS ICE
21 Ship Street, Brecon, LD3 9AD
Tel: 01874 611 586 Open: M-Sat 9am-5.30pm

6 Leisure Quest:
17 Crymlyn Parc, Neath, SA10 6DG
Tel: 01792 646 647

7 Leisure Quest:
Parc Tawn, Swansea, SA1 2AL
Tel: 07192 646 647

8 Crickhowell Adv: GEAR CAMS
14 High Sreet, Abergavenny, NP7 4RY
Tel: 01873 856 581

9 Wolf Rok Ltd:
1 St. Mary's Street, Carmarthen, SA31 1TN
Tel: 01267 238 822

10 Global Gear:
6 Pen y Bryn, Brecon, LD3 7RN
Tel: 01874 410 983

LLANGORSE ROPE CENTRE

CLIMBING CLUBS - WEBSITE KEYWORDS
ABERYSTWYTH-MC, GWENT-MC, SOUTHWALES-MC,
SWANSEA ROCK AND HILL-C

Basic gear / local books   Good UK gear / UK books   Big range / Europe books   Expert range / Worldwide

1 - PLYMOUTH
2 - BRISTOL/YEOVIL
3 - GUILDFORD
4 - MAIDSTONE
5 - LONDON
6 - IPSWICH
7 - OXFORD
8 - GLOUCESTER
9 - SOUTH WALES
10 - NORTH WALES
11 - BIRMINGHAM

Dedicated Bouldering (Square metres) — Climbing wall - Sector by sector analysis

Grotto	Freeform Rock	Texture Panel	Flat Panel	Brick	Woody	Campus Board	Climbing Walls	Bouldering Sqm (B)	Climbing Total Sqm (C)
50	18	28	0	0	15	0	① WICC	111	1408
27	137	34	0	27	0	0	② Llangorse	225	617
20	0	0	0	67	0	0	③ Pontypridd Univ.	87	263
40	70	37	0	0	0	0	④ Aberystwyth Univ.	147	147
0	0	0	0	74	0	0	⑤ Swansea Farm.	74	138
0	0	0	0	0	0	0	⑥ Swansea Univ.	0	84
0	0	0	0	0	0	0	⑦ Cardiff-C.View	0	143
0	0	0	0	0	0	0	⑧ Brecon Wall	0	60
0	0	0	0	0	0	0	⑨ Machynlleth Wall	0	57

Sector by sector analysis
Categories: Instructional / T/R Bouldering — Top Rope-insitu / Leading — Lead-Tilting / Competition — Exterior
(Sector Height - Individual lines - Total routes in sector) — Sector Sq.m M

① WICC
TP 12-6-18	84	FP 12-8-24	120	FP 12-50-150	768	TP 12-8-32	134	TP 16-4-12	96	TP 19-4-8	95

② Llangorse
FP 7m-9-18	77	TP 7m-5-15	49	TP 8m-3-6	32	TP 6-11-11	84	TP 13-5-10	78	TP 12m-5-5	72

③ Pontypridd Univ.
TP 8m-3-8	40	TP 8m-4-8	32	TP 8-5-10	48	TP 8m-2-4	24	TP 8m-3-6	32

④ Aberystwyth Univ.

⑤ Swansea Farm.
B 4-1-3	12	B 3m-2-4	12	B 5-6-10	40

⑥ Swansea Univ.
B 9m-3-6	50	B 9m-2-4	34

⑦ Cardiff-C.View
TP 5m-6-25	45	FR 5-2-4	15

⑧ Brecon Wall
TP 8m-2-3	20	TP 8-4-8	40

⑨ Machynlleth Wall
FR 5m-2-4	10	FR 5m-3-6	20	FR 5m-2-6	12	FR 5m-2-12	15

1 - PLYMOUTH · 2 - BRISTOL/YEOVIL · 3 - GUILDFORD · 4 - MAIDSTONE · 5 - LONDON · 6 - IPSWICH · 7 - OXFORD · 8 - GLOUCESTER · 9 - SOUTH WALES · 10 - NORTH WALES · 11 - BIRMINGHAM

LLANGORSE ROPE CENTRE

1 - PLYMOUTH
2 - BRISTOL/YEOVIL
3 - GUILDFORD
4 - MAIDSTONE
5 - LONDON
6 - IPSWICH
7 - OXFORD
8 - GLOUCESTER
9 - SOUTH WALES
10 - NORTH WALES
11 - BIRMINGHAM

TRELEWIS ★★★★

① *Welsh International Climbing Centre*

Taff Bargoed Centre, Trelewis, Treharris, Mid Glamorgan, CF46 6RD

Tel: 01443 710 749

Access: 5.3 miles SSE of Merthyr Tydfil. From the A470 (Cardiff-Merthyr) exit onto the A472 at Treharris. Signs may lead you to the centre if they are still all there. Otherwise, you need the next valley to the East with the B4255 from Nelson, to Trelewis, then the centre is on the L, just before Bedlinog. You can drive in from the N over the hills, but you need a good map (Nice scenic drive though)

P Free parking

Ad; £7.00

Memb; £5.00

One off- 3 hr sat; £12 ~ (ouch!)

Mon - Fri / 9am - 10pm;

Sat & Sun / 9am - 6pm

An outstanding indoor facility consisting of many different sections. The bouldering was limited to fun sections and soft woody, but is perhaps undergoing revamping. The leading here is the big expanse and of fantastic height throughout. Even all the short routes are 10 metres. A fantastic combination of panels and textures, with a breathtaking competition sector to test anyone. A full on venue that is a lead climbers paradise.

1 - PLYMOUTH

2 - BRISTOL/YEOVIL

3 - GUILDFORD

4 - MAIDSTONE

5 - LONDON

6 - IPSWICH

7 - OXFORD

8 - GLOUCESTER

9 - SOUTH WALES

10 - NORTH WALES

11 - BIRMINGHAM

WELSH INTERNATIONAL CLIMBING CENTRE

LLANGORSE **

(2) Llangorse Rope Centre
Gilfach Farm, Llangorse, Brecon
Beacons National Park, LD3 7UH
Tel: 01874 658 272
www.activityuk.com
Access: 5 miles E of Brecon. From
Abergavenny, take the A40 past
Crickhowell, then for 5 miles just past big
bends and turn R onto the B4560. After
2.7 miles the centre is signposted on the
R and before the village of Llangorse.
P £ free, car park is past reception
Ad; £4 ~ Kid; £3.50
Membership £1
One off- all day visit £5
Mon - Sat / 9.00am -10pm;
Sun/ 9am - 5pm;
*This must be 'the' best kids climbing
centre in the UK. A huge labyrinth of
cellars and caves, beneath the organic
smelling riding stables, gives a true
goblin colony of little climbing monsters;
and even a terrific Welsh Dragon to crawl
over. There is a huge cavernous pit with
rocky blocks to claw up, and finally end
up seemingly miles up. Also an outdoor
ropes course that impresses. There is a
serious climbing area too for the expert,
which is worth investigating. Casual
climbing evenings and local climbing
clubs meet here. Busy during school
holidays.*

INTRO kids club

FRIENDLY CASUAL EARTHY WEIRD

PONTYPRIDD WALL

PONTYPRIDD **

(3) Pontypridd Wall
Sports Centre, University of
Glamorgan, Pontypridd, CF37 1DL
Tel: 01443 482 681
www.glam.ac.uk/sports
Access: 1.4 miles SE of
Pontypridd. Exit the A470 at
Treforest and follow signs to the
University, Sports centre is just S
of Treforest station and up the hill
to the W.
P £ Park in main student car park
by the roundabout.
Ad & Kid; £2.60 (40mins)
Membership £6
One off- 3 hr visit ~ £16.40 (ouch!)
Mon - Fri / 8.30am -10.30pm;
Sat/ 9.45am - 8pm;
Sun/ 9.45am - 9pm;
Wall is in a multi-use sports hall
and is not always available for
climbing. Ring for availability.

PONTYPRIDD WALL

*A good modern wall is a nice combination of features and plenty of room for bolt on holds. A good
overall height and plenty of room for quite a few people to use the wall. Ring for popular useage
times. Upstairs is a corridor with technical traversing and good fun on inset pieces of natural stone.
Old fashioned but still packs a punch, especially when using the deep pointing just for the fingertips.*

1 - PLYMOUTH | 2 - BRISTOL/YEOVIL | 3 - GUILDFORD | 4 - MAIDSTONE | 5 - LONDON | 6 - IPSWICH | 7 - OXFORD | 8 - GLOUCESTER | 9 - SOUTH WALES | 10 - NORTH WALES | 11 - BIRMINGHAM

1 - PLYMOUTH

2 - BRISTOL/YEOVIL

3 - GUILDFORD

4 - MAIDSTONE

5 - LONDON

6 - IPSWICH

7 - OXFORD

8 - GLOUCESTER

9 - SOUTH WALES

10 - NORTH WALES

11 - BIRMINGHAM

LLANGORSE ROPE CENTRE

ABERYSTWYTH *
④ *Aberystwyth Climbing Wall*
Sports Centre, University of Wales,
Aberystwyth, Ceredigion SY23 4BZ
Tel: 01970 622 280
Access: 1 mile ENE of town ctr. From
the centre, leave on the A487 and follow
signs to the University.
🅿 £ free, 100 yds in Cage car park.
Ad; £3 ~ Kid; £3
Membership; £5
One off visit; £8 (Ouch)
Mon - Fri / 9am -9pm;
Sat - Sun/ 9am - 4pm;
*A brand new conversion of a squash court
into a bouldering room. Details unavailable
at present - but is proving popular.*

SWANSEA
⑤ *Clyne Farm Centre*
Westport Avenue, Mayals, Swansea,
SA3 5AR
Tel: 01792 403 333
Access: 4.3 mile WSW of Swansea.
Take the coast road A4067 from town
towards Mumbles. Turn R onto the B4436
Bishopstown rd, then soon after turn R
into Westport Ave. Drive to the far end
and the centre.
🅿 £ free
Ad; £2.50 ~ Kid; £2.50
Mon - Sun / 9am -8pm;
*A fun activity centre that offers horse
riding, archery, canoeing, and climbing
for kids. Set in a lovely position high up
with great views. A small farm barn has
been adapted to offer fun climbing and
adds to the general activities. A bit slippy
in places but hopefully will get some new
grippy holds.*

SWANSEA
⑥ *University Wall*
Sports Ctr. Univ. of Wales-Swansea,
Sketty Lane, Swansea, SA2 8PP
Tel: ?
Access: 3 mile WSW of Swansea. Take
the coast road A4067 from town towards
Mumbles and the University is on the
R. The sports ctr is past the Univ and
beneath the new swimming ctr.
🅿 £ free
Ad; Closed
Mon - Sun / Closed
An old wall that may get rejuvinated!

CARDIFF

⑦ Channel View Centre

Jim Driscoll Way, Grangetown, Cardiff
CF11 7HB
Tel: 029 2037 8161
Access: 1.5 miles SSW of Cardiff.
Difficult! From the main A4232 (On the way to Penarth) going towards follow signs to Grangetown and locate A4160 (Penarth Road). Turn SW off this onto Coronation Rd, go down this and take the 7th turn on R (Avondale Rd), and you will see the big red building of the Ctr soon on the L.

🅿 £ free but area is risky. ✖
Ad; £2.90 ~ Kid; £2.10
Mon - Sun / 9.30am -10.30pm
Fri eve: 5.30pm youths only.
An old wall of real rock inserts and concrete textured areas. It has been revamped and modernised for kids and friendly use - masses of brightly coloured holds. 4 Belay machines. A nice friendly wall for kids and a great introductory wall. Lots of technical traversing in the mid grades for adults too.

BRECON

⑧ Brecon Wall

Brecon Leisure Ctr, Penlas Brecon,
Cerrigochion Rd, Brecon, LD3 9LR
Tel: 01874 623 677
Access: 1 mile ENE of town Ctr. Enter town from the East on the B4601, you will see the brown signs to the leisure centre pointing to the R before the ctr.

🅿 £ free
Ad; £2.50 ~ Kid; £2.50
Mon - Tue / 7am -10pm;
Wed - Thu / 7am -11pm;
Fri / 7am -9pm;
Sat / 8am -8pm; Sun 8am -7pm
Casual climbing only if a member of staff is present or a qualified instructor is present.
A small dedicated top roping room at a modern and active leisure ctr. Good area for quiet instruction, useful to groups with an instructor. Basic routes on basic panels but with a reasonable length suitable for beginners.

MACHYNLLETH *

⑨ Machynlleth Awesome Wall

Canolfan Hamdden, Bro Ddyfi,
Aberystwyth Rd, Machynlleth, SY20 8ER
Tel: 01654 703 300
Access: Village Centre, follow signs
🅿 £ Pay and display but refunded 🅿
Ad; £2.55 ~ Kid; £2.30
Mon - Fri / 10am -10pm;
Fri / 10am -6pm;
Sat / 10am -8pm
A small bouldering - top rope wall in a quiet part of the leisure ctr. A top roping bar with easy access makes this a nice venue for introducing beginners in a confident surrounding. No bolt ons but plenty of natural features and hundreds of rocky crimps. A fun juggy roof and a nice leaning wall for the better climbers. Small but good quality all the same, worth a play. During term time 6-8pm Monday, there is a club with instructor.

BRECON WALL

MACHYNELLTH WALL

SWANSEA - CLYNE FARM WALL

1 - PLYMOUTH
2 - BRISTOL/YEOVIL
3 - GUILDFORD
4 - MAIDSTONE
5 - LONDON
6 - IPSWICH
7 - OXFORD
8 - GLOUCESTER
9 - SOUTH WALES
10 - NORTH WALES
11 - BIRMINGHAM

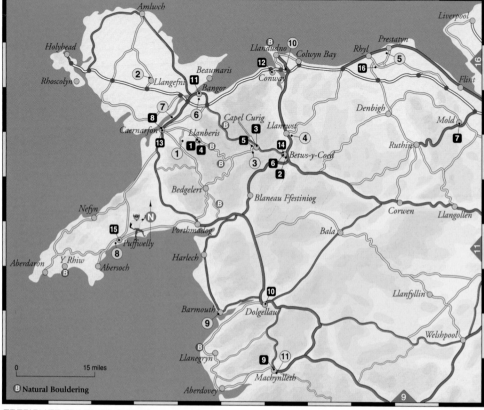

Left margin tabs: 1 - PLYMOUTH | 2 - BRISTOL/YEOVIL | 3 - GUILDFORD | 4 - MAIDSTONE | 5 - LONDON | 6 - IPSWICH | 7 - OXFORD | 8 - GLOUCESTER | 9 - SOUTH WALES | 10 - NORTH WALES | 11 - BIRMINGHAM

B Natural Bouldering

SPECIALIST CLIMBING SHOPS:

1 V 12 Outdoor: SHOES ROPES GEAR CAMS BOOKS ICE
High Street, Llanberis, LL55 4EN (Just up from Pete's Eats)
Tel: 01286 871 534 Open: M-Fri 9.30am-5.30pm, Sat 9-6pm, Sun 9-5pm

2 Cotswold Rock: SHOES ROPES GEAR CAMS BOOKS ICE
Holyhead Road, Betws-y-Coed, LL24 0AY (Down the road from main store)
Tel: 01690 710 234 Open: M,T,T,Su 9-6pm; W 10-6pm, F,Sa 9-7pm

3 Joe Brown: SHOES ROPES GEAR CAMS BOOKS ICE
Capel Curig, LL24 0EN (Around the back of the two little shops at Jtn.)
Tel: 01690 720 205   Open: M-Fri 9.30am-5.30pm, Sat 9-6pm, Sun 9-5pm

4 Joe Brown: SHOES ROPES GEAR CAMS BOOKS ICE
High Street, Llanberis, LL55 4HA (Just down a bit from Pete's Eats)
Tel: 01286 870 327 Open: M-Fri 9.30am-5.30pm, Sat 9-6pm, Sun 9-5pm

5 Ellis Brigham:
Llugwy Terrace, Capel Curig, LL24 0EP
Tel: 01690 720 232

6 Ultimate Outdoors:
Holyhead Road, Betws-y-Coed, LL24 0AY
Tel: 01690 710 555

7 Out There: SHOES ROPES GEAR CAMS BOOKS ICE
Ruthin Road, Mold, CH7 5LH (At Loggerheads Country Park)
Tel: 01352 810 458   Open: 11am - 4pm (unless we are out climbing)

8 Copa: SHOES ROPES GEAR CAMS BOOKS ICE
40 Stryd Fawr, Caernarfon, LL55 1RH (Within old town walls by East Gate)
Tel: 01286 672 900 Open: 9-5pm; Tue-Sat (Winter), Mon-Sun (Summer)

9 Greenstiles Cycles/Outdoor: GEAR CAMS BOOKS ICE
7 Heol Penrallt, Machynlleth, SY20 8AG
Tel: 01654 703 543 Open: M-Sat 9.30am-5.30pm, (Sun 10-4pm - in season)

10 Cader Idris Outdoor Gear:
Eldon Square, Dolgellau, LL40 1PS
Tel: 01341 422 195

11 The Great Arete:
307-309 High Street, Bangor, LL57 1UL
Tel: 01248 352 710

12 Conwy Outdoor Shop:
9 Castle St. Conwy, LL32 8AY, LL32 8AY
Tel: 01296 738 314

13 14th Peak:
9 Palace Street, Caernarfon, LL55 1RR
Tel: 01286 675 124

14 Snowdon Ranger:
Holyhead Road, Betws-y-Coed, LL24 0BW
Tel: ?

15 14th Peak:
14 Y Maes, Pwllheli, LL53 5HD
Tel: 01758 614 441

16 Adventure Kit UK:
Coed Parc, Rhuddlan, LL18 5UE
Tel: 01745 591 501

CLIMBING CLUBS -
WEBSITE KEYWORDS
CLWYD-MC
NORTH WALES-MC

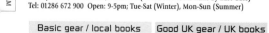

Basic gear / local books   Good UK gear / UK books   Big range / Europe books   Expert range / Worldwide

Dedicated Bouldering (Square metres) — Climbing wall - Sector by sector analysis

Key: Bouldering Sqm. | Climbing Total Sqm. | Instructional | Top Rope-insitu | Lead-Tilting | Exterior
T/R Bouldering | Leading | Competition | Sector Sq.m M
(Sector Height - Individual lines - Total routes in sector)

Grotto	Freeform Rock	Texture Panel	Flat Panel	Brick	Woody	Campus Board	Climbing Walls	B	C	Sector analysis
9	11	0	94	14	16	3	① Beacon Wall	147	610	TP 4m-5-16 (32); FP 6m-5-5 (30); FP 6m-6-11 (49); TP 8-7-21 (64); FP 9-7-21 (68); FP 11-17-51 (220)
0	0	0	0	0	0	0	② Llangefni	0	220	B 11-7-14 (220)
33	0	43	0	0	0	0	③ Capel Curig	76	213	TP 10m-3-4 (40); TP 9m-2-4 (22); TP 7-4-8 (25); TP 10-4-8 (50)
0	0	84	0	0	0	0	④ Llanrwst	84	141	TP 7m-1-3 (7); TP 7m-2-2 (14); TP 7-2-4 (18); TP 7-2-4 (18)
24	0	46	0	0	0	0	⑤ Prestatyn Leisure	70	136	TP 6m-3-6 (18); TP 6m-7-21 (48)
0	37	0	0	0	3	0	⑥ Bangor Univ.	40	120	FP 6m-3-5 (20); FP 8m-2-5 (24); FP 8m-2-4 (16); FP 8m-2-4 (20)
0	10	0	0	0	0	0	⑦ Plas Menai	10	88	FR 6m-5-8 (36); FR 7-4-7 (42)
0	0	0	0	0	0	0	⑧ Pwllheli	0	84	B 6m-2-6 (18); B 9-2-10 (27); B 10-4-12 (40)
15	42	0	0	0	0	0	⑨ Barmouth	57	57	FR 4m-2-6 (10)
0	6	0	0	0	0	0	⑩ Llandudno	6	66	TP 4m-3-9 (12); FP 5m-3-9 (15); FP 6m-1-3 (6); FR 6-1-3 (6); FR 7-3-12 (21)
0	0	0	0	0	0	0	⑪ Machynlleth Wall	0	57	FR 5m-2-4 (10); FR 5m-3-6 (20); FR 5m-2-6 (12); FR 5m-2-12 (15)

Top tips - *Welsh translations:* **Leisure Centre** - *Canolfan Hamdden*
Climbing Centre - *Canolfan Dringo*

THE BEACON WALL

1 - PLYMOUTH
2 - BRISTOL/YEOVIL
3 - GUILDFORD
4 - MAIDSTONE
5 - LONDON
6 - IPSWICH
7 - OXFORD
8 - GLOUCESTER
9 - SOUTH WALES
10 - NORTH WALES
11 - BIRMINGHAM

1 - PLYMOUTH

2 - BRISTOL/YEOVIL

3 - GUILDFORD

4 - MAIDSTONE

5 - LONDON

6 - IPSWICH

7 - OXFORD

8 - GLOUCESTER

9 - SOUTH WALES

10 - NORTH WALES

11 - BIRMINGHAM

THE BEACON - MAIN WALL

CAERNARFON ***

① The Beacon Climbing Centre

Ceunant, Caernarfon, Gwynedd LL55 4SA

Tel: 01286 650 045

www.beaconclimbing.com

Access: 3.8 miles ESE of Caernarfon. Turn right out of Pete's Eats in Llanberis and head out of town going towards Caenarfon on the A4085. After 3 miles you will enter Llanrug, just before this turn L onto a small road towards Waunfawr. This road goes uphill and the centre is on the L after about 2 miles.

P £ free

Ad; £4.50 ~ Kid £3.50 No memb.

Mon - Sun / 10am - 10pm;

Winter - 11am-10pm. Open Bank holidays.

A very good wall that caters for kids, learners, adults and really dedicated climbers. A good extensive bouldering area with a real slate practise section. Fun top roping chimneys with totem poles for kids. A weird tree slab and other fun items. Lead sector is 11m but still packs a good punch and feels quite demanding enough with the acute angles, thankfully ample jugs are usually well supplied. Also a cafe and chill out space next to the climbing area, a very thankful wet weather refuge.

INTRO ADV kids club

CALM CASUAL EARTHY SERIOUS QUIET

LLANGEFNI

② Llangefni Climbing Wall

Plas Arthur Leisure Centre, Llangefni, LL77 7QX

Tel: 01248 722 966

Access: 300 yds WNW of town ctr. Leave the main A55 on the A5114 into the town ctr. Turn L onto the high st, and then continue straight up the hill. The road bears slightly around to the R and then back left; and becomes Cildwrn Road. The centre is soon seen on the L, set back.

P £ free

Ad; £5.00 ~ Kid £2.50

Mon - Fri / 12am - 10pm;

Sat - Sun / 9am - 5pm;

Open 9am in school holidays.

A very old style wall that was state of the art - a very long time ago; the kids on Anglesey deserve better. A good height and a big expanse of wall. Rock inserts and no bolt ons. Brick pointing is too good for any use either. You need slings for top girder belay points. It does have some fiendishly hard top rope routes - as eliminates. The wall clashes with badminton courts so ring for availability.

 SWIM LEISURE

QUIET GRIPPING

1 - PLYMOUTH 2 - BRISTOL/YEOVIL 3 - GUILDFORD 4 - MAIDSTONE 5 - LONDON 6 - IPSWICH 7 - OXFORD 8 - GLOUCESTER 9 - SOUTH WALES 10 - NORTH WALES 11 - BIRMINGHAM

CAPEL CURIG **
③ *Plas-Y-Brenin Wall*

Plas-Y-Brenin National Mountain Centre,
Capel Curig, Conwy, LL24 0ET
Tel: 01690 720 214
Access: 200 yds SW of city ctr. Leaving the giant metropolis of Capel Curig and travelling W on the A4086, the road soon goes through a couple of bends with a big white outdoor centre on the L. Enquire at the reception at the front.

🅿 £ free at present, but keep an eye out for kniving National park schemes that could apply to open roads someday.

Ad; £3 ~ Kid; £3
Mon - Sun / 8am - 10.30pm

A good facility in a full-on mountaineering centre. Essentially a bouldering wall with great spongy, bouncy matting - boing, boing. At first, the plentiful supply of giant holds may seem weird, but seek further and you can find some really good problems, especially as the small crimps are hardly ever used by the beginners - who mainly utilise this wall. The leading wall feels impressive, and is enough for most leaders. A really handy wall to know about. Generally - either very quiet, or very busy.

LLANRWST *
④ *Llanrwst Wall*

Dyffrn Conwy Leisure Centre, Nebo Road, Llanrwst, Conwy, LL26 0SD
Tel: 01492 642 028
Access: 0.5 mile SW of village centre. Coming from Betws-Y-Coed on the main A470, just before the town, you turn sharp right - backwards almost, onto the B5427 (Nebo Rd). After 400 yds you will see a big new centre with a rather grand drive. This leads to the school and the leisure ctr.

🅿 £ free

Ad; £3.50 ~ Kid; £3.50
Mon - Fri / 3.30pm - 10pm
Sat - Sun / 10am - 4pm
10am - 3.30pm School use.
For group use during school time, please ring for possible extra availability.

The centre has a mezzanine floor with a nice bouldering traverse wall. These are all different and of a good sand-resin mix to give nice climbing. Plenty of bolton placements also in this 19m long section. Great scope for bouldering. Leading section is small, but again is well textured and has a nice open feel to it. Should suit both beginners and experienced climbers.

CAPEL CURIG WALL *(There is soft matting here, even though everyone seems to be wearing helmets!)*

1 - PLYMOUTH
2 - BRISTOL/YEOVIL
3 - GUILDFORD
4 - MAIDSTONE
5 - LONDON
6 - IPSWICH
7 - OXFORD
8 - GLOUCESTER
9 - SOUTH WALES
10 - NORTH WALES
11 - BIRMINGHAM

1 - PLYMOUTH

2 - BRISTOL/YEOVIL

3 - GUILDFORD

4 - MAIDSTONE

5 - LONDON

6 - IPSWICH

7 - OXFORD

8 - GLOUCESTER

9 - SOUTH WALES

10 - NORTH WALES

11 - BIRMINGHAM

PRESTATYN *
⑤ *Prestatyn Wall*
2 Princes Drive, Prestatyn, Denbighshire, LL19 8RS
Tel: 011745 855 632
Access: 400 yds SW of town centre. From the town ctr, take the main road towards Meliden (Meliden Road - strange eh!), and soon you can turn R onto Princes Drive and the centre.

🅿 £ free
Ad; £2.75 ~ Kid; £2
Mon - Fri / 1pm - 10pm
Sat & Sun / 9am - 5pm
Holidays 10am-10pm; the centre is shared with the local school. During hours it is best to ring and check for availability.
A converted squash court with textured walls. We did not manage to get to this centre but feel that it is a good fun venue and has an encouraging management. There are some 12 top ropes in place, along with some bouncy crash pads, and a small grotto bouldering area.

DEEP-MATS LEISURE

INTRO kids club 🚿 T

FUN BRIGHT QUIET

BANGOR **
⑥ *Bangor Wall*
University Climbing Wall, Sports Ctr of Maes Glas, Rhodedd Road, Bangor LL57 2E8
Tel: 01248 382 571
Access: 0.5 mile SW of town centre, right at the top of the hill. From the town centre, you need to go South and up the hill and locate Friddoedd Road, the follow signs to University and ask for Maes Glas sports centre.

🅿 £ local pay and display
Ad; £3.45 ~ Kid; £1.95
Mon - Fri / 9am - 10pm
Sat & Sun / 9am - 5pm
A big chamber with an orange glow from the lights, slightly weird but still good fun. A mixture of leading and bouldering, and general work out. The bouldering wall may be small, but it's one of the best in the country - texture to die for. No bolt ons, but crimps and pockets to keep you amused for hours, if only there was more of this. The leading takes second fiddle and is more instructional to freshers. Don't shy away from the awesome campus board.

 Insitu   Hire  DEEP-MATS 🚿 T

LEISURE

CASUAL EARTHY FRIENDLY GLOOMY INTENSE

BANGOR WALL

1 - PLYMOUTH | 2 - BRISTOL/YEOVIL | 3 - GUILDFORD | 4 - MAIDSTONE | 5 - LONDON | 6 - IPSWICH | 7 - OXFORD | 8 - GLOUCESTER | 9 - SOUTH WALES | 10 - NORTH WALES | 11 - BIRMINGHAM

CAERNARFON
⑦ *Plas Menai Climbing Wall*

Plas Menai National Watersports Ctr,
Llanfair, Caernarfon, LL55 1UE
Tel: 01248 670 964
Access: 2.4miles NE of Caernarfon.
Leave town on the A487 towards
Bangor, after about 2 miles the centre
is signposted to the L (towards the
sea).
🅿 £ free.
Ad; £2.30 ~ Kid; £2.30
Mon - Sun / 7pm - 9pm
The wall is used by the centre for
teaching. It can be used by other
groups in the day if available, please
ring first.

*A nice little room, specially built
for teaching (i.e. warm and dry), in
traditional climbing style. The wall is
made from natural Welsh dolerite that
forms good traditional climbing moves,
and even allows for leader placed
protection practise. A series of low bolt
on plastic holds gives an easy traverse
for kids. Good for beginners ropework
and belay techniques.*

   SWIM

PWLLHELI *
⑧ *Pwllheli Climbing Wall*

Canolfan Hamdden Dwyfor, Heol Hamdden/Recreation Road, Pwllheli, LL55 5PF
Tel: 01758 613 437
Access: 0.75 mile SW of town ctr. Follow signs to golf course/leisure ctr. from the town
centre. 🅿 free on site.
Ad; £4.00 ~ Kid; £4.00   Mon - Sun/ 8am - 9pm   Situated in a sports hall and is not
always available - ring for availability. Instructor session on Monday night with gear
supplied. At other times can be used by groups with a qualified instructor only.

*An old fashioned
wall with natural
rock inserts, not
that easy - not
that hard. A little
fun overhang
and a high belay
platform makes
this a welcome
wet weather
teaching venue.
Natural slots for
practicing gear
placement on a
top rope.*

BARMOUTH

(9) *Barmouth Wall*

Pavillion Leisure Centre, The Promenade,
Beach Road, Barmouth LL42 1NF
Tel: 01341 280 111
Access: Right in the middle of the seafron
of Barmouth.

🅿 £ free in car park behind centre for users
only, local pay and display.

Ad; £4 ~ Kid; £2.50   Group discount

Mon - Sun / 10am - Late

*A small dedicated little tiny room for
bouldering. A rock concrete surface with
not that many pieces of inset natural stone.
Good steep sections but limited. Good for a
work out, but not over friendly for kids. Worth
a play on a wet day if your in Barmouth
though.*

CASUAL FUN

LLANDUDNO JUNCTION *

(10) *Llandudno Climbing Wall*

Canolfan Hamdden/Leisure Centre,
Llandudno Junction, Conwy, LL31 9XY
Tel: 01492 583 592
Access: 0.5 mile S of town ctr. Approach
from the main A55 whizzy road (Via
Colwyn Bay). Pass the A470 turn off,
then take the last roundabout before the
tunnel under the river Conway. Turn R into
Llandudno J, and the leisure ctr. is on your
left immediately.

🅿 £ free.

Ad; £3.50 ~ Kid; £3.50

Mon - Fri / 10am - 10pm
Sat - Sun / 10am - 6pm
Mon,Tues & Thurs 6.30-9.30pm - club
only

*A nice open wall in the foyer to the leisure
ctr. Intended for kids introduction to
climbing and having fun. Not a venue for
the serious climber for more than half an
hour. Great for a give-it-a-go whirl.*

  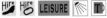

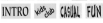

INTRO   kids club   CASUAL   FUN

MACHYNLLETH

(11) *Machynlleth Climbing Wall*
See South Wales section - 9.

BARMOUTH WALL

LLANDUDNO JUNCTION WALL

1 - PLYMOUTH
2 - BRISTOL/YEOVIL
3 - GUILDFORD
4 - MAIDSTONE
5 - LONDON
6 - IPSWICH
7 - OXFORD
8 - GLOUCESTER
9 - SOUTH WALES
10 - NORTH WALES
11 - BIRMINGHAM

1 - PLYMOUTH

2 - BRISTOL/YEOVIL

3 - GUILDFORD

4 - MAIDSTONE

5 - LONDON

6 - IPSWICH

7 - OXFORD

8 - GLOUCESTER

9 - SOUTH WALES

10 - NORTH WALES

11 - BIRMINGHAM

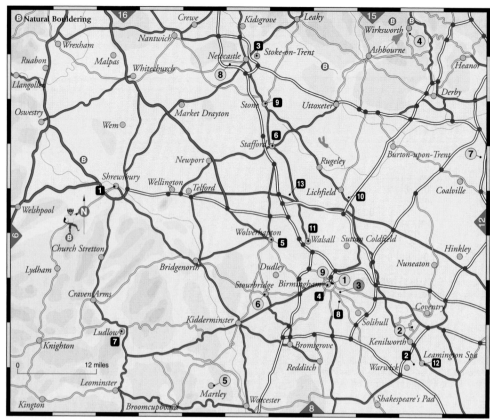

SPECIALIST CLIMBING SHOPS:

1 High Sports: SHOES ROPES GEAR CAMS BOOKS ICE

51-52 Wyle Cop, Shrewsbury. SY1 1XJ
Tel: 01743 231 649 Open: M-Sat 9-5.30pm

2 Escape 2 SHOES ROPES GEAR CAMS BOOKS ICE

29 Emscote Rd, Warwick, CV34 5QH (1/2 way between Warwick & Leam-Spa)
Tel: 0800 0286 836 Open: M-Fri 9.15am-6pm, Thurs-7pm, Sun 10.30-4.30pm

3 Mountain Fever: SHOES ROPES GEAR CAMS BOOKS ICE

25 Brunswick Street, Stoke on Trent, ST1 1DR
Tel: 01782 266 137 Open: M-Sat 9.30am-5.30pm

4 Snow & Rock:

14 Priory Queensway, Birmingham, B4 6BS
Tel: 0121 236 8280

5 White Mountain: SHOES ROPES GEAR CAMS BOOKS ICE

31 Stafford Street, Walsall, WS2 8DG (opposite leather museum)
Tel: 01922 722 422 Open: M-Sat 9.30am-5.30pm

6 Stafford Outdoor Leisure: SHOES ROPES GEAR CAMS BOOKS ICE

38 Mill Street, Stafford, ST16 2AJ
Tel: 01785 240 594 Open: Mon-Sat 9am - 5.30pm

7 Base Camp:

Ludlow Business Park, Ludlow, SY8 1XE
Tel: 01584 875 755

8 Taunton Leisure:

1045 Stratford Road, Birmingham, B28 8AS
Tel: 0121 777 3337

9 Outdoor Pursuits Co-Op: SHOES ROPES GEAR CAMS BOOKS ICE

24, Radford Street, Stone, ST15 8DA (Top end of town by Police station).
Tel: 01785 818 500 Tue-Fri 10am-5.30pm, Sat 9am-5.30pm

10 Ellis Brigham:

Leisure Island, Tamworth, B79 7ND
Tel: 01827 59047

11 White Mountain: SHOES ROPES GEAR CAMS BOOKS ICE

22 Worcester St, Wolverhampton, WV2 4LD (City centre)
Tel: 01902 773 395 Open: M-Sat 9.30am-5.30pm

12 Lockwoods: SHOES ROPES GEAR CAMS BOOKS ICE

125-129 Rugby Road, Leamington Spa, CV32 6DJ (300yds SW of A445-A452 jtn)
Tel: 01926 339 388 Tue-Fri 9am-6pm, Sat 9am-5.30pm

13 The Beaten Track UK:

6 High Green Court, Cannock, WS11 1AB
Tel: 01543 578 412

14 Hi-Peak Leisure Ltd:

Clough Street, Stoke on Trent, ST1 4AS
Tel: 01782 268 102

15 Jacksons of Old Arley:

Springhill, Coventry, CV7 8HN
Tel: 01676 540 878

Basic gear / local books   Good UK gear / UK books   Big range / Europe books   Expert range / Worldwide

Dedicated Bouldering (Square metres)

Grotto	Freeform Rock	Texture Panel	Flat Panel	Brick	Woody	Campus Board
28	0	28	28	0	0	0
50	60	0	0	0	0	0
14	44	0	0	0	0	0
15	59	0	0	0	0	0
0	24	23	0	0	0	0
42	0	51	0	66	0	0
0	0	0	0	0	0	0
0	48	0	0	24	0	0
0	60	0	0	0	0	0

Climbing wall - Sector by sector analysis

Bouldering Sqm. Climbing Total Sqm.

(Sector Height - Individual lines - Total routes in sector)

Climbing Walls		Instructional / T/R Bouldering		Top Rope-insitu / Leading		Lead-Tilting / Competition		Exterior / Sector Sq.m M
① The Rock Face	B 84 · C 858	FP 7-24-81 (203)	TP 7-12-26 (98)	TP 14-14-30 (196)	FP 11-3-7 (39)	FP 14-6-17 (98)	FP 20-6-20 (140)	
② Bear Rock	B 110 · C 470	FR 6m-6-20 (72)	FP 10-3-14 (42)	FP 10m-9-36 (116)	TP 10m-1-5 (10)	TP 10-2-4 (20)	TP 13-5-17 (100)	
③ Ackers Wall	B 58 · C 390	FR 6m-7-14 (54)	FR 7m-3-6 (46)	B 7-22-44 (196)	B 7-2-4 (36)			
④ Wirksworth	B 74 · C 201	FP 10m-2-7 (24)	FP 10m2-5 (26)	FP 10-1-3 (10)	TP 10-5-16 (52)	FP 10-1-4 (15)		
⑤ Martley	B 47 · C 185	FR 8m-1-3 (8)	TP 8-4-10 (38)	TP 11-6-15 (50)	TP 8-5-11 (42)			
⑥ Stourbridge	B 159 · C 159							
⑦ Shepshed	B 0 · C 84	B 7m-1-2 (14)	B 7m-2-2 (14)	B 7m-2-2 (28)	B 7m-3-3 (28)			
⑧ Keele	B 0 · C 72							
⑨ Aston Univ.	B 57 · C 60							

CLIMBING CLUBS - WEBSITE KEYWORDS

BEWDLEY & DISTRICT-MC, BROMSGROVE & REDDITCH-MC, COVENTRY-MC, HINKLEY-MC, LICHFIELD-MC, NUNEATON-MC, SHREWSBURY-MC, SOLIHULL-MC, THE MOUNTAIN CLUB, WALSALL ROCK & ICE-MC, WARWICK-CC, WOLVERHAMPTON-MC, WREAKIN-MC

BEAR ROCK - COVENTRY

1 - PLYMOUTH | 2 - BRISTOL/YEOVIL | 3 - GUILDFORD | 4 - MAIDSTONE | 5 - LONDON | 6 - IPSWICH | 7 - OXFORD | 8 - GLOUCESTER | 9 - SOUTH WALES | 10 - NORTH WALES | 11 - BIRMINGHAM

BIRMINGHAM - THE ROCK FACE

BIRMINGHAM ***

① The Rock Face

Birmingham Climbing Centre, Jennens Road, Millenium Point, Birmingham, B4 7QT

www.rockface.co.uk

Tel: 0121 359 6419

Access: 0.5 mile NE of New Street Stn (Birm-Ctr). Approach from M6 via A38(M)-Aston Expressway. Leave motorway at Dartmouth Circus, outer ring road (A4540) direction Coventry-Small Heath. After 0.35 mile you reach the roundabout of Jennens Road, turn R towards City centre and the wall is soon seen on the Left. (100 Yds).

P Free parking in centre car park, ✳ limited

Ad; £6.80 ~ Kid £6.30

Memb; £5.00

One off- 3 hr sat; £11.80 ~ (ouch!)

Mon - Fri / 10am - 10pm;

Sat & Sun / 10am - 8pm

(10am-6pm in summer)

A big climbing centre by any standards offerng a great variety of different routes and plenty to tire you out. A well organised venue that caters for instruction and teaching with special separate areas. The bouldering area is very good but surprisingly tiny for such a big wall; the main focus is on big, long leading routes. The wall fortunately managed to get an ex-competition lead -bulging sector that is plenty steep enough for most experts.

BIRMINGHAM - THE ROCK FACE: Bouldering area and separate teaching room.

1 - PLYMOUTH
2 - BRISTOL/YEOVIL
3 - GUILDFORD
4 - MAIDSTONE
5 - LONDON
6 - IPSWICH
7 - OXFORD
8 - GLOUCESTER
9 - SOUTH WALES
10 - NORTH WALES
11 - BIRMINGHAM

ACKERS WALL - Small Heath

COVENTRY ***
② *Bear Rock Indoor Climbing Centre*
Sports Centre, University of Warwick, Coventry, CV4 7AL
Tel: 024 7652 4880
Access: 2.6 miles SW of Coventry City Ctr. Find the A45 which circumnavigates the S side of Coventry. Leave this on the A429 towards Kenilworth (very straight road). Continue for 1.2 miles then turn R and follow signs to University. Locate multi storey car park No. 8. Park here and the sports centre is obvious.
🅿 £ Mon-fri 7am-4pm Pay-display.
Ad; £4.75 Weekdays ~ Kid; £3.45
£3.95 weekends
Mon - Fri / 7.30am -9.30pm;
Sat / 9.00am -5.30pm;
Sun / 10.00am -7.30pm;
A very good wall that offers both leading and bouldering. The cave-grotto sector has a good challenging roof covered in chunky holds and a few less pleasant. The side walls have very accomodating vertical routes for beginners, whilst the central competition is superbly demanding for the the experts. A big wall, but in big demand.

INTRO ADV kids club SWIM LEISURE

CASUAL FUN SERIOUS BUSY

BIRMINGHAM-SMALL HEATH *
③ *Ackers Wall*
The Ackers, Golden Hillock Road, Small Heath, Birmingham, B11 2PY
Tel: 0121 772 5111
www.ackers-adventure.co.uk
Access: 2.3 miles SE of B-Ham City ctr. Leave the Centre R-Road on the A45 going east. After 1 mile you arrive at the big roundabout at Small Heath. Turn R onto the B4145 towards Sparkhill (S). This is Golden Hillock Road, you go over the railway and canal, then contine for a few hundred yards and the centre is signposted to the left. The centre is set quite a long way back in the woods and is part of a ski slope little centre. The drive in past lots of broken glass is a bit worrying, but you actually can park very near the wall.
🅿 £ Free ✖
Ad £2.50 ~ Kid; £1.50
Mon - Fri / 10am -9pm;
Sat & Sun/ 10am - 5pm;
A substantial and good outdoor facility. There is a nice introduction slope set back to one side of the main climbing towers. It has some surprisingly good bouldering around it too. The main structure is classic 1980's and is brick with inset pieces of natural stone. A superb effort in a difficult urban area. Ideal for a lovely summer evening or a crisp and sunny spring day.

5 INTRO ADV kids club CALM BRIGHT QUIET OPEN FEEL

WIRKSWORTH **
④ *Wirksworth Wall*
Section 15 - Sheffield-Peaks

MARTLEY **
⑤ *Martley Wall*
Section 8 - Gloucester

STOURBRIDGE *
⑥ *Crystal Leisure Wall*
Crystal Leisure Centre, Bell Street, Stourbridge, DY8 1AE
Tel: 01384 812 910
Access: 50 yds W of High St. in town centre. Locate the clockwise directional, one way system in Stourbridge; circulate until 9 o'clock (not literally, nit-wit), where a road leads into the town centre and a multi storey car park opposite the leisure centre.
Ⓟ £ Pay-diplay, not refundable. ✸
Ad; £2.70 Weekdays ~ Kid; £2.15
Mon - Sun / 9.00am -11.00pm;
Mon 6-8pm course only
Tue - 6-8.30 course only
Room can be hired totally so ring to check if you are wanting just casual climbing.
A small excellent bouldering facility in a converted squash court. A nice mixture of textured panels and natural stone insets makes this a demanding wall for anyone. The good roof grotto is fun too. There are facilities for 5 top ropes with just a single bolt at the top.

DEEP-MATS INTRO SWIM LEISURE
QUIET CASUAL 🖼 📺 🍴 ♨ 🛒

SHEPSHED
⑦ *Hind Leys Wall*
Section - 12 Leicester

KEELE
⑧ *Keele Wall*
The Leisure Ctr, Keele University, Newcastle-Under-Lyme, ST5 5BG
Tel: 01782 583 368
Access: 2 miles WSW of Town Ctr. Leave town on the A525 going W towards Madeley. After 1.5 miles the University is signposted on the L. Follow signs to the Sport Ctr in the NW part.
£ Unknown
Ad; £2.50 Weekdays ~ Kid; £1.60
Mon - Sun / Early - late
A featured wall with natural rock inserts, fortunately not too steep since many of the holds resemble slippy bananas. Chech the route book out for all the local problems. Situated on a balcony overlooking the sports hall - good for viewing aerobics classes.

BIRMINGHAM - ASTON *
⑨ *Aston Uni - Wall*
Sports Ctr, AstonUniversity, Birmingham, B4 7ET
Tel: 0121 359 3611
Access: Access: 0.5 mile NE of New Street Stn (Birm-Ctr). Opposite the Rock Face almost.(300 Yds). From the R/F go across Jenners Road and down the small road on the L of the black horse pub. Take the road with the bar-gate soon on the L, this leads past the hockey pitch on the R, where the sports hall is set back to the L.
Ⓟ £ Free on Univ car park after 4.45pm Ⓟ at other times locally
Ad; £2.40 Weekdays ~ Kid; £1.20
Mon - Fri / 10am - 10pm
Sat - Sun/ 10am - 5pm
A freeform bendcrete bouldering wall that is popular with students and handy to know about if the bouldering gets too busy at the Rockface. Also lots of other sporting activities for everyone.

DEEP-MATS SWIM LEISURE
CASUAL FUN 📺 ♨

1 - PLYMOUTH

2 - BRISTOL/YEOVIL

3 - GUILDFORD

4 - MAIDSTONE

5 - LONDON

6 - IPSWICH

7 - OXFORD

8 - GLOUCESTER

9 - SOUTH WALES

10 - NORTH WALES

11 - BIRMINGHAM

STOURBRIDGE WALL

12 - LEICESTER

13 - NORWICH

14 - HULL

15 - SHEFFIELD

16 - LIVERPOOL

17 - LEEDS

18 - LANCASTER

19 - DARLINGTON

20 - KESWICK

21 - NEWCASTLE

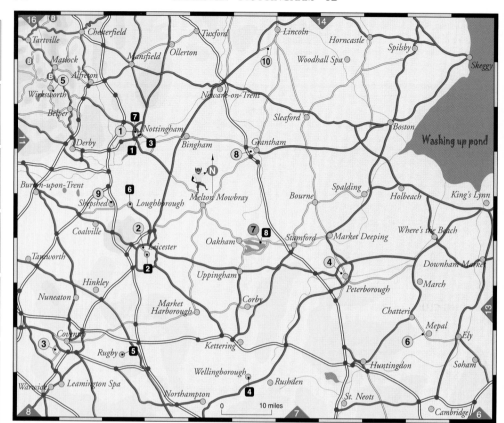

SPECIALIST CLIMBING SHOPS:

1 Castle Mountain & Moor: SHOES ROPES GEAR CAMS BOOKS ICE
40-44 Maid Marion Way, Nottingham, NG1 6GF (Inner ring road-West side)
Tel: 0115 941 4059   Open: M,T,T,F,Sat 9am-5.30-pm, Wed 10-6pm; Sun 11-4pm

2 Canyon Mountain Sports: SHOES ROPES GEAR CAMS BOOKS ICE
92 Granby Street, Leicester, LE1 1DJ (Next to City art gallery & Plantagenet pub)
Tel: 0116 255 7957   Open: Mon 9.30-5.30pm, Tue-Sat 9.00-5.30pm

3 Nevisport
21 St Peter's Gate, Nottingham, NG1 2JF
Tel: 0115 950 3455

4 Tradewinds Outdoor Ctr: SHOES ROPES GEAR ICE
4 Park Road, Wellingborough, NN8 4PG
Tel: 01933 276 632   Open: M-Fri 9.30am-5.30pm; Sat 9am-5pm

5 White and Bishop:
29-31 Clifton Road, Rugby, CV21 3PY
Tel: 01788 579 476

6 At The Mountain:
52 Sparrow Hill, Loughborough, LE11 1DE
Tel: 01509 212 868

7 Nottingham Climbing Centre: SHOES ROPES GEAR BOOKS
Haydn Road, Nottingham, NG5 1EB
Tel: 0115 924 5388   Open: Mon-Fri 10am - 10pm , Sat & Sun 10am-7pm

8 The Rock Blok:
Bull Brigg Lane, Whitwell, Rutland Water, LE15 8BL
Tel: 01780 460 060

9 Decathlon:
Ikea Retail Park, Nottingham, NG16 2RP
Tel: 0115 938 2020

ROCKBLOK

Basic gear / local books   Good UK gear / UK books   Big range / Europe books   Expert range / Worldwide

Dedicated Bouldering (Square metres)   Climbing wall - Sector by sector analysis

Grotto	Freeform Rock	Texture Panel	Flat Panel	Brick	Woody	Campus Board	Climbing Walls	Bouldering Sqm	Climbing Total Sqm
28	0	280	0	0	0	0	(1) Nottingham	B 300	C 530
52	12	76	0	20	0	0	(2) Leicester - Tower	B 162	C 485
50	60	0	0	0	0	0	(3) Bear Rock	B 110	C 470
37	0	0	0	27	0	6	(4) Peterborough	B 70	C 201
15	59	0	0	0	0	0	(5) Wirksworth	B 74	C 185
0	0	0	0	0	0	0	(6) Mepal	B 0	C 123
0	0	0	0	0	10	0	(7) Rock Blok	B 0	C 122
0	0	0	0	0	0	0	(8) Grantham	B 0	C 120
0	0	0	0	0	0	0	(9) Shepshed	B 0	C 84
0	0	0	0	0	0	0	(10) Lincoln	B 0	C 72

Sector types: Instructional   Top Rope-insitu   Lead-Tilting   Exterior   T/R Bouldering   Leading   Competition   Sector Sq.m M

(Sector Height - Individual lines - Total routes in sector)

Climbing Walls	Sector 1	Sq.m	Sector 2	Sq.m	Sector 3	Sq.m	Sector 4	Sq.m	Sector 5	Sq.m	Sector 6	Sq.m
(1) Nottingham	TP 7-4-13	35	FP 7-9-29	56	TP 7m-1-3	7	TP 7m-6-17	56	FP 9-3-6	36	FP 8-5-14	40
(2) Leicester - Tower	TP 5m-6-20	38	FR 6-8-24	54	TP 12m-5-26	60	TP 14-4-12	75	TP 15-3-10	60	TP 15-3-12	36
(3) Bear Rock	FR 6m-6-20	72	FP 10-3-14	42	FP 10m-9-36	116	TP 10m-1-5	10	TP 10-2-4	20	TP 13-5-17	100
(4) Peterborough	FP 6m-3-12	24	FP 8m-7-28	48	FP 6-5-20	36	TP 5-1-30	12	TP 12-3-12	24		
(5) Wirksworth	FP 10m-2-7	24	FP 10m-2-5	26	FP 10-1-3	10	TP 10-5-16	52	FP 10-1-4	15		
(6) Mepal	FR 5m-3-3	15	FR 5m-1-5	15	FR 5m-5-16	25	FR 6m-3-6	18	TP 10m-3-9	50		
(7) Rock Blok	FR 8m-4-8	24	FR 8m-3-6	24	FR 8m-3-9	40	FR 8m-2-4	24				
(8) Grantham	FP 8-15-30	120										
(9) Shepshed	B 7m-1-2	14	B 7m-2-2	14	B 7m-2-2	28	B 7m-3-3	28				
(10) Lincoln	B 8m-9-18	72										

CLIMBING CLUBS - WEBSITE KEYWORDS

BOWLINE-CC (Leicester), HINKLEY-MC, FRAYEDNOTTS-MC
NUNEATON-MC, RUGBY-MC

NOTTINGHAM CLIMBING CENTRE

12 - LEICESTER | 13 - NORWICH | 14 - HULL | 15 - SHEFFIELD | 16 - LIVERPOOL | 17 - LEEDS | 18 - LANCASTER | 19 - DARLINGTON | 20 - KESWICK | 21 - NEWCASTLE

12 - LEICESTER

13 - NORWICH

14 - HULL

15 - SHEFFIELD

16 - LIVERPOOL

17 - LEEDS

18 - LANCASTER

19 - DARLINGTON

20 - KESWICK

21 - NEWCASTLE

LEICESTER WALL

NOTTINGHAM ***

① The Nottingham Climbing Centre

The Sports Ground, Haydn Road, Sherwood,
Nottingham, NG5 1EB
www.nottingham-climbing.co.uk
Tel: 0115 924 5388

Access: 2 miles NNW of City Ctr. Easiest
approach is from West side -Outer ring road
(Western Boulevard-A6514). Find the A611
Hucknall Rd, and go towards City Ctr, after
0.7 mile turn R into Haydn Road, the centre
turning is 600yds on the R. (Can also be
accessed by the B682 Nottingham Road
- from the WB)

P £ free

Ad; £5.50 ~ Kid £3.00
Memb £2.50 for life.
3hr-sat-pm-one off, £8.00

Mon - Fri / 10am - 10pm;
Sat - Sun / 10am - 7pm; (10-6pm B-Hols)

*A top class bouldering centre, run by
Derrick Bolger - a climbing legend! Here you
experience just how good problems can be, set
on a straightforward climbing wall; flat panels
are set alight by the ingenuity of route setting.
A good earthy feel to the centre, and some
quite punchy little leading walls give an all
round appeal. A good place to pick up tips on
climbing, nice and friendly no matter what ever
standard you climb to.*

LEICESTER ***

② The Tower Climbing Centre

Leciester Leys Leisure Ctr, Beaumont Way,
Beaumont Leys, Leicester, LE4 1DS
Tel: 0116 233 3074

Access: 2 miles NNW of City Ctr. From the M1,
go to the Groby Jtn on the A46 via A46-A50.
Continue on the A46 to the next Jtn. at Anstey,
turn towards Lecis CC on the A5630 Anstey
Lane. Very shortly turn L at a roundabout onto
Heacam Drive. This leads to the centre soon on
the right, set back behind the big superstore-
(Tesco at present).

P £ free in main car park

Ad; £4.50 ~ Kid £3.00
No memb

Mon, Thur/ 4pm - 10pm; (Kid club sat)
Tue, Wed, Fri/ 12pm - 10pm;
Sat / 10am - 5.30pm Sun / 12pm - 7.30pm

*A good all round centre with 3 separate areas; a
good bouldering terrace with a nice cave sector;
a special room for group instruction on sensible
angled rock and medium height; a giant room
with huge leading walls that can frighten you. A
well run and dedicated climbing centre.*

NOTTINGHAM WALL

LEICESTER WALL

LEICESTER WALL

12 - LEICESTER
13 - NORWICH
14 - HULL
15 - SHEFFIELD
16 - LIVERPOOL
17 - LEEDS
18 - LANCASTER
19 - DARLINGTON
20 - KESWICK
21 - NEWCASTLE

COVENTRY ***
③ *Bear Rock Climbing Wall*
See section 11 - Birmingham

PETERBOROUGH **
④ *Peterborough Climbing Wall*
Peterborough Climbing Wall, next to
Edith Cavell Hospital, Peterborugh
PE3 6UZ
Tel: 01733 560 303 Mob: 07803
726 664
Access: 1.7 miles NW of town Ctr.
Approach from A47 bypass to the
N. Turn off at Jtn with A15, and go
towards town Ctr. Soon you see the
hospital on your right and the wall is
to the left of it, next to some playing
fields.
🅿 £ free
Ad; £4.50 ~ Kid £4.50
Mon - Fri / 7pm - 10pm;
Sat - Sun / 1pm - 9pm;
Open at other times by arrangement.

PETERBOROUGH - GROTTO

A championship style squash court has been transposed into a superb climbing venue, one of the best conversion of its style in the country. A nice mixture of freeform with sensible sized holds, even a giant hanging stalictite. Plenty of good features such as an adjustable panel, bachar ladder etc. give it a good earthy feel to this happy and relaxed venue. Upstairs a superb grotto tube to keep the gorillas happy. Good matting. Run by local climbers who certainly know what you need at your local wall.

         DEEP-MATS INTRO ADV CASUAL EARTHY FRIENDLY FUN

PETERBOROUGH WALL

WIRKSWORTH **
(5) *Wirksworth Climbing Wall*
See section 15 - Sheffield

ELY-MEPAL *
(6) *Mepal Climbing Wall*
Mepal Outdoor Centre, Chatteris Road,
Mepal, CB6 2AZ
Tel: 01354 692 251
Access: 6.6 miles WNW of Ely. Leave Ely
on the A142 towards Chatteris. After 5 miles
you pass the village of Mepal on your R. Go
over the very straight rivers and then you
see an overlarge teepee on the left, the wall
is inside this.
P £ free
Ad; £3.50 ~ Kid £3.50
Mon - Sun / 9am - 5.30pm
Tuesday - open climbing evening. For
further evening use ring the centre for up to
date arrangements & details.
Sat & Sun mornings; there are family activity
days to encourage all family fun across a
whole range of activities.
*A good facility with a rough bouldering
area plus a curved and stylish leading
area. Small but good and inventory. Simple
panels have enough texture for using
footholds only routes. Cool in any season
as air flows through the teepee quite freely.
(Temperature rises rapidly with altitude.)
A bit weird because of road noise, but a
welcome addition to the area. Kids must be
accompanied by an adult.*

INTRO ADV CALM NOISY GLOOMY

OAKHAM - RUTLAND WATER
(7) *Rockblok Climbing Wall*
The Rockblok, Whitwell, Rutland Water LE15 8BL
Tel: 01780 460 060
Access: 4 miles E of Oakham. Take the A606
along the N side of Rutland Water from Oakham.
In 4 miles arrive at Whitwell village where a
turning on the R leads to the wall and the lake.
P £ Pay and Display
Ad; £5 ~ Kid £5
Memb £5
One off - 3hr sat afternoon £10
Mon - Sun / 9am - 6pm
Instructor on site everyday offering taster
sessions, floodlit but ring to check for instructors.
*A lovely fun climbing obeslisk overlooking Rutland
Water. Kids seem to love it, and at 8 metres it is
certainly challenging for the beginner. A nice play
for the intermediate on a nice sunny day. The
routes are nicely set for beginners to enjoy and
get a good work out, with not a crimp in sight. A
ladder inside the tower for access to abseil and
general ease of instruction.*

INTRO ADV kids club OPEN FEEL

MEPAL WALL

GRANTHAM
(8) *Grantham Climbing Wall*
Meres Leisure Ctr, Trent Rd,
NG31 7XQ
Tel: 01476 581 930
Access: 1.3 miles WSW of
Grantham ctr. Exit A1 at the
A52 turn off towards town ctr.
After 0.6 mile, turn R at the
big roundabout onto Barrowby
Gate The curves round for
0.6 mile to the main Barrowby
Road (Dysart Road). Do a
quick L, then R into Trent Rd
and the LC
P £ free
Ad; £5.05 ~ Kid £3.05
Mon - Sun / 9am - 10pm
Kids must be 8 years old, ring
for a come & try session.
*A separate climbing room
allows for good climbing fun
- unchecked as yet by JW.*

INTRO kids club

CASUAL FUN

LINCOLN
(10) *Lincoln Climbing Wall*
North Kesteven Leisure Ctr.
Tel: 01522 883 311
A flat wall with a few brick
holds. *The area desperately
needs a local wall.*

SHEPSHED
(9) *Shepshed Climbing Wall*
Hind Lees Community College, Forest St,
Shepshed, LE12 9DB
Tel: 01509 504 511
Access: 0.4 miles NNE of Shepshed Village
ctr. Follow high street to the very top end, &
the College is around to the R.
P £ free
Ad; £1.75 ~ Kid £1.25
Groups by arrangement
Mon - Fri / 3.30pm - 9.30pm
Sat - Sun / Daytime
*An old brick wall climbing wall that still seems
popular and is well used. Available for group
use with a qualified instructor.*

 INTRO LEISURE   GLOOMY QUIET

SHEPSHED WALL

12 - LEICESTER
13 - NORWICH
14 - HULL
15 - SHEFFIELD
16 - LIVERPOOL
17 - LEEDS
18 - LANCASTER
19 - DARLINGTON
20 - KESWICK
21 - NEWCASTLE

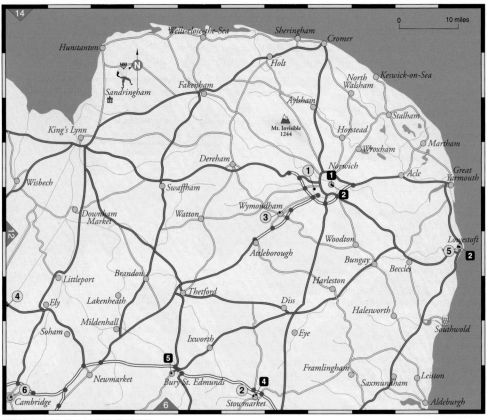

SPECIALIST CLIMBING SHOPS:

1 Venturesport: SHOES ROPES GEAR CAMS BOOKS ICE
17 Westlegate, Norwich, NR1 3LT
Tel: 01603 613 378 Open: Mon-Sat 9am-5.30-pm, Thurs -7pm

2 Sam Hook Sports:
131/132 Bevan Street, Lowestoft, NR32 2AQ
Tel: 01502 565 821

3 Norwich Camping Co:
54-6 Magdalen Street, Norwich, NR3 1JE
Tel: 01603 615 525

4 Outdoor People:
Stowupland Road, Stowmarket, IP14 5AH
Tel: 01449 675 511

5 Stepping Out:
55 St John's Street, Bury St Edmunds, IP33 1SN
Tel: 01284 763 150

CLIMBING CLUBS - WEBSITE KEYWORDS
NORWICH CAVING & CLIMBING CLUB, STOWMARKET-MC
UEA ROCKCLIMBING & MOUNTAINEERING CLUB

BOREAL

Basic gear / local books   Good UK gear / UK books   Big range / Europe books   Expert range / Worldwide

Dedicated Bouldering (Square metres) — Climbing wall - Sector by sector analysis

Grotto	Freeform Rock	Texture Panel	Flat Panel	Brick	Woody	Campus Board	Bouldering Sqm. / Climbing Total Sqm. *Climbing Walls*	Instructional / T/R Bouldering	Top Rope-insitu / Leading	Lead-Tilting / Competition	Exterior / Sector Sq.m M
							(Sector Height - Individual lines - Total routes in sector)				
21	0	0	0	0	0	0	① *Norwich UEA* — B 21 — C 240	FR 9m-3-15 [45]	FR 9-5-18 [73]	FR 11-1-4 [11]	FR 11-4-12 [50]	FR 11-3-10 [40]
0	0	28	40	0	0	0	② *Stowmarket* — B 68 — C 178	FP 7m-2-5 [18]	FP 7m-1-3 [7]	TP 6-5-15 [30]	TP 6-4-16 [30]	TP 7-2-12 [25]
0	0	15	0	10	0	0	③ *Wymondham* — B 25 — C 135	B 4m-3-5 [16]	TP 7-2-7 [22]	TP 10-2-4 [20]	TP 7-2-10 [22]	TP 10-4-6 [30]
0	0	0	0	0	0	0	④ *Mepal* — B 0 — C 123	FR 5m-3-3 [15]	FR 5m-1-5 [15]	FR 5m-5-16 [25]	FR 6m-3-6 [18]	TP 10m-3-9 [50]
0	0	0	0	0	0	0	⑤ *Lowestoft* — B 0 — C 110	FP 9m-2-6 [15]	TP 9-2-9 [28]	B 9m-3-4 [28]	TP 10m-3-8 [30]	
0	0	0	0	0	0	0	⑥ *Cambridge* — 0 — C 109	TP 4m-3-9 [14]	FR 5-10-30 [60]	FR 5m-3-9 [15]	FR 5m-2-12 [20]	

UEA WALL (Dave Reeve climbing)

12 - LEICESTER | 13 - NORWICH | 14 - HULL | 15 - SHEFFIELD | 16 - LIVERPOOL | 17 - LEEDS | 18 - LANCASTER | 19 - DARLINGTON | 20 - KESWICK | 21 - NEWCASTLE

NORWICH ***
(1) UEA Wall - The Peak
University of East Anglia, Watton Road, Norwich NR4 7TJ
Tel: 01603 592 398
Access: 2.5 miles WSW of City Ctr. West approach is from A47
Norwich bypass. Locate the B1108 that comes into town from
9 o'clock, take this and after 1.4 miles (Past Colney), you go
up a hill and the Univ is on the R and the sports centre is sign
posted. The main road B1108 continues to the outer ring road
(at 2nd roudabout). This is generally a good access way for
points East.
P £ free, but you have to collect a ticket from reception,
otherwise pay up. **P**
Ad; £3.50 ~ Kid; £3.50
Memb £0.50
Mon - Sun / 7.30am - 10pm
st to ring and check for availability.

UEA WALL (Olie the happy boulderer)

*This brand new giant sports centre must be the envy of all
Universities of the UK, with an olympic size swimming pool
and just about every other sporting facility. The climbing wall is
superbly situated opposite the cafe and restaraunt area, and
has a nice comfortable feel to it. Awash with lovely sunshine
and daylight, due to the huge windows. It is a wall that looks
bigger than it is, but in saying that, still feels big and exhausting.
A small grotto is very good for warming up, with excellent mats.
The lead areas are comfortably angled, with a few testing steep
sections to aspire to. A lovely all round facility.*

STOWMARKET **
(2) The Cragg Section 6 - Ipswich

Insitu DEEP-MATS SWIM LEISURE ♫ INTRO ADV kids club ⟨☁⟩ T I●I ▦ FUN CASUAL BRIGHT GLOOMY HUMID

UEA WALL

UEA WALL

12 - LEICESTER

13 - NORWICH

14 - HULL

15 - SHEFFIELD

16 - LIVERPOOL

17 - LEEDS

18 - LANCASTER

19 - DARLINGTON

20 - KESWICK

21 - NEWCASTLE

STOWMARKET WALL

LOWESTOFT WALL

WYMONDHAM **

(3) *Wymondham Climbing Wall*
Wymondham Leisure Ctr. Norwich
Road, Wymondham NR18 0NT
Tel: 01953 607 171
Access: 600 yds NE of village ctr. Is
signposted from the village ctr. and is
next to Wymondham high school.
P £ free.
Ad; £4.00 ~ Kid; £2.30
Mon, Wed, Fri / 7am - 10pm
Tue / 7am - 6.30pm (Courses till 10pm)
Thur / 7am - 8.30pm
Sat / 9am-5.30pm, Sun 9am-9.30pm
The wall often closes around 4-5pm on
Bank holidays.
*A big wall that is impressive and
certainly tests your stamina. A nice
dedicated wall at the end of a sports
ctr. and is separated by a barrier and
netting. Good textured panels make
up for the relatively few bolt ons. Not a
huge amount of climbing, but high in
quality and taxing for most. A lot quieter
than UEA, and handy to know about for
some laid back climbing.*

6   DEEP-MATS   SWIM   LEISURE
INTRO   ADV   CALM 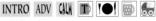

ELY - MEPAL *
(4) *Mepal Climbing Wall* - Section - 11

LOWESTOFT *
(5) *East Face Indoor Climbing Wall*
Waveney Sports Ctr, Water Lane,
Lowestoft, Suffolk, NR32 2NH
Tel: 01502 563 829
Access: 0.6m NNW of Lowestoft Stn.
Take the main A1117 bypass to the
N side of the River (Oulton Broad). At
the 3rd roundabout, turn R onto A1144
(Normanston Drive?). Pass another
roundabout (Road becomes St. Peter
St.) and shortly Water Lane is on the L.
P £ free.
Ad; £4.00 ~ Kid; £3.00
Memb £ 0.45
Mon - Fri / 8am - 10.30pm
Sat - till 10pm; Sun till 5pm
*A well situated full height wall in a large
sports hall. Built up to the ceiling - how
intelligent. Very high quality textured
panels allow a vast option of routes.
System allows panels to be changed
from time to time - excellent idea. Hall
is sometimes used for events so ring for
availability. Top ropes insitu.*

Insitu   INTRO   kids club   SWIM   LEISURE
   CASUAL FUN QUIET

CAMBRIDGE *
(6) *Climbing Wall* - Section - 6

12 - LEICESTER

13 - NORWICH

14 - HULL

15 - SHEFFIELD

16 - LIVERPOOL

17 - LEEDS

18 - LANCASTER

19 - DARLINGTON

20 - KESWICK

21 - NEWCASTLE

WYMONDHAM WALL

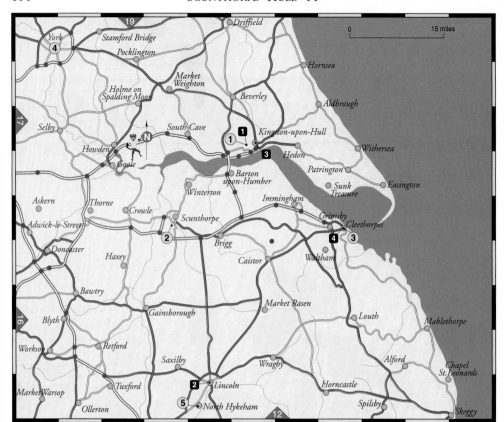

SPECIALIST CLIMBING SHOPS:

1 Rock City: SHOES ROPES GEAR CAMS BOOKS ICE
Hawthorne Avenue, Hull, HU3 5JX (Inside the climbing wall centre)
Tel: 01482 223 030   Open: Mon-Fri 10am-10pm, Sat 10-8pm, Sun 10-10pm

2 Linsports:
21-23 Silver Street, Lincoln, LN2 1EX
Tel: 01522 524 674

3 Wet and Wild Adventure Sports
619 Anlaby Road, Hull, HU3 6SU
Tel: 01482 354 076

4 Kingsway Sports:
139 Grimsby Road, Cleethorpes, DN35 7DG
Tel: 01472 601 616

12 - LEICESTER
13 - NORWICH
14 - HULL
15 - SHEFFIELD
16 - LIVERPOOL
17 - LEEDS
18 - LANCASTER
119 - DARLINGTON
20 - KESWICK
21 - NEWCASTLE

CLIMBING CLUBS - WEBSITE KEYWORDS
SCUNTHORPE-CC
LINDSEY-CC

Basic gear / local books   Good UK gear / UK books   Big range / Europe books   Expert range / Worldwide

Dedicated Bouldering (Square metres)   Climbing wall - Sector by sector analysis

Grotto	Freeform Rock	Texture Panel	Flat Panel	Brick	Woody	Campus Board	Climbing Walls	Instructional / T/R Bouldering	Top Rope-insitu / Leading	Lead-Tilting / Competition	Exterior / Sector Sq.m M
								(Sector Height - Individual lines - Total routes in sector)			
159	0	0	96	0	0	2	① Rock City - Hull B 257 C 1111	FR 10-12-48 · 200 FP 11-6-12 · 75	FP 10-8-16 · 124 FP 11-5-15 · 86	FR 12-12-24 · 204	FP 15-8-24 · 165
0	0	0	0	0	0	0	② Scunthorpe B 0 C 178	B 7-10-20 · 70	TP 7m-3-9 · 21	TP 7m-3-9 · 21	
0	0	0	0	0	0	0	③ Cleethorpes B 0 C ?				
0	0	0	0	0	0	0	④ York B 0 C ?				
0	0	0	0	0	0	0	⑤ Lincoln B 0 C 72	B 8m-9-18 · 72			

LINCOLN WALL

GROTTO AT ROCK CITY - HULL

12 - LEICESTER   13 - NORWICH   14 - HULL   15 - SHEFFIELD   16 - LIVERPOOL   17 - LEEDS   18 - LANCASTER   19 - DARLINGTON   20 - KESWICK   21 - NEWCASTLE

12 - LEICESTER

13 - NORWICH

14 - HULL

15 - SHEFFIELD

16 - LIVERPOOL

17 - LEEDS

18 - LANCASTER

19 - DARLINGTON

20 - KESWICK

21 - NEWCASTLE

HULL ****

① **Rock City Climbing Centre**
Hawthorne Ave, Hull, HU3 5JX
Tel: 01482 223 030
Access: 2.5 miles WSW of Hull ctr.
Approach from the A63 fast whizzy road.
Pass under the Humber bridge, then take
the 2nd exit after 3 miles. (Sign Quay and
KC stadium). Turn L at Jtn, then follow
signs to the centre (about 500 yds).
🅿 Free parking ✴
Ad; £7.00 Kid£ 5.50
Memb; £10.00 per year
One off- 3 hr sat; £7 special
Mon - Fri & Sun / 10am - 10pm;
Sat / 10am - 8pm

*The place to come if you want plenty to
go at and get completely exhausted. More
than enough here for a lifetime. Big walls
in the lead sector, plus lots more new
developments in this cavernous hangar.
Pride goes to the bouldering; a superb
grotto with natural jugs and texture, then
upstairs a flat woody style bouldering wall
for comp problems. Matting is very good
and superbly positioned. A truly superb
intense climbing venue.*

SCUNTHORPE *

② **West Common Youth Club**
West Common Lane, Scunthorpe, DN17
1DS
Tel: 01724 865 407
Access: 1 mile SSW of Station. Take
the M181 to the big roundabout W of
Scunthorpe. Turn R onto the A18 towards
Sth. Follow this for about 2 miles to a big
roundabout with the A159. Turn R down
the A159 (Ashby Rd). After a few hundred
yards turn R onto West Common Lane,
leading to the centre after a short while!
🅿 Free parking ✴
Ad; £1.00
Thurs / evening

*This is a sports centre for Youths up to
25 years old. Avaliable for group use with
instructor, ring for availability.*

*An old vertical brick wall in a sports hall has
been added to with textured panels to start
getting it up to speed. A handy local venue
to know about for kids wanting to have a go
at climbing.*

YORK

⑤ Wall got stolen! by developers!
See section - 19

LINCOLN

⑥ **Lincoln Wall**
North Kesteven Leisure Ctr.
Tel: 01522 883 311
A flat wall with a few brick holds. *The area desperately needs a local wall.*

CLEETHORPES **

③ **Lindsey Climbing Wall**
The Lindsey School, Grainsby Ave,
Cleethorpes, DN35 9NX
Tel: 01742 500 123
Access: 1 mile SW of Cleethorpes town ctr
& Station. Approaching from the S, leave
the A16 near Waltham and cut up to town
on the A1098. This comes to a junction
with supermarket on the R (Tesco!) go
straight on (Taylors Ave). After 500 yds
turn L onto Middle Thorpe, then 2nd R is
Grainsbly Ave and the school is on the R.
The wall is in the sports hall.
🅿 Free parking
Ad; £1.00
Memb; £10.00 per year
Thurs / 7.30pm - 9.30pm;

The wall is in the school, which allows use
by the members of the Lindsey climbing
club, a chirpy and happy bunch that
welcome new members.

*A good little wall that is the height of the
sports hall. There is an opportunity to lead
climbs here, but the general form is to use
big and deep crash pads and enjoy some
airy bouldering. The wall seems to keep
growing additions with new tufas arriving
as we write this up. An enthusastic bunch
of climbers.*

12 - LEICESTER

13 - NORWICH

14 - HULL

15 - SHEFFIELD

16 - LIVERPOOL

17 - LEEDS

18 - LANCASTER

19 - DARLINGTON

20 - KESWICK

21 - NEWCASTLE

ROCK CITY - HULL

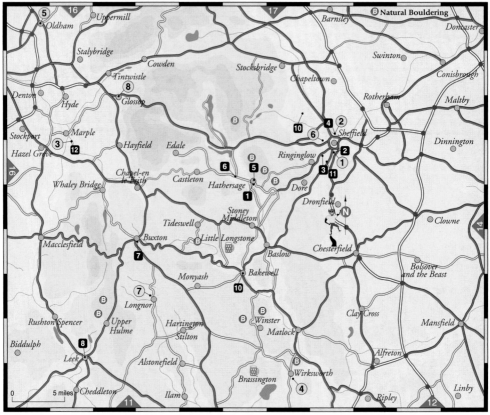

SPECIALIST CLIMBING SHOPS:

1 Outside: `SHOES` `ROPES` `GEAR` `CAMS` `BOOKS` `ICE`
Main Road, Hathersage, S30 1BB (Next to filling station with cafe upstairs)
Tel: 01433 651 936 Open: Mon-Sun 9.30am-5.30pm

2 Rock Sport - Edge: `SHOES` `ROPES` `GEAR` `CAMS` `BOOKS` `ICE`
John Street, Sheffield, S2 4QU (Just up the road from Shef United ground)
Tel: 0114 275 8899 Open: Mon-Fri 10am-8.30pm, Sat 9.00-6pm, Sun 10-5pm

3 Rock Sport - Psalt: `SHOES` `ROPES` `GEAR` `CAMS` `BOOKS`
392 Psalter Lane, Sheffield, S11 8UX (Jtn with Eccleshall Rd-Rte to Fox House)
Tel: 0114 266 7333 Open: Mon-Fri 9.30am-6.30pm, Sat 9.00-6pm, Sun 10-5.30pm

4 Crag X: `SHOES` `ROPES` `GEAR` `CAMS` `BOOKS`
The Foundry, Unit 2, 43 Mowbray St. Sheffield, S3 8EN
Tel: 0114 276 9741 Open: Mon 12-6, Tue-Thur 12-8pm, Fri 11-5, W/E 10-6pm

5 Nevisport: `SHOES` `ROPES` `GEAR` `CAMS` `BOOKS` `ICE`
The Square, Hathersage, S32 1BB
Tel: 01433 659 666 Open: M-Fri 9-5.30 (Wint) M-Sun 9-6 (rest of yr)

6 Hitch & Hike: `SHOES` `ROPES` `GEAR` `CAMS` `BOOKS` `ICE`
Mytham Bridge, Bamford, S30 0BH
Tel: 01433 651 013 Open: Mon-Sun 10am-5.30pm

7 Jo Royle: `SHOES` `ROPES` `GEAR` `CAMS` `BOOKS` `ICE`
6 Market Place, Buxton, SK17 6EB
Tel: 01298 25824 Open: Mon-Sat 9.30am - 5.30pm, Sun 10am-4pm

8 Reaching New Heights: `SHOES` `ROPES` `GEAR` `CAMS` `BOOKS` `ICE`
Fountain Street, Leek, ST13 6JS
Tel: 01538 373 854 Open: M-Sat 9-5.30; (Wed 9-3pm) Sun 10-2; Longer in summer

9 Decathlon:
Eyre Street, Sheffield, S1 4QZ
Tel: 0115 938 2020

10 The Peak Store: `SHOES` `ROPES` `GEAR` `CAMS` `BOOKS` `ICE`
Bridge St, Bakewell, DE45 1DS
Tel: 01629 815 681 Open: Mon-Sun 9am-5.30pm (Wint 10-5pm, S&S 9.3-5.30pm)

11 Foothills: `ROPES` `GEAR` `CAMS` `BOOKS` `ICE`
11 Edgedale Road, Sheffield, S7 2BQ
Tel: 0114 258 6228 Open; Mon-Fri 10am-6pm, Sat 9-5pm

12 Rope Race: `SHOES` `ROPES` `GEAR` `CAMS` `BOOKS` `ICE`
The Goyt Mill, Upper Hibbert Lane, Marple, Stockport, SK7 6HX
Tel: 0161 426 0226 Open: Mon-Thu 10-10pm, Fri 10-9pm, Sat & Sun 10-6pm

CLIMBING CLUBS - WEBSITE KEYWORDS
PEAK-CC, PARNASSUS-MC (Sh), CASTLE-MC (Sh),
ARETE-MC (Barnsley)

Basic gear / local books	Good UK gear / UK books	Big range / Europe books	Expert range / Worldwide

12 - LEICESTER
13 - NORWICH
14 - HULL
15 - SHEFFIELD
16 - LIVERPOOL
17 - LEEDS
18 - LANCASTER
19 - DARLINGTON
20 - KESWICK
21 - NEWCASTLE

Dedicated Bouldering (Square metres)

	Grotto	Freeform Rock	Texture Panel	Flat Panel	Brick	Woody	Campus Board	Climbing Walls	Bouldering Sqm (B)	Climbing Total Sqm (C)
1	162	70	0	88	10	0	0	Edge - Sheffield	330	957
2	0	94	0	0	54	30	2	Foundry - Sheffield	180	903
3	0	70	56	0	0	9	0	Rope Race	135	563
4	15	59	0	0	0	0	0	Wirksworth	74	185
5	0	0	0	0	0	0	0	Oldham	0	142
6	15	102	0	18	0	0	0	Matrix - Sheffield	135	135
7	0	12	0	95	0	0	0	Longnor	64	64
8	0	64	0	0	0	0	0	Glossup	646	64

Climbing wall - Sector by sector analysis

(Sector Height - Individual lines - Total routes in sector)

	Instructional / T/R Bouldering		Top Rope-insitu / Leading		Lead-Tilting / Competition		Exterior (Sector Sq.m M)
1 Edge - Sheffield	TP 11-8-24 (110)	FP 10-10-30 (130)	TP 12m-2-8 (36)	FP 12-12-36 (216)	FP 15-5-15 (75)	TP 15-3-10 (60)	
2 Foundry - Sheffield	FP 9m-5-15 (83)	FP 9-4-12 (56)	FP 9-12-36 (147)	FP 12-12-23 (192)	FP 11-8-30 (165)	FP 17-4-5 (80)	
3 Rope Race	FP 9m-4-14 (50)	FP 9-7-21 (77)	TP 9m-6-20 (81)	FP 10m-1-4 (20)	FP 13-3-12 (65)	FR 18-4-16 (135)	
4 Wirksworth	FP 10m-2-7 (24)	FP 10m-2-5 (26)	FP 10-1-3 (10)	TP 10-5-16 (52)	FP 10-1-4 (15)		
5 Oldham	TP 4m-2-6 (11)	TP 4m-2-8 (11)	TP 4-7-28 (30)	TP 5-10-40 (60)	TP 6-5-8 (30)		

FOUNDRY HEADWALL - THE FIRST MAINSTREAM UK CLIMBING WALL

17 - LEICESTER
13 - NORWICH
14 - HULL
15 - SHEFFIELD
16 - LIVERPOOL
17 - LEEDS
18 - LANCASTER
119 - DARLINGTON
20 - KESWICK
21 - NEWCASTLE

SHEFFIELD ★★★★

① The Edge Climbing Centre
John Street, Sheffield, S2 4QU
Tel: 0114 275 8899
Access: 1.2 mile SSW of City ctr. Approaching from the A625 (Peaks in the rain), arrive at the ring road and turn R. At the next roundabout, turn R onto Bramall Lane, continue out of town and John St. is on the right opposite the Football stadium.

P £ free, in centre car park.
Ad; £6.50 ~ Kid; £4.50
One off visit; £6.50
Mon - Fri / 10am -10.30pm;
Sat - Sun/ 10am - 8.30pm;
Summer time closes 6pm Sat & Sun

A complete climbing centre that offers everything for the full on climber. The bouldering room is an overhang that defies description, with its size and expanse, and also superb springy matting. There is also a superb freeform bouldering area for the not so strong. The lead walls are all huge, and some just keep overhanging for ever. Some of the large walls are also hydraulic so the angles can be changed. A very good all round centre for anyone.

Insitu Hire Hire DEEP-MATS
INTRO ADV kids club T ｜●｜
CALM SERIOUS EARTHY BRIGHT GLOOMY BUSY

EDGE Boulder room　　　*EDGE Woodie Grotto*

EDGE - Lead area

12 - LEICESTER   13 - NORWICH   14 - HULL   15- SHEFFIELD   16 - LIVERPOOL   17 - LEEDS   18 - LANCASTER   19 - DARLINGTON   20 - KESWICK   21 - NEWCASTLE

12 - LEICESTER

13 - NORWICH

14 - HULL

15 - SHEFFIELD

16 - LIVERPOOL

17 - LEEDS

18 - LANCASTER

119 - DARLINGTON

20 - KESWICK

21 - NEWCASTLE

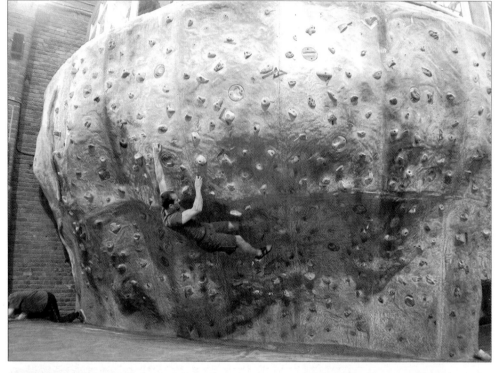

SHEFFIELD ****

② The Foundry

45 Mowbray Street, Sheffield S3 8EN
Tel: 0114 279 6331
Access: 1 mile NNW of City ctr.
Approaching from the A625 (Very
damp Peak District), arrive at the
ring road and turn L. At the next
roundabout (A57 & University) turn R
and go down Brook Hill that becomes
Brook Lane. Straight over the next
r-bout into Tenter WBar, then straight
over the next r-bout into Corporation
St. This carries on for 800 yds and
over the river Don, then turn L into
Mowbray St. The centre is along on the
L, set back in a small yard.
P £ free, in busy car park. Locally 🔀
Ad; £6.50 ~ Kid; £3.50
Memb £1 for life £7.50 one off visit
Mon - Fri / 10am -10.00pm;
Sat - Sun/ 10am - 8.00pm;

This wall was inspired by Jerry Moffatt,
and was the first major privately owned
indoor climbing wall in Britain. Since
it first began, there have been many
extra improvements with and alterations;
now with the back furnace room that
concentrates on good sustained
routes, and extra height on the comp
wall to blast anyones forearms. It still
fortunately retains a lovely open feel to
it with the big central room, and offers
plenty of routes across all the grades.
The bouldering area of the Wave seems
small by todays giant standards, but
has stood the test of time and is still as
popular as ever.

INTRO ADV kids club OPEN FEEL
FUN CASUAL BRIGHT BUSY INTENSE

12 - LEICESTER
13 - NORWICH
14 - HULL
15 - SHEFFIELD
16 - LIVERPOOL
17 - LEEDS
18 - LANCASTER
19 - DARLINGTON
20 - KESWICK
21 - NEWCASTLE

12 - LEICESTER

13 - NORWICH

14 - HULL

15 - SHEFFIELD

16 - LIVERPOOL

17 - LEEDS

18 - LANCASTER

19 - DARLINGTON

20 - KESWICK

21 - NEWCASTLE

HIGH WALL - ROPE RACE WALL - MARPLE

MARPLE ****

③ Rope Race Climbing Centre

The Goyt Mill, Upper Hibbert Lane, Marple Stockport SK7 6HX
Tel: 0161 426 0226

Access: 1.2 mile SE of Marple-Rose Hill Station. Approach
from the West on the A626 Stockport Road, continuing past
Marple Rose Hill stn. for 200 yds to a 3 way forking junction.
Bear fully right and take Church Lane for 100 yds. Then turn R
into Hibbert Lane, follow this for 0.8 mile to when it passes over
the canal and becomes Upper Hibbert Lane. The big building
on the R is the old Goyt Mill. Pass it and then turn into Sunwell
Terrace and you should see the sign for the centre and park in
the big main car park or as directed.

P £ free

Ad; £6.50 ~ Kid £5.00

Mon - Thurs/ 10am - 10pm; Fri till 9pm.

Sat - Sun / 10am - 6pm;

*A big old Mill has been turned into a huge variety of uses. Some
good parts have been snapped up by the Rope Race climbing
centre and form a 4 storey, warren of bouldering caves, top
rope and leading walls, and a giant shaft that seems to go on
forever. The centre managment is also up for improvement and
continually add and build more bits on, so keeping up with them
is always fun. Offering a full range of courses this is a fully blown
climbing centre to look up.*

ROPE RACE WALL

12 - LEICESTER · 13 - NORWICH · 14 - HULL · 15 - SHEFFIELD · 16 - LIVERPOOL · 17 - LEEDS · 18 - LANCASTER · 19 - DARLINGTON · 20 - KESWICK · 21 - NEWCASTLE

12 - LEICESTER
13 - NORWICH
14 - HULL
15 - SHEFFIELD
16 - LIVERPOOL
17 - LEEDS
18 - LANCASTER
19 - DARLINGTON
20 - KESWICK
21 - NEWCASTLE

WIRKSWORTH **
④ *Wirksworth Wall*

Wirksworth Leisure Centre, Hannage Way, off
Water Lane, Wirksworth, Derbyshire, DE4 4JG
Tel: 01629 824 717
Access: 500 yds SE of village centre. From the
centre, head out towards Derby on the main road
going South B5023. After about 0.5 mile signs
should point to the leisure centre - which is off to
the left. The wall is in the big large building above
the tennis courts.

P £ free.

Ad; £4.70 ~ Kid; £2.35

Sometimes there are special offers for a quickie!

Mon - Thur / 8am - 10.30pm (7am Tue & Thurs!!!!)
Fri / 8am - 9.30pm
Sat / 8am - 5.30pm
Sun / 9am - 7.00pm

*A purpose built climbing room that is a descent size
and an excellent place to get out of the miserable
weather - ocoassionally possible in this part of
the world. Also a fun place to go anyway. A good
bouldering wall offers a host of natural problems,
as well as the coloured nasties. The leading areas
have some nice texturing and give the middle grade
climber a lovely variation of routes to go at. May get
additions!*

insitu 3 DEEP-MATS SWIM LEISURE
INTRO ADV kids club T 🍽
BRIGHT FRIENDLY CASUAL FUN

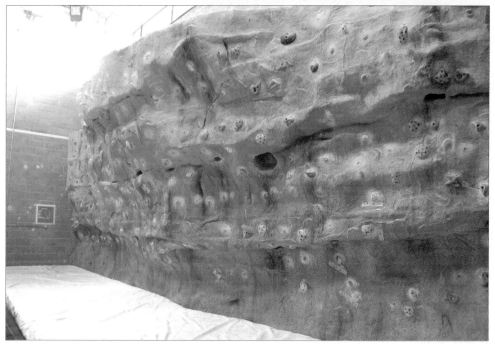

WIRKSWORTH BOULDER & LEAD WALL

12 - LEICESTER

13 - NORWICH

14 - HULL

15 - SHEFFIELD

16 - LIVERPOOL

17 - LEEDS

18 - LANCASTER

119 - DARLINGTON

20 - KESWICK

21 - NEWCASTLE

OLDHAM **
⑤ *The Oldham Wall*
Oldham Sports Centre, Lord St, Oldham
OL1 3HA
Tel: 0161 911 4090
Access: Middle of town centre on the North side. Easiest approach is to locate the town centre bypass, then head in towards the town centre from the West. You need to find the start of the A671 Rochdale Road going N, then soon turn off R onto St. Mary's Way that leads to Lord St and the leisure centre which is signposted.
🅿 £ Local pay and display
Ad; £3.60 ~ Kid; £1.70
Memb £1 for life
Mon - Thur / 9am - 10.30pm; Fri till 9pm
Sat / 9am - 5pm, Sun till 9pm
Groups need to phone and book in advance.
A very good bouldering facility - or top roping wall. Good solid and highly textured panels offer a huge variety of problems, plus a good selection of bolt on holds to help beginners, and ease the steeper sections. Plenty of lower off points to facilitate safe bouldering in the higher sections.

  DEEP-MATS SWIM LEISURE
INTRO ADV kids club
CASUAL FUN FRIENDLY

SHEFFIELD **
⑥ *Matrix Bouldering Wall*
Goodwin Sports Centre, University of Sheffield, Northumberland Road, Sheffield S10 2TZ
Tel: 01248 382 571
Access: 1.3 miles WSW of City centre. From the A6134 ring road, turn off at the A57 (Glossop) and is signposted University. Take the turning on the right in about 100 yds, Northumberland Road. The first entrance 100 yds on the R is to the sports centre, don't drive in. You have to park on the roads locally. The wall is between the recreation and pool of the sports centre, go to reception first.
🅿 £ local with difficulty in the day
Ad; £3 ~ Memb £2
Mon - Fri / 9am - 10pm
Sat & Sun / 9am - 5pm
A very good and purely bouldering area with a laid back feeling to it. Also a very handy room for the student that just needs their hourly fix of cranking between lectures. Good texturing and some bulging grotto areas make this an excellent place to work out. Doesn't have the pszazz of the big Sheffield walls, but is a quality alternative.

INTRO kids club DEEP-MATS
CASUAL EARTHY

LONGNOR
⑦ *Upper Limits*
Upper Limits, Unit 1, Buxton Road, Longnor, nr Buxton, Derbs, SK17 0NZ
Tel: 01298 83149
Access: Next to the fire Station in the middle of the village. Arrive at Longnor from the wild moors. From the crossroads in the centre of town, take the B5303 towards Buxton and very soon turn L after the fire station.
🅿 £ free
Ad; £4.00 ~ Kid; £2.75
Memb £?
Mon - Sun / 10am - 4pm;
Wed till 1pm
Mon, Wed, Fri / 6pm - 9.30pm
A small little multi activity centre offering courses in climbing, caving, archery and team challenges. Designed for kids and youth groups with aid from rural regeneration schemes. The wall is small and offers a variety of fun bouldering that is ideally suited to kids.

INTRO ADV kids club
CASUAL FUN

LONGNOR WALL

MATRIX WALL

OLDHAM WALL

GLOSSUP **
⑦ *Glossup Bouldering Wall*

Glossup Leisure Centre, High Street East, Glossup, Derbs. SK13 8PN   Tel: 01457 863 223
Access: 300 yds East of town Ctr. From the town ctr by the Station, head off on the A57
(Sheffield) and very soon you will see the Leisure Ctr on the R.

LEISURE 🚿 🚌 CASUAL INTENSE
QUIET

GLOSSUP WALL

🅿 £ The centre has free parking
but often fills up, parking locally is
not usually a problem, watch out for
any restrictions.
Ad; £2.20 ~ Kid £2.20
Mon - Fri / 9am - 10.30pm
Fri 4.30-5.30 only half the wall
available.
Sat / 9am - 8pm Sat / 9am - 9pm
A small bouldering wall, but very
well suited to the applied boulderer.
Nicely set on a mezzanine level,
the wall can be used at nearly any
time. It is a freeform with an array
of pockets and tufas, designed on
a Buoux-Chorro style. It may be
old fashioned with out bolt ons, but
it packs a certain punch of reality,
especially with steep lockoffs; just
like real 7a sport climbing. There
is a 300 problem guide that can be
purchased for £2, making the visit
well worthwhile and adding a lot of
fun. (100 probs below UK T-5c)

12 - LEICESTER

13 - NORWICH

14 - HULL

15 - SHEFFIELD

16 - LIVERPOOL

17 - LEEDS

18 - LANCASTER

19 - DARLINGTON

20 - KESWICK

21 - NEWCASTLE

12 - LEICESTER
13 - NORWICH
14 - HULL
15 - SHEFFIELD
16 - LIVERPOOL
17 - LEEDS
18 - LANCASTER
19 - DARLINGTON
20 - KESWICK
21 - NEWCASTLE

SPECIALIST CLIMBING SHOPS:

1 Rope Race: SHOES ROPES GEAR CAMS BOOKS ICE
The Goyt Mill, Upper Hibbert Lane, Marple, Stockport, SK7 6HX
Tel: 0161 426 0226 Open: Mon-Thu 10-10pm, Fri 10-9pm, Sat & Sun 10-6pm

2 Cotswold: SHOES ROPES GEAR CAMS BOOKS ICE
6A Oxford Road, Manchester, M1 5QA
Tel: 0161 236 4123 Open: M,W,F,S 9-5.30; Tue 9.30-5.30, Th 10-7, Sun 11-4pm

3 Snow & Rock: SHOES ROPES GEAR CAMS BOOKS ICE
Princess Parkway, Didsbury, Manchester, M20 8ZE
Tel: 0845 100 1020 Open: Mon-Fri 10-7pm, Sat 9.30-6.30pm, Sun 11.30-5.30pm

4 North West Face: SHOES ROPES GEAR CAMS BOOKS ICE
St. Anns Church, Winwick Rd, Warrington, WA2 7NE
Tel: 01925 650 022 Open: Mon-Fri 10am-10pm, Sat & Sun 10-6pm

5 Climb Rochdale: SHOES ROPES GEAR CAMS BOOKS
11-131 School Lane, Rochdale, OL16 1QP
Tel: 01706 524 450 Open: Mon-Fri 10am-10pm, Sat & Sun 10-8pm

6 Adapt Outdoor: SHOES ROPES GEAR CAMS BOOKS ICE
5 Richmond Street, Liverpool, L1 1EE
Tel: 0151 709 6498 Open: M-Fri 9-5.30 Sun 11-4pm

7 Paul Braithwaite: SHOES ROPES GEAR CAMS BOOKS ICE
Rhodes Bank, Oldham, OL1 1TA
Tel: 0161 620 3900 Open: M-Fri 9.30am-5.30pm

8 Ellis Brigham: SHOES ROPES GEAR CAMS BOOKS ICE
211 Deansgate, Manchester, M3 3NW
Tel: 0161 834 7278   Open: Mon-Sat 9am - 6pm, Sun 11am-5pm

9 Alpenstock: SHOES ROPES GEAR CAMS BOOKS ICE
35 St. Petersgate, Stockport, SK1 1DH
Tel: 0161 480 3660 Open: M-Fri 9.30am-5.30pm

10 Ellis Brigham: SHOES ROPES GEAR CAMS BOOKS ICE
73 Bold Street, Liverpool, L1 4EZ
Tel: 0151 709 6912 Open: Open: Mon-Sat 9am - 6pm, Sun 11am-5pm

11 Campcraft : SHOES ROPES GEAR CAMS BOOKS ICE
96-98 Newport Street, Bolton, BL3 6AB (100m from train station)
Tel: 01204 524 504 Open: M-Sat 9am-5pm (Mon, Tue, Thu, Fri, till 5.30pm)

12 Adventure Centre Ltd:
Manchester Road, Warrington, WA1 3BE
Tel: 01925 411 385

13 Ellis Brigham: SHOES ROPES GEAR CAMS BOOKS ICE
Duke Street, Castlefields, Manchester, M3 4NF
Tel: 0161 833 0746 Open: Mon-Sat 9am - 6pm, Sun 11am-5pm

14 Nevisport: SHOES ROPES GEAR CAMS BOOKS ICE
53 Stamford New Road, Altrincham, WA14 1DS
Tel: 0161 928 6613 Open: Mon-Sat 9am - 5.30pm

15 Camp & Climb: SHOES ROPES GEAR BOOKS ICE
95-97 Brook Street, Chester, CH1 3DX
Tel: 01244 311 174 Open: Mon-Sat 9am - 5.30pm

16 Ellis Brigham:
7 Northgate Street, Chester, CH1 7HA
Tel: 01244 318 311

Basic gear / local books   Good UK gear / UK books   Big range / Europe books   Expert range / Worldwide

Dedicated Bouldering (Square metres)

Climbing Walls	Grotto	Freeform Rock	Texture Panel	Flat Panel	Brick	Woody	Campus Board	Bouldering Sqm. (B)	Climbing Total Sqm. (C)
1 Awesome Walls	292	52	0	57	10	12	4	417	1198
2 North West Face	10	0	21	0	0	0	0	56	741
3 Rope Race	0	70	56	0	0	9	0	135	563
4 Climb Rochdale	97	45	0	90	0	0	0	232	439
5 Chester-Walls	0	0	0	0	0	20	0	20	322
6 Salford-Univ.	30	10	56	20	0	0	0	116	265
7 Balderstone	28	35	0	0	0	10	0	63	186
8 Broughton	8	90	0	50	0	20	2	170	0
9 Southport	0	0	10	22	0	0	0	32	142
10 Oldham	0	0	0	0	0	0	0	0	142
11 Vernon-Anfield	0	0	30	0	40	0	0	70	114

Climbing wall - Sector by sector analysis

(Sector Height - Individual lines - Total routes in sector)

Climbing Walls	Instructional / T/R Bouldering	Top Rope-insitu / Leading	Lead-Tilting / Competition	Exterior			Sector Sq.m
1 Awesome Walls	FP 6-6-15 (48)	FR 11-7-14 (75)	FP 6-16-48 (132)	FP 11-9-18 (155)	FP 14-12-36 (252)	FP 17-4-9 (119)	
2 North West Face	FP 11-4-11 (54)	FP 7-17-44 (175)	FP 12-7-18 (120)	FP 12-4-12 (72)	TP 12-4-12 (60)	TP 12-11-38 (204)	
3 Rope Race	FP 9m-4-14 (50)	FP 9-7-21 (77)	TP 9m-6-20 (81)	FP 10m-1-4 (20)	FP 13-3-12 (65)	FR 18-4-16 (135)	
4 Climb Rochdale	FP 7m-2-6 (21)	FP 7m-1-1 (7)	TP 7-4-12 (28)	FP 8-4-12 (40)	FP 9-6-18 (72)	FR 9-5-15 (39)	
5 Chester-Walls	FP 7-6-18 (49)	FP 9m-3-9 (73)	FP 8-5-15 (64)	FR 8-2-4 (40)	FP 9-3-10 (36)	FP 9-4-12 (40)	
6 Salford-Univ.	TP 5-3-6 (20)	FP 8m-3-6 (32)	FP 8m-4-6 (32)	FR 10m-2-6 (20)	TP 9m-4-10 (10)		
7 Balderstone	FR 5m-2-4 (20)	FR 7m-3-9 (28)	FP 7m-4-16 (35)	FR 7m-3-14 (32)	FR 8m-1-4 (8)		
8 Broughton							
9 Southport	TP 5m-2-6 (15)	FP 5m-2-6 (15)	TP 5m-5-15 (40)	TP 6m-2-10 (18)	FR 11m-1-2 (22)		
10 Oldham	TP 4m-2-6 (11)	TP 4m-2-8 (11)	TP 4-7-28 (30)	TP 5-10-40 (60)	TP 6-5-8 (30)		
11 Vernon-Anfield	TP 5m-2-6 (20)	FR 6m-3-9 (24)					

17 Field & Trek:
188 Deansgate, Manchester, M3 3NE
Tel: 0161 834 5707

18 Outdoor Action:
214 Stamford Street, Ashton under Lyme, OL6 7QB
Tel: 0161 343 2151

19 Field & Trek:
46 Bridge street, Chester, CH1 1NQ
Tel: 01244 340 666

20 Decathlon:
Georges Road, Stockport, SK4 1DN
Tel: 0161 476 9600

CLIMBING CLUBS - WEBSITE KEYWORDS

CHESTER-MC, KARABINER-MC, LANCASHIRE-MC,
MERSEYSIDE-MC, LANCASHIRE CAVING & CC,
OLDHAM-MC, ST.HELENS-MC, SUMMIT-MC (Southport),
VAGABOND-MC, GWYDYR-MC (Wirral),
INNOMINATA-MC (Cheshire)

12 - LEICESTER | 13 - NORWICH | 14 - HULL | 15 - SHEFFIELD | 16 - LIVERPOOL | 17 - LEEDS | 18 - LANCASTER | 19 - DARLINGTON | 20 - KESWICK | 21 - NEWCASTLE

AWESOME WALLS

12 - LEICESTER
13 - NORWICH
14 - HULL
15 - SHEFFIELD
16 - LIVERPOOL
17 - LEEDS
18 - LANCASTER
19 - DARLINGTON
20 - KESWICK
21 - NEWCASTLE

LIVERPOOL ****

① *Awesome Walls Climbing Centre*
St. Albans Church, Athol St. off Great Howard
Street, Liverpool L5 9XT
Tel: 0151 298 2422
Access: 1.5 miles NNW of City Centre. Just
a short way SW of Sandhills Stn. Central
Liverpool is a maze of roads, work your way
out to the A565 going N towards Crosby, this
road is Gt. Howard St. After 1 mile from the
Centre look out for the church on your R. If
you cross Sandhills Lane, you've gone 0.5
mile too far.

P Free parking ✹ ✹
Ad; £6.00
Memb; £5.00
One off- 3 hr sat; £6
Mon - Fri / 10am - 10pm;
Sat & Sun / 10am - 6pm

Insitu ☞ **6**☞ **Hire** ☞ **Hire** ☞ **DEEP-MATS**

INTRO **ADV** kids club **T**

CASUAL **FRIENDLY** **EARTHY** **SERIOUS** **GRIPPING**

An awesome wall that lives up to its name in every shape and form, but also is designed with intelligence and appreciation that beginners need introductory walls of easy angle and good selections of holds. There is a nice and earthy feel to this gigantic church, especially with the sobering freeform bouldering sectors, looming over you. The crypt has just opened up with a gigantic 250 sqm of grotto bouldering -wow. Beginners will enjoy the 10m freeform pyramid, and stamina freaks can have a complete overdose on the giant competition sectors, with the headwall being something quite special. It actually has a 6c on it, if you can believe that !

THE CRYPT
A HANGOUT TO   FOR

12 - LEICESTER

13 - NORWICH

14 - HULL

15 - SHEFFIELD

16 - LIVERPOOL

17 - LEEDS

18 - LANCASTER

19 - DARLINGTON

20 - KESWICK

21 - NEWCASTLE

AWESOME WALLS - LIVERPOOL

WARRINGTON ***
② *North West Face*
St. Anns Church, Winwick Road,
Warrington, WA2 7NE
Tel: 01925 650 022

Access: 0.7 mile NNW of town centre.
Easiest approach from the N via M62.
Exti at Jtn 9, Head S on the A49 towards
Warrington Centre. Pass a multitude of
shopping vistas and fast food fat feeding
frenzies; after 1.8 miles you will see th
church on the R side of the road. (10 mins
walk from Warrington Central stn).

P Free ✱ not bad but don't take risks.
Ad; £6 ~ Kid (under 12's); £5
Membership Day £1, Life £10
One off- 3 hrvisit £7
Mon - Fri / 10.00am -10pm;
Sat - Sun/ 10am - 6pm;

*An impressive wall by any standard, and
one that certainly looks a lot bigger than it
actually it (It's pretty big anyway, so treat
that comment academicalliey). Superbly
exhausting in the huge array of 12 metre
routes. A small bouldering-warm up section
that is pure quality of texture panels and a
good straighforward woodie, not so steep
and with plastics. Plenty of routes in all
standards, and an excellent place to train
for the stamina routes outside. There are
planned improvements in the pipeline, so
keep a keen eye on the developments.
(Jacquzzi and palm trees!)*

INTRO kids club 💿 FRIENDLY CASUAL BRIGHT

MARPLE ****
③ *Rope Race Climbing Centre*
See section 15 Sheffield-Peak District.

WARRINGTON WALL

WARRINGTON - BOULDER WARM UP WALL

12 - LEICESTER
13 - NORWICH
14 - HULL
15 - SHEFFIELD
16 - LIVERPOOL
17 - LEEDS
18 - LANCASTER
19 - DARLINGTON
20 - KESWICK
21 - NEWCASTLE

NORTH WEST FACE - WARRINGTON

12 - LEICESTER

13 - NORWICH

14 - HULL

15 - SHEFFIELD

16 - LIVERPOOL

17 - LEEDS

18 - LANCASTER

19 - DARLINGTON

20 - KESWICK

21 - NEWCASTLE

12 - LEICESTER

13 - NORWICH

14 - HULL

15 - SHEFFIELD

16 - LIVERPOOL

17 - LEEDS

18 - LANCASTER

19 - DARLINGTON

20 - KESWICK

21 - NEWCASTLE

CLIMB ROCHDALE - LEADING WALL

ROCHDALE ***

④ *Climb Rochdale Climbing Centre*
Apollo House, 11-31 School Lane,
Rochdale, Lancs OL16 1QP
Tel: 01706 524 450
Access: 300 yds South of the town Ctr.
Approaching from the M62, exit at Jtn
20 and head towards Rochdale on the
A627(M). At the main roundabout filter
L to the next big roundabout, then turn
R towards centre (A58). After 0.6m
on this dual carriageway, turn R onto
Drake Street (Broadfield Parking sign).
Follow this for 500 yds and School lane
is on the L. The building is obvious
on the R.
P £ free and limited in the centre.
Local parking but keep an eye on
restrictions.
Ad; £5.50 ~ Kid; £5.00
Mon - Fri / 10am -10pm
Sat & Sun / 10am -8pm

CLIMB ROCHDALE - KIDS WARM UP AREA

A superb purpose built climbing centre that is perfectly aimed at all round climbing, appealing to kids, families and boulderers. The whole building is very well organised with a whole array of bouldering areas that accomodate all tastes of vertical balance problems, to a giant extreme and demanding wave, all with excellent matting. The leading area is fun and not at all intimidating. A great benefit to the area, and a fantastic commitment to kids enjoyment.

CLIMB ROCHDALE - JAWS, THE WAVE

12 - LEICESTER
13 - NORWICH
14 - HULL
15 - SHEFFIELD
16 - LIVERPOOL
17 - LEEDS
18 - LANCASTER
19 - DARLINGTON
20 - KESWICK
21 - NEWCASTLE

12 - LEICESTER

13 - NORWICH

14 - HULL

15 - SHEFFIELD

16 - LIVERPOOL

17 - LEEDS

18 - LANCASTER

19 - DARLINGTON

20 - KESWICK

21 - NEWCASTLE

CHESTER **

⑤ *The Walls Climbing Centre*

Chester Bank Business Park, River Lane, Saltney, Cheshire, CH4 8SL

Tel: 01244 682 626

Access: 1.4 miles WSW of Chester City centre. Leave the C-Ctr inner ring road on the A483 Wrexham road, cross over the River Dee, and then turn R at the big roundabout onto the A5104 (Broughton). After 1 mile pass under the railway and river lane is soon on the R.

🅿 £ free

Ad; £6.00 ~ Kid £6.00

Memb £10 a year. One off visit - 3 hr - £6

Mon - Fri / 5pm - 10pm;

Sat / 10am - 6pm; Sun / 10am - 5pm;

There are plans to move the centre to Wreham in a few years time, so either ring to check or visit our website.

Can be used for groups by prior arrangement at other times outside opening hours.

A friendly centre that should appeal to beginners and those wanting a club - friendly atmosphere and are not hyped up by cutting edge climbing. A whole series of walls set up for top rope (no leading allowed), but all with top ropes provided. A small 45º woodie for the enthusiastic. A centre that very much extends to outdoor climbing on real cliffs!

INTRO   ADV   kids club   FRIENDLY   CASUAL   FUN   BRIGHT

MANCHESTER - SALFORD **

⑥ *Salford University Wall*

Tom Husband Leisure Centre, University Road, Salford, Manchester, M5 4WT

Tel: 0161 737 6206

Access: 1.5 miles WNW of Manchester City Ctr. Easist approach from the end of M602, turn L into Albion way A5063, after 0.4 mile, bear L on the A6 (Broad St) heading out of town for 300 yds. Then turn R onto the main road Frederick Road (B6186). Go over railways and take 3rd road on the R, Wallness Lane and signposted Peel Park Campus. Follow this for 300 yds and park in Northern Car park.

🅿 £ Charge (2) but reduced a lot (0.50) after 6pm

Ad; £4 ~ Kid £2 No memb.

Mon - Fri / 9.45am - 10pm;

Sat / 9.45am - 5pm; Sun / 9.45am - 4pm;

A very good use of space to offer a wide variety of bouldering and full on routes. Panels are heavily textured and offer plenty of footwork variations. The big 5th section is also just high enough to be demanding for most casual climbers. Small, cozy and friendly.

INTRO   SWIM   LEISURE

FRIENDLY   CASUAL   FUN

SALFORD WALL

12 - LEICESTER

13 - NORWICH

14 - HULL

15 - SHEFFIELD

16 - LIVERPOOL

17 - LEEDS

18 - LANCASTER

19 - DARLINGTON

20 - KESWICK

21 - NEWCASTLE

ROCHDALE *

⑦ *Balderstone Climbing Wall*

Balderstone Technical College, Queen Victoria Street, Rochdale, OL11 2HU
Tel: 01706 751 500

Access: 1.3m SSE of town centre. From the end of the A627(M), turn R at the 1st big roundabout, then immediately L onto the A664 Queensway, (Dual carriageway). After 0.7 mile you arrive at the tfc-lts with the A671, turn R onto the Oldham Road. QV-st. is 300 yds on the R. Go into the 1st entrance which leads through to the end and the sports hall-community ctr.

P £ free

Ad; £3.50 ~ Kid £2.40

Mon - Fri / 6pm - 10pm;
Sat / 9am - 3.30pm;
Sun / 10am - 4pm;

Open at other times by appointment booking only as the sports hall is used by school, also ring on Sunday to check.
A wall with lots of good plus points. The bouldering is very good with a superb grotto section, but no crash pads so you will need a spotter. The lead walls are well textured and fun, if only they were higher. The hall remains chilly. In essence, you need to put a lot into your climbing here to get a lot out of it. A good group teaching facility.

4.

INTRO CASUAL GLOOMY QUIET

BALDERSTONE WALL

BROUGHTON WALL

MANCHESTER - BROUGHTON **
⑦ Broughton Power Climbing Wall
Broughton Recreational Ctr, Camp Street,
Lower Broughton, Mancs. M7 17T
www.broughtonpower.co.uk
Tel: 0161 792 2375
Access: 1.5 mile NW of city ctr. Follow
approach as for Salford Univ Wall but
continue along Frederick road, which
turns into Camp St for 0.5 mile and the
centre is on the R. You can access from
the other end which runs into A56 (J17-
M60)
🅿 £ free 🏔
Ad; £3.50 ~ Kid £2.00
Mon - Fri / 9am - 10pm; Fri 9pm
Sat / 9am - 3.30pm;
Sun / 8.30am - 6pm;
*A full on hard bouldering centre with over
700 set problems on natural rock. Insets
on a 70º wave leaning wall. Excellent
fingertip and power building ctr. A new
addition of a superb comp-cube. Also don't
miss out on a superb 43º woodie cellar
which is centrally heated and has nice
smooth holds for skin care. Please ask at
reception for the bouldering guide.*

EARTHY INTENSE SERIOUS INTENSE GLOOMY

SOUTHPORT *
⑨ Southport Climbing Wall
Southport YMCA, 81 Hoghton Street,
Southport, PR9 0PR
Tel: 01704 538 317
Access: 500 yds N of town Ctr. From the
town ctr. main N-South drag, head up
N for 500 yds to and turn R at the fire
Station into Houghton St, the YMCA is
just on the R.
🅿 £ free in limited spaces, local
restrictions. (free after 6pm M-Fri!)
Ad; £3.50 ~ Kid £3
Mon - Fri / 9am - 10pm;
Sat & Sun/ 9am - 7pm;
*A really good example of a converted
squash court, and one of the best in
the country. A superb use of space and
great fun for kids. Adults will enjoy the
fingertip textured surface too. Kids have
a real ambition to work for here on the 11
metre roof! A great place to play on a wet
afternoon.*

Insitu ⚓  LEISURE

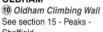 INTRO ADV Kids Club FRIENDLY FUN

OLDHAM
⑩ Oldham Climbing Wall
See section 15 - Peaks -
Sheffield

LIVERPOOL - ANFIELD*
⑪ Vernon Sangster Climbing Wall
Vernon Sangster Community Sport Ctr,
Priory Rd, Stanley Park, Anfield L4 2SL
Tel: 0151 263 0491
Access: 500 yds NE of Liverpool Footy G.
Head into Liverpool on the A580 from the
M57, after 4 miles Priory Rd is on the L,
and the sports ctr is the 0.5m set back on
the R, with footy ground beyond.
🅿 £ free, 🏔 if a match is on, its busy.
Ad; £2.50 ~ Kid £2.00
Mon - Fri / 9am - 10pm;
Sat / 9am - 3pm;
Sun / 12pm - 7pm;
The whole area is due in the future for
redevelopment, so ring to check first.
*The end of a communal sports hall that
can be separated out by netting. A nice
small facility which is a good size for group
basic introduction. A bit old fashioned but
offers some good challenges. The steep
boulder wall is pure quality, lovely. and a
crimpers paradise. Verdict - small & cute.*

DEEP-MATS

FRIENDLY CASUAL QUIET GLOOMY

12 - LEICESTER
13 - NORWICH
14 - HULL
15 - SHEFFIELD
16 - LIVERPOOL
17 - LEEDS
18 - LANCASTER
19 - DARLINGTON
20 - KESWICK
21 - NEWCASTLE

SOUTHPORT WALL (Inset Vernon Sangster Wall)

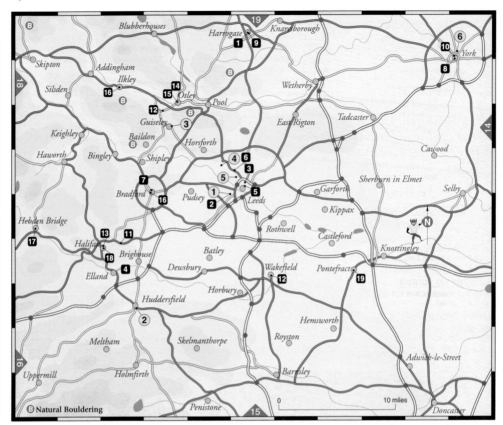

ⒷNaturalBouldering

12 - LEICESTER
13 - NORWICH
14 - HULL
15 - SHEFFIELD
16 - LIVERPOOL
17 - LEEDS
18 - LANCASTER
19 - DARLINGTON
20 - KESWICK
21 - NEWCASTLE

SPECIALIST CLIMBING SHOPS:

1 Cotswold: `SHOES` `ROPES` `GEAR` `CAMS` `BOOKS` `ICE`
8-10 West Park, Harrogate, HG1 1BL
Tel: 01423 701 100 Open: M,W,F, 9-5.30pm, Tu 9.30-5.30, Th 10-7, Sa 9-6, Su 11-5

2 Leeds Wall: `SHOES` `ROPES` `GEAR` `CAMS` `BOOKS` `ICE`
100a Gelderd Road, Leeds, LS12 6BY
Tel: 0113 234 1554 Open: Mon-Fri 10-9.30pm, Sat & Sun 10-7pm

3 Nevisport: `SHOES` `ROPES` `GEAR` `CAMS` `BOOKS` `ICE`
34 Woodhouse Lane, Leeds, LS2 8LX
Tel: 0113 244 4715 Open: Mon-Sat 9-5.30pm, Wed-10am, Sun 11.30-4pm

4 BAC: `SHOES` `ROPES` `GEAR` `CAMS` `BOOKS` `ICE`
BAC Outdoor Leisure Ltd. Central Hall, Elland, HX5 ODF (1 mile from J24-M62)
Tel: 01422 371 146 Open: Mon-Fri 9-5.30pm, Sat-5pm, Sun 1-5pm

5 Centresport: `SHOES` `ROPES` `GEAR` `CAMS` `BOOKS` `ICE`
57-59 New Briggate, Leeds, LS1 6AS (opposite grand theatre & Harveys wine bar)
Tel: 0113 245 2917 Open: Mon-Sat 9-5.30pm

6 True North:
26 Otley Road, Leeds, LS6 2AD
Tel: 0113 230 2696

7 Allan Austin:
4 Jacob Street, Bradford, BD5 7LX
Tel: 01274 728 674

8 Nevisport:
8 St. Sampson's Square, York, YO1 8RN
Tel: 01904 639 567

9 Nevisport:
71 Station Parade, Harrogate, HG1 1ST
Tel: 01423 562 874

10 Outdoors:
Micklegate, York, YO1 6JH
Tel: 01904 653 567

11 Adventure Outdoors:
Tan House Mill, Hipperholme, HX3 8EH
Tel: 01422 203 491

12 Kenmar Camping & Leisure:
Pontefract Road, Wakefield, WF4 1LW
Tel: 01924 864 494

13 Springfield Camping:
Luddenden Foot, Halifax, HX2 6AR
Tel: 01422 883 164

14 Face West Ltd:
336 Bradford Road, Otley, LS21 3LT
Tel: 01943 461 474

15 Chevin Trek Ltd:
34 Gay Lane, Otley, LS21 1BR
Tel: 01943 851166

16 Base Camp:
13 Leeds Road, Ilkley, LS29 8DH
Tel: 01943 816 011

`Basic gear / local books`   `Good UK gear / UK books`   `Big range / Europe books`   `Expert range / Worldwide`

Dedicated Bouldering (Square metres)   Climbing wall - Sector by sector analysis

Grotto	Freeform Rock	Texture Panel	Flat Panel	Brick	Woody	Campus Board	Climbing Walls (B = Bouldering Sqm / C = Climbing Total Sqm)	Instructional / T/R Bouldering	Top Rope-insitu / Leading	Lead-Tilting / Competition	Exterior / Sector Sq.m M
103	63	0	0	0	0	6	① The Leeds Wall — B 172 / C 1067	FP 9-8-12 (90) · FP 12-4-6 (48)	FP 12-9-26 (168) · FP 14-9-20 (136)	FP 12-8-18 (144) · FP 15-16-47 (309)	
16	55	23	0	12	0	0	② Huddersfield Wall — B 106 / C 318	TP 8m-2-6 (24) · TP 10-1-3 (13)	FP 10-5-10 (60) · TP 10-2-6 (20)	FP 10-3-8 (40) · FR 11-4-14 (55)	
40	0	0	0	42	0	0	③ Guiseley Wall — B 82 / C 220	B 6-13-50 (138)			
0	0	84	42	0	0	0	④ Leeds Carnegie — B 126 / C 126				
0	40	0	0	40	0	0	⑤ Leeds Univ. — B 20 / C 322				
0	0	0	0	0	0	0	⑥ York St. John — B 0 / C 60	TP 6-9-27 (60)			

(Sector Height - Individual lines - Total routes in sector)

17 Rock Bottom Outdoor Equipment:
19c Crown Street, Hebden Bridge, HX7 8EH
Tel: 01422 844 500

18 Hill & Dale:
Hill & Dale, 39 Burnley Road, Halifax, HX6 2TL
Tel: 01422 833 360

19 Crossley Tordoff:
Jubilee Way, Pontefract, WF8 1DB
Tel: 01977 702 002

CLIMBING CLUBS - WEBSITE KEYWORDS
YORKSHIRE-MC, VIBRAM-MC, CALDERDALE-MC, CRAVEN-MC, GRITSTONE CLUB, YORK-MC, VERTICALLY CHALLENGED-CC (Guiseley)

12 - LEICESTER · 13 - NORWICH · 14 - HULL · 15 - SHEFFIELD · 16 - LIVERPOOL · 17 - LEEDS · 18 - LANCASTER · 19 - DARLINGTON · 20 - KESWICK · 21 - NEWCASTLE

12 - LEICESTER
13 - NORWICH
14- HULL
15- SHEFFIELD
16 - LIVERPOOL
17 - LEEDS
18 - LANCASTER
19 - DARLINGTON
20 - KESWICK
21 - NEWCASTLE

LEEDS WALL - Freeform boulder sector

LEEDS ****

① *The Leeds Wall*

100a Gelderd Road, Leeds, West Yorkshire, LS12 6BY www.theleedswall.co.uk

Tel: 0113 234 1554

Access: 1.5 miles SW of the City Centre. A morass of roundabouts and flyovers are set on the west side of Leeds, so good luck. Geldered Road is the main A62 and runs parallel to the M621 towards Gildersomewhereoranother. A good tip is to leave the M621 at Jtn 1, exit to the North, and then at the 1st roundabout (100 yds) turn R into Geldered Rd, and the wall is soon on the L.

P £ free, not bad but be cautious

Ad; £6.80 ~ Kid (under 16); £4.50 Memb £2; One off visit £8.50

Mon - Fri / 10am - 10pm Sat & Sun / 10am - 8pm (Winter) Sat & Sun / 10am - 6.30pm (Summer)

A superb specialist climbing centre that is the result of a climbers co-operative in Leeds. Designed by climbers who climb hard, but still has plenty of climbing in the vertical areas and introductory level. A couple of giant bouldering grottos are enough for anyone to beef up. The lead wall of 14-15 metres is demanding and simply fantastic, the perfect length for an indoor lead.

Insitu 8 Hire Hire AUTO BELAY DEEP-MATS INTRO ADV kids club T CASUAL BUSY FUN INTENSE GRIPPING SERIOUS CALM

LEEDS WALL

LEEDS WALL - No place for a slouch (Dave Speakman climbing)

12 - LEICESTER

13 - NORWICH

14 - HULL

15 - SHEFFIELD

16 - LIVERPOOL

17 - LEEDS

18 - LANCASTER

19 - DARLINGTON

20 - KESWICK

21 - NEWCASTLE

12 - LEICESTER
13 - NORWICH
14 - HULL
15 - SHEFFIELD
16 - LIVERPOOL
17 - LEEDS
18 - LANCASTER
19 - DARLINGTON
20 - KESWICK
21 - NEWCASTLE

HUDDERSFIELD WALL

HUDDERSFIELD ***

(2) *Huddersfield Climbing Wall*
Kirklees Active Ctr, Huddersfield Sports Ctr, Southgate, Huddersfield, HD1 1TW
Tel: 01484 223 630
Access: 0.5 mile miles SW of town ctr. The A629 from J24 of the M62 is a relatively pain free approach to the town ctr ring road. Follow this around to the East. At the A629 Sheffield turn off (5 o'clock), continue drifting around the ring road and follow signs immedieately for the leisure ctr.
P £ Pay & display with vigorus wardens.
Ad; £3.95 ~ Kid; £3.00
Mon - Fri / 7.30am - 10pm
Sat / 9am - 8pm; Sun/ 8.30am - 9pm
Under 16's must be with an adult.
A well matted out bouldering area allows for the full use of the 5 metre height. Not many features but plenty of good bolt-ons. A nice big airy space, sets an arena with nice long routes. An interesting arête feature gives some demanding diedre routes. A good wall for kids and all levels of climbing.

GUISELEY *

(3) *Guiseley Climbing Wall*
Aireborough Leisure Ctr, The Green, Guiseley, Leeds, LS20 9BT
Tel: 01943 877 131
Access: Just to the south of the town centre. Situated on the N side of the main drag and signposted.
P £ free.
Ad; £3.30 ~ Kid; £1.80
Mon - Sun / 8.30am - 10.30pm
A small square room with lots of natural rock holds. Mainly used for bouldering but no crash pads at present. A good place to polish your technical wall climbing skills, plus a good selection of grippy bolt-ons for beginners. A handy and quiet venue to instruct beginners.

LEEDS *

(4) *Carnegie Climbing Wall*
Carnegie Sports Ctr, Becket Park Campus, Headingley, Leeds, LS6 3QS
Tel: 0113 283 3160
Access: 3 miles NW of the City Ctr. Retreat from dripping Ilkley on the A660 into Leeds. Cross over the A6120 outer ring. After 1 mile and still on the Otley Road, turn R onto Church Wood Av, (St. Chad's Drive from the S) which leads to the sports ctr.
P £ free! we think!
Ad; £3
Mon - Fri / 8am - 10pm
Sat / 9am - 7pm; Sun / 9am - 9pm;
We were unable to get to this venue, but we have understood there to be a dedicated room for bouldering that is a mixture of textured and flat panels with bolt on holds. No higher than 4m high, and about 6 X 12 metres in size.

There are plans to develop a big climbing centre in York, but this may be 12-20 months away, check this and the 6 monthly free printout updates, on our website - www.jingowobbly.com

LEEDS

(5) Leeds University Climbing Wall *

Physical Education Ctr, Leeds University, Woodhouse Lane, Leeds LS2 9JT

Tel: 0113 233 5080

Access: 0.5 mile NW of the City Ctr. From the inner ring road, exit on the A660 (Skipton), which is Woodhouse Lane. Follow signs.

P £ pay & display   Ad; £3.50

Mon, Tue, Thur, Fri / 11am - 2pm   Wed / 11am - 5pm; Tue, Thur, / 5pm - 7.30pm

A very old bouldering wall in 2 sections. A brick corridor slippery area, and a textured panel wall, with a few overhanging bits, backing its other side. Handy for students to work off stress.

YORK

(6) York St. John College Climbing Wall

York St. John College, Lord Mayors Walk, York, YO31 7EX

Tel: 01904 716 508 for information (development office)

Access: 0.5 mile N of the City Ctr. Find the inner ring road to its most northern part (York Minster) and turn up Clarence Road, car park on left. College is opposite.

P £ local pay & display   Ad; £ don't know

Access uncertain, but possible. College is encouraging public use, certainly in weekends and holidays, but obviously not in preference to students needs. Please ring

A small wall in a sports centre.

LEEDS UNIVERSITY WALL

GUISELEY WALL

12 - LEICESTER   13 - NORWICH   14 - HULL   15 - SHEFFIELD   16 - LIVERPOOL   17 - LEEDS   18 - LANCASTER   19 - DARLINGTON   20 - KESWICK   21 - NEWCASTLE

SPECIALIST CLIMBING SHOPS:

1 Ultimate Outdoors: SHOES ROPES GEAR CAMS BOOKS ICE
15 New Street, Lancaster, LA1 1EG (Right in town Centre, just off Market Sq.)
Tel: 01524 66610 Open: M-Sat 9am - 5.30

2 Ultimate Outdoors: SHOES ROPES GEAR CAMS BOOKS ICE
1 Coach Street, Skipton, BD23 1LH (In town centre)
Tel: 01756 794 305 Open: M-Sat 9am - 5.30 Sun 10am-4pm

3 Fell & Mountain: SHOES ROPES GEAR CAMS BOOKS ICE
38a Water Street, Accrington, BB5 6PX (Just off centre)
Tel: 01254 390 986 Open: M-Sat 9am - 5.30

4 Homebarn: SHOES ROPES GEAR CAMS BOOKS ICE
Unit 1, Homebarn, Clapham, LA2 8EA
Tel: 015242 51162 Open: M-Sun 10-5pm

5 Inglesport: SHOES ROPES GEAR CAMS BOOKS
11 The Square, Ingleton, North Yorkshire. LA6 3EB
Tel: 01542 41146 Open: M-Fri 9am - 5.30 Sat & Sun 8.30am-6pm

6 Outdoor Action: SHOES ROPES GEAR CAMS BOOKS ICE
26-32 King Street, Blackburn, BB2 2DH
Tel: 01254 671 945 Open: M,T,W - F, S 10am-5.30pm; Wed 10-12.30pm

7 Cave and Crag: SHOES ROPES GEAR CAMS BOOKS ICE
Market Place, Settle, BD24 9ED
Tel: 01729 823 877 Open: M-Sun 10-5.30pm

8 Alpine Climbing: SHOES ROPES GEAR CAMS BOOKS ICE
Alpine Climbing & Ski Centre, 193 Church Street, Blackpool, FY1 3NY
Tel: 01253 624 307 Open: M-Sat 9am - 5.30

9 Angling & Hiking Centre: SHOES ROPES GEAR CAMS ICE
275/277 Rawlinson Street, Barrow in Furness, LA14 1DH
Tel: 01229 829 661 Open: M-Sat 9am - 5.30

10 Boyces: SHOES ROPES GEAR CAMS ICE
44 Manchester Road, Nelson, BB9 7EJ
Tel: 01282 614 412 Open: M-Sat 9am - 5pm; Tues 9am-1pm

11 Out & About: SHOES ROPES GEAR CAMS BOOKS ICE
25 Breck Road, Poulton le Fylde, FY6 7AA
Tel: 01253 892 445 Open: M-Sat 10-5pm

12 Ellis Brigham:
Haslingden Old Road, Rossendale, BB4 8RR
Tel: 01706 223 150

13 The Furness Rambler :
19 New Market Street, Ulverston, LA12 7LQ
Tel: 01229 580 898

14 Outdoor Action:
132 Church Street, Preston, PR1 3BT
Tel: 01772 561 970

15 Compass Point:
10 Market Square, Lytham, FY8 5LW
Tel: 01253 795 597

16 Onward and Outward:
32 King Street, Clitheroe, BB7 2EP
Tel: 01200 429 977

Basic gear / local books   Good UK gear / UK books   Big range / Europe books   Expert range / Worldwide

Dedicated Bouldering (Square metres)   Climbing wall - Sector by sector analysis

Grotto	Freeform Rock	Texture Panel	Flat Panel	Brick	Woody	Campus Board	Climbing Walls	B (Bouldering Sqm)	C (Climbing Total Sqm)	Instructional / T/R Bouldering	Top Rope-insitu / Leading	Lead-Tilting / Competition	Exterior
57	0	32	33	0	12	0	① Kendal Wall	B 134	C 764	FP 7m-6-18 (49) · TP 7-14-42 (105)	TP 10-12-48 (135) · FR 10-8-32 (101)	FR 10-6-24 (40)	FP 20-9-36 (200)
20	94	12	14	0	0	0	② Ingleton	B 140	C 603	FP 8-12-34 (94) · FP 9-6-16 (63)	TP 6-5-12 (42) · TP 10-16-63 (170)	TP 12-3-8 (24)	TP 12-5-20 (70)
24	40	0	0	0	0	0	③ Preston	B 64	C 271	TP 5m-3-9 (20) · FR 7-9-36 (77)	TP 10-9-25 (110)		
53	76	0	0	0	0	0	④ Blackburn YMCA	B 129	C 229	FP 10m-1-2 (20) · TP 10-6-15 (80)			
153	0	0	28	0	0	0	⑤ Boulder UK	B 181	C 181				
0	0	58	0	24	0	0	⑥ Clitheroe	B 82	C 166	B 8m-2-8 (24) · FP 8m-2-7 (20)	FP 8m-5-15 (40)		
10	35	75	0	0	0	3	⑦ Burnley-Barden	B 123	C 123				
28	18	15	30	0	0	0	⑧ Lancaster Univ.	B 91	C 111	FR 5m-4-12 (20)			
0	0	24	18	0	0	0	⑨ Barrow	B 42	C 77	FP 9m-1-5 (14) · FP 9m-2-6 (21)			
10	0	40	0	0	0	0	⑩ Blackpool	B 50	C 75	FP 5m-4-12 (25)			

(Sector Height - Individual lines - Total routes in sector)   Sector Sq.m / M

CLIMBING CLUBS - WEBSITE KEYWORDS

PRESTON-MC,
FYLDE-MC

KENDAL WALL - Freeform boulder section

12 - LEICESTER · 13 - NORWICH · 14 - HULL · 15 - SHEFFIELD · 16 - LIVERPOOL · 17 - LEEDS · 18 - LANCASTER · 19 - DARLINGTON · 20 - KESWICK · 21 - NEWCASTLE

12 - LEICESTER
13 - NORWICH
14 - HULL
15 - SHEFFIELD
16 - LIVERPOOL
17 - LEEDS
18 - LANCASTER
19 - DARLINGTON
20 - KESWICK
21 - NEWCASTLE

KENDAL ****
① *Lakeland Climbing Centre*
See section 20 - Lake District.

INGLETON ***
② *Ingleton Wall*
The Co-op Yard, Ingleton, Yorkshire, LA6 3EB
Tel: 015242 41146
Access: Right in the centre of Ingleton. Go first to the shop-cafe of Inglesport, to register, which is 50 yds from the wall on the main high street.
🅿 Free parking in yard
Ad; £5.00 ~ Kid; £4.00
Mon - Thurs / 9am - 10.30pm;
Fri - Sun / 9am - 6pm

A rabbit warrent of chambers, towers in this unique climbing centre. Developed by local climber Alan Steele - bit by bit, there always appears another great sector just around the corner. Some very good surfaces for bouldering, and nice angles too. Leading is often from one wall to another, and is a completely 3 dimensional experience. Colourful to say the least, and amusingly thematic. Definitely worth a visit. Cafe above shop is a good place to chill out if its cats and dogs.

INGLETON - A bouldering sector

INGLETON CLIMBING WALL (Sarah Harrison climbing)

12 - LEICESTER

13 - NORWICH

14 - HULL

15 - SHEFFIELD

16 - LIVERPOOL

17 - LEEDS

18 - LANCASTER

19 - DARLINGTON

20 - KESWICK

21 - NEWCASTLE

Left sidebar tabs:

12 - LEICESTER
13 - NORWICH
14 - HULL
15 - SHEFFIELD
16 - LIVERPOOL
17 - LEEDS
18 - LANCASTER
19 - DARLINGTON
20 - KESWICK
21 - NEWCASTLE

PRESTON ***

③ *Preston Wall*

West View Leisure Centre, West View, Ribbleton,
Preston, Lancs, PR1 5EP
Tel: 01772 796 788

Access: 1.3 mile WNW of Preston centre. Coming into
Preston on the A59 from J31 off the M6, turn R at the
big roundabout after 1 mile, onto the A5085. After 0.5
mile you will come to the B6243, here you turn L onto
Ribbleton Lane, and the centre is soon on the R and is
signposted.

P £ free, car park.

Ad; £3 ~ Kid; £1.50
Registration fee £1.60
One off- 3 hr visit £4.60

Mon - Sun / 9.00am -10pm;

*This is a leisure centre that takes climbing seriously,
which is a lovely refreshing attitude and one to
be thankful for. The wall has had a long history of
development and will most probably be added to in the
the near future. There are some excellent free standing
bouldering areas with good, deep crash pads. Some
of the walls are shortish but of excellent texture and
quality.The main lead section provides plenty of punch
and is a mean angle. A good history of route setting
here too by some well known names.*

6 DEEP-MATS SWIM LEISURE
INTRO kids club
CASUAL FUN FRIENDLY SERIOUS GLOOMY

BLACKBURN **

④ *Blackburn YMCA Wall*

Clarence Street, Blackburn, BB1 8AN
Tel: 01254 51009

Access: 400 yds NNW of town centre. From the very
central town centre head out on the A677 (Preston
New Road) for a very brief while (if you get to the 2
roundabouts you've gone too far), then bear R onto
Shear Bank Road. Very soon Clarence Road is on
the R and the YMCA is just on the L.

P £ Park outside if restrictions allow and dodgy
characters don't seem too off putting. There is a car
park around the back.

Ad & Kid; £3.80

Mon - Fri / 10am - 9.30pm;
Sat & Sun / ring for use availability

*An old fashioned classic bendcrete wall, but classic
because it's really good for bouldering and has
superb natural problems if you get off on crimping like
a demon. The room is sort of weird, but then that's the
attraction, you find good weird problems on this sort
of territory. Not to be overlooked. There is a large flat
wall also in a separate room with very slightly textured
panels for leading on. You have to work exceptionally
hard at the inspiration levels on this structure - the
ultimate test.*

DEEP-MATS
QUIET SERIOUS GLOOMY INTENSE EARTHY

BLACKBURN YMCA WALL

PRESTON WALL (Nice to see that wall has priority over the ceiling)

12 - LEICESTER

13 - NORWICH

14- HULL

15 - SHEFFIELD

16 - LIVERPOOL

17 - LEEDS

18 - LANCASTER

19 - DARLINGTON

20 - KESWICK

21 - NEWCASTLE

12 - LEICESTER   13 - NORWICH   14 - HULL   15 - SHEFFIELD   16 - LIVERPOOL   17 - LEEDS   18 - LANCASTER   19 - DARLINGTON   20 - KESWICK   21 - NEWCASTLE

BLACKBURN ***

⑤ *Boulder UK*

10a Heaton Street, Blackburn, BB3
Tel: 01254 693 056
www.boulderuk.com

Access: 250 yds SW of town Ctr. Exit M65 on Jtn 4 or 5 and head into town centre. From Jtn 5, come in on the A6177 which eventually runs into the one way system (just past the canal), and turn L into Russell St. This then crosses the A666 dual carriageway (Jtn4) and becomes Freckleton St and goes over the railway, then twists down to the main A674 (King St.) Turn Right here onto King St, then go past the one way going off Rt, and Heaton St is the next on the R.

🅿 £ meters in day time ✳ ✳ 🌡

Ad; £5.50 ~ Kid; £4.50

Mon - Fri / 12pm -10pm;
Sat - Sun/ 10am - 8pm;

A highly professionally run bouldering wall run by world class boulderers. On average, 45 problems are set om a monthly basis V2-V10. Very soft and bouncy matting, ideal for the commited boulderer.

HIRE **DEEP-MATS** Ⓣ

INTRO FRIENDLY SERIOUS

BOULDER UK (Alison Martindale flowing and giving it rockall)

CLITHEROE **
⑥ *Roefield Wall*

Roefield Leisure Centre,
Edisford Road, Clitheroe, Lancs
BB7 3LA

Tel: 01200 442 188

Access: 1 mile WSW of
Clitheroe. From the town centre,
head out to the West on the
B6243 towards Longridge. The
centre is in about a mile on the
R side.

P £ a small charge that most
is often refundable by using
the centre.

Ad; £4.00 ~ Kid; £3.00
Memb; £2
One off visit £6

Mon - Fri / 7am - 7pm;
Sat / 9am - 5pm;
Sun/ 9am - 9pm;

DEEP-MATS LEISURE

INTRO ADV kids club

T QUIET

CASUAL FUN FRIENDLY INTENSE

PRESTON WALL

A dedicated climbing room that gives some good scope for fun. One wall is bouldering to a good height on very nicely textured panels. A medium height leading and top roping wall is just at a good steep angle to compensate for the limited distance. They like using lots of holds here so its good for beginners. The more discerning just have to think a bit more.

CLITHEROE WALL

12 - LEICESTER

13 - NORWICH

14 - HULL

15 - SHEFFIELD

16 - LIVERPOOL

17 - LEEDS

18 - LANCASTER

19 - DARLINGTON

20 - KESWICK

21 - NEWCASTLE

12 - LEICESTER
13 - NORWICH
14 - HULL
15 - SHEFFIELD
16 - LIVERPOOL
17 - LEEDS
18 - LANCASTER
19 - DARLINGTON
20 - KESWICK
21 - NEWCASTLE

BURNLEY WALL

BURNLEY *
⑦ *Barden Wall*

Barden Community Association, Barden High School, Heald Rd,
Burnley BB10 1JB
Tel: 01282 831 394
Access: 1.5 mile N of Burnley T-ctr. Leave the M65 at Jtn 12,to
the S on the A682 heading towards Burnley. After 1.5 mile on the
Colne Rd, turn R onto Windermere ave. After 0.5m this crosses
Barden Lane (with Rail Bridge to R), and becomes Heald Rd, the
school is on the L. (Barden Lane goes up to the Main A56/682,
also links to the E, going over the M-Way to become Greenhead
Lane and to A6068)
🅿 £ free
Ad; £2.00; Memb £3; One off visit £5
Mon - Fri / 9.15am - 10pm
Sat - Sun / 9.15am - 8.30pm
Wed 6-7pm Girls club only, Sat 9-12.30 club only.
A small room that is dedicated to high intensity and quality
bouldering. Excellent crash matting on the whole area and useful
for the grand 4.6 metre height. Well laid out and every hold
numbered (700), no shortage of features either. Great fun and
well worth a wet afternoon. There are facilities to top rope, with
easy ways up too. A good wall that is both easy and hard. The
room is sometimes used by the school and is of limited size, so
can only cope with so many, ring to check.

FUN CALM CASUAL EARTHY FRIENDLY GLOOMY

LANCASTER *
⑧ *Lancaster University Wall*

Centre for Sport, Lancaster University,
LA1 4YN
Tel: 01524 594 000
Access: 2.8 miles S of Lancaster. Exit M6
at Jtn 33 (Town ctr is slow and tortuous),
then follow the A6 North. After 2 miles the
Univ. is on the R, signs to sports ctr.
🅿 £ Pay & display but refundable.
Ad; £3.30; Kid £1.45;
Mon - Fri / 8.30am - 10.15pm;
Wed-open 11am; Fri close 9.15pm
Sat / 8.30am - 7.15pm
Sun / 9.30am - 5.30pm
A converted squash court and filled with
bouncy foam. A quite different and testing
wave end for the hard addicts. Two other
walls with some 150 problems in the T4c-6a
category. Mostly flat panel in the other parts
with a small amount of texture. A good
boulder venue.

CASUAL FRIENDLY FUN INTENSE

LANCASTER WALL

BARROW IN FURNESS *
 Barrow-Park Wall
Park Leisure Centre, Greengate St,
Barrow-in-Furness, Cumbria LA13 9DT
Tel: 01229 871 146
Access: 1 mile N of town Ctr. Approach
Barrow on the A590, and turn L onto
Abbey Road. After a while! then turn R
onto Park road and the centre is about
200 yds on the R.
P £ free
Ad; £2.20; Kid £1.30;
Mon - Fri / 7.30am - 9pm;
Sat - Sun / 9am - 6pm
Under 16 must be accom. by an adult.
A small but worthwhile local climbing
wall that is very useful to the local
climbers. A small 2 route lead tower in
a sports hall does conflict with other
sports, so ring for availability. Separate
on an upstairs mezzanine, is a nicely
textured bouldering area in two sections
- wave and flat form. Big enough to work
on some good power, but you must be
determined to make it interesting.

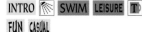

BARROW WALL

BLACKPOOL
 Blackpool Climbing Wall
Blackpool Leisure Ctr, West Park Drive, Blackpool, FY3 9HQ   Tel: 01253 699 900
Access: 1.3 mile East of town Ctr. From the J4 (End) of M55, take the A583 towards
town. After 2 miles, take R/H lane to turn R (Sign to Stanley Park. At a mini roundabout
turn L onto West Park Drive and is soon on the R.   £ free
Ad; £3.20; Kid £2.50;   Mon - Sun / 8.30am - 10.30pm;
A small room with a 5 metre high top roping wall, 2 small bouldering walls and a grotto.
There are plans afoot here!

12 - LEICESTER
13 - NORWICH
14 - HULL
15 - SHEFFIELD
16 - LIVERPOOL
17 - LEEDS
18 - LANCASTER
19 - DARLINGTON
20 - KESWICK
21 - NEWCASTLE

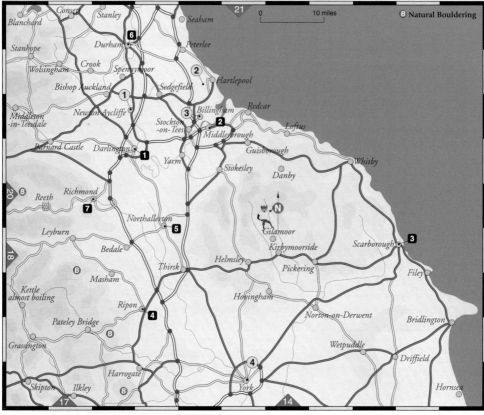

SPECIALIST CLIMBING SHOPS:

1 Simpsons Sports: SHOES ROPES GEAR CAMS BOOKS ICE
26a Post house Wynd, Darlington, DL3 7LR (From town clock-directly West)
Tel: 01325 381 068 Open: Mon-Sat 9-5.30pm

2 Nevisport:
100 Newport Road, Middlesbrough, TS1 5JD
Tel: 01642 248 916

3 Crag and Moor: ROPES GEAR CAMS BOOKS ICE
38 Victoria Road, Scarborough, YO11 1SD
Tel: 01723 368 777 Open: Mon-Sat 9-5.30pm

4 Rock Bottom Outdoor Equipment:
6 Westgate, Ripon, HG4 2AT
Tel: 01765 602 656

5 Yorkshire Rambler:
110 Garthway arcade, Northallerton, DL7 8NS
Tel: 01609 780 894

6 Scout& Guide Shop:
47 North Bailey, Durham, DH1 3ET
Tel: 0191 375 7400

7 Alt-Berg: BOOKS
14 Finkle Street, Richmond, DL10 4QB
Tel: 01748 826 922

CLIMBING CLUBS - WEBSITE KEYWORDS
BRIDLINGTON WALKING &-CC, CLEVELAND-MC,
EAST YORKSHIRE MOUNTAINEERING & CAVING CLUB
CLEVELAND-MC

Basic gear / local books   Good UK gear / UK books   Big range / Europe books   Expert range / Worldwide

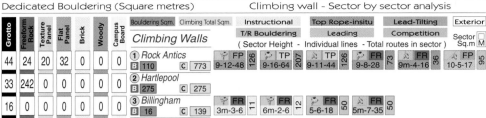

Dedicated Bouldering (Square metres) — Climbing wall - Sector by sector analysis

Grotto	Freeform Rock	Texture Panel	Flat Panel	Brick	Woody	Campus Board	Climbing Walls			Instructional		Top Rope-insitu		Lead-Tilting		Exterior
							Bouldering Sqm. Climbing Total Sqm.			T/R Bouldering		Leading		Competition		Sector Sq.m ☐ M
							(Sector Height - Individual lines - Total routes in sector)									
44	24	20	32	0	0	0	① Rock Antics	B 110	C 773	FP 9-12-48 [126]	TP 9-16-64 [207]	TP 9-11-44 [126]	FR 9-8-28 [73]	FR 9m-4-16 [36]	FP 10-5-17 [95]	
33	242	0	0	0	0	0	② Hartlepool	B 275	C 275							
16	0	0	0	0	0	0	③ Billingham	B 16	C 139	FR 3m-3-6 [11]	FR 6m-2-6 [12]	FR 5-6-18 [50]	FR 5m-7-35 [50]			
0	0	0	0	0	0	0	④ York St. John	B 126	C 126	TP 6-9-27 [60]						

12 - LEICESTER

13 - NORWICH

14 - HULL

15 - SHEFFIELD

16 - LIVERPOOL

17 - LEEDS

18 - LANCASTER

19 - DARLINGTON

20 - KESWICK

21 - NEWCASTLE

12 - LEICESTER
13 - NORWICH
14 - HULL
15 - SHEFFIELD
16 - LIVERPOOL
17 - LEEDS
18 - LANCASTER
19 - DARLINGTON
20 - KESWICK
21 - NEWCASTLE

NEWTON AYCLIFFE ***
① Rock Antics
Newton Aycliffe Leisure Centre, Beveridge Arcade, Newton Aycliffe, Durham, DL5 4EH
Tel: 01325 320 683
Access: Slap, bang in the town centre. The A167 has a looping road from N-South, the B6443. At around the centre of this on a roundabout, turn W onto Stephenson Way and the Leisure Centre is soon on the R. Park behind it, then find the entrance which is in the shopping precinct.
🅿 £ free.
Ad; £6 ~ Kid; £4
Memb; £4
One off visit; £10
Mon - Fri / 10am - 10pm
Sat / 10am - 9pm   Sun / 10am - 5pm
A surprising full on rocky centre, tucked upstairs in a shoping center takes you by surprise, a whole world in itself. A very good array of walls all over the place with everything from simple to freeform bouldering, and a huge list of top rope routes. The perfect centre for anyone, who gets a bit too tired on mega long routes. A good all round family, kids centre that should appeal to the majority of climbers. Expect the kids to burn you off here.

HARTLEPOOL **
② Summerhill Park Boulders
Summerhill Visitor Centre, Sunhill Drive, Catcote Road, Hartlepool, TS25 4LL
Tel: 01429 284 848
Access: 2 miles WSW of town ctr, just S of West Park. The main A689 comes up into Hartlepool from the S, keep on for a bit and about 1 mile before the t-ctr turn L onto Owton Manor Lane, then R onto Catcote Road, the L into Sunhill Drive.
🅿 £ free, but the main gates get locked up in the evening, so be sure to park outside these.
Ad; Free, free, free
Mon - Sun / Open
Visitor Centre; Mon - Sun / 9-5
May-Aug - 9-8pm.
Individual public access only.
The biggest group of outdoor man made boulders in the UK, and in a lovely setting. Summerhill is a 100 acre site that has been transformed as an educational outdoor sport and conservation area. There are 8 large boulders including a large hippo style one. A lovely place to boulder on a summers day or evening. Dries very quickly and with plenty of good problems. Worth bringing your pad for the few grotto probs.

BILLINGHAM *
③ Billingham Wall
Billingham Forum Leisure Centre, Town Centre, Billingham, Cleveland TS23 2LJ
Tel: 01642 551 381
Access: Right in the town centre but on the East side. Well signposted
🅿 £ free
Ad; £2.40 ~ Kid; £1.65
Mon - Sun / 7.30pm - 10pm
A converted squash court by Bendcrete, rock texture and inserts of natural stone. no bolt-ons unfortunately. A good selection of teaching slabs and fun tufas. A small room and a fair adaptation. Some good hard boulder problems but limited as quite a lot of the area is instructional. No deep pads and you are best off bringing a top rope.

YORK
④ York St. John College Wall
See Leeds section - 17

BILLINGHAM WALL

12 - LEICESTER

13 - NORWICH

14 - HULL

15 - SHEFFIELD

16 - LIVERPOOL

17 - LEEDS

18 - LANCASTER

19 - DARLINGTON

20 - KESWICK

21 - NEWCASTLE

ROCK ANTICS WALL

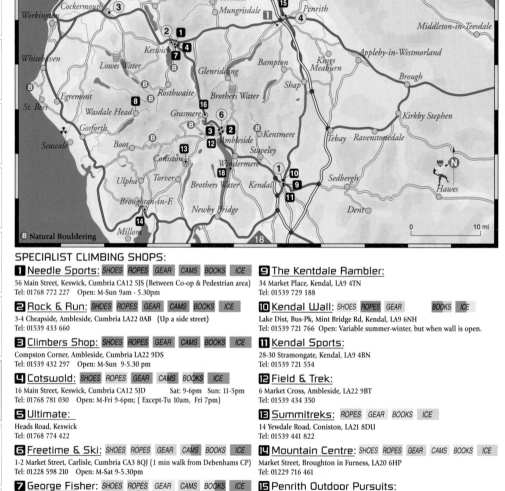

12 - LEICESTER
13 - NORWICH
14 - HULL
15 - SHEFFIELD
16 - LIVERPOOL
17 - LEEDS
18 - LANCASTER
19 - DARLINGTON
20 - KESWICK
21 - NEWCASTLE

SPECIALIST CLIMBING SHOPS:

1 Needle Sports: `SHOES` `ROPES` `GEAR` `CAMS` `BOOKS` `ICE`
56 Main Street, Keswick, Cumbria CA12 5JS (Between Co-op & Pedestrian area)
Tel: 01768 772 227   Open: M-Sun 9am - 5.30pm

2 Rock & Run: `SHOES` `ROPES` `GEAR` `CAMS` `BOOKS` `ICE`
3-4 Cheapside, Ambleside, Cumbria LA22 0AB   (Up a side street)
Tel: 01539 433 660

3 Climbers Shop: `SHOES` `ROPES` `GEAR` `CAMS` `BOOKS` `ICE`
Compston Corner, Ambleside, Cumbria LA22 9DS
Tel: 01539 432 297   Open: M-Sun 9-5.30 pm

4 Cotswold: `SHOES` `ROPES` `GEAR` `CAMS` `BOOKS` `ICE`
16 Main Street, Keswick, Cumbria CA12 5JD   Sat: 9-6pm   Sun: 11-5pm
Tel: 01768 781 030   Open: M-Fri 9-6pm; (Except-Tu 10am, Fri 7pm)

5 Ultimate:
Heads Road, Keswick
Tel: 01768 774 422

6 Freetime & Ski: `SHOES` `ROPES` `GEAR` `CAMS` `BOOKS` `ICE`
1-2 Market Street, Carlisle, Cumbria CA3 8QJ (1 min walk from Debenhams CP)
Tel: 01228 598 210   Open: M-Sat 9-5.30pm

7 George Fisher: `SHOES` `ROPES` `GEAR` `CAMS` `BOOKS` `ICE`
2 Borrowdale Road, Keswick, Cumbria CA12 5DA
Tel: 017687 72178   Open: M-Sat 9am-6pm; -5,30pm (W) Sun: 10.30-4.30pm

8 The Barn Door Shop:
Wasdale Head, Seascale, CA20 1EX
Tel: 01946 726 384

9 The Kentdale Rambler:
34 Market Place, Kendal, LA9 4TN
Tel: 01539 729 188

10 Kendal Wall: `SHOES` `ROPES` `GEAR` `BOOKS` `ICE`
Lake Dist, Bus-Pk, Mint Bridge Rd, Kendal, LA9 6NH
Tel: 01539 721 766   Open: Variable summer-winter, but when wall is open.

11 Kendal Sports:
28-30 Stramongate, Kendal, LA9 4BN
Tel: 01539 721 554

12 Field & Trek:
6 Market Cross, Ambleside, LA22 9BT
Tel: 01539 434 350

13 Summitreks: `ROPES` `GEAR` `BOOKS` `ICE`
14 Yewdale Road, Coniston, LA21 8DU
Tel: 01539 441 822

14 Mountain Centre: `SHOES` `ROPES` `GEAR` `CAMS` `BOOKS` `ICE`
Market Street, Broughton in Furness, LA20 6HP
Tel: 01229 716 461

15 Penrith Outdoor Pursuits:
37 Middlegate, Penrith, CA11 7PT
Tel: 01768 891 383

15 Summitreks:
2 College Street, Grasmere, LA22 9SZ
Tel: 01539 441 822

Basic gear / local books	Good UK gear / UK books	Big range / Europe books	Expert range / Worldwide

Dedicated Bouldering (Square metres) | Climbing wall - Sector by sector analysis

Grotto	Freeform Rock	Texture Panel	Flat Panel	Brick	Woody	Campus Board	Climbing Walls	Instructional / T/R Bouldering	Top Rope-insitu / Leading	Lead-Tilting / Competition	Sector Sq.m
57	0	32	33	0	12	0	**1 Kendal** — B 134, C 764	FP 7m-6-18 (49); TP 7-14-42 (105)	TP 10-12-48 (135); FR 10-8-32 (101)	FR 10-6-24 (40); FP 20-9-36 (200)	
16	0	0	0	0	13	3	**2 Keswick** — B 32, C 308	FP 6m-9-18 (18); TP 5-16-48 (85)	FP 6m-5-15 (36); TP 6m-9-27 (60)	FR 6m-2-6 (12); FP 7m-4-14 (35)	
16	0	0	92	0	0	0	**3 Cockermouth** — B 108, C 265	FR 6-18-99 (132); FR 5m-4-16 (25)			
25	14	0	0	0	0	0	**4 Penrith** — B 39, C 207	FP 8m-3-12 (17); FP 8m-4-16 (40)	FP 7m-4-14 (35); FP 8m-4-16 (48)	FR 8m-3-12 (28)	
12	16	0	0	0	0	0	**5 Carlisle - Sands** — B 28, C 164	FR 6m-1-2 (6); B 7m-4-12 (46)	FP 7m-3-4 (21); FP 7m-3-9 (28)	TP 7m-6-11 (35)	
20	0	0	20	80	0	0	**6 Ambleside** — B 120, C 120				
0	0	0	0	0	0	0	**7 Carlisle-St.Aidan's** — B 00, C 109	FR 5m-3-6 (23); FR 5m-3-7 (20)	FR 6m-2-6 (12); FR 6m-1-2 (12)	FR 7m-4-12 (42)	

(Sector Height - Individual lines - Total routes in sector)

17 Summitreks:
Compston Road, Ambleside, LA22 9DJ
Tel: 01539 441 822

18 Stuart's Sports:
32 Lake Road, Bowness on Windermere, LA23 3AP
Tel: 01539 443 001

[1] Mountain Exhibition: CLIMBER'S information
Rheged, Redhills, Penrith, Cumbria CA11 0DQ Tel: 01768 868

CLIMBING CLUBS - WEBSITE KEYWORDS
EDEN VALLEY-MC (Penrith Wall), CARLISLE-MC
FELL AND ROCK-CC (General), KESWICK-MC

KESWICK WALL, The bouldering sector; Gaz Turner

12 - LEICESTER | 13 - NORWICH | 14 - HULL | 15 - SHEFFIELD | 16 - LIVERPOOL | 17 - LEEDS | 18 - LANCASTER | 19 - DARLINGTON | 20 - KESWICK | 21 - NEWCASTLE

12 - LEICESTER
13 - NORWICH
14 - HULL
15 - SHEFFIELD
16 - LIVERPOOL
17 - LEEDS
18 - LANCASTER
19 - DARLINGTON
20 - KESWICK
21 - NEWCASTLE

KENDAL****

① *The lakeland Climbing Centre*
Lake District Business Park, Mintbridge
Road, Kendal, Cumbria LA9 6NH
Tel: 01539 721 766
Access: 1 mile NNE of Kendal T/centre.
Take the main A6 from the town centre
going N towards Shap, Mintbridge rd.
leads directly off A6 on the left.
P Plenty of free parking
Ad; £7.00 ~ Kid; £6.00 ~ no 1st time fee.
Mon / 4pm-10pm; Tue-F/ 10am-10pm
Sat, Sun & B.hol/ 10am-7pm
Summer changes: (May-Aug)
Closed Mon; S,Sun, BH 10am-5pm
*A superb facility offering a complete
range of climbing to everyone. There are
4 different areas: a very good bouldering
grotto room; a bigger bouldering area
with easier problems; a top roping in-situ
room, excellent for beginners; and the
main wall area. This massive competition
wall is breathtaking, steep and desperate.
This section also has big windows, giving
it a nice and airy feeling.*

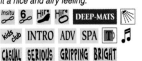

KESWICK**

② *Keswick Climbing Wall*
Southey Hill, Keswick, Cumbria CA12 5NR
Tel: 017687 72000
Access: 500 yds NW of T/centre.
Southey Hill leads N, off Main Street just
past the mini roundabout (Co-op).
P Free parking
Ad; £4.25 ~ Kid; £2.75
no 1st time fee.
Mon - Sun / 10am - 9pm
*A very good indoor facility, right in the
heart of Keswick, and a blessing for
those rare days that it rains in the Lake
District! It offers a great day out for a lot
of people and is consequently popular
(gets busy and quite noisy with kids).
The wall is unfortunately quite low, and
is limited because of this, and hence it is
angled at beginners rather than cutting
edge climbing. It works exceptionally well
for kids, and anyone who is less than an
expert (good steep woody though). Plenty
to climb for a day. No exterior light, and a
bit strange with heavy orange lighting.*

COCKERMOUTH **

③ *Cockermouth Climbing Wall*
Cockermouth leisure Centre, Castle Gate
Drive, Cockermouth, Cumbria. CA13 9JR
Tel: 01900 823 596
Access: 500 yds SE of T/centre. Follow
the brown signs for the sports centre.
P Free parking
Ad; £2.00 ~ Kid; £1.30
no 1st time fee.
Mon - Fri / 8am -10pm
Sat - Sun / 9am - 5pm
*An excellent and wonderfully vertical,
inside natural gritstone wall, giving
superb bouldering (2 clips to the top for
the fainthearted). A large old fashioned
brick section and a very worn and
polished bendcrete form, gives very
hard bouldering. A nice change from a
converted squash court, "odd" but very
good and demanding for the fingers. This
old wall proves that plastic doesn't match
up to real rock for quality, fingertip training.*

12 - LEICESTER

13 - NORWICH

14 - HULL

15 - SHEFFIELD

16 - LIVERPOOL

17 - LEEDS

18 - LANCASTER

19 - DARLINGTON

20 - KESWICK

21 - NEWCASTLE

KENDAL WALL, Competition sector

12 - LEICESTER
13 - NORWICH
14 - HULL
15 - SHEFFIELD
16 - LIVERPOOL
17 - LEEDS
18 - LANCASTER
19 - DARLINGTON
20 - KESWICK
21 - NEWCASTLE

EDEN VALLEY WALL

CARLISLE**

⑦ *St. Aidan's Climbing Wall*

St. Aidan's County High School Sports Centre.
Victoria Place, Carlisle, Cumbria CA1 1LY
Tel: 01228 607 469
Access: 1/2 mile yds E of city centre. From M6
(J43) The Warwick Road (A69) leads to City
Centre. Just Past the Football ground, then at
lights, turn R into Victoria Place, carry on past
school entrance and to sports Centre on the L.
🅿 Free parking.
Ad; £3.50 ~ Kid; £2.50
no 1st time fee.
Mon - Fri / 5pm -9pm (8pm-Last-E)
Sat - Sun / 10am -5pm (4pm-Last-E) In school
holidays, ring to check for extra opening times.
*A very good real rock textured wall. Lots of small
features, but not enough for fully textured routes
in general. Good steep parts, with any of the
routes getting nasty by using plastic hand holds
only. Short in height but a great looking wall and
lots of fun climbing. Situated in a main sports
hall, but well designed netting allows for climbing
during any event (Perhaps not archery!). Notes:
sometimes the wall is fully booked by a group, so
phone first.*

 INTRO ADV SWIM LEISURE

 CASUAL FRIENDLY OPEN FEEL

ST. AIDAN'S WALL

THE SANDS WALL

PENRITH **
④ *Eden Climbing Wall*
Penrith Leisure Centre, South End Road, Penrith. CA11 8JH
Tel: 01768 863 450
Access: 800 yds S of T/centre. Take the A66 ring road to the south, and come in on the A6, centre is just on the left
P Free parking
Ad; £2.55 ~ Kid; £1.30
no 1st time fee.
Mon - Fri / 10am - 9.30pm
Sat - Sun / 10am - 9pm
It's not the biggest wall in the world, but every square millimetre of it is good. A very good small rock textured bouldering wall with excellent features and properties. Very good leading area with demanding and everchanging routes. Limited height, but some texturing on the panels to add some lovely hands only routes. Good for a wet day anytime.

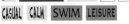

CARLISLE *
⑤ *The Sands Climbing Wall*
Sands Leisure Centre, Hardwicke Circus, Carlisle, CA1 1JQ
Tel: 01228 625 222
Access: 500 yds E of city centre. Go to the giant roundabout in the town centre A7/A595, the centre is on the NE side.
P Free parking in L/centre spaces only; free with admission for 3 hours, pay and display car parks next to centre also.
Ad; £2.55 ~ Kid; £1.55
£1 deposit for a tag to climb
no 1st time fee.
Mon - Sun / 9.30am -10.30pm
A wall of multi stage development. The original DR inset pieces of stone slab sector still gives a good area for novices to be taught, along with a funky littly grotto. The improvements to the central area still make this a worthwhile wall; the nice central panel sector gives a good work-out for those long winter evenings. The nosiest wall in Britain. Behind the curtain in the sports hall, there is a fitness area where the boppy music tends to get blasted out. Sometimes has competitions on a Sat afternoon & is not big enough for casual climbing - ring to check.

AMBLESIDE*
⑥ *St. Martins College Climbing Wall*
St. Martins College, Rydal Road, Ambleside. LA22 9BB
Tel: 015394 30210
Access: 300 yds NW of t/centre. From TC 1 way (climbers shop), go N on A591; after 10 yds turn R and bear L to go up Nook Lane. Go up here for 250 yds and the Hall is on the L (grey pebbeldash).
P Free parking by hall.
Ad; £3 ~ Kid; £3   no 1st time fee.
Mon - Thu/ 1.30pm -9.30pm   Fri / 1.30pm -7pm   Sat / 12pm -5pm   Sun Closed.
During the college holiday times, opening hours are reduced, phone for availability.
A purpose built wall of the 1980's, a bouldering room with natural rock insets. Now with additional bolt ons, it gives a great variety and endless range of vertical problems. It still demands good technique and with plenty of local rock holds, will do marvels for training on the E1-2 style, Lake District classics.

AMBLESIDE - ST. MARTIN'S COLLEGE WALL

12 - LEICESTER
13 - NORWICH
14 - HULL
15 - SHEFFIELD
16 - LIVERPOOL
17 - LEEDS
18 - LANCASTER
19 - DARLINGTON
20 - KESWICK
21 - NEWCASTLE

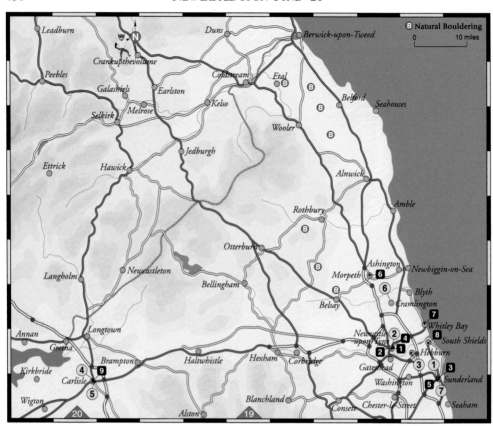

12 - LEICESTER

13 - NORWICH

14 - HULL

15 - SHEFFIELD

16 - LIVERPOOL

17 - LEEDS

18 - LANCASTER

19 - DARLINGTON

20 - KESWICK

21 - NEWCASTLE

SPECIALIST CLIMBING SHOPS:

1 Wild Trak: SHOES ROPES GEAR CAMS BOOKS ICE
60 - 62 St Andrews Street, Newcastle-upon-Tyne, NE1 5SF
Tel: 0191 261 8582 Open: Mon-Sat 9-5.30pm

2 LD Mountain Centre: SHOES ROPES GEAR CAMS BOOKS ICE
34 Dean Street, Newcastle-upon-Tyne, NE1 1PG
Tel: 0191 232 3561 Open: Mon-Sat 9-5.30pm, Thurs till 7pm, Sun 11-5pm

3 Chapel Rock Shop: SHOES ROPES GEAR CAMS BOOKS ICE
29 Stockton Road, Sunderland, SR2 7AQ (200m from metro interchange)
Tel: 0191 567 4199 Open: Mon-Sat 10-5.00pm

4 Nevisport:
22 Saville Row, Newcastle-upon-Tyne, NE1 8JE
Tel: 0191 232 4941

5 Reynolds Outdoor Centre:
6-7 Derwent Street, Sunderland, SR1 3NT
Tel: 0191 565 7945

6 Northumbria Mountain Sports:
The Chantry, Morpeth, NE61 1PJ
Tel: 01670 513 276

7 Outdoor World:
49 Ilfracombe Gardens, Whitley Bay, NE26 3LZ
Tel: 0191 456 6402

8 McReds Ramble In:
72 Dean Road, South Shields, NE33 4AR
Tel: 0191 456 6402

9 Freetime & Ski: SHOES ROPES GEAR CAMS BOOKS ICE
1-2 Market Street, Carlisle, Cumbria CA3 8QJ (1 min walk from Debenhams CP)
Tel: 01228 598 210 Open: M-Sat 9-5.30pm

SUNDERLAND WALL

Basic gear / local books   Good UK gear / UK books   Big range / Europe books   Expert range / Worldwide

Dedicated Bouldering (Square metres) | Climbing wall - Sector by sector analysis

Grotto	Freeform Rock	Texture Panel	Flat Panel	Brick	Woody	Campus Board	Climbing Walls (B / C)	Instructional / T/R Bouldering	Top Rope-Insitu / Leading	Lead-Tilting / Competition	Sector Sq.m
0	0	0	113	0	0	4	① Sunderland B 117 C 892	FP 6m-6-24 | 72 — FP 6-4-12 | 30	FP 10-6-18 | 85 — FP 10-7-21 | 90	FP 16-6-18 | 112 — FP 23-14-30 | 368	368
87	161	60	0	0	0	3	② Newcastle-Berg B 308 C 308				
0	0	0	0	43	0	0	③ Hebburn B 43 C 202	TP 6m-2-8 | 18 — TP 6-10-40 | 69	TP 7m-5-15 | 36 — FP 6m-2-5 | 18	TP 6m-2-8 | 18	
12	16	0	0	0	0	0	④ Carlisle - Sands B 28 C 164	FR 6m-1-2 | 6 — B 7m-4-12 | 46	FP 7m-3-4 | 21 — FP 7m-3-9 | 28	TP 7m-6-11 | 35	
0	0	0	0	0	0	0	⑤ Carlisle-St.Aidan's B 28 C 109	FR 5m-3-6 | 23 — FR 5m-3-7 | 20	FR 6m-2-6 | 12 — FR 6m-1-2 | 12	FR 7m-4-12 | 42	
0	0	0	0	0	0	0	⑥ Cramlington B 00 C 80	TP 8m-5-15 | 40 — TP 8m-5-15 | 40			
0	0	0	0	0	0	4	⑦ Sund-Leisure B 00 C 80	B 8-10-20 | 80			

(Sector Height - Individual lines - Total routes in sector)

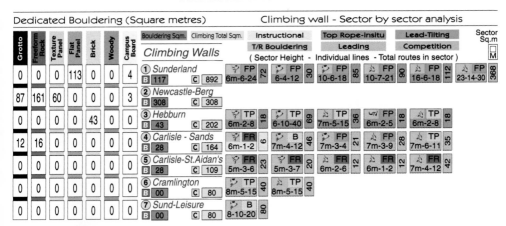

CLIMBING CLUBS - WEBSITE KEYWORDS
NORTHUMBRIAN-MC
WANNEYS-MC

berghaus

BERGHAUS WALL

12 - LEICESTER | 13 - NORWICH | 14 - HULL | 15 - SHEFFIELD | 16 - LIVERPOOL | 17 - LEEDS | 18 - LANCASTER | 19 - DARLINGTON | 20 - KESWICK | 21 - NEWCASTLE

12 - LEICESTER

13 - NORWICH

14 - HULL

15 - SHEFFIELD

16 - LIVERPOOL

17 - LEEDS

18 - LANCASTER

19 - DARLINGTON

20 - KESWICK

21 - NEWCASTLE

SUNDERLAND ***
① *Sunderland Climbing Wall*
Doxford Works, Pallion Quay, SR4 6TQ
Tel: 0191 514 4234
Access: 1.5 mile WNW of T-ctr. Approach
is to take the A1231 along the N side of
the River to Southwick, then cross S (Q-
Alex-bridge), and turn R onto the B1405.
Wall is soon signposted on the R.
🅿 Free parking outside. 🔆
Ad; £7.00 ~ Kid; £5.00
Mon - Fri / 10am -10pm
Sat - Sun / 10am -8 pm
*WHOPPING Big, is your first impression
of this wall without doubt. Then again,
the size of the shed it's in, it pre-warns
you. A fantastic development for the area
and in its very early stages. An entirely
flat panel construction, that is obviously
entirely dependent upon the route setters
ingenuity. The same with the bouldering
areas too. Certainly with good climbers in
control, this place could zing, lets hope.*

CARLISLE *
④ *Sands Wall*
See section - 20 - Keswick

CARLISLE **
⑤ *St. Aidan's Wall*
See section - 20 - Keswick

NEWCASTLE-UPON-TYNE ***
② *The Berghaus Climbing Wall*
Eldon Leisure Centre, Eldon Sq, NE1 7XY
Tel: 0191 232 5917
Access: City Centre, 500 yds NNE of
Stn.. Park in Entrance is upp & off
Grainger St, on SW side of centre.
🅿 Lots of pay and display multi storey. 🔆
Ad; £3 ~ Kid; £2.20
Mon - Thu/ 9am -10pm, Fri 8pm
Sat / 9-6pm & Sun 9-7pm
*A highly dedicated bouldering area built
by bendcrete at their peak in the moulded
concrete phase. Very popular and has
its own little guidebook, definitely worth
getting. Warm, popular and superbly good.
Always worth checking out for a crank.*

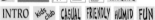

CRAMLINGTON **
⑥ *Concordia Climbing Wall*
Concordia L.Ctr, Forum Way, NE1 7XY
Tel: 01670 717 423
Access: Town Centre. 🅿 Free
Ad; £2.95 ~ Kid; £2.10
Mon - Fri / 9am -10.30pm
Sat / 9-9.30pm & Sun 9-10.30pm
*A popular and busy little climbing wall of
some nice textured panels, with lots of
routes.*

HEBBURN *
③ *The Clegwell Climbing Wall*
Clegwell Community Association,
Mountbatten Ave, Hebburn, NE31 2QU
Tel: 01228 625 222
Access: Good luck! Get a map from
streetmap.co.uk. The center is behind
the Hebburn Comp-school, just S of the
A185 towards Monkton, but you have to
navigate through the houses to find ctr.
🅿 Free parking. 🔆
Ad; £2.50 ~ Kid; £2.00
Mon / 7-9pm adults
Tue / 4.45-7pm kids, 7-9 general
Thur / 4.45-9pm general
*A highly enthusiastic little activity centre,
with a group of very keen climbers who
have given some lovely climbing life to this
little sports hall. A badminton court area
has rock walls all around, posters and lots
of climbing info. Something here for most
and welcoming.*

SUNDERLAND
⑦ *Crowtree Climbing Wall*
Crowtree L-Centre, Sund, SR1 3EL
Tel: 0191 553 2600
Access: Town Centre.
Ad; £5 per hour for entire wall use
Mon - Sun/ 8am -10pm
In a sports hall, so ring to book first.
An old style vertical wall, use for groups.

HEBBURN WALL

12 - LEICESTER

13 - NORWICH

14 - HULL

15 - SHEFFIELD

16 - LIVERPOOL

17 - LEEDS

18 - LANCASTER

19 - DARLINGTON

20 - KESWICK

21 - NEWCASTLE

SUNDERLAND WALL

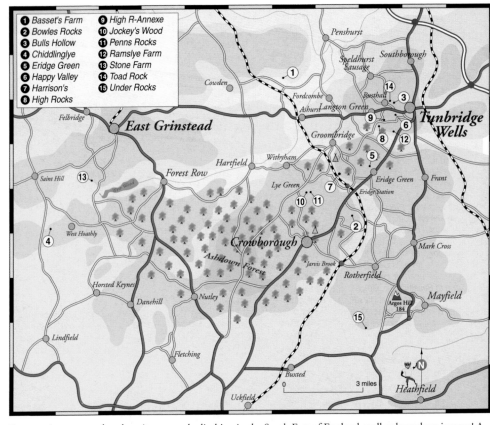

Some cynics may say that there is not much climbing in the South East of England, well at least there is some! A few weekends spent in the area will either hook you, or send you off in search of bigger and wetter places. The climate for this wine growing region is very good indeed; however, the winter is still wet and most of the rocks stay damp with green moss on them. In spring, the sun shines and instantly you have a chirpy little climbing playground that offers hundreds of small routes. The rock is very soft, and erosion is a big problem and issue. You must use a top rope, and protect the top edge from wear. There is also no abseiling, and it is essential to always walk down after a climb. The climbing is superbly technical and provides a whole array of intensive test piece routes. Beginners will struggle here because the angle is always steep. Best grades are t5a-6a.

Julie Tullis Memorial Campsite.
(01/1-31/12)
Harrison's Rocks, Groombridge
There is a large car park at the entrance to the woods that surround the rocks. To the right of the car park, are around 20 level camping pitches in the trees. Very tranquil and peaceful but can get busy at weekends. At the car park toilet block there are hot water facilities for washing up. Pay the warden who visits in the morning.

Goldsmith Campsite. (02/1-31/12)
Crowborough
01892 664 827
A caravan and camping posh site nearby with facilities, 0.4m NW Crowborough.

SANDSTONE
SOUTH-EAST-ENGLAND
Topo guidebook
338 pages - Colour
150 colour photos
A5 - Flexiback
Pub-2000
by Jingo Wobbly
(David Atchison-Jones)

The very first Jingo Wobbly topo guidebook has a refreshing layout, with very clear and easy to use diagrams. A lavish production with enticing colour photos. Bouldering included with a full tick & graded list of routes, plus history of 1st ascents.

2,3, 5,6,7,8,9,12,13,14,15

SOUTHERN
SANDSTONE
Text guidebook
288 pages - B &W
A few colour photos
Pocket - 165 x 105mm
Pub-1995
by the Climbers Club
(M.Vetterlein)

A book with most climbs & to all the cliffs in the area - with or without access possibility. It does the job if you already know the routes. Handy little pocket size, but difficult to use if you don't know the area like the back of your hand. A good section on radical chalk climbing, eek!

1 - 15, plus south coast cliffs too!!!!

① BASSET'S FARM ROCKS

San 〈3〉 👟 | Alt-60m | 6m | 8.5

| 24 | -- | 🧗 | 🏛 |

A medium sized wall offering quite a few climbs in the lower quality range. The place is quiet, and the rock is very sandy. Often gets overgrown in late summer and is high mosquito territory. On private ground, but a public footpath runs beneath the crag. Worth being discreet, and with care to the area.
Map: OS.188 (Landranger) 491 414
Dir: 7m WNW of Tun Wells. Take the A264 due west from TW, passing through Ashurst after 6 miles, under railway, then on for 0.5m. Turn R to Blackham, after 0.6m bear R over a railway, soon follow the road sharp R. After 0.4m, turn L towards Chiddingstone. After 0.7m turn L towards Cowden at White post; after nearly a mile road drops down to Bassett's Far. Go past and at a bend in the road shortly after, you will see a footpath leading off to the R. Take this and the crag is 500 yds further on the left.

② BOWLES ROCKS**

San 〈1〉 👟 | Alt-80m | 10m | 8.2

| | 170 | 30 | 🧗 | Q-D |

A superb outcrop and the best quality rock in the local area. Bowles is an outdoor centre with its own little dry ski slope and indoor swimming pool for canoe practise. A small charge is made for climbing, but there are toilets up at the top; and the whole place is kept immaculately clean. Belays are provided at the top and must be used. In places there are signs of rock wear, but in general there are still lots of crimples for your fingertips. The skill is to find the correct ones before your strength runs out. Nice for a picnic, but can get busy on a Sunday.
Map: OS.135 (Explorer) 543 330
Dir: 3m SSW of Tunbridge Wells. Follow A26(Crowborough) SW, past Eridge station for 0.7m, then turn left(Bowles outdoor centre). A road leads to the centre 0.5m, enter and park. The rocks are up the track past the road barrier, about 100 yds on.

③ BULLS HOLLOW ROCKS

San 〈3〉 👟 | Alt-90m | 8m | 8.4

| 70 | -- | 🧗 | ⚅ |

One of those outcrops that is 'not' on many peoples 'must go back there in a hurry list.' An old quarry that is very sandy and has mainly vertical routes. It also seems to be a natural seepage dip and stagnent water collection point. It is in the process of being cleaned up but don't hold your hopes too high. In a really dry spell it does give some very good and technical routes. The Toad Rock Retreat pub around the corner is often the better bet.
Map: OS.135 (Explorer) 569 394
Dir: 1m W of Tunbridge Wells. Take A 264(East Grinstead). 300yds past the Spa Hotel turn right(Denny Bottomroad). This leads to some twisting downhill bends, park either in the small space on the bend, or further on down on the right, leaving the driveway clear. A path leads down to the the right into the trees for the rocks; from the bend as you approach in the car.

BOWLES ROCKS, the Eastern end.

KENT/SUSSEX · DORSET · CORNWALL · DEVON · BRISTOL · SOUTH-WALES · MID-WALES · NORTH-WALES · LEICESTER · PEAKS · YORK-LANCS · CLEVELAND · KENDAL · LAKES · PENRITH · NEWCASTLE

④ CHIDDINGLYE WOOD ROCKS

San (15)- 👟 Alt-130m 6m 8.2 | 26 | 10 | ☀ | HBall

Some very good climbing to be found on this small but rambling outcrop. Was once deep in the woods and secluded. The area has now been cleared and can easily be located on a good footpath. Is on private land, and climbing is not encouraged. Rock is fragile, but a nice place for a walk.
Map: OS.135 (Explorer) 348 324

⑤ ERIDGE GREEN ROCKS *

San ⊗- 👟 Alt-110m 9m 8.3 | 160 | -- | ☀ | Pump

These rocks are now in a local wildlife conserve, and parts are forbidden to be climbed upon (Plants growing on the rock)-with local notices. The climbing is superb, but the rock is exceptionally soft so care must be taken. Even falling on a top rope will damage this rock, so please climb only on routes you will easily cruise and do not work on any routes here. The rock is not strong enough to support bouldering.
Map: OS.135 (Explorer) 555 356
Dir: 2.3m SW of Tun Wells. Take the A26 to Eridge (Crowborough), turn R down the side of the church on a lane that goes to the crag in 500m. Car park to the R, rocks go on for about 1 mile.

⑥ HAPPY VALLEY ROCKS *

San (5)- 👟 Alt-120m 3-7m 8.3 | 12 | 20 | ☀ | 🔄

Some small and fun little rocks on a little hillside that give a nice evening of easier bouldering. Falling into the ferns and down the hill is a local speciality. Also with a solitary tower, and a handful of demanding t5c desperates. Definitely a top rope needed.
Map: OS.135 (Explorer) 565 392
Dir: 1m W of Tun Wells. Down the track by St. Pauls Church before Rusthall common. Within 400 yds.

⑦ HARRISONS ROCKS ***

San (15)- 👟 Alt-100m 11m 8.1 | 350 | 40 | Sloper | 🙂

This is the most popular and well known crag in the SE of England. A long rambling crag with over 300 routes and countless variations. Most of the climbs are excellent, and are spread over all the grades. There are many classics which are now worn away and require high levels of technique to easily dispense with. The rocks are sometimes damp and need a good dry spell to gain their full merit, especially in the harder grades and where trees encompass the cliff. You need a few slings to set up top ropes on the trees and bolt belays provided. Please read local code of conduct on the notice boards in car park.
Map: OS.135 (Explorer) 530 350
Dir: 2m W of Tunbridge Wells. Take the A264(East Grinstead) from Tunbridge Wells. After 2.5m B2188 to Groombridge, fork left at mini roundabout, over railway; 200 yds - then fork R(Eridge) and in 70yds turn R into a lane signposted (?) Harrisons Rocks and Birchden Wood. Park in car park; footpath is from the bottom Left and well worn. Car park is used by dog walkers so don't be put off by busyness.

Open fun climbing at Harrison's, with a group of hecklers on hand; PHILLIPA t6a.

Eridge Green, looking just that in high summer.

WOOLY BEAR t6b, a Harrisons classic testpiece route; Angela White - crimping

CELEBRATION t5c, High Rocks; Paul from Brighton

⑧ HIGH ROCKS**

Some superb climbing here in the higher grades. A labyrith of dark chimneys offer the only really easy routes. For the rest it is steep and impending walls that get a bit slime ridden due to loss of control with the trees in the outcrop. Some wedding areas have been cleared and give lovely climbing on crisp and brittle pockets. Can often be quiet and beautiful. Cliff is on private land. There is a small charge to climb and you can use the facilities at the High Rocks Inn opposite. You have to get permission to climb the day before by ringing 01892
Map: OS.135 (Explorer) 348 324
Dir: 2m W of Tunbridge Wells, take the A264 and after 1 mile turn L and follow signs to High Rocks.

⑨ HIGH ROCKS ANNEXE

A group of very small buttresses that are tucked away in the trees. You could forget about these but there are some lovely short routes for either - easier grades or completely desperate slab climbs. You need to get permission to climb from the house above. Go back to the triangle then up the hill, the bungalow is on the bend.
Map: OS.135 (Explorer) 562 385

⑩ JOCKEY'S WOOD ROCKS

Some good short routes, powerful and steep, also well shaded in summer. On private land, only climb if you get permission in writing from Penn House.
Map: OS.135 (Explorer) 516 346

⑪ PENNS HOUSE ROCKS

Some lovely rocks in Penn House Garden, private - no permission. Short and excellent climbing of - historic.
Map: OS.135 (Explorer) 520 346

Stone farm Pinnacle

⑫ RAMSLYE FARM ROCKS

Nobody seems to know who owns the land here. Nobody seems to mind anyone climbing, there are only a handful of short climbs; fun all the same. Bouldering is in the lower grades.
Map: OS.135 (Explorer) 568 379

⑬ STONE FARM ROCKS

Good, oversize boulders set in the side of a hill, high up and with lovely views. Good climbing in the lower grades, and some lovely easy bouldering. Rock is soft, so please be careful in setting up your top ropes, and no abseiling at all.
Map: OS.135 (Explorer) 382 347
Dir: 2.3m SSW of East Grinstead. Situated at overlooking the west end of the Weir wood reservoir. A track leads off to the W going up the hill on the L, park just below the house on a lane.

⑭ TOAD ROCK BOULDERING

Toad rock is a giant soft pinnacle, with a barrier to prevent climbing. Around the area are lots of little pieces of rock to clamber all over. A kids little circuit can be worked out, along with some hard problems too.
Map: OS.135 (Explorer) 596
Dir: 1.5 miles W of T Wells. Take the A264, to Denny bottom, Toad Rock.

⑮ UNDER ROCKS

The setting of these rocks is idyllic, the rock is good but soft. Climbing here on a sunny day is unrivalled anywhere in South East England. Unfortunally, the outcrop only offers a handful of climbs, most of which in essence are 5c and above.
Map: OS.135 (Explorer) 555 264
You need the Jingo guidebook.

UNDER ROCKS in spring

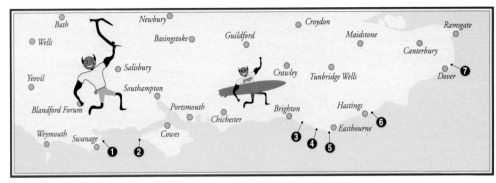

❶ OLD HARRY ROCKS *

A splendid pinnacle off Studland may proove unpopular with the National Trust. Simutaneous abseil descent.
Map: OS.195 (Landranger) 055 826

❷ THE NEEDLES *

A ridge up from one of the most famous landmarks in Britain. A difficult expedition, but one to remember.
Map: OS.196 (Landranger) 293 849

❸ SALT DEAN *

This is completely barmy climbing by the sea. Overhanging dry ice climbing using the soft chalk to claw your way up. Routes have been equipped, but whole sections of the cliffs fall down from time to time. Do not to miss out.
Map: OS.198 (Landranger) 385 018

❹ SEVEN SISTERS

Only a single route on this whole piece of coastline, highly scary and not without danger.
Map: OS.199 (Landranger)

❺ BEACHY HEAD *

Formidable and huge cliffs tower over the 120m drop down to the lighthouse below. Often with landslides!
Map: OS.199 (Landranger) 384 852

❻ ECCELSBOURNE-HASTINGS

Congealed mud, is a reasonable view.
Map: OS.199 (Landranger) 837 102

❼ DOVER - ST. MARGARETS * *

Popular with lots of climbs, all a bit crazy and dangerous; addictive!
Map: OS.179 (Landranger) 380 470

SALTDEAN CLIFF, The Pleasure Dome

KENT/SUSSEX · DORSET · CORNWALL · DEVON · BRISTOL · SOUTH-WALES · MID-WALES · NORTH-WALES · LEICESTER · PEAKS · YORK-LANCS · CLEVELAND · KENDAL · LAKES · PENRITH · NEWCASTLE

MASSIVE ATTACK, Saltdean; Mark Garthwait, photo Dave Pegler

HORNY L'IL DEVIL s-7a, Stair Hole East; An onsight splash

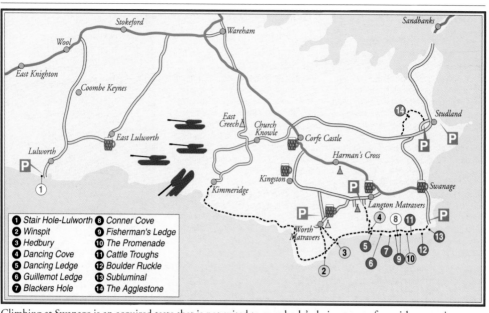

Map Key:

1. Stair Hole-Lulworth
2. Winspit
3. Hedbury
4. Dancing Cove
5. Dancing Ledge
6. Guillemot Ledge
7. Blackers Hole
8. Conner Cove
9. Fisherman's Ledge
10. The Promenade
11. Cattle Troughs
12. Boulder Ruckle
13. Subliminal
14. The Agglestone

Climbing at Swanage is an acquired taste that is not suited to everybody's desire; some of us wish to continue living, just a little while longer. The rock is limestone which forms in a blocky structure, unlike Malham cove with its thick and solid, massive seam. The limestone that forms the blocks is quite strong, and indeed, the blocks themselves have rippled edges which interlock quite well. However, you do get sediment run out that makes the gaps and cracks expand at a regular rate. In turn, large sections of the cliffs fall down periodically, taking existing climbs into the deep blue sea. Nothing is permanent in the Swanage game, and you are well to remember that. The plus side, is that you have a terrific expanse of coastline which is vertical for just about it's entire length from Swanage to Worth Matravers. In some areas there are serious bird restrictions, so if ever in doubt, keep away from Swanage during the period March 1st until July 31st. There is a big difference between placing natural gear in the rock here; and finding it to work in the event of a fall. You get a very high rate of runners pulling through the rock and people getting killed! Most top climbers, simply do not fall off. Some of the cliffs are very serious, and you need a good apprenticeship in crawling up vertical mud to top out. Often, climbers will leave the abseil rope in place, even setting up a top belay ready when they get near to the top. The last 30ft of the Boulder Ruckle, can be frightening - at the very least! The areas with sport climbing are very popular and deservedly so. These routes are not big or intimidating, and offer some very good and intensive moves that soon get you puffing. Because the access to the routes involves complicated abseils, with no easy escape routes; getting hold of a guidebook before you come is essential for most climbers. The area is popular, and books are often out of print and unavailable.

INTO THE BLUE
Topo & Text guide
98 pages - B&W
Good colour photos
A5 - Paperback
Pub-1996
by Climbers Club
(J. Cook, S. Taylor
M. Robertson)

The guidebook that has attracted so many people into Deep Water Soloing. A really good little guidebook that shows you all about this wet summer activity. Essential to know about the good spots over nice deep water. Good photos to entice toe dipping - or more.

 1 & 8 plus many more small venues

PORTLAND AND SWANAGE
Text guidebook - 2 parts
Pocket - 165 x 105mm
Due 1994-5-6 ?
Swanage section reprinted and some are in circulation as a paperback.
by the Climbers Club

DORSET
TOPO guidebook
A5
Due 1995-6-7 ?
by Rockfax

!

KENT/SUSSEX · DORSET · CORNWALL · DEVON · BRISTOL · SOUTH-WALES · MID-WALES · NORTH-WALES · LEICSETER · PEAKS · YORK-LANCS · CLEVELAND · KENDAL · LAKES · PENRITH · NEWCASTLE

① STAIR HOLE*

Lime ⑦ | Alt-0m | 23m | 7.5
25 | --

Once upon a time you could climb here and there are still the stainless steel bolts in the rock to prove it. Lovely short routes that sweep out into overhanging roofs. Climbing is not allowed at the moment. DWS though still goes on regularly and seems to escape the attention of the authorities. A good spot with plenty of splash potential. The other cliffs in the close area are really terrible so don't bother.
Map: OL15 (Explorer) 822 798
Dir: 500 yds S of the giant car park in Lulworth cove. A footpath leads over the hill and the climbing is on the seaward side of the twin holes.

② WINSPIT QUARRY

Lime ⑯ | Alt-40m | 22m | 7.7
30 | --

A small quarry that is popular with a lot of climbers. The rock itself is variable and you need the good bolts that are insitu; even so - the whole block can pull away at times. The cliff is tucked in the hill a bit and out of the wind, so can be good on a cold day. There is a bigger quarry opposite but undeveloped.
Map: OL15 (Explorer) 977 762
Dir: 1m south of Worth Matravers. From the pub follow the lane down and to the green, keep following the road down which becomes the footpath down to Winspit, with the Quarry on the L.

DANCING LEDGE

③ HEDBURY QUARRY

Lime ⑱ | Alt-40m | 20m | 7.7
17 | --

A small quarry not that different from Winspit and often a bit quieter than Dancing Ledge Cove
Map: OL15 (Explorer) 992 768
Dir: 300 yds West of Dancing ledge.

④ DANCING LEDGE COVE*

Lime ⑳ | Alt-30m | 15m | 7.7
33 | --

Nothing much to look at; you even might turn away in disgust. The climbing is very good though, so it is worth getting stuck in. Nice and technical, and sustained for the short distance. Very popular, in fact - one of the most popular crags in Britain.
Map: OL15 (Explorer) 997 769
Dir: 1m S of Langton Matravers. From the village a short road goes through a gate and to a parking spot just beyond spyway house. Follow footpath and signs to Dancing Ledge (popular trail).

⑤ DANCING LEDGES

Lime ⑳ | Alt-5m | 15m | 7.7
35 | 25

A very popular spot for beginners. Easy to set up a top rope and a nice scramble down. Some caves also give very good sport routes. Swimming spot too. Bouldering from ledge for fun.
Map: OL15 (Explorer) 997 768

INSECT GRAVEYARD s-6b, Winspit Quarry; Mark Scott

DAYLIGHT ROBBERY s-6c, Dancing Ledge Cove; Thomas Jacobson

The Square and Compass pub in Worth Matravers, is a truly historic and traditional ale house. It's position overlooks the golden fields down to the sea, and enjoys the soft evening glow of summer sunsets. The whole position and ambience of the village and pub, has an air of freedom to it, not entrapped by a ghastly themed, brewing-munching enterprise. It's quirky with no bar, just a couple of serving hatches, and the range of ciders is to die for. It also gives over a room for a quaint, but very interesting rural museum; an intrigue that includes parts of everything from the local area. You will find stone cutting gatherings here, live music bands, and climbers who have managed to get back from the Boulder Ruckle, still alive - needless to say, they all need a good couple of drinks.

❻ GUILLEMOT LEDGE *

Lime	25		Alt-0m	65m	7.8

60			∞

The central area below the quarry with 20 routes is not affected by the bird ban. (01/03~31/07). This is a big cliff that is protected by a large platform, well above high tide. Big and impressive climbing with some routes being, full on adventures. A good place to explore and make the transition from dangerous - to really dangerous routes.
Map: OL15 (Explorer) 001 768
Dir: 300 yds East of Dancing Ledge

❼ BLACKERS HOLE AREA *

Lime	40		Alt-0m	55m	7.8

100			∞

The cliff is in two parts. The left side is huge and impresive and needs abseil descent, also has a bird ban (01/03~31/07). To the right side of the main giant hole, you can walk-scrambe down to quarries with routes. There is a huge expanse of coastline running east that offers a complete mixed bag of routes. Good for an easy descent, wow factor for the ascent!
Map: OL15 (Explorer) 008 767 (descent)
Dir: 800 yds East of Dancing Ledge.

GUILLEMOT LEDGE - top

BLACKERS HOLE, *intimidating but a great pool to swim in.*

KENT/SUSSEX | DORSET | CORNWALL | DEVON | BRISTOL | SOUTH-WALES | MID-WALES | NORTH-WALES | LEICSETER | PEAKS | YORK-LANCS | CLEVELAND | KENDAL | LAKES | PENRITH | NEWCASTLE

⑧ CONNER COVE**

| Lime | (40) | | Alt-0m | 20m | 7.6 |

| | | 25 | -- | | HBall |

A great spot made famous by the deep water soloing festivals that have taken place. A very airy solo gets you down to the bottom where you can comfortably traverse along the cliff in a low sea. The opportunities are great to climb up above the deep pool here. Caution is still needed to get away from the rock if you fall, and hitting the water correctly is crucial. A good summer spot.
Map: OL15 (Explorer) 012 768
Dir: Best approach from Swanage.

⑨ FISHERMANS LEDGE**

| Lime | (40) | | Alt-0m | 55m | 7.8 |

| | | 130 | -- | | ⊙ |

The whole area either side of Conner Cove is referred to as Fishermans Ledge. To the west are very good quality rock walls, mainly vertical and with some wide ledges at the bottom for convienent abseil approach. To the east of Conner Cove are some spectacular overhanging areas that give plenty of E4's for a hungry appetite.
Map: OL15 (Explorer) 012 768
Dir: 1.2 mile W of Swanage car park, just beyond the 1 mile set of pylons.

⑩ THE PROMENADE**

| Lime | (30) | | Alt-0m | 30m | 7.8 |

| | | 80 | | | ⊙ |

One of the first ever sport climbing areas on the south coast. A very good and in there spot for hard climbing, with nearly 99% of the routes having been rebolted with stainless staples. Good in the higher grades and with strong and powerful routes. The east approach, is just a scramble down to a big long platform - promenade, just above the sea.
Map: OL15 (Explorer) 015 767
Dir: 400 yds before the pylons a scooped bay can be scrambled down.

⑪ CATTLE TROUGHS*

| Lime | (25) | | Alt-0m | 30m | 7.8 |

| | | 25 | -- | | ☀ |

A very lovely and tranquil spot on this fearful part of coastline. Some easy angled bays at last, offering the lower grade climber some good possibilities. Still, the dangers are there of poor gear, and often it is difficult to find and place - so beware. Some of the routes are not that long, but you need to walk a long way back to find a belay - so communicating with beginners can be tricky on some routes.
Map: OL15 (Explorer) 015 766
Dir: 1m west of car park, 2 big scoops.

CATTLE TROUGHS; The platform is nice and high above the sea

FREEBORN MAN s-6c, Conner Cove; Tim Emmett

DEEP WATER SOLOING FESTIVAL; climbers everywhere

KENT/SUSSEX · DORSET · CORNWALL · DEVON · BRISTOL · SOUTH-WALES · MID-WALES · NORTH-WALES · LEICSETER · PEAKS · YORK-LANCS · CLEVELAND · KENDAL · LAKES · PENRITH · NEWCASTLE

⑫ BOULDER RUCKLE**

The Ruckle as it is known, is famous for terror and anguish - a must if you're into that sort of thing. Some of the most famous climbs, fell into the sea a few years ago. The whole area stretches for some 600 yards. The lower rock is medium to poor, but outstandingly deteriorates as you near the top! There are no easy ways out, leave an abseil rope in place. Not for beginners - remotely.
Map: OL15 (Explorer) 023 768
Dir: Area west of Subluminal

⑬ SUBLUMINAL*

A good small cliff that is very popular. Near to the car park, and with good rock for the area. Areas to the east have bird restrictions so stick to the popular areas. Escape can be made up an easy route (diff).
Map: OL15 (Explorer) 029 769
Dir: About 150 yds west of lighthouse.

BOTANY BAY HVS t-5a. Subluminal; Kelvin Charman

⑭ THE AGGLESTONE

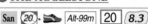

A fun lump of sandstone on the middle of a moor with a lovely setting.
Map: OL15 (Explorer) 025 827

THE AGGLESTONE; a small amount of fun bouldering on this soft lump of rock; Rebecca Hossack

Portland in so many ways, is the opposite to Swanage. You have lost the lovely coastline, peppered with arable fields and soft country pubs, linked by quiet lanes that fan out from Corfe Castle. Here you enter Weymouth and are instantly thwarted by exceptionally slow moving traffic, content in crawling along at a snails pace. Arriving at Portland Bill, its history of stonework, quarrying, military stronghold and prison; - is somewhat evident. There are no campsites on this island which is a pity, since travelling here daily, is not one of life's greatest pleasures. The up side of the down side, is that if the island had become private years ago, it's position is so fabulous that with investment, you would have some of the most expensive real estate around. For sure, you wouldn't be able to even pay to get across the causeway, let alone touch the cliffs. The southern part of the Island is lovely and wild, where the grass is almost kept short and vibrant by the constant battering of the wind. You plip over the edge, and down the tiny paths that lead to the cliffs, and your whole world changes. The wind is gone, the houses that win no architectural awards disappear; you hear the cawing of the sea gulls, and the smell of the sea, oozes up from the seaweed below. It truly becomes a magical place. The rock on the cliffs at Portland is very varied, but nowhere could you classify it as good. The lower strata at sea level is blocky, and quite similar to Swanage. Then at mid level, you come across some really dodgy putty and sand mix, that belies climbability, and is seen in abundance at Wallsend Cove. At the top level, the rock does actually veer towards respectability. With the placement of stainless steel bolts in secure resin, climbing can be made enjoyable, but not without risk. Holds break here quite often, even whole parts of the cliff fall down, so don't be surprised to see bolts in rock on the beach. It's a transient place that might not win your heart, but still makes you come back, time and time again, simply for great fun.

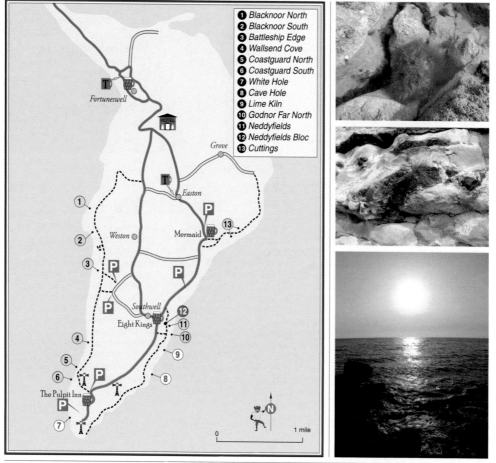

1 Blacknoor North
2 Blacknoor South
3 Battleship Edge
4 Wallsend Cove
5 Coastguard North
6 Coastguard South
7 White Hole
8 Cave Hole
9 Lime Kiln
10 Godnor Far North
11 Neddyfields
12 Neddyfields Bloc
13 Cuttings

Seaweed at Wallsend Cove; Rock and Sunset at Coastguard Cliff

KENT/SUSSEX | DORSET | CORNWALL | DEVON | BRISTOL | SOUTH-WALES | MID-WALES | NORTH-WALES | LEICESTER | PEAKS | YORK-LANCS | CLEVELAND | KENDAL | LAKES | PENRITH | NEWCASTLE

HOT FROM THE FORGE ~ 7a, Blacknoor North~ Sandy Ogilvie

① BLACKNOOR NORTH**

Lime [15] Alt-60m 25m **7.6**
| | 80 | -- | | |

This is one of the most popular parts to Portland with a few classic routes on flowstone tufas, such as Reptile Smile. There are no shortage of routes with stars and the equipment is generally very good. A wide path at the bottom allows easy chilling out. The top end faces north west and stays cool in the early afternoon sun, whilst the belayer gets a good tanning. It has also a big pinnacle that gives anyone an easy photo opportunity. The rock here is the best on the island.
Map: OL15 (Explorer) 677 715
Dir: Aproach as for Battleship cliffs but carry on along the tops and past an old lookout bunker and concrete fort. The slope eventually becomes easy angled to descend.

② BLACKNOOR SOUTH**

Lime [10] Alt-50m 30m **7.7**
| | 100 | -- | | |

A broken area with quite an assortment of routes for all different levels of climber. Easily located from above and includes the big giant fallen slab down at sea level. Only a handful of routes to the N part have a bird restriction. Some long routes but mostly shorter around the 15m length. The base of the cliff is a bit rough and tumble, not the ideal spot for a picnic.
Map: OL15 (Explorer) 679 712
Dir: Aproach for all Blacknor and Battleship cliffs. Park by the road and head out towards the cliff top coast path. Go north to an old quarry that has a footpath leading down to the cliffs.

③ BATTLESHIP EDGE*

Lime [10] Alt-40m 20m **7.7**
| | 50 | -- | | |

A very nice small cliff that is decptively difficult, and rather more technical than you expect. The climbing is very good and sustained for the short distance that you get here. Quite a reasonable base at the bottom. The cliff seems to attact wind and is not sheltered, but then when the wind stops it can be a real sun trap, very variable.
Map: OL15 (Explorer) 677 710
Dir: From the parking on the road, vault the stile, then take the footpath straight over to the cliff edge where you can find the descent by some boulders acroos the path.

Wallsend Cove in the background   *SOMETHING OR ANOTHER s-7b/c, Coastguard North; Annete Sinclair*

Time to exit COASTGUARD SOUTH, the platform is tidal to say the least.

④ WALLSEND COVE*

| Lime | 20 | | Alt-20m | 30m | 7.9 |

| | | 150 | -- | Pump | |

This cove is large and with a huge amount of rockfall and big blocks strewn all over the place. Lots of routes in the higher grades, but lots of rock that is highly indifferent. Scary for some, yet happiness for others. When it's good here, it's really good - but at other times you should only proceed with caution. For the most part, it's quiet and a good place to get away from the crowds. Getting to the bottom and scrambling along the boulders is a workout in itself. Some areas have bird restrictions at certain times if the birds nest, see local indicators for this.
Map: OL15 (Explorer) 697 678
Dir: Approch with someone who knows the area and the routes.

⑤ COASTGUARD NORTH

| Lime | 12 | | Alt-0m | 20m | 7.9 |

| | | 40 | -- | | |

A reasonable cliff for the island, but not one to visit on your first trip, you wouldn't be that impressed. The plus part is in the climbing moves and parts of some of the routes. Other parts are near-on congealed sand, and glued up weetabix. Will suit a like minded characher perhaps. Position is fab and relatively quick to get to. I'm still to be convinced by this little spot.
Map: OL15 (Explorer) 675 693
Dir: There is a really dangerous gully that dirctely descends to this, but you are better advised to approach via the normal coastguard approach and go easily along the sea platform.

⑥ COASTGUARD SOUTH**

| Lime | 12 | | Alt-0m | 25m | 7.6 |

| | | 60 | -- | | |

The best placed cliff on the island, down by the sea with lovely rockpools and often very sheltered. Tidal though. The rock is good but the cliff is generally unstable. The big orange areas are where there used to be some really good and interesting climbs! Some very good climbs in the lower grades that are pure enjoyment. Not to be missed.
Map: OL15 (Explorer) 670 690
Dir: At present there are a few free parking spaces on the bend in the main road. From here a path leads up and over the hill, then a very steep and intimidating path drops down to an easy descent.

⑦ WHITE HOLE

| Lime | 10 | | Alt-0m | 12m | 7.7 |

| | | 35 | | DWS | |

Right down at the very tip of Portland, the land slopes away to give some very small but atmospheric cliffs. The water is not too deep so you do need to have a good high tide for the small amount of DWS that there is. Approach to all routes is by abseil with the easiest escapes being around 6b. There are a good selection of short routes 6b-7a that will keep you busy for a while.
Map: OL15 (Explorer) 675 684
Dir: From the bottom of the giant pay carpark, head directly west to the sea, then you can skittle along to tops going in a northerly direction with the climbing beneath you.

MAGICAL MR. MESTOPHELES s-6c, Wallsend South; Lee Hogarth

A typical busy day at GODNOR FAR NORTH

⑧⑨ CAVE HOLE & LIME KILN

Two very good venues for some DWS and with deep water for most part. Cave Hole is not the quickest place to get to, but on the other hand that makes it nice and quiet. Good morning sunshine. The area can seep quite badly in winter. Getting familiar with the Lime Kiln first, is a good introduction to the more serious DWS exploits of the area. Protected from the west, there is also good swimming on this side.
Map: OL15 (Explorer) 687 692

⑩ GODNOR FAR NORTH

The most popular sea cliff on the whole of Portland. A lovely little sport venue with good clip-up routes for lower grade climbers. The top of the cliff has rare plants so don't top out, just thread and lower off both bolts. Hack along the rock beach is a bit naff, watch the ankles. Most of the routes are non-tidal.
Map: OL15 (Explorer) 691 698

⑪ NEDDYFIELDS

A cliff in two halfs, the bottom is about as dodgy as it comes and needs a good health warning. The top has a strong band of impeccable rock. This is where you get the hard moves and thankfully good gear. Cliff has big cracks behind it, so watch this space!
Map: OL15 (Explorer) 691 701

⑫ NEDDYFIELDS BOULDERING

There is a terrace at the top of the Neddyfields cliff that offers some really good and popular bouldering. A mixture of vertical problems on flowstone and crimps. A good place to practise your slapping techniques.
Map: OL15 (Explorer) 691 701

⑩ THE CUTTINGS *

There are two parts to the Cuttings, where an old railway used to run. The routes are on the land side, with a high bank opposite for an excellent viewing gallery. Some very good routes on hollow sounding rock in lots of places. There are also some shorter routes on the new cuttings to the south. These have a nicer position overlooking the sea. A good selection of shortish routes in the lower grades not to be overlooked. Popular.
Map: OL15 (Explorer) 700 715

NEDDYFIELDS BOULDERING AREA; Gordie Lees

JULIE OCEAN s-6c+, Neddyfields Main Cliff; Lee Hogarth

TATER-DU CLIFF

The area to the west of Penzance is - West Penwith; the land that reaches far out into the Atlantic, and hides away from England. Every time I go there I have a great time, and end up questioning myself as to why I don't go there more often. It's simply a long drive, make no mistake; but the landscape is extrodinarily beautiful, and the only sign of industrial past, are old relics in decay. The weather can be iffy, true. But it's the most southerly part of the UK and temperatures are always going to be pleasant. Even though the area is wild and wind swept, you really can climb here on good days, for most of the winter. The rock is mostly granite, but not without other volcanic types of greenstone and kilas slate. It's a mixed bag of single and multi-pitch routes down here; the 'full on' trad style, often needing a bold, yet 'competent' approach. Thankfully there's a lot of climbing in the lower grades, for the majority of climbers to enjoy. There are masses of cliffs to explore; it's one of Britain's best climbing areas.

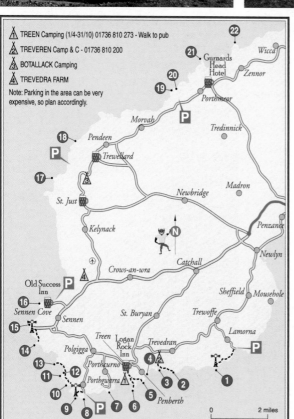

TREEN Camping (1/4-31/10) 01736 810 273 - Walk to pub

TREVEREN Camp & C - 01736 810 200

BOTALLACK Camping

TREVEDRA FARM

Note: Parking in the area can be very expensive, so plan accordingly.

❶ Tater-Du
❷ Saint Loy
❸ Porthguarnon Cove
❹ Penberth
❺ Cribba Head
❻ Logan Rock
❼ Levan's Wall
❽ Hella Point
❾ Chair Ladder
❿ Fox Promontory
⓫ Carn Barra
⓬ Zawn Kelly
⓭ Carn Lês Boel
⓮ Pordenack Point
⓯ Land's End
⓰ Sennen Cove
⓱ Carn Kenidjack
⓲ Carn Vellan
⓳ Great Zawn
⓴ Bosigran
㉑ Gurnard's Head
㉒ Zennor Cliff

WEST CORNWALL
Text guides 1& 2
328 & 343 pages - B&W
Some colour photos
Pocket size 165 x 105
Pub-2000 by Climbers Club

2 guidebooks that come together in a plastic wrap around. Very handy small size for the multi pitch routes of Bosi and Chair Ladder.

G-03a △ 1 - 22 + more & Lizard.

CORNISH ROCK
Phototopo guide
266 pages - B&W
Some colour photos
Hardback A5
Pub-1996 - Cicerone

A fresh feel local book, that is very clear & with big topos. Very handy(except for Chair L) & nice to browse. Lots of info from local guru Rowland Edwards.

G-03b △ 1,2,5,7,8,9 - 22 (Good route selection)

❶ TATER-DU *

Voluntary bird restriction: 1/3 - 1/7
A truly beautiful spot down by the sea that needs the sun out to prevent depression setting in. Climbing is very nice but the rock is brittle. You need some big chunky gear here. Approach to the west of the cliff is possible, but fraught with danger. Somewhere to really get away from it all. Good and easy slabs, grippy and blocky overhangs, nice sea level traversing. Cliff is semi tidal.
G03a,b; Map: OL15 (Explorer) 439 231
Approach is from Lamorna

❷ SAINT LOY *

A small cliff that is slightly reminiscent of the larger Bosigran - in shape and climbing style. Overlooking the bay, it is a quiet cliff. The harder climbs are very bold and will not be suited to most tastes.
G03a,b; Map: OL15 (Explorer) 414 228
Dir: Best to visit when camping locally.

❸ PORTHGUARNON COVE *

A reasonable cliff that is in 3 separate tiers, and gives plenty of climbs in the lower grades that are short but still interesting. Only the bottom tier is affected by the sea. The situation is beautiful and a great place for a day outing. A separate abseil rope can be very handy to set up, for a common descent on the routes, especially from the top tier. There is an easy access up to the right if the sea allows.
G03a; Map: OL15 (Explorer) 412 229
Dir: Best to visit when camping locally.

❹ PENBERTH COVE

A very good diddy cliff that is always popular with beginners, and others wanting to set up convienient top roping. Sunny, quiet, sheltered and entertaining. Good swimming in the bay too. Short climbs. Nice bouldering.
G03a; Map: OL15 (Explorer) 404 226
Dir: From carpark at Treen, walk down to the cove, signposted.

❺ CRIBBA HEAD

The whole headland has climbing on it and accounts for a few longer routes of varying quality. The piéce de resistance is the giant 15m pillars at the top, leaning the weird side of vertical. Position is everything here. Climbing is cracky, or arête style that is best on a top rope.
G03a; Map: OL15 (Explorer) 403 224
Dir: An amaizing trip to the headland.

❻ LOGAN ROCK

This is a very striking headland and a popular tourist spot, so don't expect to be on your own here. Not many 'official and proper' routes, but a good place to climb around and seek out a lot of technical climbs on excellent slabs. Also some zawns with lots of smaller routes, plus walls with routes in the easier grades. Bouldering on the upper tier.
G03a; Map: OL15 (Explorer) 397 220
Dir: Follow the others.

KENT/SUSSEX · DORSET · CORNWALL · DEVON · BRISTOL · SOUTH-WALES · MID-WALES · NORTH-WALES · LEICESTER · PEAKS · YORK-LANCS · CLEVELAND · KENDAL · LAKES · PENRITH · NEWCASTLE

KENT/SUSSEX

DORSET

CORNWALL

DEVON

BRISTOL

SOUTH-WALES

MID-WALES

NORTH-WALES

LEICSETER

PEAKS

YORK-LANCS

CLEVELAND

KENDAL

LAKES

PENRITH

NEWCASTLE

PORTHGUARNON COVE

CRIBBA HEAD (top)

7 LEVAN'S WALL**

A good area with a whole mixture of routes on various walls, routes 10m-40m. Some are partially tidal and others are not. A very good sun trap and near to the beach if others want to go swimming and generally sunbathe and do some beach bouldering. The routes are mainly on cracks and in the higher grades, with a few exceptionally difficult problems.
G03a,b; Map: OL15 (Explorer) 385 217

8 HELLA POINT*

This point consists of two mounds of granite. A lovely place to scramble and climb around in the summer. The climbing is sort of intermitent, but is nice and quiet - instead of Chair Ladder. A bit scrappy but useful to know about for those interested in something apart from route ticking.
G03a,b; Map: OL15 (Explorer) 371 214
Approach via *car park* at Porthgwarra

9 CHAIR LADDER***

This is without doubt the best cliff in Cornwall and the whole southern coast of England. It is big and grand, overlooking the sea with a series of giant buttresses that defy belief as to how they still stand up! You can scramble down to the tidal base quite easily in parts, and the bottom is relatively friendly at low tide. Tides are important, simply to gain access to all of the routes. The multi pitch routes however, soon get you away from the wet tidal bottom anyway. The easy routes are classics; the harder ones are still very good but often involve some tricky boulder style moves that may not be well protected. For real beginners an abseil rope can be very handy to secure the descent to the base of some sectors. There is also a sector called Zawn Rinny, for those seeking intense adventure!
G03a,b; Map: OL15 (Explorer) 366 215
Approach via *car park* at Porthgwarra, then hack up the giant hill to the west, the navigate to the top of Gwennap head and the cliffs are pretty obvious.

10 FOX PROMONTORY*

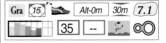

This cliff resembles a fin sticking out on a promontory, and has climbing on both sides of it. Sunny and pleasant on the south, cold dark and blackness on the north side in winter. Great in a hot summer but can seep and stay quite miserable at other times. It's not truly north facing so it isn't that bad. Good face and crack climbing. The base of the cliff is tidal and you are a bit restricted if you get it wrong.
G03a,b; Map: OL15 (Explorer) 361 223

11 CARN BARRA**

A very good cliff for the low extreme climber, not that much for the low grade climber. Definitely bring an ab-rope here. A good low platform so you can climb in most states of the tide. A real sun trap and one of the best winter venues. Rough rock to the touch, especially if you have to struggle!
G03a,b; Map: OL15 (Explorer) 359 226

HELLA POINT

SOUTH FACE DIRECT VS t-4c, Chair Ladder; Andy Prosser

⑫ ZAWN KELLYS *

Gra	20	👟	Alt-0m	40m	7.4
▁▃▅▃▁		15	--	🏊	Zzz

One of those places with not many routes, but simply out of the way and superb to visit and climb. Tidal and needs a calm sea. Around the corner is Zawn Frank is around the corner and somewhat atmospheric - climbs of great quality and room for some really desperate lines.
G03a,b; Map: OL15 (Explorer) 358 227
Approach via car park at Porthgwarra.

⑬ CARN LÊS BOEL *

Gra	25	👟	Alt-0m	55m	7.3
▁▃▅▅▃▁		25	🤽	🏊	∞

Voluntary restriction 1/3-1/7. This area has some classic lines in the hard extreme grades on paradise wall that shouldn't be missed. There is also an area called seal cave and badlands. All need a calm sea and are more easily accessed with an extra abseil rope. Not a cliff for beginners. You also get seals living in the cave which breed in September and October, so please do not go swimming in there which could affect the natural breeding cycle.
G03a,b; Map: OL15 (Explorer) 357 252
Approach either from Portgwarra or Land's End, a long hike regardless.

⑭ PORDENACK POINT * *

Gra	12	👟	Alt-0m	35m	7.3
▁▃▅▅▃▁		70	--	🏊	🡥

A very good and popular crag, away from the melé at Land's End fortunately. Just about something for everyone here. The easier routes tend to be on the short 10-15m side; some very good middle grade classics. A tidal platform but not too badly affected though.
G03a,b; Map: OL15 (Explorer) 347 242

⑭ LANDS END * * *

Gra	3	👟	Alt-0m	75m	7.6
▁▃▅▅▃▁		70	🏊	∞	👻

A very big area of climbing to the west side of the Hotel area. Lots of different cliffs, and plenty in all grades. Rock is very indifferent. An abseil rope is very useful. Plenty of atmospheric climbs, and in bad weather, highly dangerous! Worth a really good exploration.
G03a,b; Map: OL15 (Explorer) 347 242
Dir: Parking is usually free if you are only climbing, tell them politely.

⑨ SENNEN COVE * * *

Gra	10	👟	Alt-0m	40m	7.1
▁▃▅▅▅▃		200	200	🏊	HBall

You can't descibe Sennen in a nutshell. No route here gets 3 stars, but all combined together, certainly give you a top quality place to visit. Plenty of easy routes in the lower grades, all approachable from a scramble down, and all non tidal. The cliff is on many terraces, all which offer a huge amount of bouldering at all grades. The more you look for, the more you find. Many of the problems are quite highball and you should have combination mats and spotters. In summer it can easily get too hot, in winter the sea spray can make it hopeless. A good selection of harder routes, using non exisiting crimps.
G03a,b; Map: OL15 (Explorer) 347 262
Approach via car park in Sennen. For quick access go via the low rocks. At high tide this is impossible and you have to hike over the headland.

Side tabs: KENT/SUSSEX · DORSET · CORNWALL · DEVON · BRISTOL · SOUTH-WALES · MID-WALES · NORTH-WALES · LEICSTER · PEAKS · YORK-LANCS · CLEVELAND · KENDAL · LAKES · PENRITH · NEWCASTLE

Highball bouldering on the lower tiers at Sennen; Mark Edwards

⑲ GREAT ZAWN *

Gra	13	👟	Alt-0m	80m	7.2
	30		⚭	💀	

Steep, imposing, intimidating - the list of adjectives goes on and on with this place. A fabulous piece of rock that offers some really good climbing. Many classic routes here in the E3-4 category that were once the classic hardest routes of the country. A bit dark and dingy, so the routes often remain damp. Impressive if you like commiting and hard climbing. Abseil approach to one side, and giant abseil for the back of the zawn.

Map: OS.--- (Explorer) 415 368

⑰ CARN KENIDJACK *

Sla	5	👟	Alt-0m	50m	7.4
	30	--	🧗	💀	

A cliff in two parts. The main cliff is a giant slab that seems to have just enough holds to make it comfortable, if you are a good climber with a sound head. Otherwise it feels run out. Not typical slate; like dolerite with lots of incut pockets, good to climb on but don't run to good gear. The bay at the bottom is protected from the sea and is generally non tidal. Also you have the seadreams cliff (tidal), that offers some good shorter 20m routes.

G03a,b; Map: OL15 (Explorer) 366 215

⑱ CARN VELLAN

Sla	10	👟	Alt-0m	60m	7.4
	25		😃	💀	

Ho, Ho, Ho - you're having a laugh. A cliff to intimidate the unintimatdateable. Killas slate at its most expressive. A big spurter cliff with some stupendous lines that scream out into the giant overhanging wall. A very atmospheric place whilst it stays up!

G03a,b; Map: OL15 (Explorer) 366 215

KENT/SUSSEX | DORSET | CORNWALL | DEVON | BRISTOL | SOUTH-WALES | MID-WALES | NORTH-WALES | LEICSETER | PEAKS | YORK-LANCS | CLEVELAND | KENDAL | LAKES | PENRITH | NEWCASTLE

㉑ GURNARD'S HEAD**

| San | 15 | 👟 | Alt-0m | 40m | 7.7 |

| 22 | | |

A very thrilling and exciting place to be in a big sea, then go quickly back up to the pub. The giant black cave has a square cut roof and the waves thunder in, giving a giant booming sound constantly, ominously sounding out the toil of your doom - if you get things wrong here. The climbing is good, if just a bit too hard for most. There are a couple of easier classics, and it's worth the trip here just to do them. Anyone into DWS might find their utopia here, if the sea is quiet and the tide is high enough.
G03a,b; Map: OL15 (Explorer) 432 385
Approach after parking near the Gurnard's Head Hotel, a footpath leads down to the long promontory, access from the north side for ease.

㉒ ZENNOR CLIFF*

| Sla | 15 | 👟 | Alt-0m | 70m | 7.8 |

| 20 | | |

Things are starting to deteriorate and this is just about the last area you will want to travel to before the cliffs turn to squidge. Dark black rock that seems to be a cross between slate and sandstone, and that is pretty forboding and gathers lichen in the top parts. At least the angle is better and offers some good climbing in the lower grades. Climb with caution though.
G03a; Map: OL15 (Explorer) 447 392

㉒ BOSIGRAN***

| Gra | 14 | 👟 | Alt-40m | 60m | 7.1 |

| | 90 | | | Ouch |

A very good cliff with something for everyone. Slabs and easy crack lines for beginners, intimidating walls with little gear for injury addictive bods, big capping roofs for awkward, thrutch seeking exponents. From a distance, the whole cliff looks naff and boring, yet up close it rears up giantly above your head and is bound to impress. Not affected by tide, and protected from any cold north easterly wind that might blow. A very popular cliff for the area and deservedly so. A lot of cliff that takes quite a lot of exploration, and make sure that you don't miss out on the seaward cliff which is tidal.
G03a,b; Map: OL15 (Explorer) 366 215
Approach via NT car park at the top.

THE GHOST E3 t-5b, Bosigran; Bob Bradley (Top)

KENT/SUSSEX · DORSET · CORNWALL · DEVON · BRISTOL · SOUTH-WALES · MID-WALES · NORTH-WALES · LEICSETER · PEAKS · YORK-LANCS · CLEVELAND · KENDAL · LAKES · PENRITH · NEWCASTLE

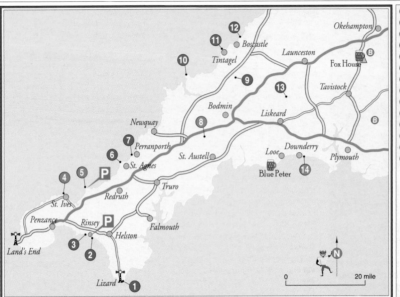

Legend:
1. Pen Olver
2. Trewavas
3. Basher's Harbour
4. Clodgy Point
5. Godrevy Point
6. Carn Gowla
7. Cligga Head
8. Roche Rock
9. Devil's Jump
10. Pentire Head
11. Tintagel
12. Bukator
13. Cheesewring
14. Downderry

① PEN OLVER

Sch	15		Alt-0m	15m	7.5

| | | 34 | -- | | |

We don't have a lot of information about climbing on the Lizard. This cliff looks like a good bet for anyone wanting a nice selection of easy routes that are in a good position. The cliff is tidal but not too badly affected. Many of the harder routes around this area get weird grades!
G03a; Map: 203 (Landranger) 712 117

② TREWAVAS

Gra	17		Alt-40m	20m	7.5

| | | 80 | -- | | |

A selection of small cliffs grouped together that comes well recomended to us by local climbers and guides, and handy to know about. More of an inland cliff and unusual because of this for the area. Quite steep rock. The majority of climbs are around the 10-15m height, but there are a few harder climbs up to 20 metres high.
G03a; Map: 203 (Landranger) 596 264
Approach via car park at Rinsey head.

③ BASHER'S HARBOUR *

Gra	7		Alt-0m	30m	7.4

| | | 37 | -- | | |

A superb cliff, to quote Rowland Edwards after a recent spell of adding some new routes. Tidal but protected from big sea swells. For most of the routes you have to abseil in from stakes. A very attractive cove with excellent features; corners, cracks and routes following strong lines. Good for the middle grade climber.
G03a; Map: 203 (Landranger) 588 272
Approach via car park at Rinsey head.

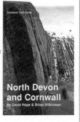
Sidebar (left margin): KENT/SUSSEX, DORSET, CORNWALL, DEVON, BRISTOL, SOUTH-WALES, MID-WALES, NORTH-WALES, LEICESTER, PEAKS, YORK-LANCS, CLEVELAND, KENDAL, LAKES, PENRITH, NEWCASTLE

4 CLODGY POINT

A small but worthwhile bouldering area. Not big, but some steep and technical problems.
Map: 203 (Landranger) 507 414
Dir: 1m NW of the centre of St. Ives. Park somewhere and then find the footpath out to the point.

5 GODREVY POINT

The best known bouldering in the area. Slate that is by the sea and affected by the tide. You can get wet and slippery rock on humid days, so it is best in the warm evening with a bit of a breeze.
Map: 203 (Landranger) 347 262
Approach via car park (Free after 5pm) at the headland of Godrevy point.

6 CARN GOWLA *

About 2m of coastal cliffs at St Agnes head, mostly around 350ft high offering plenty of multi pitch routes on quite good rock. Not really a place for the novice but has many HVS and Extreme's, a very notable classic America E3 situated on the North side of the head, the best rock. Very impressive scenery here without the crowds makes a real epic very possible, even probable. If the sea gets rough pray that your leader is having a good day, and you've got your jumars. Long double ropes advisable here, also additional ropes for abseil to leave in place etc. Cliff stays damp for several days so go in a good spell. Good luck.
G03c; Map: OS.200 (Landranger) 698 512
Dir: 10m N of Redruth. From A 30 at Three Burrows take the B3277 to St Agnes, take a minor road up onto the headland to parking. places near the coastguard lookout.The cliffs are on the North and the West side, explore at will.

7 CLIGGA HEAD

A mixture of cliffs, worthwhile - popular.
G03c; Map: OS.204 (Landranger) 737 537
Dir: 15m NW of Truro near Perranporth. From Perr. take the B 3285 S for 1m, park. On the right is the dissused Cligga mine and the point beyond is Cligga Head, the climbs being on the N & W side.

8 ROCHE ROCKS

A small 60ft granite outcrop with lots of bouldering in a non serious enviroment. Mainly good in the lower grades, soloing and scrambling for all the family.
Map: 200 (Landranger) 992 597
Dir: 7m SW of Bodmin. Turn off the A 30 onto the B 3274 to Roche. Pass through the village to locate the rocks.

9 DEVIL'S JUMP

Granite Tors at 750 ft offer some 70 ft routes in the low grades in a very pleasant setting.
Map: OS.200 (Landranger) 103 800
Dir: 2m S of Camelford. Take B 3266 S from Camelford, 1m before Michaelstow there is a track to Trecarne. Park and walk SE up the valley for 0.5m to the rocks.

10 PENTIRE HEAD *

A whole series of north facing cliffs around 40 metres high. The 80m great wall here is perhaps the finest piece of rock in the south west of England. The situation being escapeable and not tidal, still can be desperate if your arms aren't up to it. The rock is very good, and runs to solid protection. The route up the centre Darkinbad the Bright Daylayer E4, a classic route of the South West. Best on a good summers day, can be nippy with a cold N wind
G03c; Map: OS.200 (Landranger) 924 805

11 TINTAGEL *

A very big cliff with some steep and sombre lines. You come here for a full on climbing experience and need full commitment. Difficult to access & negociate, difficult to climb. Very impressive but dark and forboding.
G03c; Map: OS.200 (Landranger) 048 892

12 BUKATOR

A cliff for those seeking the ultimate adventure. Full ice climbing gear is the rigor of the day.
G03c; Map: OS.190 (Landranger) 118 935

13 CHEESEWRING *

A Quarry offers plenty of amusement with several climbs at most grades including some good hard problems and bouldering.
Map: OS.201 (Landranger) 258 724
Dir: 7m NNE of Liskard, on Bodmin Moor at 1000ft. From Liskard go N on the B3254 for 8m to Upton Cross, turn L to Minions, 2m. The quarry lies 1m to the N of here up a track.

14 DOWNDERRY

A handy little place to know about. Down on the shingle beach, you have a series of small caves with overhanging lips that give plenty of pumpy traversing. A few other bits and pieces.
Map: 210 (Landranger) 330 538
Dir: Make your way to Downderry on the coast. At the east end of the town, the B3247 makes some hard hairpin bends to wind up the hill. From here you can get down to the beach and along to the east, and the bouldering.

KENT/SUSSEX | DORSET | CORNWALL | DEVON | BRISTOL | SOUTH-WALES | MID-WALES | NORTH-WALES | LEICESTER | PEAKS | YORK-LANCS | CLEVELAND | KENDAL | LAKES | PENRITH | NEWCASTLE

BONEHILL, Climber Dave Henderson

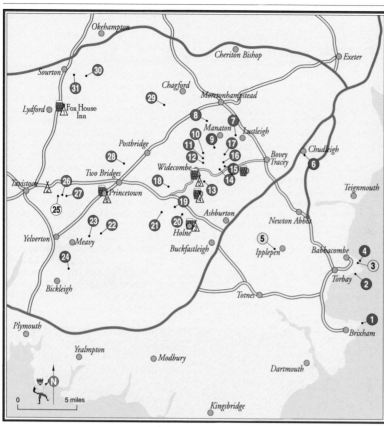

1 Berry Head
2 Daddyhole
3 Anstey's Cove
4 Sanctuary Wall
5 Torbryan
6 Chudleigh
7 Lustleigh Cleave
8 Easdon Rocks
9 Hound Tor
10 Honeybag Tor
11 Bell Tor
12 Bone Hill Rocks
13 Tunhill
14 Saddle Tor
15 Hay Tor
16 Smallacombe
17 BlackHill
18 Yar Tor
19 Luckey Tor
20 Bench Tor
21 Combestone Tor
22 Combshead Tor
23 Sheeps Tor
24 Dewerstone, The
25 Vixen Tor
26 Hucken Tor
27 Kings's Tor
28 Longaford Tor
29 Middle Tor
30 Shelstone Tor
31 Sourton Tors

KENT/SUSSEX · DORSET · CORNWALL · DEVON · BRISTOL · SOUTH-WALES · MID-WALES · NORTH-WALES · LEICSETER · PEAKS · YORK-LANCS · CLEVELAND · KENDAL · LAKES · PENRITH · NEWCASTLE

Fox House Inn.
Nr Lydford
A simple camping field behind the pub.

Lower Longford Caravan & Camping
?

Stone Camping at Holne
(01364 631 544)
A small campsite attached to a camping barn. Pub with superb food a few mins walk.

Lower Aish Camping
(01364 631 544) *Open Mar - Oct*
At Poundsgate, inexpensive and near pub

Cockingford Caravan & Camping
Widecombe TQ13 7TG
(01364 621 258) *Well run and busy site at the heart of the moors. Apr-Oct*

Plume of Feathers Pub
(01822 890 240)
A camping field nearby - open all year

Camping Barns:
*Stone/Holne: 01364 631 544
Hound Tor: 01647 221 202
(1 mile ENE of Hound Tor)*

Good local topo website
www.javu.co.uk

South Devon has been famous for indifferent trad climbing in the past. It has now come to the forefront of bouldering in the UK and is a really popular venue with good landings. The granite is very rough on the hands, but has the great benefit of excellent friction.

SOUTH DEVON & DARTMOOR
382pages - B &W
A few colour photos
Pocket - 165 x
105mm
Pub-1995
by Cordee
(Nick White)

A good overall guidebook - just to the trad routes in the area; it will certainly navigate you to all the routes. Optimistic! with a huge number of climbs, that won't appeal to everyone.

G-04a ⚠ 1-6,15,23,24 + esoterics

The scenery is also fabulous, and as wild as any Yorkshire or Derbyshire moor. There is no guidebook at present for the bouldering, but you'll find no shortage of good web links and topo downloads. The rocks dry out very quickly with the usual strong south-westerly breeze. For the top level 7b upwards, there are some super little venues for a blast. For the lower grade trad climber, the Dewerstone is a must on anybody's tick list. Many of the other sea cliffs are a bit on the wild & intrepid side, so adventure with plenty of caution. The trad routes on the granite tors need plenty of cams for protection, plus the grains of rock can shatter, and make the cams slip - think first! Definitely an area worth full investigation.

KENT/SUSSEX | DORSET | CORNWALL | DEVON | BRISTOL | SOUTH-WALES | MID-WALES | NORTH-WALES | LEICESTER | PEAKS | YORK-LANCS | CLEVELAND | KENDAL | LAKES | PENRITH | NEWCASTLE

❶ BERRY HEAD**

| Lime | 10 | | Alt-0m | 70m | 7.7 |

| 46 | | | DWS |

Bird restriction 15/3 - 31/7 total
This is the major cliff of the area and has a style of climbing that is unique; generally of giant handholds on a weird shattered rock. There are all sorts of problems here with tides etc, and if the sea gets up. There is no retreat from many of the routes, and you need to be a competent climber to even dream of coming to climb here. An ideal place for those searching out their inner soul. Covered in bird dung and pretty smelly too. More pleasant is the vast range of deep water soloing in the near area. (E2-ish)This is great fun and worth a play in a hot august, great cave.
G04a; Map: 202 (Landranger) 947 565
Dir: 2m NE of Brixham. From the town Berry Head is signposted, park on Berry Head common. Go through the steel gate that prevents tourists from rolling down the hill and over the edge.

❷ DADDYHOLE AREA

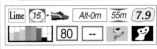

| Lime | 15 | | Alt-0m | 55m | 7.9 |

| 80 | -- | | |

This area consists of four minor cliffs; Meadfoot Quarry, & London Bridge, Telegraph Hole, all around 80ft and one major cliff, Main Cliff, east facing and set just above the high tide line. There is little below VS on the main cliff and indeed the harder routes are often referred to as serious! For the other cliffs there are plenty of diffs etc. The traverse of the area is The Watchtower a 600ft VS+ possible at high tide, and south facing.
G04a; Map: 202 (Landranger) 928 628
Dir: 7m SE of Torquay.

❸ ANSTEY'S COVE*

| Lime | 10 | | Alt-60m | 25m | 7.3 |

| 14 | | Pump | |

Two small cliffs set high up on the hillside overlooking Anstey's cove. SW and SE facing to either get the sun or keep the shade. Nice and steep with classic hard limestone, technical moves. Bolting is nothing to write home about and certainly won't impress those used to European bolting. A cliff that lives in a bygone era and hasn't passed through the trad stage yet, slip making a clip here, and you will happily spend the rest of your life in a wheelchair!
G04a; Map: 202 (Landranger) 935 650
Dir: Just S of Babbacombe. Park near the DIY centre and take a track-path to the top of the headland, where a fence on the right signals the top of the cliff. Steps lead down that are closed because of landfall - climbers should be able to manage this. Hiking up from the cove is a real sweat.

BERRY HEAD, Cave Wall - the main central area.

AVENGED s-7c+, Empire Wall, Anstey's Cove; Caedmon Mullin - inspecting

THREAD FLINTSTONE s-7b, Torbryan Quarry; Caedmon Mullin

④ SANCTUARY WALL

An impressive piece of rock that has a lot of hard routes on. If you are into E6 climbing and need adrenalin, this is your party time.
G04a; Map: 202 (Landranger) 937 651
Dir: On the sealevel down towards Long Quarry Point. (There is climbing here, but it's way dodgy and higly reccomendable)

⑤ TORBRYAN QUARRY*

A fun little venue that falls in the middle. Hardly good enough to travel a big distance for, but then again - when you find it on your doorstep, what a fantastic few hours you can have here. A complete dissaray of bolts and needs a complete overhaul - what a mess. The climbing is excellent with very good pumpy routes on vertical rock. Small flowstone crimps, but plenty of holds in general. In time will become a classic tiny crag no doubt.
G04a; Map: 202 (Landranger) 824 665
Dir: Take the steep road from Ipplepen towards Torbryan, at the top of the hill fork left, then go down into the woods and park just before the hairpin bend that would take you to Torbryan. On the L is a gate and footpath that leads up to the quarry in minutes. Park responsibly

⑥ CHUDLEIGH

The icons say it all! Truly a horrible crag with little or no merit for the majority of climbers. A complete embarrasment. Rock like this is soft and lends itself to high polish, gear is not easy to place or find. All the routes in the lower grades are highly dangerous. Accidents are just waiting to happen to low grade climbers on this cliff - Don't be the next statistic. Loose, overgrown etc.
G04a; Map: 202 (Landranger) 864 788

⑦ LUSTLEIGH CLEAVE*

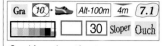

Good for a day at least.
Map: OL28 (Explorer) 722 815

⑧ EASDON ROCKS

Good fun. Park responsibly please
Map: OL28 (Explorer) 729 822

⑨ HOUND TOR**

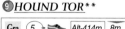

An excellent place with tons for everyone. Lots of rocks scattered about the top of the moor and really gritty.Usually a tea van in the car park.
Map: OL28 (Explorer) 742 790

LIMBO DANCER t-5c, Hound Tor; Dave Henderson

⑩ HONEYBAG TOR

Gra [15] Alt-445m 10m **7.3**
20 ☀ Zzz

Nice spot and out of the way, quiet.
Map: OL28 (Explorer) 729 787

⑪ BELL TOR

Gra (5) Alt-400m 3m **7.3**
10 Sloper Ouch

The small neighbour to Bonehill
Map: OL28 (Explorer) 731 778

⑫ BONE HILL ROCKS**

Gra (1) Alt-393m 3m **7.1**
10 150 Fun **Q-D**

One of the best bouldering venues on the moors, with routes too.
Map: OL28 (Explorer) 732 774

⑬ TUNHILL

Gra (15) Alt-380m 3m **7.3**
25 ☀ Zzz

Not to be forgotten, nice and quiet.
Map: OL28 (Explorer) 731 758

⑭ SADDLE TOR*

Gra (5) Alt-428m 7m **7.3**
25 ☀ **Q-D**

A superb spot with lots of problems in the harder grades. The tor bulges out and gives plenty of viscious starts. Can be really nippy as there is little way of getting out of the wind here. Don't miss a few problems lurking in the near area.
Map: OL28 (Explorer) 751 763

⑮ HAY TOR**

Gra (10) Alt-457m 22m **7.2**
50 25 ☀

A truly fantastic spot, right on top of the moors. Haytor stands high but can easily be reached in minutes from the car. There are two separate crags that have different characters. Hay Tor is the upper cliff and somewhat more friendly of the two - not that friendly would be a particularly good word for any Dartmoor granite. Low man is a giant brooding slab that has some hard and nasty routes on. Placing gear on either of these cliffs is difficult and energy consuming. These cliffs can find the achillies heel of most climbers. If you visit and cruise here, you're doing well. A magical place all the same.
G04a Map: OL28 (Explorer) 757 771

BONEHILL BOULDERING; Dave Henderson

DON'T STOP NOW E2 t-5c, West Face, Haytor; non stop solo-Dave Henderson

Sidebar tabs (left margin): KENT/SUSSEX · DORSET · CORNWALL · DEVON · BRISTOL · SOUTH-WALES · MID-WALES · NORTH-WALES · LEICESTER · PEAKS · YORK-LANCS · CLEVELAND · KENDAL · LAKES · PENRITH · NEWCASTLE

⑯ SMALLACOMBE*

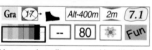

Gra 17 · Alt-400m · 2m · 7.1 · -- · 80 · Fun

Very good quality rock and bouldering here. Quite low and short problems, but good landings and plenty of slopers and traversing. Quite spread out area.
Map: OL28 (Explorer) 754 784

⑰ BLACK HILL

Gra 5 · Alt-400m · 3m · 7.2 · -- · 20 · Fun

A good and compact small area that can easily be combined with a visit to Smallacombe.
Map: OL28 (Explorer) 763 789

⑱ YAR TOR

Gra 5 · Alt-410m · 3m · 7.2 · -- · 10 · Fun

A small bouldering area, small.
Map: OL28 (Explorer) 678 741

⑲ LUCKEY TOR

Gra 20 · Alt-200m · 12 · 7.2 · -- · -- · Fun

A climbing venue.
Map: OL28 (Explorer) 685 721

⑳ BENCH TOR

Gra ? · Alt-312m · ? · 7.2 · -- · ? · Fun

A climbing area with routes from diff to E grades.
Map: OL28 (Explorer) 691 716

㉑ COMBESTONE TOR

Gra 1 · Alt-356m · 3 · 7.2 · -- · 20 · Fun

A bouldering area by the parking spot.
Map: OL28 (Explorer) 670 719

㉒ COMBSHEAD TOR

Gra 20 · Alt-320m · 7 · 7.1 · -- · 50 · Fun

A stunning setting away from it all, some of the best bouldering on the moors. Worth the walk in - uphill-ish.
Map: OL28 (Explorer) 587 688

㉓ SHEEPS TOR*

Gra 10 · Alt-370m · 9m · 7.2 · 35 · 25 · HBall

A very good small crag of very compact and entirely different granite. It has formed like extruded columns, and is in basalt type - flat columns. Very smooth and technical, offerering a whole variety of routes that lean out steeply at the top. You can place good gear on some of the routes, others need a top rope or very bold-highball approach. Nice situation. Limited parking and please make sure not to block the road.
G04a Map: OL28 (Explorer) 566 682

㉔ THE DEWERSTONE**

Gra 15 — Alt-200m 55m 7.2 · 90 · — · Ouch

A very good cliff indeed and popular with climbers for many years now. A venue that is steep but broken enough with cracks to give good climbing that offers itself to natural protection devices.
G04a Map: OL28 (Explorer) 539 638

㉕ VIXEN TOR*

Closed to public access at present. The tor itself is a grand piece of rock and one of the finest on Dartmoor. It may be opened up under the access of the new CROW access agreement. Please check to see that all is in order first. A shame not to climb here, but respect any agreement please.
G04a Map: OL28 (Explorer) 542 743

㉖ HUCKEN TOR

Gra 15 — Alt-287m 3 7.2 · — · 2 · Fun

Bouldering, nothing too brilliant and be with delicate access. Tread with care.
Map: OL28 (Explorer) 550 738

㉗ KINGS TOR*

Gra 18 — Alt-380m 5m 7.1 · — · 60 · Zzz

A really good little bouldering venue with a host of problems. Gets good sun and in a lovely position.
Map: OL28 (Explorer) 557 738

㉘ LONGAFORD TOR

Gra 25 — Alt-507m 4m 7.2 · — · 30 · Zzz

A remote bouldering spot, to be combined with Littaford tor.
Map: OL28 (Explorer) 616 779

㉙ MIDDLE TOR

Gra 5 — Alt-410m 3 7.1 · — · 10 · Zzz

A bouldering venue with a fantastic roof, some rave about this place, others definitely don't.
Map: OL28 (Explorer) 669 858

㉚ SHELSTONE TOR

Gra 25 — Alt-410m ? 7.1 · — · 30 · Zzz

Very good bouldering here. Quite low and short problems, but good landings and plenty of slopers; not to all tastes.
Map: OL28 (Explorer) 557 898

㉛ SOURTON TORS

Gra 16 — Alt-440m 5 7.2 · — · 50 · Zzz

A good amount of accessable bouldering, just a hike up to it, big wow view.
Map: OL28 (Explorer) 544 899

KINGS TOR, Luc Percival

Jingo climbing the rock at COMPASS POINT, new wave for sure!

North Devon is somewhere that definitely has a charismatic flavour of its own. There is a range of rock types from the sublime to the ridiculous, it can be play time or a complete death trap. There is also the island of Lundy which is situated some 15 miles northwest of Hartland Point, and has dramatic granite scenery that you just don't find on the mainland. The atmosphere of North Devon changes dramatically with the seasons. In summer the whole area is invaded by holiday makers, especially with surfers at Bude and Croyde. There is a relaxed manner to the scene; floppy billabong clad blonds, swish around the bars and hide mysteriously behind cool shades and bronzed sun tans. Cliffs like Baggy are bathed in sun and offer superb routes with tidal beaches at the bottom, everyone at the ready for a quick dip if it simply gets too hot. Outside of the summer holidays, life starts to cool down a bit, the winds pick up and the ominous clouds roll in. The majority of the cliffs face west and north, and they sulk in a shady sombreness of cold mornings. It is in some ways it's a real Jeckyll and Hyde flavour - when the sun goes in, they seem to grow bigger and bigger, and get nastier and nastier. Anything loose, seems even looser; the stakes at the top belays, seem to have rusted through or have disappeared, and the last runner you have placed 10 metres below, will always fall out when the going is getting gnarly. For many climbers, this is why they love the North Devon coastline; the desolation, the quietness, the total commitment of a soul searching experience on a route. It certainly, is that. The rock is immensely variable. It can be a compacted sandstone, at Compass Point it has worn into fabulous shapes, curves and inlets. At other places like Screda Point, the rock is exceptionally strong, though still dark and satanic. The coastal land, is nearly always comprised of shale and mud, but it's the promontory's which are the resolute veins of hard rock that battle against the sea, and manage to stand upright in defence. The finest example of these are at Lower Sharpnose, where two fins - 100 feet high, stand magnificently proud, leaving you open mouthed and aghast that they still are standing. They won't be there forever, that's for sure, so if you want to tick anything here, do it this year; it might have fallen down - next year!

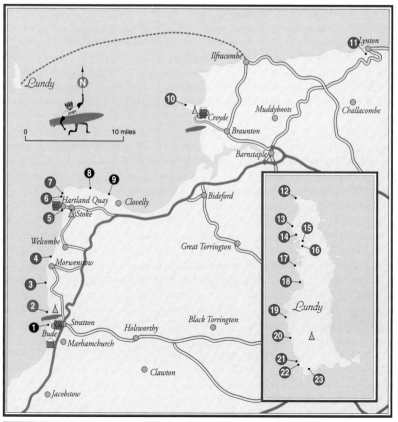

1. Compass Point
2. Menachurch Bloc
3. Sharpnose, Lower
4. Marsland
5. Screda Point
6. Dyer's Lookout
7. Smoothlands
8. Exmansworthy
9. Blackchurch
10. Baggy Point
11. Valley of the Rocks
12. North West Point
13. Arch Zawn
14. Torrey Canyon Bay
15. Diamond
16. Devil's Slide
17. Beaufort Buttress
18. Jenny's Cove
19. Battery Point
20. The Old Light
21. Goat Island
22. Montague Steps
23. Devil's Limekiln

△ Croyde: No shortage of campsites.
△ Hartland: Camping at Hartland and Stoke with pubs nearby.
△ Bude: Surfing and summer campsites
△ Lundy: Camping by booking only

❶ COMPASS POINT

San	(12)	🥾	Alt-0m	30m	**8.5**

| | | | **25** | -- | 🧗 | 🙂 |

A highly soft, sandstone fin, that gives a good selection of climbs to those who seek an early retirement from life. The climbing is actually very good and with good sandstone moves; falling off doesn't bear thinking about. Whole cliff is highly unstable.
G04a; Map: 190 (Landranger) 099 064

❷ NORTHCOTT-MAER

San	(5)	🥾	Alt-0m	30m	**8.4**

| | | **40** | **40** | 🧗 | 🙂 |

An area with some good bouldering spread out all along the coast here. Some on isolated blocks on the shingle beach, other sections as short walls at the base of the cliffs. Routes tend to be in the E4-E6 and very serious.
G04a; Map: 190 (Landranger) 201 080
Park at Northcott mouth and explore to the south along the coastal path.

V7 NORTHCOTT; Simon Young cranking

❸ LOWER SHARPNOSE*

San	(17)	🥾	Alt-110m	50m	**8.0**

| | | **45** | -- | 🧗 | Pump |

Some big fins that give excellent climbing, though somewhat difficult, and need a very steady head. Highly sustained for the finger muscles, and nervousness cells. Tidal dependent.
G04a; Map: 190 (Landranger) 195 127

❹ MARSLAND*

San	(?)	🥾	Alt-0m	30m	**8.2**

| | | **30** | -- | 🧗 | ⚭ |

These have been recommended to us by some friends. Lovely slabs with some very good routes in the lower grades, tidal, and a nice position. A series of fins going out in a row.
G04a; Map: 190 (Landranger) 206 174

LOWER SHARPNOSE

SCREDA POINT NEEDLE HS -t4b; Simon Young

⑤ SCREDA POINT*

A superb few pieces of rock on this small headland. The sea pinnacles offer some lovely smaller routes in the diffs and severe grades, a lovely situation and tidal. You need a big sling to arrange an abseil from the top. The main cliff has very good quality rock and is full of E1-4 slab routes, on the bold side (top rope poss) Bouldering in a small cave beneath car park area. This can get damp with seepage and level changes with the height of the shingle beach. Worth knowing about though.
G04a; Map: 190 (Landranger) 223 245
Dir: just down from the car park at Hartland Quay (pub also).

⑥ DYER'S LOOKOUT

There are two locations worth a detour here; Dire's Leadout tells you about one, plenty of E silly's. The other is Barnacle slab that offers a good couple of 80ft hard severe routes and a few harder lines. Cold and sombre.
G04a; Map: 190 (Landranger) 224 256
Dir: Just N of car park at Hartland Quay

⑦ SMOOTHLANDS

Worth a mention for just the couple of routes that are here, classics of their kind and totally impressive. A large black and blank wall gives a handful of E5-6 routes in a dark position.
G04a; Map: 190 (Landranger) 226 266
Dir: A bit further N of car park at Hartland Quay

⑨ EXMANSWORTHY

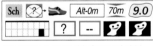

We had to include this for good old times sake. Routes come and go as the cliff falls down periodically. Proceed with caution!
G04a; Map: 190 (Landranger) 278 270

⑩ BLACKCHURCH

Tales of climbing here are varied, if it's adventure you require, have a look. Not a popular cliff, so you won't have to que for routes generally.
G04a; Map: 190 (Landranger) 299 267

⑩ BAGGY POINT**

San	(17)		Alt-0m	45m	8.0
		100			

The cliff is in two parts. The PROMON-TORY is huge and impresive and needs abseil descent, also has a bird ban *(15/03~31/07)*. You really want an extra rope since the top is very suseptable to getting ropes stuck. If the grass is wet, you can even need a rope to get to the descent. The slab routes are fantastic and everyone is worth doing. Some are very frightening and bold, go easy. The other cliff - KINKY SLABS, does not have a bird ban. Here the rock is a lot softer and there are some pleasant, easier slab routes.

G04a; Map: 180 (Landranger) 419 406

⑪ VALLEY OF THE ROCKS

?		Alt-0m	30m	?
	?	--		

Some climbing here apparently
Map: 180 (Landranger) 710 497

TWINKLE TOES VS t-4c, Promontory, Baggy Point; Alex Flemming

LUNDY, is a small single island, about half a mile wide and 4 miles long. It's far enough from Devon to be completely isolated and feel like another country. I've landed here on a hot day in summer, and it feels just like a small Mediterranean island. It just lacks the smell of cooking with sun dried tomatoes, oregano and pasta - if only. The one thing that Lundy is not, is modern. It survives, simply because of the Landmark Trust, who look after and manage the island in the interest of wildlife and nature conservation for the National Trust. Lundy benefits hugely from this, and as a result, has none of your usual, dire tourist trappings. The island seems to work very well with only a limited number of people staying on it at one time. There is a strict restriction on numbers of people staying at the island, so you are well advised to book up in advance. There is a

SATAN'S SLIP E1 5a. Devil's Slide, Lundy. Adam Hudson

small campsite, and there are also a number of cottages that can be rented by the week. Certainly when the weather turns hostile, there is very little to do and some comfort of rooms, heat etc. is a worthwhile consideration for a week. Since the island is a major nesting site for birds, climbers do not really visit until the restrictions are over at the end of July. By contacting the Landmark Trust, you will be able to get a full list of restrictions and they can fully advise you about the island and travel etc. The climbing is on good, solid granite. It is fair to say that 95 percent of the routes are in the extreme grades, since the granite here does tend to be very blank and is made up of very smooth blocks. It would be a waste of space here to describe individual cliffs, you'll come here for a week, or not. If you only climb in the diff and severe grades, there are a good selection of routes for a single trip, but not

FOCAL BUTTRESS, Devil's Limekiln, Lundy

KENT/SUSSEX
DORSET
CORNWALL
DEVON
BRISTOL
SOUTH-WALES
MID-WALES
NORTH-WALES
LEICSETER
PEAKS
YORK-LANCS
CLEVELAND
KENDAL
LAKES
PENRITH
NEWCASTLE

a huge amount. The guidebook to the island gives very few stars to any of the easy routes which is a bit unfair. I am sure that many lower grade climbers will find these routes fantastic and enjoyable. Part of the whole fun on Lundy, is the exploring the entire coastline of the island. With a group you can hire a boat to take a trip around the island and go fishing at the same time, an excellent way of having a day off and getting a better view of the cliffs.

LANDMARK TRUST (manages the island for the NT) Shottesbrooke, Maidenhead, Berkshire, SL6 3SW 01628 825 925

www.landmarktrust.co.uk

(Sometimes in winter, you can even fly from Hartland Point and have lunch on the island at the Marisco Tavern)

LUNDY
288 pages - B &W
A few colour photos
Thin Pocket size
165 x 105mm
Pub-1994 - reprinted
by Climbers Club
(Gary Gibson
Paul Harrison)

A handy book, even though it's not up to date, it has all the information that most climbers need, and contains just about all the routes worth doing. (You'll need a week to read through it!)

G-04b ⚠ All cliffs on Lundy.

CONTROLLED BURNING E3 t-6a, Torrey Canyon, Lundy; Gary Gibson

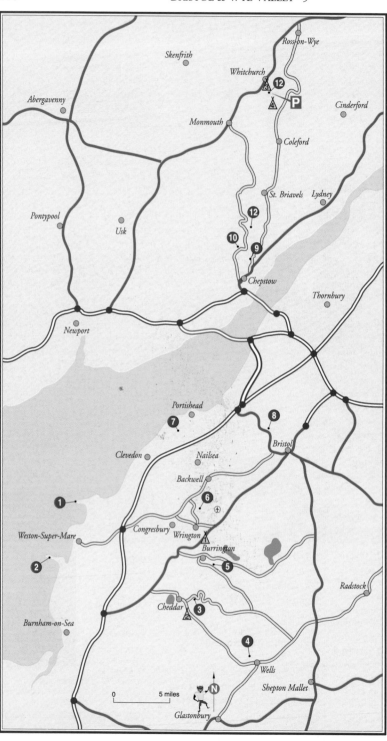

1 Sand Point
2 Brean Down
3 Cheddar Gorge
4 Split Rock Quarry
5 Burrington Combe
6 Goblin Combe
7 Portishead Quarry
8 Avon Gorge
9 Wintour's Leap
10 Wyndcliffe
11 Shorn Cliff
12 Symonds Yat

Brook Lodge
Caravan & Camping
Cowslip Green.
28/2 - 1/11
01934 862 311

Cheddar ?

Symonds Yat Camping
(by the river and busy
with canoes) Walk to
the pub though.

Campsite near
Hillersland

I find it hard to get enthusiastic about climbing in the Bristol Gorge and Wye Valley. Having spent a huge amount of my climbing learning years in both areas, the routes always seemed to involve considerable hard work and very little pleasure. It simply is pretty dangerous climbing in this area, and a issue that no climber should take lightly. Climbing with trad gear is dangerous at the best of times, and just about any climber who is into trad in a big way, usually gets a real high from the danger. If you don't get an enormous high from danger, and the fear of being impaled on a rock spike gets to you, then give this area a miss. Trad climbing can be fun and glorious, such as on the sea cliffs of Pembroke; if you are driving, then keep going. Over there, the rock is roughened by the sea salt and climatic elements, so when you hang off a hold to place a needy piece of protection, your hand will stay firmly gripping the rock and your feet will adhere beautifully to the crozzels on the footholds. These grains of limestone sometimes crumble beneath your weight as you place the gear, giving you a bit of a fright - it's something that you get used to and learn to cope with. The routes at Pembroke are also quite steep, and with good cracks, so you can place good gear, and the absorption system of ropes, nuts and belays tend to work very well. Climbing is fun at Pembroke and never too problematic, you are in a lovely location which is essential for your belayer. On the average trad route, you will spend about 5 times as much time and energy placing gear, as actually climbing. The belayer must be provided for, looked after and pampered; hence the superb view and lovely sea air, peace and quiet for the 45 min belay duration. All in all, Pembroke dishes up all the right ingredients. Trad climbing in the Bristol area is something completely different, and if you are coming out of a climbing wall, then you need to know think carefully about it. The rock in this area is smooth limestone, and is not that friendly since it doesn't run to good incuts. You generally find slope'y smooth holds, the kind that really polish up like a mirror, handy for those adjusting their make up. The cracks are very tight seamed, giving almost no chance to place nuts, and with marginal holding possibilities when you do. Cams slide off the slippery surfaces too. You also have to place the gear, balancing on really polished footholds. Avon gorge gets the full sun too, so when you are slipping around, you can sweat up really badly on the polished holds. The view for the belayer is pretty awful, and the constant din from the traffic is mind numbing, don't worry, just another hour before your turn - bet you can't wait. The gorge also has the added attraction of some impaling metal spikes sticking out of the rock, a gem that Trad climbers enjoy the extra thrill from. A quick trip to the Wye Valley soon solves the noise problem. There however you have a new nicety - loose rock, and I mean loooooose. When you are trying to place a nut behind a loose block, the loose block you are holding works loose, and your nerves and chattering teeth are left on the, somewhat loose side. In talking to a lot of different climbers, the overall opinion is that the whole area is not ideally suited to a trad climbing arena like gritstone or juggy Pembroke.

The BMC opinion at present, is that it shouldn't change. Most climbers are out bouldering and don't care either way anyway, I don't mind either. I just ask that if ever anyone does turn an area into a sport climbing arena, that they do it properly and for all climbers of every level, diff upwards. Some photos to show what good 15mm resin bolts with inset heads, actually look like.

THE BOLT DEBATE, will Cheddar be bolted up or cocked up?
This area wanted to ban chalk! Bristol & controversy, inexorably linked.

AVON & CHEDDAR
Text guidebook
2 Volumes
224 & 242 pages - B &W
A few colour photos
Pocket - 165 x 105mm
Pub-1992
by the Climbers Club
(M.Crocker)

A double guidebook to
area. A lot of text and a
lot of high extreme grades. Generally - if it
doesn't get E5, it doesn't get any stars; if you
don't crank this hard, you won't find the author
sympathing with you.

G-05a ⚠ 1,2,3,4, 8 plus esoterics

WYE VALLEY
Text guidebook
336 pages - B &W
A few colour photos
Pocket - 165 x 105mm
Pub-1997
(John Wilson)

This guidebook is simply
full of text. If you want
to read for hours upon hours, then this is the
guidebook for you. A great work of computer
text output, very difficult to use and fathom out;
filled with extreme climbs.

G-05b ⚠ 9, 10,11 - plus esoterics

SYMONDS YAT
Text guidebook
? pages - B &W
A few colour photos
Pocket - 165 x 105mm
Pub-?
by the Climbers Club
(?)

A whole guidebook dedicated to this crag. It
apparently now deserves a whole guidebook.
The last 34 pages in the 1977 Wye valley
guidebook, did it complete justice. The only
guidebook to the cliff.

G-05c ⚠ 12

❶ SAND POINT

A small amount of climbing in the upper grades that maybe of use to someone living or working in the area.
G05a(C); Map: 182 (Landranger) 324 661

❷ BREAN DOWN

A variable crag of variable quality.
G05a(C); Map 182 (Landranger) 290 588

❺ CHEDDAR GORGE*

This is a beautiful limestone gorge that rises up 100 metres from the valley floor. It faces north, and is extremely cold and shivvery. Added to this, climbing is not allowed during the peak tourist season of *1/3 - 21-10 - no climbing*. The rock is quite brittle and shattered, with sections liable to fall down - hence summer closure. There are plans to bolt up and stabilise various areas, let us see what happens?
G05a(C); Map 182 (Landranger) 472 542

BRAINBITER E2 t-5c, Cheddar Gorge; Damion Carroll

KENT/SUSSEX · DORSET · CORNWALL · DEVON · BRISTOL · SOUTH-WALES · MID-WALES · NORTH-WALES · LEICESTER · PEAKS · YORK-LANCS · CLEVELAND · KENDAL · LAKES · PENRITH · NEWCASTLE

SPLIT ROCK QUARRY

KENT/SUSSEX | DORSET | CORNWALL | DEVON | BRISTOL | SOUTH-WALES | MID-WALES | NORTH-WALES | LEICESTER | PEAKS | YORK-LANCS | CLEVELAND | KENDAL | LAKES | PENRITH | NEWCASTLE

4 SPLIT ROCK QUARRY

Lime	15		Alt-60m	20m	7.6
	12	--		

The wall of a disused quarry is superb for climbing on. Steep wall routes that rely on some crozzly texture and some very small holds. There are a few embarrasing haphazard bolts. The norm is to top rope until the crag gets properly equipped.
G05a; Map 182 (Landranger) 539 471
The old lane to the quarry from the west has been blocked, so either walk in on the footpath or drive up via the east. Seek local knowledge.

5 BURRINGTON COMBE

Lime	?		Alt-50m	?	?
	?	?		

Some small cliffs in this area give good bouldering and some short climbs of varying difficulty.
Map 182 (Landranger) 477 585

6 GOBLIN COMBE

Lime	10		Alt-50m	25m	7.8
	55	--		

Some nice cliffs in the woods that are cloaked in ivy and suffer a bit. Loose in parts, and generally of variable quality.
Map 182 (Landranger) 470 653

7 PORTISHEAD QUARRY

Lime	?		Alt-50m	50m	7.7
	20	--		

Not a bad quarry, in need of sorting out.
Map 182 (Landranger) 457 747

ARMS RACE E3 t-5c, Avon Gorge; Steve Findlay

SUSPENSION BRIDGE ARETE VS, Avon gorge

KENT/SUSSEX
DORSET
CORNWALL
DEVON
BRISTOL
SOUTH-WALES
MID-WALES
NORTH-WALES
LEICESTER
PEAKS
YORK-LANCS
CLEVELAND
KENDAL
LAKES
PENRITH
NEWCASTLE

⑧ *AVON GORGE*

Lime | Alt-40m | 100m | 7.7 | 300 | -- | 90db

This is an immensely variable cliff; in fact there are about 7 different sectors that all need separate descriptions. The busy road beneath makes for a good reason to stay away. Some parts are 8.5 on the rock stability scale, so be warned. The rock does not lend itself to natural protection, and climbing here is exceptionally dangerous. Climbing well below your grade is adviseable. The expanse of the place and exposure is superb and memorable. A place to have great memories - so long as you are still in one piece. Many of the classics are really polished, to make the thrill factor even higher! In some places, there are still the old quarrying metal spikes sticking out, ready to impail a falling climber. My advice is to keep driving to anywhere else!
G05a; Map 182 (Landranger) 562 743

⑨ *WINTOUR'S LEAP*

Lime | Alt-60m | 80m | 7.8 | 200 | -- | Pump

Oh dear, oh dear, oh dear - it's still up. I really thought it would have fallen down since the 1st edtion of our Crag guide to England and Wales, some 16 years ago. Well, several sections at least have fallen down at least, and many more should be on there way soon. If you want to get crushed on falling lumps of limestone, try your luck on this heap of tottering muck. Only the very best areas of the crag get our 7.8 stability scale; others creak into the mid 8's. Sure you can have some good climbing here, but you have to be an adrenalin junkie. In the low grades, the climbing is nice but the gear is abominable, and you don't find any placements for any cams all. Here; it's all balls and no nuts!
G05b; Map 162 (Landranger) 542 948

⑩ *WYNDCLIFFE*

Lime | ? | Alt-50m | 40m | 8.3 | 30 | --

Just so you know the score.
G05b; Map 162 (Landranger) 527 974

⑪ *SHORN CLIFF*

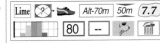
Lime | Alt-70m | 50m | 7.7 | 80 | --

Some good routes here but a very overgrown cliff and can seep quite a lot. May get popular in years to come with development. Has possiblilities.
G05b; Map 162 (Landranger) 542 993

⑫ *SYMONDS YAT*

Lime | 8 | Alt-70m | 35m | 7.7 | 60 | --

A popular cliff with beginners and groups. Justifiably so because there is some fun climbing here. Easy to manage and set up top ropes.
G05c; Map 162 (Landranger) 563 157

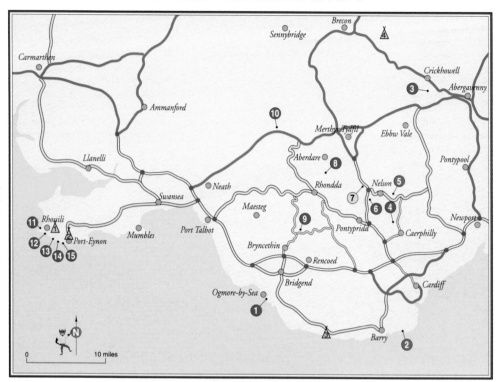

1 Ogmore
2 Sully Island
3 Llangattock
4 Llanbradach Q.
5 Penallta
6 Navigation Quarry
7 The Gap
8 Cwmaman Main Q.

9 Cwm Dimbath
10 Dinas Rock
11 Rhosilli
12 Fall bay
13 Great & Little Tor
14 Three Cliffs
15 Pennard

www.sportsclimbs.co.uk
topo downloads for sport climbing in the
South Wales region

Caravan & Camping - Pitton

Port Eynon Caravan & Camping

Llantwit Major - Acorn Caravan & Camping
1/3-31/10   Tel: 01874 658 283

Llangorse - Lakeside Caravan & Camping Park
31/3-31/10   Tel: 01874 658 226

GOWER & SE WALES
Full - route List
Bound floppy book
366 pages - B&W
Some colour photos
Pocket size 165 x 105
Pub-1991 by South Wales
Mountaineering Club

A simple book, text printout
style, with a handful of diagrams
on the big cliffs. Difficult to find.

G-06a   1 - 15 & a lot of esoterica

No shortage of great cream teas on the Gower.

This area does not rate very highly for climbing - period; we told you so. You can certainly find some good climbing, but don't get your hopes up. The big cliff is Ogmore, and it's very impressive. The tide here is also impressive, with up to a 30 foot range, so be very careful. Ogmore is grand and deserves a visit by any climber, for at least a whole weekend. The valleys themselves have a few natural outcrops, but mainly offer quarries that are being equipped, bit by bit. The future is uncertain here and we are waiting to see what development happens. The new South Wales Mountaineering Club guide book, is now approaching prolonged immanency (it has been for 2 years). The Gower peninsular is a tiny little haven, especially for those wanting some sandy beaches, peace and quiet. The climbing is good, but really small. Ideal for families and those just beginning, only wanting 8-10 metre routes. Anything bigger, is generally loose and gripping. The area deserves a good inclusion in this guidebook, but with sensible reservation.

GIANT KILLER E5 t-6a, Dinas Rock; Pat Littlejohn

❶ OGMORE**

| Lime | 10 | 👟 | Alt-0m | 40m | **7.8** |

| | 200 | -- | 🖐 | 🐾 |

The premier cliff in the south east of
Wales by quite a long way. Apart from a
few short routes at the sides, you need
to be a comfortable HVS leader to get
much out of a visit here. If you are, then
you should be able to get right into the
Ogmore experience of very steep and
juggy climbing. E3/4 is the grade to
really get cranking here, not so much
of the technical difficulty but stamina in
placing gear at a very steep angle. The
rock is very stratafied and a good set of
medium to large cams are very useful.
A helmet for the belayer can also be
quite a good precaution. Tides here
come in very fast and completely cut
you off, expect a complete epic if you're
not up to the required standard.
G06a; Map: 170 (Landranger) 875 738
*Dir: 5m SW of Bridgend. Take the B
4524 to Southerndown, then a small
lane to Dunraven Bay, car park, here
the cliffs run NW for about 1m.*

❷ SULLY ISLAND

| Lime | ? | 👟 | Alt-0m | ? | **?** |

| | | -- | ? | 🐾 |

A small good bouldering area but is
only accessible at low tide.
Map: 171 (Landranger) 167 670
*Dir: 4m E of Barry on the coast. From
Barry towards Cardiff on the A 4055
for 2m turn R onto the B 4267 for 1.7m
through Sully. Turn R to reach the coast
and Sully Island in 600 yds.*

❸ LLANGATTOCK

| Lime | 8 | 👟 | Alt-400m | 9m | **7.8** |

| | 130 | -- | 🐾 | 🗑 |

A beautiful position but generally north
facing and not very friendly unless
you get caught in a heatwave during
summer. Nearly all the routes are very
short and slabby in nature. Placing
gear is very difficult and falling off is not
adviseable. The blank bigger walls of
around 20m, offer some brilliant climbing; but it's a trad venue at the moment
where leading is a completely harrowing experience. For groups, top ropes
can be set up quite easily and walking
down around the side is practical.
*Groups: Because the outcrop is used a
lot by groups, you need to book first to
stop overcrowding. Ring 01873 810 149
(Crickhowell Adventure gear).*
Map: 161 (Landranger) 215 147
*Dir: Negociate your way to a high park-
ing spot near to the cliffs. 8mins to the
L and 14 mins to the right.*
*Breacon Beacons Wardens:
01874 624 437*

LLANGATTOCK; one of the steeper and totally frightening sections!

❹ LLANBRADACH QUARRY

There is climbing here with menace and an attitude. Might not be your cup of tea, esoteric

G06a; Map: 171 (Landranger) 146 895

❺ PENALLTA

A good, small crag that is popular with beginners, and has some good bouldering too.

G06a; Map: 171 (Landranger) 138 952
Dir: 7m NNW of Caerphilly. Take the A 469 N to Ystrad Mynach then take a small road through the village due N towards Gelligaer for about .3m and turn L into a housing estate and park at the far end. The crag is NW from here.

❻ NAVIGATION QUARRY

Some routes here of a good length. Some of the slabs are badly protected so come prepared.

G06a; Map: 170 (Landranger) 090 935

⑦ THE GAP

Simply, the most popular crag in SE Wales, bring trad gear as well.

G06a; Map: 170 (Land) 080 693 or 963

FALL BAY, a lovely sandy beach with the cliffs behind

❽ *CWMAMAN MAIN QUARRY*

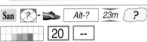

San	？	👟	Alt-200m	23m	？
			20	--	

Apparently there are some hard routes here, those seeking should enquire further.
G06a; Map: 170 (Explorer) 998 992

❾ *CWM DIMBATH*

San	？	👟	Alt-?	23m	？
			20	--	

Climbing here!
G06a; Map: 170 (Explorer) 951 896

❿ *DINAS ROCK*

Lime	？	👟	Alt-100m	42m	7.6
			80	--	

A good old tottery limestone cliff that has been climbed all over with trad routes. Unpopular.
G06a; Map: 170 (Explorer) 913 080

YELLOW WALL, a fest for those who enjoy tottery instability

⑪ *RHOSILLI*

These are the some small and fun cliffs that offer climbing to both beginners and E2-4 climbers. Nothing brilliant, but the positionis lovely and the walk is one of the shortest in the area.

G06a; Map: OL164 (Explorer) 406 877

⑫⑬ *FALL BAY - GREAT TOR**

Lime	20	👟	Alt-0m	20m	7.8

| | 150 | -- | | |

A beautiful stretch of coastline that is unspoilt, calm and friendly. The climbing is highly varied. At sea level the rock is very good, and you are blessed with short, 10m routes that are mostly easy angled, great for beginners. Going east; Yellow wall has some harrowing harder climbs. On the upper tiers, the rock gets a lot poorer and flakey, so watch out. You eventually get to Great tor and little tor, where again, short stuff by the sea is the best bet.

G06a; Map: OL164 (Explorer) 414 874

⑭⑮ *THREE CLIFFS & PENNARD**

A fabulous pic-nic and climbing area, for the family who like beaches and nothing too difficult or harrowing. Three cliffs is home to a few easy classic routes, and the longest quality routes on the Gower. Tidal so watch it. Further along the coastline is Pennard. It is high up and overlooks the area - lovely. Here the routes are steeper and more intimidating, but not that difficult. Sea gull attack, being my most dangerous suffering to date.

G06a; Map: OL164 (Explorer) 538 878

Side tabs: KENT/SUSSEX · DORSET · CORNWALL · DEVON · BRISTOL · SOUTH-WALES · MID-WALES · NORTH-WALES · LEICESTER · PEAKS · YORK-LANCS · CLEVELAND · KENDAL · LAKES · PENRITH · NEWCASTLE

ARCH SLAB Severe, Three Cliffs; Jonathon Delamont

PLEASURE DOME E3 t-6a, Stennis Head; Jason Porter

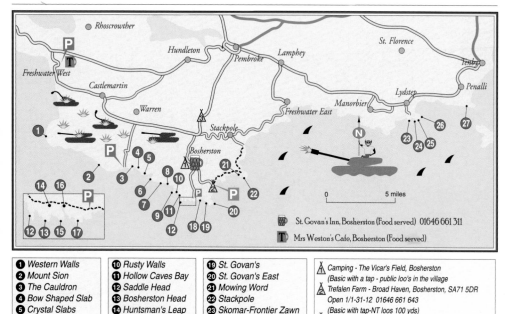

St. Govan's Inn, Bosherston (Food served) 01646 661 311
Mrs Weston's Cafe, Bosherston (Food served)

❶ Western Walls	❿ Rusty Walls	⓳ St. Govan's
❷ Mount Sion	⓫ Hollow Caves Bay	⓴ St. Govan's East
❸ The Cauldron	⓬ Saddle Head	㉑ Mowing Word
❹ Bow Shaped Slab	⓭ Bosherston Head	㉒ Stackpole
❺ Crystal Slabs	⓮ Huntsman's Leap	㉓ Skomar-Frontier Zawn
❻ Mewsford	⓯ Stennis Head	㉔ Mother Carey's Kitchen
❼ Crickmail Point	⓰ Stennis Ford	㉕ White Tower
❽ Triple Overhang	⓱ Newton Head	㉖ Lydstep Head
❾ The Castle	⓲ Trevallen Cliff	㉗ Giltar Slabs

Camping - The Vicar's Field, Bosherston
(Basic with a tap - public loo's in the village
Trefalen Farm - Broad Haven, Bosherston, SA71 5DR
Open 1/1-31-12 01646 661 643
(Basic with tap-NT loos 100 yds)
St. Petrox Caravan & Camping
Good facilities 01646 683 980

The south coast of Pembroke is without doubt, the premier trad climbing area in the whole of Britain. The photos in this guidebook should illustrate, both the wealth of different locations and styles of climbing available to every level of climber. If you combine this with the weather that this peninsular enjoys, you certainly do have a magical cocktail. It's a long way to drive to, especially at holiday time. But for some reason, most ordinary punters don't make it this far along the South Wales coast, leaving the area nice, quiet and peaceful for the climbers to enjoy. On the far left, you begin at Freshwater West, and can go rip roaring windsurfing, off a fabulous golden sandy beach that gets windblown 354 days a year. The road from Castlemartin to Bosherston is bounded on the south by an army tank range. This is a full on battle range that you can only get access to the west part by special permission at certain times, and need to go on a special briefing course to recognize unexploded nuclear bombs! The area from Stack rocks (3) to St. Govan's (20) is still in an army range but access is rarely restricted. I have never heard of this section being closed at a weekend or in the school holidays. It is limestone everywhere, and totally different to inland limestone. Here you get some lovely sweeps of flat rock, but with surface crusting to give wonderful handholds, and genuine possibilites to place natural protection. It seems to have been designed for trad climbing, so much, that I would imagine it very unlikely to ever change. The climbing is rarely technical, and only occoasionally do you have to resort to using small holds. The difficulty lies in the general angle of the rock, as it is nearly always vertical, and with no shortage of overhanging sections. You can even find 150ft overhanging routes that are only HVS. When you do get the chance to place protection, you generally have to do it hanging off your arms, with strength sapping out of your body at an alarming rate. You do see some spectacular falls of course; at least you whizz into air. Routes like the classic 'The Butcher E3' at St. Govans, recieves a very high rate of jibbering candidates each year. In the lower Severe-VS grades the angles are more pleasant, and the whole coastline is studded with fine examples of these. There have been some superb deep water soloing venues developed in the last few years, and with many more just egging to be included on the tick list. It's a great place to come and climb for a week during the summer holidays. Some of the cliffs are affected by bird bans (until mid august), but these are very well signposted at the notice boards, also with hand out maps from the car park at Broad Haven (Camping 2). Top tip; Sometimes the north coast is in full sunshine, when the south coast is in sea mist all day.

THE CAULDRON

❶ *WESTERN WALLS* * *

Lime (80) Alt-0m 30m **7.6** | 120

Bird Restriction 31/1 - 15/8; Army special permit needed. An excellent area of slabby walls that give the biggest selection of climbs in the lower grades to the whole of Pembroke. There are good tidal ledges but these don't cope with a big swell.
Map: OL36 (Explorer) 883 969

PEMBROKE
Topos & photos
Guidebook
112 pages - B &W
No colour photos
A5
Pub-1995
by Rockfax
(Alan James)

A good guidebook for climbers who haven't been here before. Well laid out and easy to use, with a plentiful selection of routes to keep you going for a full week. Doesn't have all the easier routes, but works well in combination with the other giant guidebook - buy both.

G-06b ⋀ *4-22, 24 (Selected routes only)*

❷ *MOUNT SION* * *

Lime (30) Alt-0m 55m **7.6** | 150

Bird Restriction 31/1 - 15/8; Army special permit needed. The gem crag in the range west. The cliff is in 3 sections with a very steep and overhanging central part. Definitely worth the hassle of getting a permit for.
Map: OL36 (Explorer) 913 945
Army permit ring: 01646 662 230

PEMBROKE
Full - route List
Bound floppy book
415 & 415 pages - B &W
A few colour photos
Pocket - 165 x 105mm
Pub-1995
by the Climbers Club
(J Harwood & D Viggers)

A giant double book edition gives you access to the route list of the area. Actually finding your way around with the guidebook is desperate. There are some photo diagrams but mainly relies on you knowing the classic routes.

G-06b ⋀ *1 - 27 + more.*

❸ *THE CAULDRON*

Lime (5) Alt-0m 40m **7.7** | 30

Bird Restriction 31/1 - 15/8. This is a highly atmospheric place to encounter, and not the place you want to be stuck when darkenss is falling with a big sea running. Invigourates the soul.
Map: OL36 (Explorer) 929 945
Dir: 5 mins from stack rocks car park.

❹ *BOW SHAPED SLAB* *

Lime (8) Alt-0m 50m **7.4** | 12

Bird Restriction 31/1 - 15/8. This is a highly atmospheric place to encounter, and not the place you want to be stuck when darkenss is falling with a big sea running. Invigourates the soul.
Map: OL36 (Explorer) 929 945
Dir: 5 mins from stack rocks car park.

FRESHWATER WEST BEACH

BOW SHAPED CORNER hard severe t-4b; David Laddiman

RAZZLE DAZZLE VS t-4c, Crystal Slabs; Sue Herwood

⑤ CRYSTAL SLABS *

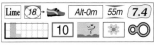

| Lime | 18 | 👟 | Alt-0m | 55m | 7.4 |

| | | 10 | | 🐍 | ☀ | 🔗 |

A giant slab that is a VS climbers dream. A lovey situation with the difficulties concentrated in the central and upper parts of the routes.
Map: OL36 (Explorer) 636 943

⑥ MEWSFORD ***

| Lime | 26 | 👟 | Alt-0m | 55m | 7.4 |

| | | 50 | 🐕 | 🏃 | 🔗 |

Bird Restriction 1/3 - 31/7; on the West face. This is one of the great cliffs in Pembroke. The rock quality is exceptional and gives excellent grips and offers plenty for gear placements. Very atmospheric. A commiting abseil in, but escape isn't that difficult. Tidal and fraught with problems if a sea is running.
Map: OL36 (Explorer) 942 938

⑦ CRICKMAIL POINT *

| Lime | 30 | 👟 | Alt-110m | 50m | 7.4 |

| | | 50 | 🏃 | ☀ | 🔗 |

This is the farthest point from just about anywhere. Stick to the track if you want to get there or back quickly. A two tier buttress that can be handy if the tides are wrong for you or the sea is tempestuous. All round fun.
Map: OL36 (Explorer) 947 938

⑧ TRIPLE OVERHANG *

| Lime | 34 | 👟 | Alt-0m | 50m | 7.4 |

| | | 20 | 🏃 | 🐕 | 🔗 |

Bird Restriction 1/3 - 31/7; r One of the classic cliffs that is impressive and superb to climb on. You can find a good selection of HVS to graduate up to. Deservedly popular.
Map: OL36 (Explorer) 949 937

A compulsory breakfast at Mrs Westons tea shoppe

KENT/SUSSEX · DORSET · CORNWALL · DEVON · BRISTOL · SOUTH-WALES · MID-WALES · NORTH-WALES · LEICESTER · PEAKS · YORK-LANCS · CLEVELAND · KENDAL · LAKES · PENRITH · NEWCASTLE

MEWSFORD POINT, West face

9 THE CASTLE *

A very good all round venue with plenty to keep a mixed group busy all day. A few of the routes nearby on the Fortress have a bird restriction but the main areas are free from our winged friends nesting fortunately. An atmospheric place on both sides, especially when they fall into shade. A very handy place to keep in - or get out of the sun. Worth the long walk in.
G06b; Map: OL36 (Explorer) 954 934

10 RUSTY WALLS *

Small but very high in quality sums this area up. Steep walls with some classic lines at E1-2. Also in the area is some really excellent DWS, very grippy rock and challenging lines.
Map: OL36 (Explorer) 956 933

11 HOLLOW CAVES BAY *

A mixed bag here. Lots of small areas that can give some shorter 20m routes of all grades. Has become popular with DWS in the last couple of years with a few special areas - especially for the harder climber.
Map: OL36 (Explorer) 957 932

12 SADDLE HEAD * * *

One of the best cliffs in Pembroke for the lower grade climber. You need a proper spring low tide to get down to the sea platform, which is a fabulous experience. From here there are stupendous climbs in the easier grades. On the upper tier you have non tidal shorter routes of all grades, steep but with chunky holds.
Map: OL36 (Explorer) 959 928

13 BOSHERSTON HEAD * *

A head with many faces, some good and some really dodgy; maybe rename it politicians head. A complete array of nooks and crannies. Easier stuff to the west and a really full on steep east face. A very difficult place to get a view of since it sticks out farther than just about anywhere else. A few classic VS routes here that are lovely.
Map: OL36 (Explorer) 961 928

14 HUNTSMAN'S LEAP * *

A zawn, completely filled with 3 star routes, awesome and sombre. It's cold and dank too, which eradicates a 3rd star. If it's a heatwave, this is the place to come. Bring a spare abseil and leave no valuables up top - right on a footpath. Belay stakes set back a bit so have full length twin 50's.
Map: OL36 (Explorer) 962 929

⑮ STENNIS HEAD***

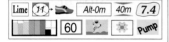
Lime (11) Alt-0m 40m **7.4** | 60 | **Pump**

(Photo at front of this section). A superb headland with some steep and wonderful routes. In many ways one of the perfect crags with great popularity. On the west side is a lovely terrace running down to the sea, and protects the cliff from even a raging sea. The routes here look very easy, but the angle is deceptive and you are soon pumped out of your brains. At the end of the headland is the Pleasure Dome wall, one of the big outings for anyone who is trying to crank E3. The east face has a selection of easier routes but still with high technical merit and will amuse the HVS aspirant. Right on the headland are a few easy severe's that are all time classics.
Map: OL36 (Explorer) 963 928

⑯ STENNIS FORD**

Lime (5) Alt-0m 45m **8.5** | 15

A bigger version of Huntsman's leap that offers very little for the lower grade climber. All the routes are long, intracate and intimidating. Hardly needs explaining that it is not very popular. Again, handy in a heatwave if Huntsman's is bulging with climbers.
Map: OL36 (Explorer) 964 929

⑰ NEWTON HEAD**

Lime (3) Alt-00m 30m **8.3** | 60 | **DWS**

Another one of those political heads. On the west face that combines with Stennis ford, you have a superb wall for DWS, that is proving to be very popular. Steep and very intimidating as you abseil in, then cast off your harness and rope to swing out into space - freaky if you're not up to it. The awesome arena prooves friendly with good holds - often! Further around the head are a good selection of different routes of mid standard. Higher up there is a tier and some 15 metre walls that give an excellent area for beginners or novices. On the east face are some steep and intimidating lines - eekk!
Map: OL36 (Explorer) 965 928

Chapel Point
The next headland along due east, has some superb steep routes, but also has a bird restriction 1/2-1/8.

KENT/SUSSEX · DORSET · CORNWALL · DEVON · BRISTOL · SOUTH-WALES · MID-WALES · NORTH-WALES · LEICESTER · PEAKS · YORK-LANCS · CLEVELAND · KENDAL · LAKES · PENRITH · NEWCASTLE

SUNSET BOULEVARD HVS t-5a, Saddle Head; Jingo solo (22 years after his 1st ascent)

JUST ANOTHER DAY E5 t-6b, Huntsman's Leap; James McHaffie

FLASHING EYEBROWS E1 t-5b deep water on-sight solo, Stennis Ford-Newton Head; Ruth Taylor

ORANGE ROBE BURNING E5 t-6a, Trevallen Cliff; Tim Emmet 'COOL MAN RESTING' with a complete hands off rest using a footjam.

THE ARROW E1 t-5b, St. Govan's Head; Yan Wang

18 TREVALLEN CLIFF***

The premier crag for the hard climber who needs to crank off dozen's of E5's every day, to stay in shape for 7b sport climbing. Nothing too steep, just mainly vertical walls with sustained fingertip pulling. The cliff is protected by a boulder beach and can be accessed for any state of the tide. Best to abseil in and take your gear with you as the top is very popular with passers by. The cliff is a real sun trap, so take plenty of sun lotion and something to drink.
Map: OL36 (Explorer) 000 000

19 ST. GOVAN'S HEAD***

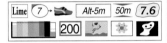

The largest cliff in the range east section of Pembroke. Easily seen when you enter the free car park. Here you have the full selection of routes in all grades. There is an awkward but possible scramble chimney descent, but many people bring an abseil rope to make life easier in tight rock shoes. There is a nice and friendly sector on a high platform, well out of tidal reach. Then the cliff starts to angle away towards the headland where it eventually becomes tidal, big and intimidating. The routes get harder and harder too.
Map: OL36 (Explorer) 975 927

20 ST. GOVAN'S EAST*

A quiet crag that is not used by so many. Just that bit too far to walk, and doesn't have too many easy routes either. Handy though if it's a bit chilly in the morning since it gets good sun and is sheltered to some extent from the westerly winds. Steep with roofs and full on bulky climbing in a superb position. Worth keeping a secret. You can scramble down to the bottom but this does need a lowish tide, wheras an abseil into the central high platform is handy.
Map: OL36 (Explorer) 976 926

21 MOWING WORD***

Bird restriction 1/2 - 31/7 Prize for the weridest cliff name in the area. A lovely peninsular that is almost vertical on all sides. The best climbing is to be found on the west face and is simply a delight. Most of the routes are classic lovely outings. Bottom is tidal and is worth the extra effort of being here at low tide for easy access to many of the routes. Routes on the east face are shorter and a lot easier.
Map: OL36 (Explorer) 992 943

22 STACKPOLE*

Bird restriction 1/2 - 31/7 & 1/3 - 15/8 This cliff is not recommended for beginners. It has a huge tidal platform that looks very welcome at low tide. It goes well under water! and the only ways up are through awesome territory. The whole cliff strata angles too steeply and often whole blocks fall into the sea. Superb all the same, but you do get a good element of risk in climbing here.
Map: OL36 (Explorer) 995 942

BLOWIN IN THE WIND E2 t-5b, Mowing Word; Dave Johnson-belay, Marion Dalgleish climbing, Al Cook (drying out after his belay fell out!)

KENT/SUSSEX | DORSET | CORNWALL | DEVON | BRISTOL | SOUTH-WALES | MID-WALES | NORTH-WALES | LEICESTER | PEAKS | YORK-LANCS | CLEVELAND | KENDAL | LAKES | PENRITH | NEWCASTLE

㉓ SKOMAR TOWERS *

| Lime | 8 | 👟 | Alt-0m | 35m | 7.6 |

60   🏊   Zzz   ∞

This area is to the west of the Kitchen, and is generally quiet and handy to get away from it all during busy periods. Frontier Zawn is here, with some impressive and demanding E2-4 routes, (Also No-man's - needing low tide and no seepage on the north wall for a bundle of E5-6 routes). The front of the towers offer a handful of good routes for the lower Severe-VS leader.
Map: OL36 (Explorer) 084 976

㉔ MOTHER CAREY'S KITCHEN ***

| Lime | 6 | 👟 | Alt-0m | 50m | 7.7 |

60   🏊   ⛏   ∞

Just what your mother wouldn't like! This is a stupendous cliff in two sections. A big wall that is vertical and has some lovely, full length classic routes. On the left side of the cliff the rock veere's towards (8.5). The main wall is very sound, but has lots of loose bits at the top. Anyone down below belaying is well advised to sport a helmet. The other cliff is the space face - east facing. Tidal, atmospheric and E4 to above demanding. There is a severe to climb the cracks and is well worth it for anyone, but don't go without a strong leader backup - there just ain't an easy way out of this place. Tidal but you can still get a lot done outside very high tide.
Map: OL36 (Explorer) 090 975

㉕ WHITE TOWER *

| Lime | 10 | 👟 | Alt-0m | 35m | 7.4 |

14   --   🏊   ❄

What a fun venue we have here. Famous for the route The Great White E7, and you need the right nuts for that one! An amazing white sheet that you just can't see from anywhere, until you're beneath it. Tidal and wow factor. There are some other easier routes in the area but they don't come recommended by repuatation.
Map: OL36 (Explorer) 092 975

㉖ LYDSTEP HEAD *

| Lime | 15 | 👟 | Alt-0m | 40m | 7.7 |

20   **DWS**   🏃   ∞

The forgotten head eh! Now brought into the modern domain by the DWS sun seekers. You can't see the climbing on this headland from anywhere, and some of the top sections leave a lot to be desired too. A superb chimney allows easy access to the NE and you can then explore at will. Still a good place to go and be away from it all.
Map: OL36 (Explorer) 094 974

㉗ GILTAR SLABS *

| Lime | ? | 👟 | Alt-0m | 40m | 7.5 |

40   ?   ❄

A range of slabs that offer a very good range of easier routes in the Diff-S category. The cliffs are situated behind and army firing range, but the footpath along the tops is apparently open at all times. Base of the cliffs is slightly tidal.
Map: OL36 (Explorer) 120 983

NEPTUNE HVS t-5a, Stackpole Head; David Tabner

MOTHER CAREY'S KITCHEN

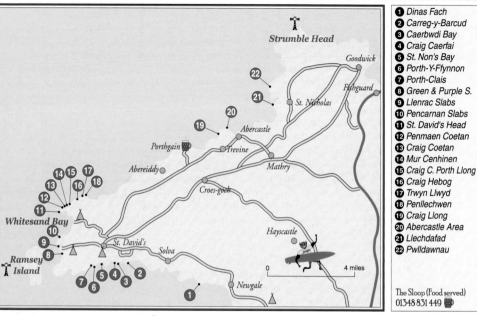

Map legend:
1. Dinas Fach
2. Carreg-y-Barcud
3. Caerbwdi Bay
4. Craig Caerfai
5. St. Non's Bay
6. Porth-Y-Ffynnon
7. Porth-Clais
8. Green & Purple S.
9. Llenrac Slabs
10. Pencarnan Slabs
11. St. David's Head
12. Penmaen Coetan
13. Craig Coetan
14. Mur Cenhinen
15. Craig C. Porth Llong
16. Craig Hebog
17. Trwyn Llwyd
18. Penllechwen
19. Craig Llong
20. Abercastle Area
21. Llechdafad
22. Pwlldawnau

The Sloop (Food served)
01348 831 449

❶ DINAS FACH

A good crag for the VS leader having a good 5 VS's about 100ft long. W facing and on a nice scenic headland out of the way make this a relaxing spot. The rock towards the top of the climbs however is not above suspicion.
Map: OL35 (Explorer) 826 227

❷ CARREG-Y-BARCUD *

San (18) → 👟 Alt-0m 30m 7.7
████ 60 👤☂ ❄ ∞

A faulous cliff in a lovely position. I still remain unconvinced by the quality of the climbing however. Protection is non existant on the slabs where the climbing is really good and technically testing. Some of the harder routes are superb, but the face routes can be suicidal. In the other areas, the moves are easy, yes, I mean really easy. A mixed bag after the high quality punch of south Pembroke, but great for a photo opportunity and a lovely day out. Some of the cracks are wide! So you may get a chance to use your number 10 friends.
Map: OL35 (Explorer) 774 242

This area remained very undisturbed and quiet during the 1980's. However, good word sneaked out and some of the cliffs have gained tremendous popularity. You are now just as likely to find, dense testosterne enriched E4 crowds at some of the more popular cliffs. It is however, far easier to escape the general presence of climbers in this area. The majority of the climbing on the north coast is sombre and needs a committed approach; especially in anything other than a heatwave. The southern part ia baked in sun and there to enjoy. Access is variable; some locals near Solva have taken to damaging cars parked in annoying places, so act conformatively - only parking in designated bays. Whitesand bay is more crowded than a Sunday in Bournemouth during a heatwave, so expect parking mayhem. If you do want to climb around St. David's head, use a convenient campsite so you can walk direct to the cliff from the teepee, and not get caught up in the angry space arguing melée. Farther up the north coast, you can escape the touroids and discover some really beautiful areas, but unfortunately, the climbing is a bit indifferent and you may have to jungle bash some 10ft ferns to escape the tops of the cliffs. Overall, the climbing is very good and there is plenty here to occupy ones interest; 'good - but not brilliant.'

❸ CAERBWDI BAY

This bay has two sets of slabs on its W side, both around 100ft, the more southernmost of these being Belly Buttress. BB is semi-tidal and an abseil rope is very useful for the descent to the sea washed platform at the bottom, and generally low grade routes. The more NE crag is Cathedral Slabs which has generally harder climbs.
Map: OL35 (Explorer) 764 242

STINGRAY E2 t-5c, Carreg-Y-Barcud; Oliver Forrest

BEYOND THE AZUMITH VS. Craig Caerfai: Jake Morgan

❹ CRAIG CAERFAI

A 130ft crag offering about 10 climbs Diff to E1 scattered quite evenly. The cliff base is easily approached but semi tidal.
Map: OL35 (Explorer) 762 240

❺ ST. NON'S BAY

Some walls and some slabs offer some nice climbing in this bay, about 30 routes up to 80 ft mainly Diffs and Severes. Non tidal and W facing.
Map: OL35 (Explorer) 753 242

❻ PORTH-Y-FFYNNON

The climbing to be found here is mainly on some 80ft slabs all of which are S facing and very accommodating. Grades range from Diff to HVS with most climbs except the hard ones being well protected. A good spot.
Map: OL35 (Explorer) 745 240

❼ PORTH-CLAIS*

A crag with about 20 routes to 70ft and all around the Severe standard, some harder and others easier. Access is made easier at low tide or with the use of an abseil rope at high tide. A very good crag.
Map: OL35 (Explorer) 743 238

❽ GREEN & PURPLE SLABS

Here lie some 100ft slabs offering a handful of lower grade routes for the taking. Non tidal and worth bringing an abseil rope.
Map: OL35 (Explorer) 724 248

❾ LLENRAC SLABS

Some nice slabs offering about 20 or so routes ranging from Diff to VS. All around 100ft and Non tidal. Often abseil is the easiest descent, bring a spare rope. A nice situation, near to the car park and W facing being semi sheltered by Ramsey Island.
Map: OL35 (Explorer) 720 255

❿ PENCARNAN SLABS

This area offers many good climbs mainly as slabs in the Diff to Severe range of about 80ft. Nearly all the routes are non tidal. A good area.
Map: OL35 (Explorer) 721 260

⓫ ST. DAVIDS HEAD

This applies to the cliffs right on the end of the W point. A small 50ft crag offering 10 or so routes, Diffs and Severes mainly. The rock is good even if the routes are not as spectacular as on the larger cliffs, and approach is made easily from the far W
Map: OL35 (Explorer) 722 278

⓬ PENMAEN COETAN

A small crag 80ft, offering some worth-while easy clims and a few VS's. West facing and on good rock this is a must.
Map: OL35 (Explorer) 724 248

⓭ CRAIG COETAN*

Bird restriction 1/2 - 31/7 An excellent crag, especialy for the low grade climber. About 20routes are below VS on this red slabby cliff. About 200ft high yet with a terrace running up it halfway to give an upper and lower tier. Good rock makes this crag very enjoyable.
Map: OL35 (Explorer) 724 282
Dir: 2.2m NW of St Davids. From the car park at Whitesands bay B 4583 take the coastal path N past the 2 bays and straight over to the cliffs past the burial chamber. The cliff easily seen from the path is recognised as a big slabby lump. Descent is made by scrambling down the gully Diff or abseil.

⑭ MUR CENHINEN*

Bird restriction 1/2 - 31/7 **A very good crag which is unseen from the land. Excellent rock. Most of the climbing here is VS-HVS with a few extremes. Being NW facing can be very chilly in the morning. The climbing becomes less well protected towards the S end of the crag, as the routes tend to get more difficult.**
Map: OL35 (Explorer) 725 283

⑮ CRAIG CARN PORTH LLONG

A large cliff offering routes up to 250ft in the middle grades, about 10 routes including some Diffs and Severes.
Map: OL35 (Explorer) 727 285

⑯ CRAIG HEBOG

A good crag with about 20 routes mainly in the Diff and Severe grades, with a few obvious VS's, 100-150ft. NW facing.
Map: OL35 (Explorer) 732 287

⑰ TRWYN LLWYD

This crag has some notable lines in the VS, HVS and E3 area. About 250ft and not tidal. Only a handful of routes though but well worth a visit. To the NE about 150 yds away there a handful of slab routes around the Severe standard, about 150ft. Indeed the coastline from here to the E head has many smaller crags, offering plenty in the way of Diffs and Severes, the most notable being Porth Llwch situated about 200 yds further on.
Map: OL35 (Explorer) 733 287

⑱ PENLLECHWEN

This crag of 80-180ft offers plenty of climbing in the Diff to VS grades. Not that good in the winter months since it is N facing and tends to get rather slippery.
Map: OL35 (Explorer) 741 291

⑲ CRAIG LLONG*

A very impressive cliff that is in two parts. The upper cliff leans dramatically out, and feels quite insecure. You're added weight won't make any difference, but that doesn't help to cure the nerves very much. The lower cliff is bulging and something out of sci-fi. Relies on insitu pegs that have all rusted through and are an embarrassment anyway - solo or be dammed. A candidate for stainless steel bolts, perhaps!!!
Map: OL35 (Explorer) 842 334

⑳ ABERCASTLE AREA

Bird restriction 1/2 - 31/7 **A nice area for the low grade climber, offering some good severes. Two cliffs Craig Ddu offering two VS climbs, 110ft and good; and the interesting headland of Ynysdeullyn, with two islands and a sea stack approachable at low tide. This offers about 15 climbs V Diff to VS, slabby routes.**
Map: OL35 (Explorer) 845 343

㉑ LLECHDAFAD

Bird restriction 1/2 - 31/7 **This steep crag of about 150ft offers about 16 routes VS up to E3 with over half being extreme. Not really affected by the tide because of a large platform beneath it. Most of the climbs can be viewed from the promontory to the S. West facing and often sunny, makes this a good spot. 500yds to the S of this crag is Carreg-Golchfa, a small 110ft promontory offering 3 routes of VDiff and Severe standard, slabby routes.**
Map: OL35 (Explorer) 880 358

㉒ PWLLDAWNAU

The cliffs here never reach higher than 200ft and the climbing tends to be around HVS or E3. A series of small bays just S of the headland of Penbwchdy gives several crags. The crags are impressive with Rainbow Zawn and Peoples Cliff being most noteworthy. Approach to most is by abseil from stakes already in place, but is rumoured that a full complement of friends are useful for belays.
Map: OL35 (Explorer) 878 371

CRAIG LLONG

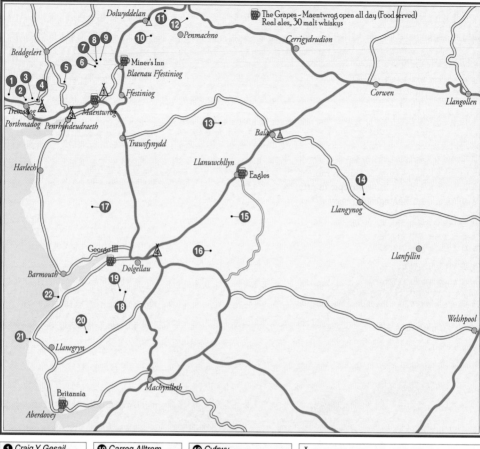

The Grapes – Maentwrog open all day (Food served)
Real ales,, 30 malt whiskys

❶ Craig Y Gesail	❿ Carreg Alltrem	⓳ Cyfrwy
❷ Craig Y Castell	⓫ Craig Rhiw Goch	⓴ Craig Yr Aderyn
❸ Craig Pant Ifan	⓬ The Tubes	㉑ Cae-Du
❹ Bwlch Y Moch	⓭ Simdde Ddu	㉒ Friog
❺ Carreg Hyll Drem	⓮ Craig Rhiwarth	
❻ Clogwyn Yr Oen	⓯ Gist Ddu	
❼ Craig Yr Wrysgan	⓰ Craig Cywarch	
❽ Upper Wrysgan	⓱ Rhinogs	
❾ Craig Y Clipiau	⓲ Craig Cau	

⛺ Llechrwd Farm, Maentwrog, LL41 4HF
Open Easter-Oct; 01766 590 240   proper site etc.
⛺ Eric Jones cafe, Bwlch Y Moch, Tremadoc
Open 1/1-31-12 Flat field, Loos, cafe & a shower!
⛺ Blaen Cefn Farm, Penrhyndeilldraeth, LL48 6NA
Open April-Oct   Tel: 01766 770 981
⛺ Dolgun Uchaf, nr Dolgellau, LL40 2AB Tel: 01341 422 269
Open 1/1-31-12, Lovely open field with full facilities.

TREMADOG
Text & bound
286 pages - B &W
A few colour photos
Pocket - 165 x 105mm
Pub-2000
by the Climbers Club
(Ferguson,Jones,Littlejohn)

A handy pocket guide to this area; just small
enough to carry on a climb. Basic text with
routes in list form; a few photo diagrams, but
terrible to find the starts of routes.

G-07a ⛺ 1 - 5, plus some in Snowdonia

MEIRIONNYDD
Text guidebook
512 pages - B &W
A few colour photos
Tome - 165 x 105mm
Pub-2000
by the Climbers Club

A massive piece of work
and a labour of love
which is difficult to find
fault with; a lot of book and a big catalogue of
routes. However, full of esoterica, short climbs,
and scrappy high E numbers.

G-07b ⛺ 6 - 20, plus ++++

LLEYN
Text - paperback

176 pages - B &W
A few colour photos
Pocket - 165 x 105mm
Pub-2002
by the Climbers Club
(Ferguson,Jones,
Littlejohn)

A handy list of routes to a very unknown area
with some useful access info and some excellent little diagrams. Appealing to new-wave
climbers.

G-07c ⛺ Lleyn Peninsular

For the record, the 53 latitude goes through Blaneau Ffestiniog, so we're treating anything between the 52nd & 53rd as mid Wales. We're also nicking some other areas, since if you base yourself in 'mid Wales,' then you will want to know about any good climbing within easy distance. The jewels are simply the cliffs of Tremadoc, where it always seems to be sunny and calm. So many climbers keep these cliffs as a last resort when the weather is awful in Snowdonia; but the climbing does warrant a special visit in itself. There are classic routes in every grade, and most are very well protected. There is a mixture of delicate and smooth slabs, overhanging sectors, and holdless grooves that will scold you calf muscles forever. It's a great place for those folk, going up through the grades of trad climbing. The Moelwyns have always been popular with first time climbers, it's a great place to experience the mountain environment, and start placing gear when the angle isn't too stiff. To the south, are the less frequented areas of the Aran hills, Rhinogs and Cadair Idris. These areas do offer some climbing, but anyone used to clean rock and easy access, will not be amused. They are high crags and demand excellent weather to enjoy anything at all. If it's that good weather, then maybe you should head off up to Cloggy anyway, and I'm not going to disagree with that. Climbing in mid Wales is more about getting away from everything, feeling totally remote and forgotten, maybe enjoying a complete epic in private. An area worth putting on the map, but knowing the weather will always keep it unspoilt, green, mossy, lichenous, damp, etc.

PINCUSHION E3 -t6a, Pant Ifan; Paul Cropper

CRAIG BWLCH Y MOCH Vector buttress

❶ CRAIG Y GESIAL*

Vol ⟨15⟩ 👟 Alt-110m | 70m | 7.2 | 50 | -- | ✳ | ⇜

Not as impressive as the other crags in the Tremadoc area but nevertheless good, sound rock and enjoyable to climb on except in mid summer when the midges really get going.
G07a; Map: 124 (Landranger) 545 411
Care in parking - do not block anything

❷ CRAIG Y CASTELL*

Vol ⟨15⟩ 👟 Alt-80m | 70m | 7.2 | 25 | Q-D | 60db | ⇜

This is the smallest of the three great cliffs at Tremadoc. The climbing is excellent and not to be missed.
G07a; Map: 124 (Landranger) 557 403
Park down at the town and not up the lane by the school.

Note: The cafe below, usually sells the local guidebook for Tremadoc plus a small selection of krabs, nuts, chalk etc.

❸ CRAIG PANT IFAN***

Vol ⟨15⟩ 👟 Alt-80m | 90m | 7.2 | 130 | Q-D | ⇜ | ☺

The other great cliff at tremadoc, not quite so popular sice it requires a 15 min walk, desperate exhaustion whew! After arriving at the crag and taking a breather it appears you are in the trees, you are, but anyway about 30ft up the routes sudden exposure is felt, making it a very enjoyable place to climb. The majority of routes here go up slabs, some smoother than others, and through overhangs yes, some tiny, others not so tiny.
G07a; Map: 124 (Landranger) 569 406

❹ CRAIG BWLCH Y MOCH***

Vol ⟨4⟩ 👟 Alt-20m | 70m | 7.2 | 135 | Q-D | 60db | ⇜

This is the finest crag in 'North Wales,' offering some of the most classic routes in the country. A long crag with several buttresses, mixed slabs and overhangs. The showpiece is the Vector Buttress, it overhangs so much it's going to fall down one day, a terrific loss - so I can only reccomend you do all the routes before it dissappears. They are all E1 upwards though, and include the classics Void E3. Cream E4, Sultans of Swing E4 and the famous Strawberries and Dream Topping E6. The VS climbs here don't give in easily. All routes are at least 2 pitch. Gets crowded here on rainy days in the mountains, the only other option being the pub, yes no option, hic; the Golden Fleece has always prooved popular in Tremadoc.
G07a; Map: 124 (Landranger) 577406

KENT/SUSSEX · DORSET · CORNWALL · DEVON · BRISTOL · SOUTH-WALES · MID-WALES · NORTH-WALES · LEICESTER · PEAKS · YORK-LANCS · CLEVELAND · KENDAL · LAKES · PENRITH · NEWCASTLE

CRAIG Y CLIPAU, t-4b solo; Jingo Jones (photo; Gary Morgan)

Carret Hyll Drem bouldering wall

⑦ CRAIG YR WRYSGAN*

A very nice cliff in an excellent position, and is less used than it's neighbour. It seems a grim haul up, but the walk is worth it. Gear is a bit sparse, but the rock texture is very nice, with small pockets often coming to the rescue.
G07b; Map: 115 (Landranger) 679 454

⑧ WRYSGAN UPPER TIER

Above the lower cliff and through the mine tunnel, is a lovely terrace that has some walls at the back, only seen from the top of the Wrysgan main cliff. A perfect place for a quiet pic-nic and some short, good routes on nice clean rock.
G07b; Map: 115 (Landranger) 676 455

⑨ CRAIG Y CLIPIAU**

Location, location, location; this cliff certainly has it. Any route up here on this exposed buttress is excellent and well worth the walk up. Unfortunately, the rock does not lend itself to much natural protection and you either stick to the easier lines, or go on a suicide mission. Does need very good weather, but a gem in such situations.
G07b; Map: 115 (Landranger) 683 458

⑤ CARREG HYLL DREM*

A very impressive crag situated right above the road. A crag of unrelenting steepness, with the bottom half staying completely dry in wet weather. Not a crag for weak arms, but a definite must for the super spurter. At the bottom right, there is a small bouldering wall that seems to stay dry in all weather. Popular and with hundreds of variation problems. A bit grotty in the rain, but lovely on a winters sunny morning.
G07a; Map: 124 (Landranger) 614 432

⑥ CLOGWYN YR OEN*

This is the farthest crag up the road from Tan Y Grisau, situated above the giant boulder by the road on the right. Slabby and superb for beginners. Popular with groups and deservedly so. Bouldering below can have a marshy landing, so bring a waterproof pad.
G07b; Map: 115 (Landranger) 675 450

Clogwyn yr Oen: Bouldering block

WHITE STREAK Hard Severe, Craig Yr Wrysgan; Gary Morgan

FRATRICIDE WALL HVS 5-5a, Carreg Alltrem, Lynn Rogers

⑩ CARREG ALLTREM

Vol 16 · Alt-350m 50m 7.6 | 20 -- ❄ Zzz

There is no quick way here from Llanberis, hence it remains one of the most beautiful spots in Snowdonia. There routes up to 150ft, but worth splitting pitches because the belay tress are set well back. Routes. The rock is excellent and runs to very sensible sized holds.
G07b; Map: 115 (Landranger) 739 507

⑪ CRAIG RHIW GOCH

Vol 5 · Alt-200m 30m 7.6 | 8 -- ❄ Zzz

A small crag situated above the Lledr River, excellent for trout fishing, whatever you do don't disturb the fish.
G07b; Map: 115 (Landranger) 767 541

⑫ THE TUBES *

Vol 10 · Alt-120m 8m 7.2 | -- 50 ❄

The new spot to go bouldering - in a dry spell that is. Esoteric spot in the hidden depths of the river Conwy, just upstream from the scenic fairy glen. A touch on the high side for some, a top rope can be handy here. Worth keeping quiet about.
G07b; Map: 116 (Landranger) 804 538

⑬ SIMDDE DDU

This is the principle crag in the Arennig range of mountains. South-east facing, with sections of clean walls about 15m high. 30 odd routes E2 upwards. High up at 750 metres.
G07b; Map: 125 (Landranger) 840 380

⑭ CRAIG RHIWARTH

A selection of esoterica crags above the tiny hamlet of Llangynog. Lots of small and scrappy cliffs offering some broken routes (20m) around E5!
G07b; Map: 125 (Landranger) Various

⑮ GIST DDU

The northern ridge of the Aran hills, is home to this cliff. East facing and high up, needs good weather. A substantial buttress, 100m high and giving around 30 routes across the grades. Fine position, but needs an exceptionally dry summer.
G07b; Map: 125 (Landranger) 873 255

⑯ CRAIG CYWARCH

A series of rambling cliffs over 120m ath the very top of the Arans. Stacks of routes, stacks of moss and vegetation too. Will come of age with global warming, watch this space.
G07b; Map: 125 (Landranger) 845 190

⑰ RHINOGS

This is about as esoteric as it gets. Superb 6m routes after walking for miles. For the enthusiast and botanist. Wellies for walk-ins are handy.

⑱ CRAIG CAU

A large and rambling 300m crag. Although there is some very good climbing to be found here, much scrambling over poor territory has to be acomplished as well. There are about 30 established routes from Diff to E3, friends are useful as is a trowel for digging out belays.
G07b; Map: 124 (Landranger) 712 122

⑲ CYFRWY

The largest stretch of crags in the area, about 800 yds long, and offering about 50 climbs, 50-130m, of all standards and very different quality. The rock often needs careful attention and one never feels really at home here. A high crag at 2000ft, not the place for a winter picnic.
Map: 124 (Landranger) 703 135

㉒ FRIOG

Some bolted routes on the railway embankment, and arches that make good bouldering, sea boulders too.

⑳ CRAIG YR ADERYN

BIRD ROCK - *Bird restriction 1/3 - 31/7, left side on the E face.* Quite a good outcrop offering three parts on which to dice with death. The Bastion is the lowest and most formidable crag about 50m high with extremes on it and HVS and VS routes up the side, and easier routes to the R. About 30 routes in all, NW facing. There is also a more sheltered Far Southern Buttress around to the R of The Bastion with a handful of 130ft Severes on it.
G07b; Map: 124 (Landranger) 643 069

㉑ CAE-DU

A small amount of bouldering on the sea boulders that is tidal. Good fun in an evening and only a short walk. *G08a;*

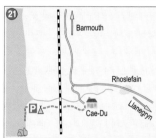

KENT/SUSSEX | DORSET | CORNWALL | DEVON | BRISTOL | SOUTH-WALES | MID-WALES | NORTH-WALES | LEICSETER | PEAKS | YORK-LANCS | CLEVELAND | KENDAL | LAKES | PENRITH | NEWCASTLE

CAE-DU Seaside bouldering and fun, a nice quiet spot and easy walk in.

KENT/SUSSEX

DORSET

CORNWALL

DEVON

BRISTOL

SOUTH-WALES

MID-WALES

NORTH-WALES

LEICESTER

PEAKS

YORK-LANCS

CLEVELAND

KENDAL

LAKES

PENRITH

NEWCASTLE

1 Porth Ysgo
2 Cilan
3 Ty'n Tywyn Quarries
4 Shale City
5 Trwyn Y Gorlech
6 Pen Y Cil

1 PORTH YSGO *

This is the place that everyone has been talking about in bouldering for the past few years. It demands a required taste, and will certainly suit those fired up on adrenalin looking for bad landings. A lot of good quality boulders down at sea level on a tidal beach. Quite a tidal range here too, so you benefit hugely from low tide. Peaceful and scenic, nothing grand but just nice. You get very good weather here in the main. The big boulders are jumbled about on top of lots of small boulders. A good warm up is spent leveling out some of the landing areas, but watch your back. Bring plenty of pads here. A great place for a day out.
G08a; Map: 123 (Landranger) 212 264

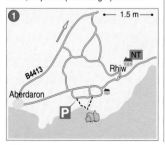

2 CILAN HEAD

Bird restriction 1/2 - 31/7 Not every area has a bird restriction, but the majority of areas do. Big cliffs up to 100m, and a very serious place to climb. Mainly abseil access and with a certain amount of uncertain rock. Varies between 7.9 and 8.5 so don't get your hopes up. An area that will suit climbers looking for something completely different and out of the ordinary! You find grades here like E2 t-5a, and E3 t-5b; so if it's serious climbing you want, play roulette today.
Map: 123 (Landranger) 292 234

3 TY'N TYWYN QUARRIES

A series of south facing quaries on the coast with some climbing in, and are not tidal. Only quarry 4 has a bird restriction. 30-70m routes, VS up to E4.
Map: 123 (Landranger) 329 304

4 SHALE CITY

The name of this cliff says it all, 60m of tottering!
Map: 123 (Landranger) 364 474

5 TRWYN Y GORLECH

Some large quarries by the sea offering quite a few routes with some lower grade routes and Severes - HVS, up to 250m high. Very broken.
Map: 123 (Landranger) 355 457

6 PEN Y CIL & PARWYD

These two crags are of instable character and worth a visit if you wish to get away from it all, there on the southernmost tip of the peninsula and quite remote. An epic here would leave you stranded perhaps for months. Pen Y Cil is about 70m and Parwyd around 150m, big, very loose, and not surprisingly serious!
Map: 123 (Landranger) 158 240

KENT/SUSSEX
DORSET
CORNWALL
DEVON
BRISTOL
SOUTH-WALES
MID-WALES
NORTH-WALES
LEICSETER
PEAKS
YORK-LANCS
CLEVELAND
KENDAL
LAKES
PENRITH
NEWCASTLE

Managing to squeeze in a few more easy problems before the tide comes in at Porth Ysgo; Jingo climbing

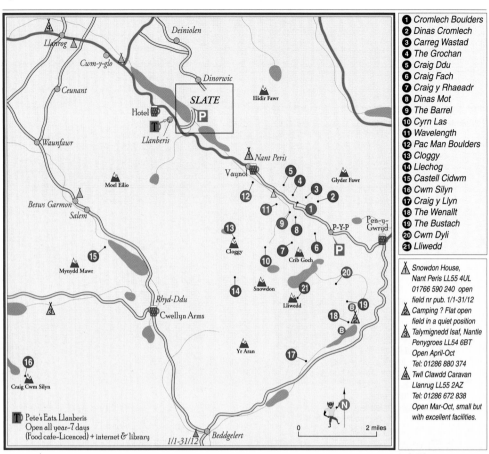

● Cromlech Boulders
● Dinas Cromlech
● Carreg Wastad
● The Grochan
● Craig Ddu
● Craig Fach
● Craig y Rhaeadr
● Dinas Mot
● The Barrel
● Cyrn Las
● Wavelength
● Pac Man Boulders
● Cloggy
● Llechog
● Castell Cidwm
● Cwm Silyn
● Craig y Llyn
● The Wenallt
● The Bustach
● Cwm Dyli
● Lliwedd

Snowdon House, Nant Peris LL55 4UL 01766 590 240 open field nr pub. 1/1-31/12
Camping ? Flat open field in a quiet position
Talymignedd Isaf, Nantle Penygroes LL54 6BT Open April-Oct Tel: 01286 880 374
Twll Clawdd Caravan Llanrug LL55 2AZ Tel: 01286 672 838 Open Mar-Oct, small but with excellent facilities.

Pete's Eats. Llanberis
Open all year-7 days
(Food cafe-Licenced) + internet & library

This area is probably the best trad climbing area in the country. There aren't that many routes surprisingly, but there is a massive quality in the depth of climbing, with excellent routes of very pure lines up the cliffs. The crags are mountain cliffs and stay wet in anything other than an excellent sunny day. Fortunately, there are a lot of climbs in the easy grades, more than you would think for the most challenging of areas. The north side of 'The Pass' gets lovely sunshine, and is a heavenly place to be, the south side is reserved for heatwaves. Cloggy, high on Snowdon is majestic, if somewhat sombre and introspective. Lliwedd is greasy, but has 100 years of stiff upper lip tradition. Diversity is the name of the game here, it's simply a tremendous location for every level of climber.

NORTH WALES BOULDERING
Topo & s/bound
304 pages - B &W
Lots of b&w photos
A5, plus pagemarkers
Pub-2004
Northern Soul
by Simon Panton

A guidebook that brings bouldering in the area up to date. Very graphic and with all the latest problems. Also in Welsh, so you can learn the local lingo - easy problem, eh!

G-08a   Lots of areas, masses of problems

LLANBERIS
Text - s/route book
306 pages - B &W
A few colour photos
Tome - 165 x 105mm
Pub-1987
by the Climbers Club

A BIG book that has lots of information and lots of routes. Not the size you want to take climbing, but handy to look at after the end of the day. A good read but newcomers may find it confusing, errors too.

G-08b   Llanberis Pass and slate

CLOGWYN D'UR ARDDU
Text - s/bound, single cliff route book
Pub-2004
by the Climbers Club

G-08c

LLIWEDD
Text - s/bound, single cliff route book
Pub-?
by the Climbers Club

G-08d

TREMADOC
Text - s/bound, area route book
Pub- 2000
by the Climbers Club

G-07a

Side tabs: KENT/SUSSEX | DORSET | CORNWALL | DEVON | BRISTOL | SOUTH-WALES | MID-WALES | NORTH-WALES | LEICESTER | PEAKS | YORK-LANCS | CLEVELAND | KENDAL | LAKES | PENRITH | NEWCASTLE

❶ CROMLECH BOULDERS*

Vol	⓪	🥾	Alt-130m	4m	7.2
▨▨▨▨		--	100	🔨	🖐

When the corner fell out of the Cromlech, it fortunately landed right next to the road in anticipation of future boulderers who didn't like walking. Som giant blocks that are great fun to boulder and climb all over. A lot of holds on them so the problems are all eliminates that you make up. In the evening the trafiic has gone and the sun sets on them till 7pm. A lovely spot and certainly the place to catch up with a few friends.

G08a; Map: 115 (Landranger) 629 565

❷ DINAS CROMLECH***

Vol	㉚	🥾	Alt-400m	100m	7.4
▨▨▨▨		55	--	❋	🍃

A super impressive cliff that looks like a open book cast in stone, set up on the side of the pass. Both open walls give incredible 150ft routes of all standards E1 upwards. The big corner itself named Cenotaph Corner by Joe Brown, one of the finest routes in Britain with the crux at the top, so guidebook needed. There are some easier routes too for the diff and severe leaders. The whole cliff gets busy and deservedly so.

G08b; Map: 115 (Landranger) 629 569

❸ CARREG WASTAD

Vol	⑳	🥾	Alt-180m	90m	7.8
▨▨▨▨		30	--	🍃	👻

This has never been a favourite cliff of mine since the rock is generally on the loose side, and the protection pos- siblilties are never great. A popular cliff all the same with a couple of fabulous routes. The severe - Crackstone Rib, being a lovely climb with stunning exposure for the grade.

G08b; Map: 115 (Landranger) 625 571

Petes Eats, Llanberis

INTENSE CONCENTRATION

RELAXED FLOW

CROMLECH BOULDERS; The great Johnny Dawes and young Jude Spancken enjoying a late evenings bouldering

KENT/SUSSEX · DORSET · CORNWALL · DEVON · BRISTOL · SOUTH-WALES · MID-WALES · NORTH-WALES · LEICESTER · PEAKS · YORK-LANCS · CLEVELAND · KENDAL · LAKES · PENRITH · NEWCASTLE

❹ THE GROCHAN**

Clogwyn Y Grochan is the undisputed steep and awkward crag of the Pass. All the holds face the wrong way and you certainly have to engange brain as you try and climb up this cliff. A handy stroll from the car and perfect for a good evening, making this a popular cliff. The rock is a funny texture of rhyolite and tends to be a bit slippery and greasy sometimes. A lot of very good climbs that can end up as nice multi-pitch epics for the timid leader. Ticking an HVS on this crag is a good landmark for your improvement.
G08a; Map: 115 (Landranger) 622 573

❺ CRAIG DDU

A crag that is lost to the Welsh weather, and is nearly always running in water, black slime and gunge. Some guide-book writers seem to like this spot, you may like it also too - I don't however. There are some pleasant lines and easier slab climbs, but the rock tends to be quite smooth and not brilliant for finding gear placements. Maybe global warming will change things; so check it out when you see palm trees sprouting up in Nant Peris.
G07b; Map: 115 (Landranger) 618 574

❻ CRAIG FACH

A small crag that is high up near the top of the pass. Some good routes and often very quiet. The cliff has a nice little left hand section which is very suitable for beginners and up to 20m high.
G08b; Map: 115 (Landranger) 634 554

❼ CRAIG Y RHAEADR

An out of the way cliff, halfway up the side of the mountain. A very wet and mostly horrible crag, fit only for frog-men. When it dries out there is some very enjoyable climbing to be had. It is said to have an unusual atmosphere! 30 routes at all grades up to 120m
G08b; Map: 115 (Landranger) 622 562

LLANBERIS PASS

❽ DINAS MOT*

Vol	15		Alt-190m	130m	7.4

	85	--		

If this cliff were in Pembroke - wow, it would be superb. Unfortunately it's not, and it faces north, hence gives me so many memories of dark and dank days in the past, freezing on belays. Multi-pitch climbing and lots of hanging around, so you need to wrap up well and come here in summer. If it's good weather and hot, then the whole cliff jumps up to 3 stars since there are some very good routes indeed, and across the whole spectrum. The front of the cliff is like a giant nose and contains some easy slab routes - which tend to be a bit run out and feel very soft if you are crusing well. To the right of the cliff is the comanding Plexus buttress, very steep and black - often seeps like hell. A mixed attraction.
G08b; Map: 115 (Landranger) 627 563

❾ THE BARREL

Vol	6		Alt-140m	3m	7.0

	--	10		Pump

A small and long barrel shaped boulder just up the hill opposite the boulders in the Pass. Technical traversing for the pump, plus some good straight up problems on crimps. A lovely setting and cool for some good bouldering. Small and nice.
G08a; Map: 115 (Landranger) 619 569

❿ CYRN LAS**

Vol	70		Alt-700m	150m	7.6

	33	--		

A fantastic high mountain crag. Over 400ft routes of absolute quality and distinction make this a must for everyone. Routes of all standards, Nearly all classics, also a very cool spot. Hot summer only, worth getting up early to slog up.
G08b; Map: 115 (Landranger) 614 561

⓫ WAVELENGTH**

Vol	10		Alt-150m	4m	7.0

	--	90		Sloper

A very good bouldering area on superb quality welsh rock. The centrepiece is the wavelength boulder, classic in size and shape and giving 12 very good problems. A lot of good boulders scattered all over the hillside with all types of problem.
G08a; Map: 115 (Landranger) 623 566
Dir: Hillside above Ynys Etws, due w of Cromlech boulders.

⓬ PAC MAN BOULDERS

A couple of boulders up on the hillside that offer some nice but short problems. V5,6,6,10,12. Only a 12 mins walk up from Nant Peris
G08a; Map: 115 (Landranger) 608 578
Dir: From Nant Peris, cross the river to the S, then follow path up to obvious boulders high up on a lumpy hill.

THE MINIMUM t-6c / V7, The Barrel; James McHaffie

KENT/SUSSEX | DORSET | CORNWALL | DEVON | BRISTOL | SOUTH-WALES | MID-WALES | NORTH-WALES | LEICSETER | PEAKS | YORK-LANCS | CLEVELAND | KENDAL | LAKES | PENRITH | NEWCASTLE

THE AXE E4 t-6a, Cloggy; Martin Crook

13 *CLOGWYN DU'R ARDDU* *

Very much an old school style crag of big multi-pitch climbs that are dark and dank. To some this is the climbing mecca, however for most of the year it is cold, wet, windy and thoroughly unpleasant. Most other sensible people view it simply; too far from the car park to find out that the routes are wet and seeping. The lower grade routes are very good and is well worth a visit if your going at VS of HVS. There are plenty of E1-2 yet very few E3-4, the hard routes on the big walls and slabs are often unprotected, and abseil inspection is advisable. If you get up really early in the morning you can catch it in sunshine, but I mean early!
G08c; Map: 115 (Landranger) 600 550

14 LLECHOG

This cliff in places is 120m high and commands a fine view. The 15 or so routes, all in the Diff, Severe standard with a few exceptions, are broken in character, but do offer some worthwhile pitches on good sound rock. At 2500ft and NE facing neccesitates some fine weather or very strong character.
G08?; Map: 115 (Landranger) 597 537

15 CASTELL CIDWM

A very awe inspiring cliff, with about 15 routes of VS upwards with reasonable protection. The cliff seems a lot biggget especially when encountering the steeep right hand section, mainly E3 to E6. SE facing with a very picturesque outlook.
G08?; Map: 115 (Landranger) 550 554
Access issue - use long way in that comes from the bottom of the lake on the western side.

OCTO HVS, Cloggy; Dave Lawson   CASTELL CIDWM

KENT/SUSSEX · DORSET · CORNWALL · DEVON · BRISTOL · SOUTH-WALES · MID-WALES · NORTH-WALES · LEICSETER · PEAKS · YORK-LANCS · CLEVELAND · KENDAL · LAKES · PENRITH · NEWCASTLE

JABBERWOCKY E2 †- 5c. Cwm Silyn: Paul Williams

⑯ CWM SILYN*

Vol	45	🥾	Alt-500m	140m	7.4
			40	--	☀	⇚

A superb area offering so much climbing in the lower grades. There are
climbs also around E1-3 but tend to
be more frightening than particulary
difficult. There are several crags all of
which though are dwarfed in quality
by CRAIG YR OGOF. The climbs on
the slabs have sparse protection but
nowhere are unduly difficult. A nice lake
for swimming in below the cliff.
G08?; Map: 115 (Landranger) 518 502

⑰ CRAIG Y LLYN

Vol	15	👟	Alt-80m	70m	7.5
			24	--	☀	Zzz

Not a crag if your going badly, the
protection here is not as forthcoming,
as one often wishes! Protection aside
its a very good crag. In the main expect
the harder routes to be more satisfying.
Quite low, fairly good on winter mornings. The crag if damp is not a sensible
place to climb.
G07a; Map: 115 (Landranger) 619 502

⑱ CLOGWYN Y WENALLT*

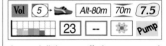

Vol	5	👟	Alt-80m	70m	7.5
			23	--	☀	Pump

A superb little crag offering some excellent VS-HVS climbs, with famous routes
such as Oxo and Bovine. 15 routes in
total VS to E5 on good, steep and well
protected rock.
G07a; Map: 115 (Landranger) 647 528

CLOGWYN Y WENALLT

⑲ CLOGWYN Y BUSTACH

Vol	⑯		Alt-170m	70m	7.7
		23	5		

A crag always remembered if only for
the usual guidebook quoted description
to the classic Diff Lockwoods Chimney,
"It is customary to do this climb by
moonlight in the worst posssible
conditions; the climbing party should
preferably be large and of large men."
The climbing is not brilliant but the 15
or so routes of Diff to HVS offer typical
mountain climbing experiences.
There are some boulder problems on
the blocks scattered below the crag
-G8a.
G07a; Map: 115 (Landranger) 651 535

⑳ CWM DYLI*

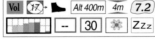

Vol	⑰		Alt 400m	4m	7.2
		--	30		Zzz

Bouldering in the middle of nowhere.
A group of boulders that offers a good
range of problems in a lovely location.
Handy for a lot of people since there
are quite a few problems here in the
lower grades. Rough rock and squidgy
landings, waterproof pad essential.
G08a; Map: 115 (Landranger) 644 545
Dir: Park at Pen-y-Pass (usually full up
in the morning). Take the lower miners
track for about 600 yds, the boulders
are over to the L just beyond the pipeline. If you get to Llyn Teyen, you have
gone too far. Midge territory.

㉑ LLIWEDD *

Vol	⑥⓪		Alt-600m	300m	7.7
		100	--		Zzz

This is the traditional crag of all Wales,
indeed the first ever authorative Welsh
guide book to be produced was of this
very crag in 1909. It is not a hard mans
crag at all, even so don't think you're
going to simply stroll up the routes.
About 300m from bottom to top and
offering many 10 pitch climbs. There
are terraces on which to crack open
a good bottle of Bordeaux and have a
jolly good lunch. So much so, that an
outing on any day other than a real
scorcher, is simply quite unpleasant.
The rock can get very greasy which
can see you dissappearing downwards
into the gloom from which you
came. Diff leaders could well find themselves in deep water, Severe standard
is best for the exploraton if this cliff.
G08d; Map: 115 (Landranger) 623 534

KENT/SUSSEX · DORSET · CORNWALL · DEVON · BRISTOL · SOUTH-WALES · MID-WALES · NORTH-WALES · LEICSETER · PEAKS · YORK-LANCS · CLEVELAND · KENDAL · LAKES · PENRITH · NEWCASTLE

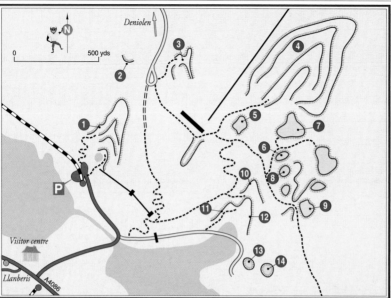

1 Vivian Quarry
2 Blast Shelter Crag
3 Bus Stop Quarry
4 Australia
5 Dali's Hole
6 Serengeti
7 California Wall
8 Never Never Land
9 Twll Mawr
10 Colossus Wall
11 Rainbow Slab
12 Rainbow Walls
13 Trango Tower
14 Peppermint Tower

HB

NORTH WALES SLATE
Text & topo book
glue/bound,
single cliff route book
Pub locally
Jones

G-08e

1 VIVIAN QUARRY*

Please no climbing above the tourist footpath and park in the car park. A popular area in the quarries with easy access, but now unpopular with expensive pay parking. Many classic lines of all difficulties. About 70 routes 80-150ft E1 to E7, the classics tending to be in the harder grades. Dries very quickly, also close for a sprint to the car in the unlikely event of rain.
G08b,e Map: 115 (Landranger) 587 605

2 BLASH SHELTER CRAG

A small 20m slab in small bay opposite The Rippled Slab offeringan E1 and a VS. Nothing stunning.
G08b,e Map: 115 (Landranger) 590 611

3 BUS STOP QUARRY

This quarry contains 2 areas; Dinorwic Needles about 80ft with about 10 routes around HVS,E2,E5 and The Rippled Slab, a fantastic 35m slab offering a handful of hardish routes with interesting run outs.
G08b,e Map: 115 (Landranger) 592 612

4 AUSTRALIA

This area consists of several walls and areas; Looning The Tube Area, Railtrack Slab, The Rognon, Gorbals Level and Skyline Buttress Level. All are around 20-30m and offer a handful of truly unmemorable climbs. The climbs are mostly around E3 except for the

Skline which has easier climbs on it.
G08b,e Map: 115 (Landranger) 598 610

5 DALI'S HOLE AREA

Beleive it or not, a surreal hole amidst the creative world of quarrymen. About 25 routes in the E1 to E4 std. 20m
G08b,e Map: 115 (Landranger) 595 606

6 SERENGETI*

Mostly 70ft climbs, a right mixture from VS to E7. Areas known as Peter Pan Wall; Seamstress Slab with The Medium and Windows of Perception, difficult climbs; Yellow wall with Loved by a Sneer, quite difficult and rumoured to have imaginary protection; and Heaven Walls, a larger 50m crag with exposure.
G08b,e Map: 115 (Landranger) 596 604

7 CALIFORNIA WALL*

A great area, not the best however but offering about 4 classics in the E5 grade. 100-200ft Wall offering itself mainly to 6a and 6b moves, Central Sadness E5 being the classic taking a line just L of centre, split by a bolt belay.
G08b,e Map: 115 (Landranger) 596 605

8 NEVER NEVER LAND

About 15 routes of all difficulties VS to E7, The route Never Never Land E5 6a being the classic, exciting as well, 50m.
G08b,e Map: 115 (Landranger) 596 604

9 TWLL MAWR**

What a crag, this quarry is definitely worth a visit. The West Wall has some of the most amazing routes in Llanberis if not the universe. The Quarryman, 300ft of E8 offers a challenge to anyone fully conversant in the powers of levitation. Pitches of 6c,6b,7a and 7b make chances of an on sight cruise of this route somewhat optimistic. The North Wall of the quarry offers some 700ft routes. of VS,E1 and E3.
G08b,e Map: 115 (Landranger) 587 605

10 COLOSSUS WALL*

A magnificent wall 50m, offering classic routes E3 to E5, not to be missed, and because of the bolt protection very popular. The very popular route Colossus E3 5c is probably the safest route in the quarries with more bolts than holds.
G08b,e Map: 115 (Landranger) 593 602

11 RAINBOW SLAB & WALL**

The best looking slab in the area offering about 15 routes in the more interesting and exciting grades. Abseil inspection thoroughly advised, with the exception of complete headcases.
G08b,e Map: 115 (Landranger) 593 601

13 TRANGO & PEPPER TOWER

Some small towers have been climbed here in the past but is banned, no great loss.

KENT/SUSSEX DORSET CORNWALL DEVON BRISTOL SOUTH-WALES MID-WALES NORTH-WALES LEICESTER PEAKS YORK-LANCS CLEVELAND KENDAL LAKES PENRITH NEWCASTLE

COMES THE DERVISH E3 - Historic photo when it was E5 t-6a (over time, the crack has widened), Vivian Quarry; Kev Reynolds

www.berghaus.com

Thomas and Alexander Huber climbing in Berchtesgaden, Germany

Photographer: Marcus Maidel

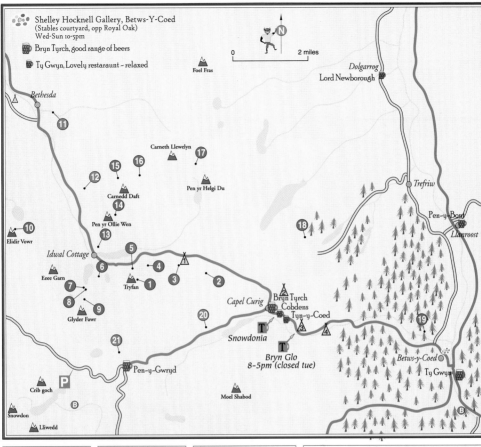

Shelley Hocknell Gallery, Betws-Y-Coed
(Stables courtyard, opp Royal Oak)
Wed-Sun 10-5pm

Bryn Tyrch, good range of beers

Ty Gwyn, Lovely restaraunt – relaxed

0 — 2 miles

❶ Tryfan East Face	❿ Pillar of Elidir
❷ Gallt Yr Ogof	⓫ Caseg Bethesda
❸ Willy's Farm	⓬ Sheep Pen Bloch
❹ Little Tryfan	⓭ Braich Ty Du
❺ Milestone Buttress	⓮ Craig Lloer
❻ Gribin Facet	⓯ Llech Du
❼ Idwal Slabs	⓰ Black Ladders
❽ Suicide Wall	⓱ Craig Yr Ysfa
❾ Glyder Fawr Main	⓲ Crafnant Eryr

⓳ Clogwyn Cyrau	
⓴ RAC Boulders	
㉑ Mallory Boulder	
㉒	

△ Gwern Gof Isaf (Willy's Farm), Capel 3miles, LL24 0EU
Open all yr: 01690 720 276   tilting field, wild, bunkhouse.
△ Bryn Tyrch Farm, Capel Curig centre, LL24
Open all yr: 01690 720 414   showers etc, bunkhouse
△ Bryn Glo Cafe camping, Capel Curig LL24 0DT
Open all yr; Tel: 01690 720 215 small space for some tents
△ Dolgam Camping, Capel Curig LL24 0DS
Open all yr; Tel: 01690 720 228 Large open field with
basic facilities - plus b&b.

OGWEN AND CARNEDDAU

Text - s/route books
212 & 206 pages - B & W
A few colour photos
Pocket - 165 x 105mm
Pub-1993
by the Climbers Club
Two area route books
sold together but sepa-
rate volumes, hefty. Lots
of good info, but still a lot of esoterica; you buy
the Ogwen and get the other for free. Photos
do not do the area any favours.

G-08f △ Trad cliffs in this area

Ogwen valley is a wild place for at least 300 days a year. If you are lucky, then you will manage to arrive here and go climbing on one of the 65 other days. Then it can be beautiful since the hills here are as close as you get to mountains in Wales. Tryfan always is inspiring with its wonderful east face, covered in climbs that just about anyone should be able to get up. There are plenty of classic trad crags only a short distance from the car, but the finesse of this region is the far away crags that remain quiet and calm. If you do get a good spell of weather, then certainly look up some of the distant high cliffs, they can offer excellent climbing. Getting the timing right is also essential, Glyder Fach and the Milestone in the afternoon light, Craig-yr-Ysfa in the clear morning sunshine, it makes all the difference. The harder climbs here tend to be dangerous, why risk it.

KENT/SUSSEX | DORSET | CORNWALL | DEVON | BRISTOL | SOUTH-WALES | MID-WALES | NORTH-WALES | LEICSETER | PEAKS | YORK-LANCS | CLEVELAND | KENDAL | LAKES | PENRITH | NEWCASTLE

DIRECT ROUTE, desperately difficult, Milestone Buttress; Jingo solo, photo Luc Percival

KENT/SUSSEX
DORSET
CORNWALL
DEVON
BRISTOL
SOUTH-WALES
MID-WALES
NORTH-WALES
LEICESTER
PEAKS
YORK-LANCS
CLEVELAND
KENDAL
LAKES
PENRITH
NEWCASTLE

OH YEAH V5 (f-6b) t-6b; Willy's Farm; Ian Hill

❶ TRYFAN EAST FACE**

Vol	60		Alt-700m	200m	7.5
		50	--	☀	≼

The East Face of Tryfan is one of the biggest and best cliffs for that real mountaineering challenge. The routes start from halfway up the face and reach 200m to the summit. Only artificial lines exceed VS in difficulty and mostly one can climb below Severe with tactful route finding. There are many Snowdonias classics on the cliff and on a good summers day the route tickers will be out in force. About 50 routes in total. The West face offers climbing of a more broken character mainly diffs in standard.
G08f; Map: 115 (Landranger) 664 594

❷ GALLT YR OGOF

Vol	18		Alt-500m	70m	7.5
		30	--	☀	≼

A good crag for beginners offering about 30 routes below E1. Not being far from the road yet reasonably unpopular are the two best features of this crag.
G08f; Map: 115 (Landranger) 693 595

❸ WILLY'S FARM - CASEG FRAITH

Vol	2		Alt-340m	5m	7.0
		10	15	☀	Sloper

A group of small cliffs that are great for beginners on routes and bouldering. Lovely rock and excellent friction and really close to the car at the campsite. Tucked away down a bit lower are a couple of boulders with some excellent problems, nothing too hard but good quality in a lovely setting.
G08f; Map: 115 (Landranger) 684 600
Park at the camping for a small fee, follow a track WSW past the hut to the boulders.

❹ LITTLE TRYFAN*

Vol	15		Alt-400m	70m	7.1
		20	--	☀	

Some great slabs for beginners to practice on. About 200ft offering about 20 routes of easy grades, but allowing for more difficult eliminates. Can get busy with teaching groups.
G08f; Map: 115 (Landranger) 672 601

❺ MILESTONE BUTTRESS*

Vol	1		Alt-350m	120m	7.5
		30	20		≼

A very good crag for the lower grades and not that far from the road; always takes longer than you think too. The rock is very clean as are the routes, very well worn and polished. Can get crowded with very slow moving parties. On the screes below there are some good boulders but you definitely want a guidebook. Landing are not so good.
G08a & f; Map: 115 (Landranger) 663 601

❻ GRIBIN FACET*

Vol	17		Alt-500m	0m	7.5
		60	--		≼

A gem of a little crag offering a very good introduction to the harder severes for the Severe leader. Lots of holds generally when you need them, but certainly a lot steeper than either the milestone or Idwal slabs. A lovely position. (Cloggy Tarw)
G08f; Map: 115 (Landranger) 650 596

ORDINARY ROUTE - Diff, Idwal Slabs in flood; Billy Bollweavil (by popular request)

⑦ *IDWAL SLABS****

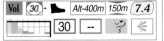

| Vol | 30 | | Alt-400m | 150m | 7.4 |

| 30 | -- | | |

The largest concentration of routes in the area. Slab routes of varing degree? This crag is good but suffers from terrible overcrowding, especially with group from centres, so much that I can reccomend any other crag in the area. However the attraction of such fine routes will attract everyone at some stage. The crag is a combination of the main slabs, with about 6 classic Diff, Severe lines; To the R is Holly Tree Wall with some fine middle grade routes. Above the main slabs there are continuation walls with some very good middle grade routes, even so a Diff route can always be taken to the very top of the cliff. About 60 routes in total offering fun for all the family. By continuing on up Glyder Fawr Upper Cliff is reached with its 20 or so routes 300ft in all grades. An expedition to the summit from the bottom of the slabs is a great mountain day.
G08f; Map: 115 (Landranger) 645 591

⑧ *SUICIDE WALL**

| Vol | 30 | | Alt-400m | 60m | 7.5 |

| 20 | -- | CRIMP | |

This is the eastern section of the Idwal Slabs, where they are anything but slabs. Vertical rock that gives very little protection and substantial rocky ground to fall on. A well named cliff that has certainly mashed up a few leaders in the past and left them in a horrible state for the rest of their lives. Good luck.
G08f; Map: 115 (Landranger) 645 591

Somebody may suggest that you have a wonderful days climbing at a place called the Devil's Kitchen, Cwm Idwal. They will promise you a deeper soul and character development - use your judgement wisely, it's the most ghastly climbing spot on the planet.

SHEEP PEN BLOCH

⑨ *GLYDER FAWR MAIN CLIFF***

| Vol | 70 | | Alt-700m | 100m | 7.6 |

| 45 | -- | | |

A real mountain crag, perhaps offering the best selection of routes below E1 in the area. About 40 to 50 routes on good rock which dry quickly after rain, and is pretty essential here. The rock is never too steep but always manages to tire the arms sufficiently during a days cragging. The situation is one of the best in Wales since you get plenty of sun! in the afternoon and it is often lovely and quiet. A very good alternative to the slabs if the weather is looking good for the day.
G08f; Map: 115 (Landranger) 656 586

⑩ *PILLAR OF ELIDIR*

| Vol | 120 | | Alt-800m | 50m | 7.5 |

| 20 | -- | | |

As far as remote crags go - this is pretty remote. About 15 stern routes Severe to E1. Also some good 70m VS slab routes. Good rock quality and a wonderful position.
G08f; Map: 115 (Landranger) 615 616

⑪ *CASEG BETHESDA*

| Vol | 12 | | Alt-160m | 4m | 7.1 |

| -- | 25 | | Zzz |

A few differerent boulders in the area to the SW of Bethesda. Get a guidebook to find them and seek out some nice fun problems. All in different grades and different styles of problems. Nothing to rave madly about, but certainly worth a crank
G08a; Map: 115 (Landranger) 000 000

⑫ *SHEEP PEN BOULDERS*

| Vol | 15 | | Alt-450m | 5m | 7.4 |

| -- | 25 | | |

It's quite amazing to find these blocks here on the side of the hill in such a fine position overlooking the Bethesda valley. Some good steep and technical problems. Landings are well iffy, so bring an army of pads and spotters for some of the problems. A great place to chill out. Good but small.
G08a; Map: 115 (Landranger) 645 623
When approaching, go back up the road from the layby and don't try to cut straight up, the slope won't stand the erosion.

AMPHITHEARTRE BUTTRESS - Diff. Craig Yr Ysfa; Dave Whitfield

⑬ CRAIG BRAICH TY DU *

Vol 5 | Alt-340m | 70m | 7.5 | 80 | --

This is a series of crags that run up the north side of the Bethesda valley, with routes of all grades but especially in the Diff-Severe standard. They start virtually at the bridge at the bottom of the mountain with small climbs and bouldering. There are about 10 cliffs in total, of reasonable size scattered across the West face of Pen Yr Ole Wen, the mountain due N of Ogwen Cottage. Nice sunny aspect, great place.
G08f; Map: 115 (Landranger) 650 610

⑭ CRAIG LLOER

Vol 70 | Alt-850m | 90m | 7.5 | 17 | -- | Zzz

A crag without difficult climbs, mainly diffs and severes. The setting here on a nice summers day is fantastic and quite secluded, and with the lovely lake down below perfect for an after climb swim. However the weather in Wales usually takes care of this en-route. Gets the morning sun and worth jumping out of bed early to take advantage of this
G08f; Map: 115 (Landranger) 661 619

⑮ LLECH DU

Vol 120 | Alt-900m | 90m | 7.5 | 40 | --

This crag is a large and powerful looking buttress tucked away in the confines of the Carneddu. It has some good hard routes on it, however they do need to be dry and even in a good summer two dry days are the minimum requirement. The climbs vary from 60m to 130m in length. Of the 40 or so climbs most are either in the Diff category or Extremes, there are others but they are few.
G08f; Map: 115 (Landranger) 664 594

⑯ BLACK LADDERS

| Vol | 120 | 👢 | Alt-900m | 130m | 7.7 |

| | | | | 20 | | -- | 🌿 | |

This cliff is really best as a winter ice climbing playground.For rockclimbing it is very broken and situated in a N facing Cwm making it dark and damp. (Called Ysgolion Duon in Welsh)
G08f; Map: 115 (Landranger) 670 632

⑰ CRAIG YR YSFA *

| Vol | 80 | 👢 | Alt-700m | 120m | 7.5 |

| | | | | 64 | | -- | ☀ | ⬅ |

To climb at Craig Yr Ysfa is one of the stepping stones in any mountain climbers lifetime.The whole crag is in two parts, the right side catching more of the early morning sun and having the best routes on it. The routes vary from 200-1000ft. It can get bitter any time other than summer as the cliff is in a wickedly drafty gully. The routes are long and warm clothing should not be left at the foot of the crag, but carried en-route in mountain style. A lot of the climbs have a superb view, but they are a bit broken and ramble.
G08f; Map: 115 (Landranger) 694 637

⑱ CRAFNANT ERYR

| Vol | 45 | 👢 | Alt-450m | 52m | 7.6 |

| | | | 30 | | -- | ☀ | 🌿 |

The best crag in the area around Llanrwst. There is plenty of climbing here for everyone. The forestry Buttress is the first encountered, and these smaller cliffs on the side with the easier routes on. They are completely diminished in stature by the South Buttress. This is "The" crag. Its big, butch and hunky. Its 20 or so routes average in at E3, but more impressive is that they average at 2 stars each. A morning crag for the sun. It can seep quite a lot so a good dry spell is useful, however some of the harder routes on the arete's dry quickly.
G?; Map: 115 (Landranger) 733 604

⑲ CLOGWYN CYRAU

| Vol | 12 | 👟 | Alt-120m | 25m | 7.4 |

| | | | 50 | | -- | ⬅ | Q-D |

Some very good small cliffs overlooking Betws Y Coed. Often popular with teaching groups from the centres. Quite solid rock and good pro make this an ideal beginners crag.
G07b; Map: 115 (Landranger) 789 571

⑳ RAC BOULDERS *

| Vol | 2 | 👟 | Alt-210m | 4m | 7.1 |

| | | -- | 70 | ☀ | Q-D |

A small group of medium sized boulders of perfect volcanic tuff rock. Good friction in parts, slippery but fun slab sections too. In nice weather the position is fabulous and only a quick sprint to the car if the weather turns. A lot of straight up problems, and many with the obligiatary Welsh sitting start. A lovely spot, please tidy up anything after you have been here.
G08a; Map: 115 (Landranger) 694 572

㉑ MALLORY BLOCK

| Vol | 30 | 👢 | Alt-450m | 5m | 7.1 |

| | | -- | 10 | ☀ | Zzz |

A single boulder, set in a distant and remote location. Some very good problems on this perfect shaped block. Excellent quality of rock and should dry quite quickly.
G08a; Map: 115 (Landranger) 662 570
Due north of the Pen-y-Gwryd hotel, off the path leading to Llyn Caseg Fraith.

RAC boulders, nr Capel Curig

KENT/SUSSEX
DORSET
CORNWALL
DEVON
BRISTOL
SOUTH-WALES
MID-WALES
NORTH-WALES
LEICESTER
PEAKS
YORK-LANCS
CLEVELAND
KENDAL
LAKES
PENRITH
NEWCASTLE

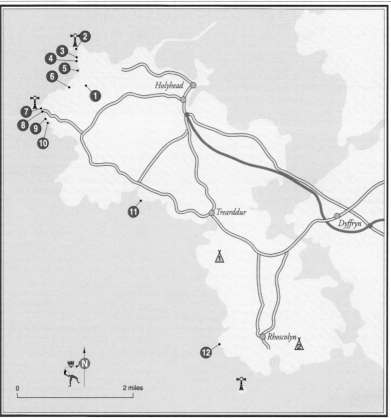

1 Holyhead Mountain
2 North Stack
3 Wen Zawn
4 Easter Island Gully
5 Gogarth Main Cliff
6 Upper Tier
7 Mousetrap Zawn
8 Red Wall
9 Castell Helen
10 Yellow Wall
11 Porth Dafarch
12 Rhoscolyn

Tyn Rhos Camping
Ravenspoint Road,
Trearddur Bay LL65 2AZ
1/3-31/10; 01407 860 369
(Large camping field and
with good facilities; 10
min walk to beach, hotel
with bar close by)

Bryngoleu Farm,
Rhoscolyn, LL65 2SJ
apr-oct; 01407 860 413

A lot of climbers have always treated Gogarth as a wet weather alternative to Snowdonia, mistake number one. Gogarth certainly gets miraculously better weather than continental Wales, and stays a lot drier because of it's minimal height above the sea. However, the rock is quartzite, and of a grey-whitish colour that merges indistinctly into the cloudy miserable sky, that will no doubt be forming the frontal system enveloping Snowdonia. You can climb of course, but will still have that dejected mournful feeling as you gaze into the panoramic greyness, tossing euphoric visions of a blue skied nirvana of the Pass in your mind. However, if you make a special trip to come climbing at Gogarth when the weather is good, then the whole place lights up with a myriad of wonderful colour that will inspire you or anyone. It is a place that really needs sunshine, yes - and lots of it. In the height of summer, the west facing main cliff becomes a furnace, and the soapy texture of the rock is a nightmare to contend with. This only lasts for a few hours, and swimming is always a good option in any case. There is a mixture of climbing here to suit even the most diverse of tastes. Anything from big overhanging zawns, to blissful slabs and ocean walls, but not forgetting the contrast of soft chewey sandwich texture in Mousetrap Zawn. The only thing it lacks are any worthwhile routes in the diffs and Severe grades. You get plenty of middle grade routes around HVS, which are fabulously steep and consume protection at an alarmingly good rate. The cliffs are covered in a green lichen, but when you get up close, this is gone from the hand and footholds of the climbs (may vary with traffic). All the cliffs have their vagaries, but you quickly learn how to cope and thrive on these. It is a great climbing location and one with a whole aura to itself. If you have ever climbed in south Pembroke, you will know how good sea cliffs are, this is certainly grander.

GOGARTH
Text & Hard bound
300 pages - B &W
A few colour photos
Small - 165 x 105mm
Pub-1990
by the Climbers Club
(Andy Newton)

A handy small guide to this area; Basic text with routes in list form; a few photo diagrams. Trying to locate the routes without prior knowledge is desperate. New guide may appear!

G-08g   All the cliffs in the area

HUNGER E5 t-6a, Gogarth Main Cliff; Jules Taylor & Mark Lynden

KENT/SUSSEX | DORSET | CORNWALL | DEVON | BRISTOL | SOUTH-WALES | MID-WALES | NORTH-WALES | LEICSTER | PEAKS | YORK-LANCS | CLEVELAND | KENDAL | LAKES | PENRITH | NEWCASTLE

❶ HOLYHEAD MOUNTAIN

There are some very useful crags here offering plenty of climbing in the lower grades V Diff - VS and a handful of easy extremes, 25-40m. Being away from the sea and not so intimidating, they offer a good days climbing for a mixed party whose cream team are fully occupied on the main cliff, scenery is a bit bland though. About 60 climbs in total, scattered all around the mountain.
Map: 114 (Landranger) 220 827

❷ NORTH STACK*

This is a cliff for the very bold leaders, with ability! The North Stack Wall does not see many falls, good job too. About 20 routes up to 50m on fairly predictable rock, that doesn't mean solid. It supports well enough, whether or not portection holds is questionable, nobody usually tests gear here. The routes are all easy E3 to not so easy E6. There are E7's and beyond for the levitation experts with big balls. Abseil approach from poles (watch the tar at the bottom, bring a rag) or some metal rings set well back. Tidal at the bottom.
Map: 114 (Landranger) 215 840

❸ WEN ZAWN**

A great area, one of the finest in Wales. This Zawn on a sunny afternoon warms even to T shirt temperature even in the coldest of winter days. There are many climbs here at all grades VS upwards. There are some quite challenging lines through some spectacular overhangs. About 30 routes up to 100m. Approach is by abseil to the tidal bottom or by scrambling down the seaward edge of Wen Slab. The slab can be climbed in almost any weather, including 60ft waves, trendy.
Map: 114 (Landranger) 215 839

❹ EASTER ISLAND GULLY**

The entrance to some very impressive rock scenery and the north end of the main cliff. A good VS to E3 area, definitly worth a visit if only for the abseil in. About 30 routes 30-90m. You can access routes on the main cliff, and the Wen slab from here, but there is no easy way out. You definitely need a spare abseil rope or two. Very atmospheric and enticing. Not good in bad weather at all!
Map: 114 (Landranger) 215 838

THE BELLS, THE BELLS E7 t-6b, North Stack Wall: John Redhead

❺ GOGARTH MAIN CLIFF***

This cliff can only be described as fantastic and worth a visit when your fit with big arms. It commands over the whole coastline and offers huge routes of up to 140m of really challenging climbing. Most of the routes are classics and recieve the afternoon sun. All are at least 2 pitches and often an abseil from the belay will deposit you in the sea. The rock is mostly sound but large bits have been known to break off with climbers attached! Friends are usefull here as well as small nuts. The tide affects the bottoms quite a lot, 2 hrs either side of HT prevents access to the main section, one can climb over the small pinnacle at the bottom of the start to the sector at high tide, to gain access on a calm day. About 70 routes with many E4,E5 climbs and a few easy E6's.
Map: 114 (Landranger) 215 835

⑥ UPPER TIER

This cliff is unafected by tides and a good introduction to the area, however the routes here are nowhere as impressive or as good as other areas. Lots of slabby climbs, steep slabs admittedly but nevertheless slabs. About 70 routes HVS upwards to E6 on reasonable rock.
Map: 114 (Landranger) 216 833

⑦ MOUSETRAP ZAWN

Bird restriction 1/2 - 31/7 This crag is actually climbed on quite frequently which is quite bizzare since the rock! is certainly awful in comparrison with most of Gogarth, anyway go for it. 300-400ft routes from a tidal base, about 20 in total. Nothing technical here, rocks not very strong see, it comes away in big chunks. Large nuts useful as well as big protection.
Map: 114 (Landranger) 205 822

⑧ RED WALL

Bird restriction 1/2 - 31/7 This area consists of two walls, Red Wall and Left Hand Red Wall. Both are serious places to climb and not without difficulty. There are about 50 extremes here and about half of them are very hard indeed. Most are about 100m involving a belay halfway up, even the second has to be a headcase. There are storys of seconds refusing to visit the crag because of the belays on some of the routes! A lot of the routes recieve three star classic status which must make them very memorable indeed. The route Red Wall itself gets E1 5a, need I say more.
Map: 114 (Landranger) 205 822

⑨ CASTELL HELEN **

A superb cliff for the climber who doesn't want to be frightened. Lovely rock in a very pleasant position makes this easily the most popular cliff in the area. About 20 routes VS to E2 and the very interesting Obelisk E5, well protected on not too steep solid rock. The base is semi tidal, a bit of a crush on a ledge at high tide, entertaining in a heavy sea though. Abseil rope useful here for top abseil. A big cliff with most routes about 80m.
Map: 114 (Landranger) 205 820

⑩ YELLOW WALL

About 10 routes in this impressive Zawn area. Routes are all E2 upwards and can entail some amusing activities if the leader of second should fall off, its quite overhanging. Routes of around 85m give plenty of climbing and an area worth savouring. In a heavy sea, spray tends to make the area quite-damp and difficult to climb.
Map: 114 (Landranger) 205 819

⑪ PORTH DAFARCH

A super little crag with a handful of climbs in the easy extreme grade, about 40ft. Quite a steep crag, good for the arms.
Map: 114 (Landranger) 233 799

⑫ RHOSCOLYN*

A good crag with lots of climbing. Some of ther climbs are definitly better than others. About 50 routes up to 150ft on fairly sound rock. South facing, worth a visit.
Map: 114 (Landranger) 257 756

NORTH WEST PASSAGE - VS, Castell Helen; Keith Robertson

KENT/SUSSEX
DORSET
CORNWALL
DEVON
BRISTOL
SOUTH-WALES
MID-WALES
NORTH-WALES
LEICSETER
PEAKS
YORK-LANCS
CLEVELAND
KENDAL
LAKES
PENRITH
NEWCASTLE

OVER THE MOON s-8a, Lower Pen Trwyn; Ben Pritchard

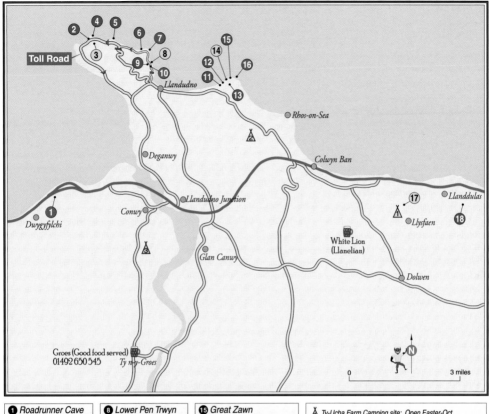

1 Roadrunner Cave	**8** Lower Pen Trwyn	**15** Great Zawn
2 St. Tudno's	**9** Upper Pen Trwyn	**16** Angel Bay
3 The Gorge	**10** Parisella's Cave	**17** Castle Inn Quarry
4 Castell Y Gwynt	**11** Craig Y Don-Upper	**18** Llandulals Cave
5 Crinkle Crags	**12** Diamond	**19**
6 Homo Sapien	**13** Meadow Walls	**20**
7 Pidgeon Cave	**14** Detritus-Atlanta	**21**

Ty-Ucha Farm Camping site: Open Easter-Oct
Tan-Y-Craig Road, Llysfaen, LL29 8UD; 01492 517 051
Dinarth Hall: Open May-Sept
Rhos-on-Sea, LL28 4PX; 01492 548 203
Conwy Touring Park: Open Apr-Oct
Trefriw Rd, Conwy, LL32 8UX; 01492 592 856

**NORTH WALES
LIMESTONE &
BOULDERING
Topo guidebook**
224 pages - B &W
A5 Paperback
Pub-1997
by Rockfax
(Alan James,
P. Evans & J Barton)

*A lot of guidebook with excellent details for
finding the cliffs and locating the routes. A
very mixed area that benefits from the topo
approach. Gives trad and sport route details,
but may well be out of date on the state of the
sport bolts with sea salt & rust etc.*

G-08g △ All these cliffs plus other minors

The climbing scene at Llandudno has always seemed bizarre compared
with the natural mountain environment of Snowdonia. Llandudno itself
is bizarre, a seaside town yet facing north and always seeming chilly. The
main climbing cliffs are on the east side of the little Orme, and are cold in
anything other than the hottest of summer days. Access is always a problem with the whole Orme, since the road around it is a toll road, and I've
witnessed ugly incidents between those that live on the Orme and tourists;
so be very aware where you park your car. You can't climb on some of the
cliffs during summer holidays even. If it's climbing hard and steep 7c/8a
routes that turns you on, then it is a good spot to visit. For other climbers,
you may well be better off visiting somewhere else. The other cliffs on the
Great Orme are very impressive and contain a host of expeditionary routes
in the very high grades. There are some good bouldering spots in this area
that have seen popularity over recent years, and give a nice alternative to
playing around on dodgy bolts. Tides are important here, but not critical
in all areas. Hard cliffs are busy, others are quiet - really quiet.

❶ ROADRUNNER CAVE

A bouldering area right next to one of the loudest roads in Wales. About 10 problems and 30 variations, all V5 and above. Slopers and dark black rock.
G08a; Map: 115 (Landranger) 744 783

❷ ST. TUDNO'S BUTTRESS

A crag in an impressive position, with good rock and routes. About 30 routes around E2-E3, with a few Severes to HVS's, 10-55m. One of the most useful places to climb with no restrictions and generally away from the touroids. The home of the famous Gritstone Gorilla, it is rumoured!
G08h; Map: 115 (Landranger) 754 843

❸ THE GORGE

A small gorge area that offers around 15 sport routes up to 6c, small and dank, 3 clip routes.
G08h; Map: 115 (Landranger) 758 843

❹ CASTELL Y GWYNT

Bird restriction some areas 1/2 - 31/7
A historic cliff with some demanding high E grade climbing. In an exceptionally cold and dank postion on the headland and never gets the sun. Home to many bird colony's and stinks to high heaven. A place you visit, are impressed, then walk away quickly - forever.
G08h; Map: 115 (Landranger) 758 846

❺ CRINKLE CRAGS

A series of small cliffs that are just above the sea and offer a wide range of climbs - up to 80 in easy to hard grades. All are abseil access down to ledges just above high tide. Not much sun.
G08h; Map: 115 (Landranger) 766 843

❻ HOMO SAPIEN

Climbing restriction all areas - School and bank holidays A series of small cliffs that are just above the road with about 60 routes. A complete jumble bag of trad and bolts in places!
G08h; Map: 115 (Landranger) 778 838

❼ PIDGEON CAVE

A big area of caves down at sea level. Face north and stay cooool. The cave itself has some juggy big routes in itself. Further along the beach are some big boulders with standard V problems on them. Quiet, but don't get caught out by the incoming tide.
G08a; Map: 115 (Landranger) 780 839

❽ LOWER PEN TRWYN *

A cliff with a lot of hard sport climbs on it, ranging from 7a-8c. About 60 routes up to 25m. The cliff faces NE and only gets the sun for a short time during early morning. It can therefore stay damp very easily and give soapy conditions for most of the climbs. A very popular spot with the very top climbers in the country. The base is tidal and you loose the climbing for about 3 hours at high tide. Apart from this there are no other restrictions. A very chilly place so bring a puffer to keep you warm between 8a redpoints or flashes.
G08h; Map: 115 (Landranger) 783 835

❾ UPPER PEN TRWYN * *

Climbing restriction all areas - School and bank holidays Some very impressive walls that don't offer anything in the remotely easy category. Big and powerful wall climbing that is demanding. A real mixture of trad and some bolts, confusing. Some of the routes are also banned, consult any local notices about this. At the bottom of the walls are some good short and steep sections that have proven popular for bouldering.
G08h; Map: 115 (Landranger) 781 837

❿ PARISELLA'S CAVES

A series of BIG caves that overhang with sloping holds everywhere. They stay dry but are miserable and dingy. The climbing is very good which you have to admit, but the prospect of onsetting permanent depression may prove too much for many. The toll road charging a few quid, may seem outrageously expensive!
G08a; Map: 115 (Landranger) 782 835

⓫ CRAIG-Y-DON

A good introduction to the climbing on the Little Ormes. About 20 routes HVS-E5 on the upper and middle tiers, 40m. On the lower tier which is tidal, there are about 10 routes around 70m E1-E5. The best routes are on the upper tier and in the E3-E5 range, however the route Hydro at E1 takes the obvious easy way up the centre of the buttress.
G08h; Map: 116 (Landranger) 812 824

⓬ THE DIAMOND

Bird restriction 1/3- 15/8 An impressive big wall offers a host of hard climbs that may have some rusty bolts in - or be around E something or another. Some of the routes were done as aid routes originally.
G08h; Map: 116 (Landranger) 813 825

⓭ MEADOW WALLS

A good little spot offering some tough little spurts. About 10 routes, E3-E5 with the easiest, Hole of Creation going straight up the middle. 20m N facing.
G08h; Map: 116 (Landranger) 817 825

⓮ DETRITUS-ATLANTA WALL * *

Bird restriction 1/3- 15/8 An area that has been developed slightly, access is very difficult as is finding the correct routes. Abseil in, about 10 sport routes in the 6b-7c league.
G08h; Map: 116 (Landranger) 815 826

⓯ GREAT ZAWN

Bird restriction 1/3- 15/8 A BIG area that is remote and full of difficulty in the ascent and even the finishing, you have to climb up to a preplaced rope on the vertical grass! About 10 mid E grade routes that might appeal to some.
G08h; Map: 116 (Landranger) 815 826

⓰ ANGEL BAY *

The area to go bouldering on the Orme and down on the beach with swimming on hand. Lots of water worn smooth rock and undercut boulders. The pebble beach changes height from time to time. You definitely want a pad here. About 60 standard listed problems from V1-V11 and countless variations.
G08a; Map: 116 (Landranger) ?

⓱ CASTLE INN QUARRY

A small quarry offering around 14 routes 5-6c About 24m and behind a pub. A good day to be had here.
G08h; Map: 116 (Landranger) 891 770

⓲ LLANDULAS CAVE

A cave overlooking the main A55. This area and a west facing wall offers about 20 sport routes in the 6a-7a range, with a couple of 7c routes just to the right of the cave.
G08h; Map: 116 (Landranger) ?

AXLE ATTACK - E5 t-6a, Upper Pen Trwyn, Matt Boyer

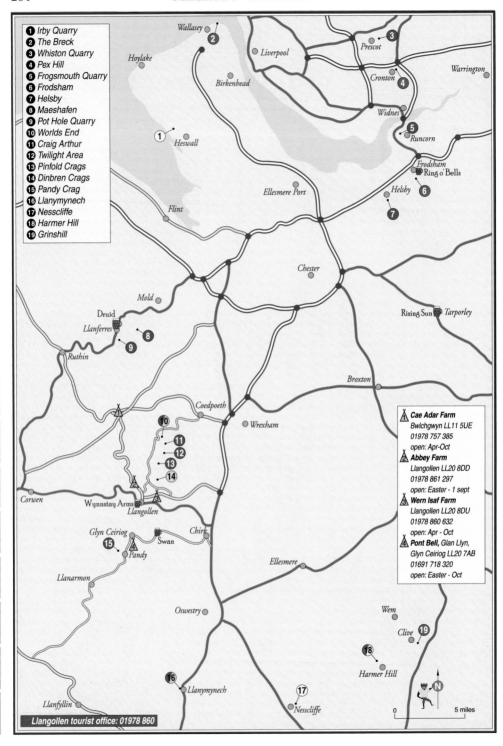

1 Irby Quarry
2 The Breck
3 Whiston Quarry
4 Pex Hill
5 Frogsmouth Quarry
6 Frodsham
7 Helsby
8 Maeshafen
9 Pot Hole Quarry
10 Worlds End
11 Craig Arthur
12 Twilight Area
13 Pinfold Crags
14 Dinbren Crags
15 Pandy Crag
16 Llanymynech
17 Nesscliffe
18 Harmer Hill
19 Grinshill

Cae Adar Farm
Bwlchgwyn LL11 5UE
01978 757 385
open: Apr-Oct

Abbey Farm
Llangollen LL20 8DD
01978 861 297
open: Easter - 1 sept

Wern Isaf Farm
Llangollen LL20 8DU
01978 860 632
open: Apr - Oct

Pont Bell, Glan Llyn,
Glyn Ceiriog LL20 7AB
01691 718 320
open: Easter - Oct

Llangollen tourist office: 01978 860

Side tabs: KENT/SUSSEX, DORSET, CORNWALL, DEVON, BRISTOL, SOUTH-WALES, MID-WALES, NORTH-WALES, LEICSETER, PEAKS, YORK-LANCS, CLEVELAND, KENDAL, LAKES, PENRITH, NEWCASTLE

Map labels: Wallasey, Hoylake, Liverpool, Prescot, Birkenhead, Cronton, Warrington, Heswall, Widnes, Runcorn, Frodsham, Ring o' Bells, Helsby, Ellesmere Port, Flint, Chester, Mold, Rising Sun, Tarporley, Druid, Llanferres, Ruthin, Broxton, Coedpoeth, Wrexham, Corwen, Wynnstay Arms, Llangollen, Glyn Ceiriog, Swan, Chirk, Pandy, Ellesmere, Llanarmon, Oswestry, Wem, Clive, Harmer Hill, Llanymynech, Nesscliffe, Llanfyllin

0   5 miles

BLACK MAGIC t-6a, Pex Hill; Joe Healey

① *IRBY QUARRY*

A sandstone quarry up to 18m high offering good climbing in the lower grades, very useful for beginners starting climbing. Top roping being very sensible.
Map: 108 (Landranger) 252 858

② *THE BRECK**

A very good bouldering area near the centre of Liverpool. There are about 50 routes of which most are around t-5c. Good sandstone and worth a visit.
Map: 108 (Landranger) 298 918

③ *WHISTON QUARRY*

A very good bouldering area near the centre of Liverpool. There are about 50 routes of which most are around t-5c. Good sandstone and worth a visit.
Map: 108 (Landranger) 298 918

GOING BAD HVS t-5a, World's End; Pete Chadwick

❹ PEX HILL *

One of the great bouldering areas in the country. Heights of the routes here varies fron 10ft to 50ft. Most of the routes are nearly always chalked up not that it matters since the holds are obvious, its getting between them that can prove awkward. A top rope is very useful for the longer routes which rarely are soloed. Enjoys quite reasonable weather. Beware of car theives. ☠ Always worth a visit. No overhangs to shelter in, only steep walls on which to boulder.
Map: 108 (Landranger) 501 887

❺ FROGSMOUTH QUARRY

About 50 climbs in this sandstone quarry mostly 5a-5c. The rock is not of sound nature and it is advisable to bring a top rope. 20-60ft high and quite steep.
Map: 108 (Landranger) 507 815

❻ FRODSHAM *

This crag consists of a series of small sandstone boulders set in the trees. There are about 8 in total of which all are good and offer plenty of fun; up to 15ft high and with a lot of roofs and grotto style moves. The climbing is generally very strenous and in the higher grades, even so there is still plenty for the enthusiastic struggler. There must be over 100 problems and countless variations. In summer its a gem, in winter it can stay rather damp as the trees enshroud the crag.
Map: 117 (Landranger) 512 753

❼ HELSBY *

A large crag with over 100 routes on it 20-40ft. The sandstone has excellent climbing properties but is very weak for protection. People do lead routes and fall off and live but you should examine the risk of erosion and any needless damage that may occur to snapping flakes and the surface texture. There are some very good problems which will test your ability to levitate. Routes at all grades. Faces W and gets the sun well, however it is very exposed, and being covered in green dust, or slime when wet, it is not the best winter crag.
Map: 117 (Landranger) 492 755

❽ MAESHAFEN

Check local access first with Bryngwyn Farm-private land. Even though this crag is a quarry it has the mood of a natural limestone escarpment with views over the surrounding countryside and not being a hole in the ground. It faces west and at 1000ft catches little bad weather compared with other areas to the S and W. The climbs vary from 40-80ft with about 80 in total in all grades. The rock in the main is clean and sound since the quarry ceased production in the last century. 5 mins from parking.
Map: 117 (Landranger) 214 615

❾ POT HOLE QUARRY

The quarry is owned by a nearby farm and the farmer has given kind consent to climbing here so far as approach is made by the recognised footpath and no litter is left. A small quarry of up to 70ft with about 30 routes of all grades. Some of the routes are top roped to avoid bolting and others can be led quite safely. The rock is very good and some interesting climbs are to be found.
Map: 116 (Landranger) 192 597

❿ WORLD'S END *

A long and rambling limestone escarpment in a beautiful setting. No shortage of routes here in all grades. If the crag were to come of age and get bolted up across all the grades, then it would transform the whole area as an attraction for every level of climber. The rock is quite shattered and hence, traditional gear is not that reliable and nervy to place or fall on. Many of the harder routes have bolts on the hard moves and hence are well protected. Good technical and fingery climbing, and mean on the joints. Because of the trees and the position in the combe, it is relatively protected and can be a lot warmer than many of the other edges in the area. A lovely morning crag.
Map: 117 (Landranger) 220 472

KENT/SUSSEX · DORSET · CORNWALL · DEVON · BRISTOL · SOUTH-WALES · MID-WALES · NORTH-WALES · LEICSETER · PEAKS · YORK-LANCS · CLEVELAND · KENDAL · LAKES · PENRITH · NEWCASTLE

CRUMPET CRACK t-5c, Helsby; Gax Healey

⓫ CRAIG ARTHUR
There could be a bird issue here 1/2 - 15/7 You can't miss this crag, its big. This 60m crag at the top of the valley feels like 1000m high and quite out there, man. Some of the best routes in the area are to be found here, also some of the hardest. There are some 40 routes here with little below E1, mostly E3 upwards. A pity since the position is sensational. The rock in parts is questionable as is the distance between some of the runners!
Map: 117 (Landranger) 224 471

⓬ TWILIGHT CRAGS
These consist of two crags facing each other. Only about 60ft high but offering about 70 really good routes on excellent limestone, to the N is the Tower Buttress, the one getting the most sun and best outlook. There is also some good bouldering to be had on the tier above these crags. A very good area.
Map: 117 (Landranger) 223 463

⓭ PINFOLD CRAGS
This crag offers over 100 routes of which most deserve merit and ascending at some point in time. Being situated high up and generally N they can be a very hostile place to climb. The rock is mostly good and offers good protection. Mainly routes in the middle and extreme grades.
Map: 117 (Landranger) 222 453

⓮ DINBREN CRAGS
A very accessable crag offering some really good climbs and quality moves, also within very close range of the car. A must for the lazy cragrat. Two walls at 90 degrees to one another. About 20 routes mainly in the harder grades, however there are some trad Severes and Diffs. For desert you can also sample the tier below and to the R, guarranteed to finish you off.
Map: 117 (Landranger) 221 445

⓯ PANDY CRAG
A quiet crag and out of the mainstream climbing activity of the area. A very nice setting and of volcanic rock. A handful of routes in the lower grades.
Map: ? (Landranger) ?

⓰ LLANYMYNECH
A large limestone crag to the west of the village of the same name, and easily seen from the car when passing. Around 100 routes, and a mixture of sport and trad climbing.
Map: ?(Landranger) ?

BOREAL

⓱ NESSCLIFFE

These cliffs are set in a lovely woodland and are now quiet since the re-routing of the A5 to quite a distance away. The rock is a bit too soft for top quality bouldering, but does offer a lot of fun problems in the middle grades. The walls are big and suicidal to attempt in the trad manner. Generally everyone top ropes here. A huge amount of damage has been done to the top of the cliff. Please bring a static rope to make a top belay, and protect the top edge with carpet.
Map: 126 (Landranger) 384 193

⓲ HARMER HILL *
A very good area and of substantially high sandstone, up to 100ft high. The best quality rock is in the lower 50ft, with bouldering too. Situated in the woods to the NW of the village. The cliff is semi quarried and part natural.
Map: ? (Landranger) ?

⓳ GRINSHILL *
Probably the best bouldering crag in the area. Sandstone of a good hard consistency, with some bulging overhanging sections. Park at the church in the village. 10-50ft high.
Map: ? (Landranger) ?

NESSCLIFFE BOULDERING

NESSCLIFFE, big walls and superb lines - soft rock though.

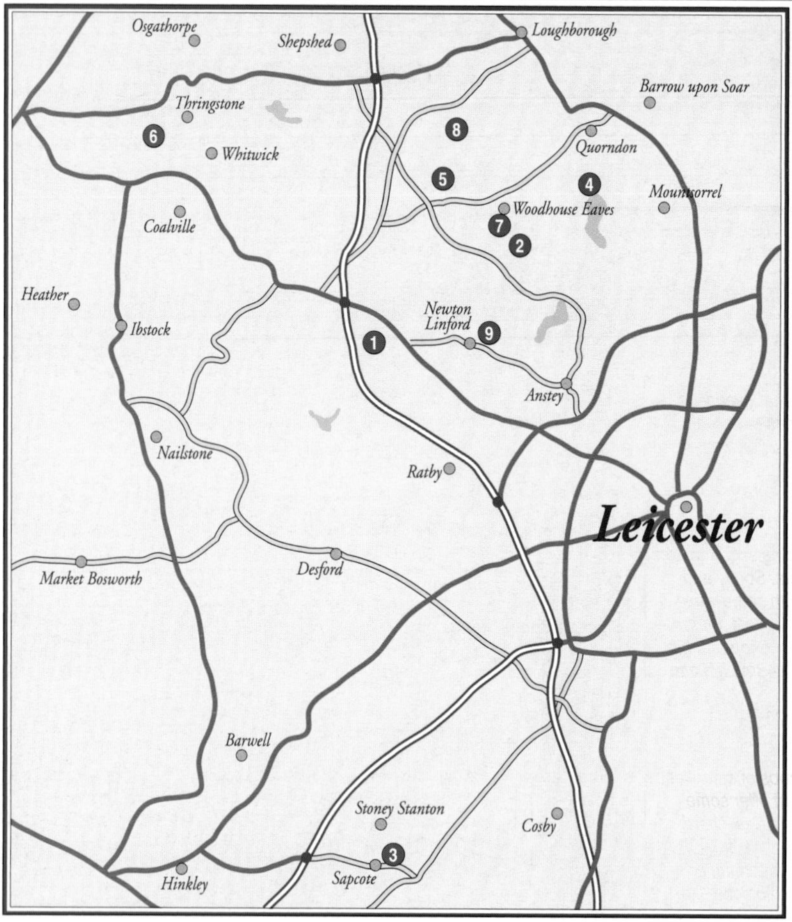

Left margin tabs: KENT/SUSSEX · DORSET · CORNWALL · DEVON · BRISTOL · SOUTH-WALES · MID-WALES · NORTH-WALES · LEICESTER · PEAKS · YORK-LANCS · CLEVELAND · KENDAL · LAKES · PENRITH · NEWCASTLE

Map labels: Osgathorpe, Shepshed, Loughborough, Thringstone, Barrow upon Soar, Whitwick, Quorndon, Coalville, Woodhouse Eaves, Mountsorrel, Heather, Ibstock, Newton Linford, Anstey, Nailstone, Ratby, Leicester, Market Bosworth, Desford, Barwell, Stoney Stanton, Cosby, Hinkley, Sapcote

Legend:
1 Markfield Quarry
2 The Brand
3 Granitethorpe Qy.
4 Craig Buddon
5 Beacon Hill
6 Cademon Wood
7 Forest Rock
8 Outwoods Crag
9 Bradgate Park

When you approach the topic of climbing in Leicestershire, you are best off seeking a fast car and whizzing off to the many of the other cliffs listed in this book. Manic zest alone should attract you to those wonderful other destinations. However, there is some good climbing to be found in this locale on the other hand, but it definitely falls into the category of 'I can't be bothered to drive very far,' and 'let's get out this evening for some pulling on little bits of rock.' With this approach, have a great fun time and really enjoy yourself here. The landscape of the area is pretty casual, with nice rolling countryside that is generally pleasant to the eye. The highest part is to the NW of Leicester, home of the old Charnwood Forest; a really dizzy height of some 900ft at Bardon Hill and Beacon Hill, both sure to keep the snow longer than most areas over the winter. From these beautiful and serene high points, the land slopes away down to working towns and industrial quarries on most sides. Blasting and chiselling always seem in a state of flux, into retirement and then back for rejuvenation. This digging out of Leicestershire has given rise to climbers hope and happiness, especially at Markham Quarry where a big dig has left a substantial climbing area of fair quality. In many other areas, you have simple little caves or vertical walls above pools. It's a mixed bag here and takes a lot of hunting around to find all the ideal little nooks and crannies. There was a guidebook to the area but unfortunately it's now out of print. The problem being the constant change of access issues making publication somewhat - ever changing and out of date. Fortunately the whole guidebook is available on the web; free, browseable and downloadable. We list the site, but also include the major crags, so that you can get appetized in hunting and looking for places to spend your lovely hot and sunny, summers evenings.

www.leicesterclimbs.f9.co.uk

❶ MARKFIELD QUARRY

The major climbing area in Leicestershire and with good public access.
Map: 129 (Landranger) 486 104

❷ THE BRAND

Access; You must get permission to
climb here first, check the website for
the correct and current number to ring
please. A good but small climbing area.
Map: 129 (Landranger) 537 132

❸ GRANITETHORPE QUARRY

A bit overgrown at present.
Map: 140 (Landranger) 495 937

❹ CRAIG BUDDON

A small granite quarry that overlooks
the reservoir and catches the evening
sun. The left side being a SSSI, so
please be careful.
Map: 129 (Landranger) 558 150

❺ BEACON HILL

A very nice small climbing site. A bit too
high for most boulderers. Soapy and
slippy style rock, but with some very
good challenges. Popular with groups.
3 different outcrops on the top of a hill,
facing most directions. 248m high and
can be a bit chilly.
Map: 129 (Landranger) 508 149

❻ CAEDMON WOOD

Small, well - little outcrops of sandstone
hidden in the woods that offer some
fun bouldering, even with a few hard
problems too. Finding the problems and
outcrops may prove as much fun as
ticking them. A very scenic spot.
Map: 129 (Landranger) 435 170 ish

❼ FOREST ROCK

Some bouldering and climbing on this
little lump of slate near the church.
Access is delicate here, so please act
courteously to ensure that the local
villagers have no axe to grind against
climbers.
Map: 129 (Landranger) 532 142

❽ OUTWOODS CRAG

A good small quarry that is popular with
groups. About 15 routes in the lower
grades up to 9m high.
Map: 129 (Landranger) 514 167

❾ BRADGATE PARK

Some good small outcrops in this area,
with Stable Pit being more notable for
good bouldering. Worth investigating.
Map: 129 (Landranger) 526 101-ish

BEACON HILL, popular with youth groups   FOREST ROCK

NEW CRAGS TO BE DISCOVERED:

USEFUL CURRY RESTAURANT NUMBERS:

KENT/SUSSEX · DORSET · CORNWALL · DEVON · BRISTOL · SOUTH-WALES · MID-WALES · NORTH-WALES · LEICESTER · PEAKS · YORK-LANCS · CLEVELAND · KENDAL · LAKES · PENRITH · NEWCASTLE

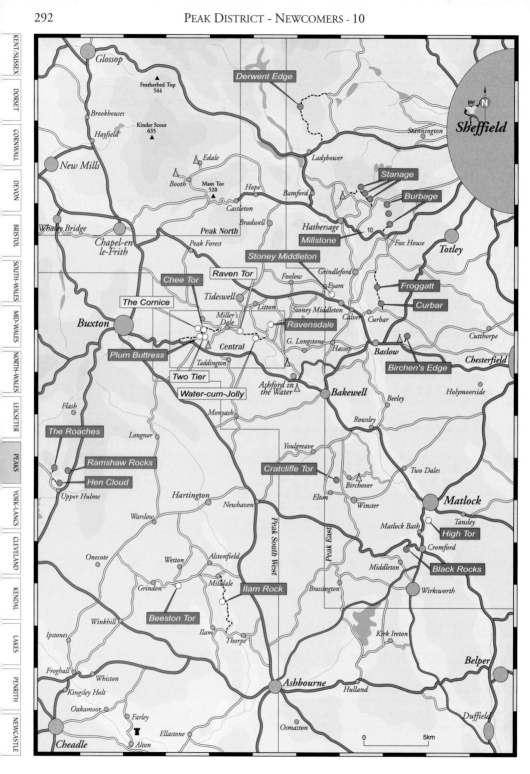

The Peak District is a very large area which we split into 4 completely separate regions. Most newcomers will not appreciate the distances involved from cliff to cliff, not withstanding that it will take 2 hours to drive from top to bottom on a busy weekend during summer. We have given a complete overview of the peak in the map opposite, so you can get a good overview and start to plan you climbing trips with ease. It is an impossible climbing area to split up easily, because of the variety in the rock, as well as the difference in climbing styles and standards that exist right next door to each other. If you live close by, then you are privileged in being able to sample cliffs at leisure and slowly discover the whole peak for yourself. The purpose of this section in our handbook, is to help those climbers easily choose cliffs that are suitable, and get the most out of the Peak.

There are two main types of rock here, gritstone and limestone. We have marked the map with white for limestone and brown for the gritstone so that you can get a quick idea where the rock types occur. The gritstone is famous for its abrasive qualities that cut up hands not used to jamming and working the painful cracks. But in addition, it does have wonderful frictional properties that are necessary to add a complete dimension to shorter climbs, giving tussle and bemusing answers to many of its classic problems. Soloing on the gritstone has always been popular, especially in the easier grades and on many of the smaller outcrops like Birchen's Edge, Burbage North and parts of Stanage. Before the invention of camming devices, many of the routes were effectively big solo's and gritstone was a highly risky place to test yourself on the upper grades. Gritstone forms in bedding planes that are anything from 1-3 ft apart, and then curve in to leave a parallel horizontal crack which often takes a hand or fist jam. You also find that the rock naturally forms into buttresses that are about 10-20ft wide and make a fine looking piece of rock that stands up in a proud manner. Nature has played a wonderful part in the moulding of the gritstone edges and no outcrop is the same, some buttresses are pleasant and have cracks the perfect width for hand jamming, and are the nice side of vertical. Others are fiendishly steep and have cracks that simply flare outwards and are just the wrong width to take a jam. Mostly it is the aretes and walls that appear striking and shout out their challenge to be climbed. You need a good assortment of natural gear plus a wealth of cams to get the best out of gritstone in a safe-ish manner. All of the grades in the guidebooks presume you have access to all the possible sizes and types of cams available, so be careful. The rock has suffered from climbers use over the years and there are many missing flakes, especially where cams have levered them off, and the insides of cracks are now ground smooth by the cams - so forget your old gear nowadays. The plus side is that climbers have resisted bolting the outcrops which would have permanently damaged the beautiful forms that gritstone weathers into.

The limestone areas are quite different, some are natural, some are quarried; and others are terribly crumbly and overgrown. There certainly isn't any strict criteria for pro or anti bolting on the limestone, simply that most of the harder routes 7b upwards, are starting to get properly bolted up with proper lower offs put in place. The limestone is found in the river valleys and consequently is mostly low down and of classic river bed consistency. It is brittle, blocky and shattered, and offers small tiny edges that are often square edged. The cliffs are also vertical with an undercut base, offering hard starts up shattered rock for most of the climbs. Placing natural protection at this angle with the dubious nature of the rock, has consequently led to widespread adoption of bolting. There are still however a few trad areas on limestone, but these are now very polished - especially in the lower grades, and are often poorly protected and not short of a few accidents every year. If you do venture onto these sorts of climbs, you are well advised to wear a helmet, especially at Ravensdale - a popular lower grade cliff.

The weather has a very large influence on climbing in the Peak District. In autumn, winter and spring, the climate is pretty hostile, and it is no mistake that bouldering has become so popular over recent years, so you can keep warm by constantly moving. Most of the gritstone is high up at over 1000ft, and exposed mostly to the westerly winds. What often happens is that the wind hits the cliffs at 90 degrees and blows straight over, so the cliff itself is often out of the wind. It's just belaying on the top which feels like a force 10 gale and can be numbingly cold. The limestone in the valleys can remain damp for quite a while, and is often in the shade and exceptionally cold. Only in summer after June do the river cliffs start to dry out after winter seepage, but can stay dry then until October. The gritstone in summer can become unbearably hot and sweaty, not to mention the midges that come out when the wind drops, with Stanage having a particular vociferous colony of nasties. Overall, the countryside is beautiful enough to enjoy in itself, the small cliffs all dotted over the landscape are simply icing on the cake.

KENT/SUSSEX · DORSET · CORNWALL · DEVON · BRISTOL · SOUTH-WALES · MID-WALES · NORTH-WALES · LEICESTER · PEAKS · YORK-LANCS · CLEVELAND · KENDAL · LAKES · PENRITH · NEWCASTLE

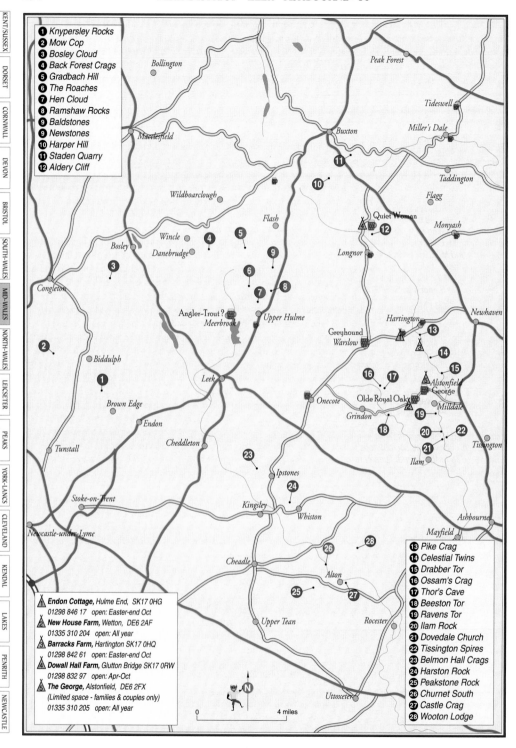

1. Knypersley Rocks
2. Mow Cop
3. Bosley Cloud
4. Back Forest Crags
5. Gradbach Hill
6. The Roaches
7. Hen Cloud
8. Ramshaw Rocks
9. Baldstones
9. Newstones
10. Harper Hill
11. Staden Quarry
12. Aldery Cliff

13. Pike Crag
14. Celestial Twins
15. Drabber Tor
16. Ossam's Crag
17. Thor's Cave
18. Beeston Tor
19. Ravens Tor
20. Ilam Rock
21. Dovedale Church
22. Tissington Spires
23. Belmon Hall Crags
24. Harston Rock
25. Peakstone Rock
26. Churnet South
27. Castle Crag
28. Wooton Lodge

Endon Cottage, Hulme End, SK17 0HG
01298 846 17 open: Easter-end Oct
New House Farm, Wetton, DE6 2AF
01335 310 204 open: All year
Barracks Farm, Hartington SK17 0HQ
01298 842 61 open: Easter-end Oct
Dowall Hall Farm, Glutton Bridge SK17 0RW
01298 832 97 open: Apr-Oct
The George, Alstonfield, DE6 2FX
(Limited space - families & couples only)
01335 310 205 open: All year

0   4 miles

Side tabs: KENT/SUSSEX, DORSET, CORNWALL, DEVON, BRISTOL, SOUTH-WALES, MID-WALES, NORTH-WALES, LEICESTER, PEAKS, YORK-LANCS, CLEVELAND, KENDAL, LAKES, PENRITH, NEWCASTLE

❶ KNYPERSLEY ROCKS

A good solid gritstone crag but set in the trees and get green and unpleasant quite often. A score of routes in the very easy grades, around 30ft. A pleasant spot, worth a visit for the low grade climber.
G10c; Map: 118 (Landranger) 900 557

❷ MOW COP

A unique rock formation The OLD MAN OF MOW, offering about half a dozen routes around 20m in the HVS category with the exception being Spiral Route at HS, the classic route of the crag. Descent is by abseil. There are some quarries nearby with about 30 routes in the middle grades of which very few have real merit. The crags are known as THE FOLLY CLIFF, HAWKS HOLE QUARRY and MILLSTONE QUARRY. They are situated beneath the castle, Folly Cliff being the most northern.
G10c; Map: 118 (Landranger) 858 576

❸ BOSLEY CLOUD

Some good climbing to be found here, but it is NE facing and can get rather lichenous. Most of the climbs are around VS with a few easier and others harder. About 20 routes in total up to 50ft on natural gritstone. There is a quarry at the N end of the hill with some routes in as well as some suspect rock. Quite good views reward the hike up to the crags. Having found the crags easily near the summit trig point one should not miss the two outcrops on the W side farther round. These are SECRET SLAB and THE CATSTONE. Both offer good routes especially 6a problems on the secret slab, worth a top rope.
G10c; Map: 118 (Landranger) 905 637

❹ BACK FOREST CRAGS

These crags offer good gritstone problems up to 20ft high in all grades. Great fun for all the family. There are about 100 problems of all sorts which come in about 30 routes. At around 1000ft they are quite exposed and best kept for a summers evening and a dry spell makes the approach walk a lot more pleasant.
G10c; Map: 118 (Landranger) 987 653

❺ GRADBACH HILL

A west facing lonely outcrop ideal for getting away from it. About 20 climbs in the lower grades with one 5c. Still plenty of bouldering though on this soung grit outcrop. Worth a visit.
G10c; Map: 119 (Landranger) 001 653

❻ THE ROACHES** **

The most popular gritstone crag in the area. The crag offers plenty for everyone to enjoy. Slabs, cracks, roofs, all are to savour. There are 300 routes and as many boulder problems. Every grades imaginable, the harder slabs mostly being top roped. The big roof is taken by The Sloth up the crack in the middle at a good HVS. There are two tiers but the bottom one tends to get green very quickly and also stay damp. SW facing and up to 100ft high, open to the elements, wonderful aspect but often wet and windy. Always worth a visit, just for the view.
G10a,b,c; Map: 119 (Landranger) 003 627

❼ HEN CLOUD *

A very impressive crag with some excellent climbing on it. There are 100 of so climbs up to E3 from Diff. However none seem to ever be easy. There are some very difficult walls for which a top rope is very handy, plus bring a 10m length of rope to help top rope as the belays are set back. Some climbs reach 30m in length. Most routes are well worth doing. The gritstone is tough on the hands. SW facing but very exposed to any bad weather that may be around, always bring a jacket. Great views.
G10b,c; Map: 119 (Landranger) 008 616

❽ RAMSHAW ROCKS *

A truly great crag to the connoisseur of gritstone. About 120 routes in all grades up to 16m. There is plenty here for all, good bouldering, big and small. The crag faces E and is quite exposed, in winter an hour can easily be enough, in summer it can offer delightful bouldering in the shade on the hot days. A lot of strength can be useful since in parts it is steep but tact and skill will soon win through as the hulks get exhausted. Very near the road, good bet if the weather might turn, at about 1400ft though and prone to wet horrible weather.
G10b,c; Map: 119 (Landranger) 019 622

KENT/SUSSEX | DORSET | CORNWALL | DEVON | BRISTOL | SOUTH-WALES | MID-WALES | NORTH-WALES | LEICESTER | PEAKS | YORK-LANCS | CLEVELAND | KENDAL | LAKES | PENRITH | NEWCASTLE

BALDSTONES

⑨ BALDSTONES-NEWSTONES *

Bird restriction 1/2 - 31/7 at the Bald-stones. The outcrop is neighboured by NEWSTONES to the S; and GIB TOR to the N, and are dealt with as one as the climbing on each is so similar, and only a minute apart. From 7-17m high there are about 50 routes and a good ton of boulder problems. All grades here from Diff upwards. East facing gritstone with good holds. About 1400ft and cold on a cool day. Definitely worth a visit for the bouldering. There are also weird rock formations for those with weird tendencies and of lurid imagination.
G10a,b,c; Map: 119 (Landranger) 019 638
G10a,b,c; Map: 119 (Landranger) 019 644

⑩ HARPER HILL QUARRY

Just you know where it is, an old dis-used quarry with some climbing.
Map: 119 (Landranger) 062 707

⑪ STADEN QUARRY

Another old disused quarry with some climbing. Please park considerately. 20 routes up to 20m, slabby and possible to set up a top rope, Severe-E3.
Map: 119 (Landranger) 080 723

⑫ ALDERY CLIFF

An old limestone quarry with about 40 climbs mainly around the VS grade. 15-35m high and mostly solid in places. There tends to be vegetation here in summer and is E facing. None of the routes are particuarly brilliant to say the least. A cliff for the enthusiastic. The crag is on private land and use is subject to sensible behaviour.
G10g; Map: 119 (Landranger) 097 663

⑬ PIKE CRAG

About 10 climbs in the VS to E2 cat-egory. Fairly solid limestone up to 20m. The crag is quite steep but generally runs to good protection. A pleasant spot.
G10g; Map: 119 (Landranger) 129 590

⑭ CELESTIAL TWINS

An open crag with some good climbing. About 20 limestone climbs around HVS to E3. A few harder and easier climbs exist. 20m high. The left of the Celestial Twins offers all the climbing. West facing and worth a visit.
Map: 119 (Landranger) 133 582

⑮ DRABBER TOR

A 25m limestone crag offering about 10 routes VS to E2 on good rock but is to be reserved for the sweltering hot summer days. Not an often visited crag since you need to wade across the river to get to it after treking a good mile and a half.
Map: 119 (Landranger) 139 570

⑯ OSSAM'S CRAG

This is a crag for the green fingered not the white fingered. There are some fair routes here and on the neighbouring crag known as THE CHIMNEY. About 15 in total from Severe to E5. A crag to get away from the crowds. 50m limestone.
Map: 119 (Landranger) 096 554

⑰ THOR'S CAVE

Some futuristic climbing here on this very impressive limestone cave. About 20 routes VS upwards. Most routes are worth doing, around 50m and pleasant. This is also a very popular tourist attraction. Worth a visit.
G10g; Map: 119 (Landranger) 098 549

18 BEESTON TOR *

One of the best limestone crags in the Peak District. The rock often runs to good pockets and good protection. About 40 routes VS upwards, mostly HVS or E3. Worth a visit at anytime. Around 70m high with most climbs running to 2 pitches. Gets the morning and early afternoon sun. The stinging nettles in summer means a big stick and long trousers for the approach; remember you still have to descend the L side of the crag in the undergrowth.
G10g; Map: 119 (Landranger) 106 541

19 RAVENS TOR

A very good steep limestone crag offering perhaps the best climbing in the Dovedale valley in the middle grades. About 25 routes VS to E5 with a few odd very easy routes! E facing and chilly on a winters day. Worth a visit though. (not to be confused with the other Raven's Tor - 8a city)
Map: 119 (Landranger) 141 539

20 ILAM ROCK

A superb 70ft spire of limestone sticking out of the river bed. Only a few routes though. The summit can be gained by a severe from the gully behind and grass ledges with interest. There are 6 extremes from E1 facing the river to the very impressive overhanging wall Eye of the Tiger E6, guaranteed flying time. Definitely worth a visit.
G10g; Map: 119 (Landranger) 142 532

21 DOVEDALE CHURCH

A group of limestone pinnacles offering about 25 routes of all standards even so the best routes are E3 upwards, however there are exceptions so make the trip. A summer crag this one and approach can be very overgrown and includes wadeing the river, not fun in winter. You could always walk across the ice. About 100ft high with the best routes on the wall facing the river. Best descent is by abseil.
Map: 119 (Landranger) 144 522

22 TISSINGTON SPIRES

A very good group of crags offering plenty of climbing, about 60 routes in total of which half are definitely worth doing. VS upwards for nearly everything, lots of good E1's and a good handful of middle grade extremes. W facing but with awkward trees and undergrowth. At the S end is the John Peel wall with the best selection of routes on the crag and the classic HVS John Peel, following the rightward curving scar.
Map: 119 (Landranger) 146 521

23 BELMONT HALL CRAGS

Some 50 ft gritstone outcrops offering excellent climbing. About 15 routes at all grades. Worth a visit.
G10c; Map: 119 (Landranger) 007 504

24 HARSTON ROCKS

A softish gritstone crag offering about 50 routes 10m in all grades. The routes tend to stay green with the exception of Harston Rock itself. This offers a hand ful of routes VS to E3 around 20m and worth a visit. The crag is hidden in trees and is best in early spring. Harston Rock itself is a gem though and well worth a visit.
G10c; Map: 119 (Landranger) 032 477

25 PEAKSTONE ROCK

A small group of rocks up to 30ft high with some suspect rock. About 10 climbs around VS. Most though tend to be technically quite hard and strength is somewhat useful, in fact brute force is even better. Good place for hulks.
G10c; Map: 119 (Landranger) 052 422

26 CHURNET SOUTH

A small variety of conglomerate - peb-bledash buttresses in the river valley offer around 40 short problems and traverses in the mid V grades. A bit out of the way and esoteric, but worth knowing about.
G10a,c; Map: 119 (Landranger) 058 430

27 CASTLE CRAG

Some good climbing to be found here, and on ALTON CLIFF which is about 500 yds to the L. Anything worthwhile is VS and above. About 17m and 15 climbs in total nearly all around HVS,5b. A couple of 5c's at Alton Cliff. Mostly walls with undercut bases, good for the arms. Worth a trip for the HVS leader.
G10a,c; Map: 119 (Landranger) 073 425

28 WOOTON LODGE CRAGS

Steep and generaly hard climbing on these two buttresses with undercut bases. About 50ft high and VS to E4. There is a small buttress however with a couple of Severes on it just up to the L of the crag. Not a bad outcrop but a bit limited.
G10c; Map: 119 (Landranger) 095 435

KENT/SUSSEX · DORSET · CORNWALL · DEVON · BRISTOL · SOUTH-WALES · MID-WALES · NORTH-WALES · LEICESTER · PEAKS · YORK-LANCS · CLEVELAND · KENDAL · LAKES · PENRITH · NEWCASTLE

Map legend (numbered locations):

1. Wharncliffe
2. Dovestones
3. Rivelin
4. Bamford Edge
5. Stanage Edge
6. Higgar Tor
7. Burbage North
8. Burbage South
9. Millstone
10. Lawrencefield
11. Froggatt Edge
12. Curbar Edge
13. Baslow Edge
14. Gardoms Edge
15. Birchens Edge
16. Chatsworth Edge
17. Stoney Middleton
18. Stoney Quarries
19. Horseshoe Quarry

20. Rheinstor
21. Robin Hood's Stride
22. Cratcliffe Tor
23. Rowtor Rocks
24. Turning Stone Edge
25. Cocking Tor
26. Pic Tor
27. Long Tor Quarrry
28. High Tor
29. Wildcat Tor
30. Willersley Rocks
31. Black Rocks
32. Harborough Rocks

T Hathersage, Longlands (Food served)
T Grindleford, at Station (Food served)
T North Lees NT, Fox House (Some food)
T Stoney Middleton, Main road (Food served)

Side tabs: KENT/SUSSEX, DORSET, CORNWALL, DEVON, BRISTOL, SOUTH-WALES, MID-WALES, NORTH-WALES, LEICESTER, PEAKS, YORK-LANCS, CLEVELAND, KENDAL, LAKES, PENRITH, NEWCASTLE

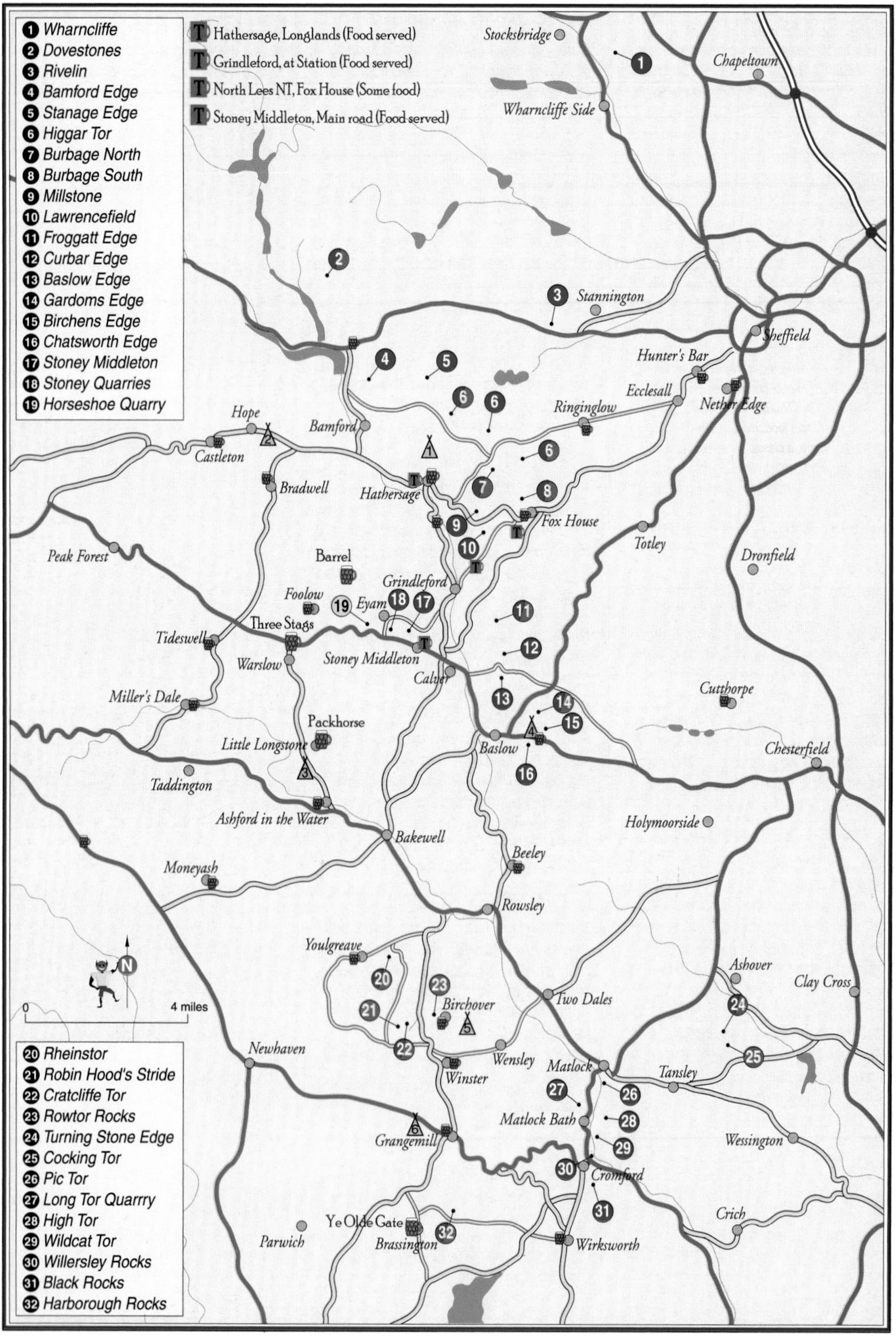

Place names: Stocksbridge, Chapeltown, Wharncliffe Side, Stannington, Sheffield, Hunter's Bar, Ecclesall, Nether Edge, Ringinglow, Hope, Bamford, Castleton, Bradwell, Hathersage, Fox House, Totley, Dronfield, Peak Forest, Barrel, Grindleford, Foolow, Eyam, Tideswell, Three Stags, Warslow, Stoney Middleton, Calver, Cutthorpe, Miller's Dale, Packhorse, Little Longstone, Baslow, Chesterfield, Taddington, Ashford in the Water, Bakewell, Holymoorside, Moneyash, Beeley, Rowsley, Youlgreave, Birchover, Two Dales, Ashover, Clay Cross, Newhaven, Wensley, Matlock, Tansley, Winter, Matlock Bath, Wessington, Grangemill, Cromford, Crich, Parwich, Ye Olde Gate, Brassington, Wirksworth

0   4 miles
N

North Lees Campsite, Hathersage, S30 1BR
01433 650 838   open: Easter-Dec

Hardhurst Farm, Borough Lane Ends, Hope,
S33 6RB   01433 620 001   open: All year

Farm Field, nr Monsal Head
?   open: ?

Eric Byne Mem. Campsite, Birchens Edge;
C/o Peak Park 01246 582 277 open: All year

Barn Farm, Birchover, DE4 2BL
01629 650 245

Grangemill, Middle Hill Farm, Grangemill,
DE4 4HY   01629 650 368   open: All year

The Barrel*, Foolow: A lovely position high
up with a great view. Practical food & good
beer.

Fox House Inn, main road to Hathersage:
Eaterie style pub, but warm and bearable

Three Stags Heads,** Wardlow: Classic old
style pub with food, real ales and
atmosphere, a classic of its kind .

Packhorse, Little Longstone; Small pub,
good food, tiny garden, quiet but calm and
nice

Ye olde Gate Inn, Brassington: Old pub,
great beer, loveley garden, smart and good
food

Barley Mow, Kirk Ireton (Just off the map to
south-Wirksworth) Really old pub with
superb real ale

BOREAL

PEAK GRITSTONE EAST

Topo guidebook
288 pages - Colour
Photo topos
A5 floppy style
Pub-2001
by Rockfax
(Chris Craggs
Alan James)

A practical guidebook to the eastern grit
edges. Easy to use and ideal for a first timer
to the edges. Thankfully reads from left to right
on Stanage, thank goodness - sanity prevails.

G-10d 〽 1-16 & 22

STANAGE

Text Route guide
372pages - B & W
Sketches & Text, some
colour photos
Pocket size & style
Pub-2002
by BMC
(David Simmonite)

The perfect book if you want complete brain
ache! Text as normal goes left to right, but
diagrams go the other way. A good authoritative
list of routes and grades, ideal for the ticker and
enthusiast. Photos are stunning and inspiring.

G-10e 〽 5 only.

MILLSTONE, FROG-GATT, CURBAR BLACK ROCKS ETC.

Guidebook
? pages -
BMC authoritative
guides
In progress

Various books

A planned edition by the BMC to cover all the
routes in the eastern grit edges of every route
done. Some current guides exist, but vary from
shop to shop, seek up to date copies.

G-10f 〽 Various concoctions

CHEQUERS BUTTRESS t-5b (V1 highball) Froggatt Edge; Choe Brooks

KENT/SUSSEX | DORSET | CORNWALL | DEVON | BRISTOL | SOUTH-WALES | MID-WALES | NORTH-WALES | LEICSETER | PEAKS | YORK-LANCS | CLEVELAND | KENDAL | LAKES | PENRITH | NEWCASTLE

QUIETUS, E3 1-6a, High Neb, Stanage; Mark Stokes

❶ WHARNCLIFFE

The most N of the Gritstone Eastern Edges offers 30-50ft climbs of variable quality. The rock is often green and is best in the hot summer months although facing SW. About 150 routes in all grades with only 20 or so of notable merit. Worth a visit if desperate.(Grit)

G10d; Map: 110 (Landranger) 300 972

❷ DERWENT EDGE*

A marvelous gritstone edge offering good sound climbing in the Diff to HVS grades. The edge consists of DOVESTONES TOR, the largest of the outcrops with about 40 routes. Other outcrops are THE WHEELSTONES, WHITE TOR and BACK TOR. All of these have good bouldering and offer plentyful entertainment. None of the outcrops exceed 40ft in height. W facing but quite high up at 1650 ft, chilly on a cold day. In a very typical peak setting.(Grit)

G10a,d; Map: 110 (Landranger) 197 898

❸ RIVELIN

At Rivelin there is an Edge about 100 routes and a Quarry 50 routes. Gritstone. The natural edge offers the best climbing and is famous for its Needle, a 20m pinnacle which can be ascended by the VS climber. Most of the climbs are in the lower grades and the less popular routes tend to get overgrown. A bit green and prone to slippery epics, also midge and mosi territory. (Grit)

G10d;Map: 110 (Landranger) 280 873

KENT/SUSSEX DORSET CORNWALL DEVON BRISTOL SOUTH-WALES MID-WALES NORTH-WALES LEICESTER PEAKS YORK-LANCS CLEVELAND KENDAL LAKES PENRITH NEWCASTLE

❹ BAMFORD EDGE

No Access 1/4 - 31/9; access only at other times for small groups by arrangement with the keeper, Tel: 0114 263 0892. A grouse moor. The gritstone here is very good and offers about 100 routes in all grades though most are below extreme. SW facing and with a superb view. Worth a visit if its a nice day. (Grit)

G10d;Map: 110 (Landranger) 208 850

❺ STANAGE EDGE**

The most famous gritstone edge in England. Over 800 listed routes in every grade. Nearly all SW facing and commanding a fine view over the Hope Valley. The rock is hard and coarse to the weak hands. There are some great three star routes here, but in general, it's the quanity of climbing is the plus point. Any bad weather can be seen coming from the W and rapid descent to the car is often a wise decision. Midges in late summer. Excellent bouldering. A must for anyone. Very busy at weekends, pay and display car parking. There are three main parts to the crag. The southern end is known as the popular end, and gets a lot of traffic. A nice selection of routes. The central area is called Plantation, and has the best bouldering of the edge. Also some superb classic aretes for highball solo's. To the north is High Neb. Here the walk is substantially longer and you can get caught out by the weather. Alternatively, it is the best place to pick up an evening breeze to combat the midges. A huge outcrop of complete variety.

G10a,d,e; Map: 110 (Landranger) 247 832

❻ HIGGAR TOR*

The steepest gritstone outcrop in England. Some classic routes that are designed to tear your hands to pieces. Rough rock. The easier routes look easy until you get halfway up, then it turns nasty, so beware of the highball enticing solo. Some nice low level bouldering. Often a quiet spot.

G10d,f; Map: 110 (Landranger) 255 819

HIGGAR TOR

❼ BURBAGE NORTH*

A fine gritstone outcrop with most probably the best rock in the area. Fantastic bouldering for any grade. About 150 routes in all grades up to 30ft but very good for the lower grade climber. SW facing and although 400m, tends to be much more sheltered than Stanage. Very quick and handy; but still investigate further along from the first sector, lots of scope and great climbing. Worth a visit.

G10a,d,f; Map: 110 (Landranger) 265 828

❽ BURBAGE SOUTH*

A NW facing crag which consists of an Edge and a Quarry, both solid gritstone. A lot of routes in the harder grades, with the Cioch Block in the Quarry being a very spectacular piece of rock. Some of the best bouldering in Derbyshire. Excellent crag. Car break-ins are a real problem with the area, so take good precautions.

G10a,d,f; Map: 110 (Landranger) 266 812

KENT/SUSSEX · DORSET · CORNWALL · DEVON · BRISTOL · SOUTH-WALES · MID-WALES · NORTH-WALES · LEICESTER · PEAKS · YORK-LANCS · CLEVELAND · KENDAL · LAKES · PENRITH · NEWCASTLE

LITTLE WHITE JUG t-4c (V0- Highball), Burbage North, Mike Loureiro

Left margin vertical tabs: KENT/SUSSEX · DORSET · CORNWALL · DEVON · BRISTOL · SOUTH-WALES · MID-WALES · NORTH-WALES · LEICESTER · PEAKS · YORK-LANCS · CLEVELAND · KENDAL · LAKES · PENRITH · NEWCASTLE

⑨ MILLSTONE EDGE **

Grit 6 · Alt-270m 35m 7.3
160 20 🏃 Ouch

Not really a crag for the beginner although only half of the 160 routes are hard. For the extreme climber this is the three star gritstone attraction, the classics London Wall, Edge Lane, Scrittos Republic and Masters Edge. All onsight possibilities for levitation expert. The easy embankment extremes with the keyhole cave area make this a great crag for the low grade extreme leader. The best quarried gritstone in England. A must for the visitor.
G10a,d,f; Map 110 (Landranger) 248 804

⑩ LAWRENCEFIELD

Grit 4 · Alt-250m 25m 7.1
70 --

A very good gritstone crag which is sheltered from the elements, everybody knows this so on windy unpleasant days don't expect to have the crag to yourself. There are about 10 different bays with the pool bay and wall dominating the outcrop. Here are some fine extremes on the back wall, none very hard. To the sides are some excellent VS and HVS routes, also some easier slabs. Very good in winter, a sun trap. Keep for the rainy or windy cold day
G10d,f: Map 119 (Landranger) 249 797

⑪ FROGGATT EDGE **

Grit 17 · Alt-230m 16m 7.0
150 35 🏃

A great crag, famous most of all for its unprotected slab routes. The edge is about 0.5m long and is broken for the first 300 yds. It then becomes more continuous. Nearly all routes can be well protected, and if not, top roping is very easy to arrange. Very quick to dry.
G10d,f: Map 119 (Landranger) 250 763

⑫ CURBAR EDGE **

Grit 6 · Alt-230m 23m 7.1
200 10 🏃

A marvellous edge, but the easy routes are fewer than of most crags, the harder routes tend to be long and sometimes very unprotected. The coldest grit edge in Derbyshire, even

though SW facing. It takes people quite a time to attune to the climbing style here. Very fine face climbing in the high grades, very high grades!!
G10a,d,f; Map 119 (Landranger) 255 755

⑬ BASLOW EDGE *

A very good edge for beginners, one of the smaller and friendlier outcrops. Nowhere is the rock really steep and the holds unuseable. About 100 climbs below E1, plenty of diffs. W facing and rarely crowded, the diff climbers retreat.
G10a,f; Map 119 (Landranger) 260 745

⑭ GARDOMS EDGE *

One of the less frequented crags, which is understandable since it does stay damp after rain for quite a while. Nevertheless the 180 or so routes offer really good climbing on sound gritstone. 30 - 60ft and covers all grades very well except the high E's. W facing but surrounded by trees.
G10a,d,f; Map 119 (Landranger) 271 732

⑮ BIRCHENS EDGE *

The! great crag for bumblies in Derbyshire. Be proud to be a Bumblie, have a great full set for breakfast. Do a few climbs, adjourn for lunch, pheasant pie and a few pints then take in a few more Diffs in the afternoon. This crag fills all those criteria. About 40ft at the highest, VS at the hardest and 400yds from the pub. About 150 climbs and SW facing.
G10d,f; Map 119 (Landranger) 280 728

⑯ CHATSWORTH EDGE

A crag not often visited since it faces virtually N and is very close to the main A 619. Nevertheless it has about 70 climbs covering most grades though the best climbing is in the lower grades. About 40ft, watch the mosquitos in late summer, they breed here.
G10d,f; Map 119 (Landranger) 275 720

⑰ STONEY MIDDLETON *

A very historic crag with some super routes in quite thrilling positions. The big walls have a midway terrace that the routes go from. They soon spurt out into space and are quite exhilarating to say the least. They used to be popular, but the routes have very polished footholds, making the placement of gear a highly risky business. Most people now avoid the danger. Keep an eye on the web in case it ever gets bolted up, would become the classic sport crag of the peak without doubt.
G10a, g; Map 119 (Landranger) 228 757

OUR FATHER E3 t-6a, Stoney Middleton; Pete O'Donovan

⑱ STONEY QUARRIES *

This is the lower part of Stoney Middleton further up the old track, and also contiues along a mid height ledget to then drop down to a small quarry by a didy power sub-station. The location is not completely inspiring, and almost awful at the electric quarry with spike to impail you! But the quality of the climbing is superb and technical. These are the most polished routes in Britain, but are highly technical and require excellent footwork and fingertip control. Sure to be the nemesis of a climbing wall thug. There are some fine big corners for lower grade climbers, and some really desperate boulder problems for the 8a brigade. When the main road is quiet and the sun is out in the spring, one could even call this place beautiful.
G10f, g: Map 119 (Landranger) 228 757

⑲ HORSESHOE QUARRIES

As far as grotty looking quarries go this one's not bad. About 70 distinctive routes which are all extreme and tend to be around E4. Anything worth climbing has lots of bolts. For the routes with less than adequate gear as viewed from below, abseil inspection seems very advisable.
G10g: Map 119 (Landranger) 208 761

VALKYRIE HVS t-5a, Froggatt Edge; Rob Wark

RHEINSTOR

20 RHEINSTOR

The crag is on private land. If visiting take care not to damage any plants etc, which would result in a likely climbing ban. A small crag that gives a handful of short, but exceptionally high quality and pocketed routes. Please do not leave any threads in place since it makes the whole area tatty and unsightly. There is some bouldering here, but completely eliminate since there are just so many jugs! (Lime)
G10a; Map: 119 (Landranger) 218 644

21 ROBIN HOODS STRIDE

This often gets grouped together with Cratcliffe tor, but is a totally different little outcrop. Some good bouldering, but not very much of it. Many holds have broken off and have worn through, so please do not use them, and treat them with a resin to protect them; good clean hand holds should not need resin. Some wild high balls if you are up for it. (Grit)
G10a; Map: 119 (Landranger) 225 623

22 CRATCLIFFE TOR *

A small crag with some classic routes but dissapointing as a whole. The rock is simply too blank and the routes are like one move wonders. The grit is good but becomes lichenous in winter and in summer it heats up to a furnace. Nothing here for the beginner, 40 routes 8-18m. There is also some bouldering to be had on boulders nearby and down at the bottom of the crag by the Hermits Cave.(Grit)
G10a,d,f; Map: 119 (Landranger) 228 623

23 ROWTOR ROCKS

Up behind the pub - The Druid (eaterie but with some charm-best sitting outside) are some small and esoteric rocks hidden in the woods. If you treat them like font, you can make a nice very easy circuit. Some grizzly roof problems too. Simply a nice place to be on a hot afternoon in the shade, with a pint so close at hand. Quote: Some jolly good bouldering on these much bouldered boulders.(Grit)
G10a; Map: 119 (Landranger) 235 622

24 TURNING STONE EDGE

A fine edge of natural grit in a very pleasant setting. About 30 climbs Diff to E2. 40ft high, good for the HS and VS climber. Some highballs too, with the slope goind down hill and you taking a roller coaster ride when you fall off. (Grit)
G10a; Map: 119 (Landranger) 342 621

25 COCKING TOR

A small gritstone Tor offering some good bouldering, high in parts.(Grit)
G10f; Map: 119 (Landranger) 344 617

CRATCLIFFE TOR - Fiver finger exercise wall.

ROADRUNNER E6 1-6b. High Tor: Andy Pollitt

26 PIC TOR *

Some good 60ft routes here around the low extremes. About 15 routes in total a VS, HVS(2), E1, E2(3), E3(4), E4(2). A sheltered crag and quite pleasant. NW facing, pocketed. (Lime)
G10g; Map: 119 (Landranger) 299 598

27 LONG TOR QUARRY

There is climbing listed here in some old guidebooks; the access situation is uncertain, please check first. Hard climbs in the top grades. Just a handful. (Lime)
Map: 119 (Landranger) 293 588

28 HIGH TOR * * *

The most impressive cliff in Derbyshire, with lots of old classic 70m routes with exposure. An unfriendly cliff, and highly dangerous to anyone coming from an indoor climbing wall. Gear is very difficult to place, and there are some big run out sections, plus many of the mid belay points have dreadful nut belays. The classic easier routes are protected with steel pitons, which sometimes are in place, making them cruisable clip-ups. Nice if you are a very good climber, but if you struggle around E1-2; it's a big risk here. The cliff is not without accidents needless to say. Road noise makes communication difficult. Gets very difficult on hot summer days and being so exposed it can get very cold. About 80 climbs.(Lime)
G10g; Map: 119 (Landranger) 298 590

29 WILDCAT TOR

The limestone alternative to High Tor for those without superhuman forearms. Unfortunaly the quality here is very poor to that of High Tor. Even so there are some very good routes and this 120ft crag offers plenty in the lower grade. There are plenty of VS, HVS routes. Of the 200 routes only 45 are extremes. The rock is very dubious in places and falling off should be treated with caution. The crag is long and rambling and not often very crowded.(Lime)
G10g; Map: 119 (Landranger) 297 575

PROMONTORY NOSE HVS t-5b, Black Rocks; Ian Parsons

Right side column tabs: KENT/SUSSEX · DORSET · CORNWALL · DEVON · BRISTOL · SOUTH-WALES · MID-WALES · NORTH-WALES · LEICSETER · PEAKS · YORK-LANCS · CLEVELAND · KENDAL · LAKES · PENRITH · NEWCASTLE

㉚ WILLERSLEY

The rocks are privately owned. It is hoped that sensible behaviour by climbers will allow the continued use of this crag. A small crag offering 50 worthwhile routes and 25 not so worthwhile. 30m in places with climbs well spread from VS upwards. Can stay damp after rain but is useful when High Tor is getting battered by icy winds. (Lime)
G10g; Map: 119 (Landranger) 298 570

㉛ BLACK ROCKS *

Some excellent gritstone rocks up to 20m offer routes of all standards. The rocks appear small at first, but upon soloing a route on sight, they take on a more interesting perspective. About 60 routes with countless variations. There are some small boulders at the bottom that are good, but not generally on the bloc-circuit. Plenty of high balls though, and big high balls at that! Although NW facing they seem to remain sheltered and warm for most of the year. (Grit)
G10f; Map: 119 (Landranger) 294 557

㉜ HARBOROUGH ROCKS

The farmer who owns the rocks does not want to be invaded and it is hoped that large groups will stay away. Small groups of countryside enthusiasts are very welcome. An excellent area of climbing on good pocketed limestone, unfortunately only 10m high, but nevertheless very worthwhile. Very good for beginners with the 50 or so routes spread from Diff to VS. Good spot and lovely to solo around in the evening sun - facing west, easy bouldering. (Lime)
G10g; Map: 119 (Landranger) 242 552

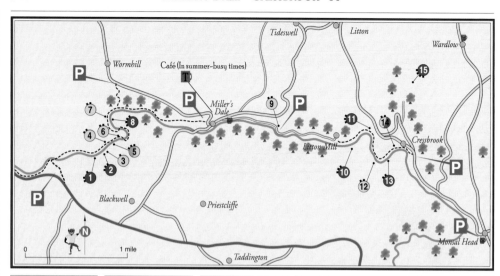

① Plum Buttress	⑥ The Nook	⑪ Jackdaw Point	**The Angler,** Miller's Dale: A basic pub that might improve.
② Moving Buttress	⑦ The Cornice	⑫ The Cornice	**Monsal Head Hotel,** Bit of an eaterie, packed with touroids
③ Long Wall	⑧ Chee Tor	⑬ Moat Buttress	**The Bull,** Wardlow: Strange opening, dull
④ The Embankment	⑨ Raven Tor	⑭ Rubicon Wall	**Three Stags Heads****, Wardlow: Just off map - excellent
⑤ Two Tier Buttress	⑩ Water Cum Jolly	⑮ Ravensdale	**Packhorse****, Little Longstone; Just off map - excellent

① PLUM BUTTRESS *

One of the most impressive pieces of rock in Derbyshire. Some classic routes here Big Plum E5 up the middle and Sirplum E1 up the RH side. About 18 70m routes in all grades E1 upwards with the addition of one classic VS. The climbing is very out there and leaders with leg wobble problems should have at least three shredded wheat for breakfast. NW facing and exposed ideal for a summers evening to round the day off in the setting sun, should exhaust you completely. (Lime)
G10g,h; Map: 119 (Landranger) 115 726

② MOVING BUTTRESS

Quite a lot of climbing here. About 50 routes of various difficulties from VS to E6 but mostly in the lower grades with a good deal of VS climbs. Little around E1,2,3. Either easy or hard. Some of the climbs worth a visit, especialy for the HVS leader.
G10g,h; Map: 119 (Landranger) 118 727

③ LONG WALL

A fair crag with some good hard routes around the s-7a/b grade. About 25 routes in total up to 20m. One of the first crags to get the sport climbing treatment. MW facing, staying cool but not cold. (Lime)
G10g,h; Map: 119 (Landranger) 122 728

④ THE EMBANKMENT

Some of the rock here is suspect whatever anybody tells you. About 10 routes, 20m high and mostly in the s-6c/7b grades. Mainly vertical climbing on small holds, technical and intricate. South east facing and goes into the shade in the mid afternoon, handy in the damper months.
G10g,h; Map: 119 (Landranger) 119 728

⑤ TWO TIER BUTTRESS **

A very good crag for todays top level sport climber and a lovely position, getting the afternoon sun. You have to wade across the water however. About 30 routes here in the s-7c/8a category. There may be some lower grade routes in the old trad style but this may well change to make it a full sport cliff in the future and bring it up to date. (Lime)
G10g,h; Map: 119 (Landranger) 122 728

⑥ THE NOOK

The crag in the dale for the Arnolds. Quite a few have been here over the years and with so much strength to spare have pulled off many of the holds making the routes now slightly difficult. Big roofs give about 10 climbs - 10m, and in the high grades. (Lime)
G10g,h; Map: 119 (Landranger) 124 731

THE GOLDEN MILE E5 t-6a, Chee Tor; Chris Hamper

⑦ THE CORNICE *

At one time an aid climbers domain. Now has given more up to free climbing, even so the L hand end is nearly always wet and is perhaps best left to underhand activities. One of the major sport climbing venues in Derbyshire, but a bit of a dump really. An ideal place to come and climb if you want to get cold, morose and be depressed. The cliff never sees the sun, and drips with water for 9 months of the year. If staying completely white and anemic is your ambition, seek this cliff out. The climbing is good however, with strong moves on steep but slightly overhanging rock. Just bring a warm jacket and strong shades, then you can't see anything and won't get so depressed. The cliff seeps and when it looks dry in june - it never is. A hot july is needed then the cliff stays dry until October. In a heatwave it is superb - but then again, this is England. Up to 25m high and sod all if you climb under 7a.(Lime)
G10g,h; Map: 119 (Landranger) 123 733

⑧ CHEE TOR *

A difficult cliff to comprehend and appraise in todays sport climbing era. Once upon a time the cliff would raise a cheer, but it is out of phase at the moment with not really any bolted routes. Some of the old traditional routes are still good, but others have a lot of polish to give the leader grief and anguish. They used to just be OK before the polish, but now most climbers prefer safer and steeper climbs. The angle of the cliff is mainly vertical and allows for good t-5c/6a climbing without having to be a power climber. Some of the easier routes in the HVS-E2 grades give pleasant memories of placing gear that should have held. Difficult to sum up since most climbers didn't fall off in the big trad era! Climb here with caution, there have been a lot of near misses. Out of the 90 listed routes, most are worth doing actually, which is very rare for any trad cliff in the Wye Valley.This large cliff sulks in some very esoteric giant rhubarb here in late summer, a botanical feast. (Lime)
G10g,h; Map: 119 (Landranger) 123 734

⑨ RAVEN TOR * *

This is the hard climbers rain retreat and power climbing arena. If you crank 8a, then this is the cliff for you. Even if you can spurt up a 7b then you're in with a good day here. Climbing here is an aqquired taste that doesn't suit all. Very steep and polished, wow - really polished - not on a Volx or Châteauvert scale mind you. Good power moves when it gets steep, crimpy like buggery at just about all other times. Some of the routes are multi-pitch and a big undertaking. About 37 routes up to 25m for the general climber. A complete clip up cliff. Park below. Famous too for the low level traversing and bouldering up the mini 8a routes. (Lime)
G10g,h; Map: 119 (Landranger) 151 732

⑩ CENTRAL BUTTRESS

The most impressive cliff in these parts. A sombre looking cliff with lots of dubious holds. Some leave this cliff never to return. The climbs are generally hard in the obvious areas of steeepness. The routes come up to expectation and are very out there in the upper reaches. A bold approach is neccesary here as is full competence in arranging protection. There are some easier routes in the wing to the R VS to E1, worth doing as well. The main cliff itself has about 25 routes 150ft and generally two pitch around the E5 grade. The L wing offers about 10 exciting E3's. A cool and creepy place to climb, best on a hot summers day, have an epic in peace. (Lime)
G10g,h; Map: 119 (Landranger) 163 729

⑪ JACKDAW POINT

The first largeish buttress on the area known as THE UPPER CIRCLE which has mostly extreme climbing on it. About 15 routes VS to E1 with a few desperates as well for good measure. 40-60ft high, little of great merit here.
G10g,h; Map: 119 (Landranger) 164 732

⑫ THE CORNICE (WCJ)

This area offers some excellent 20m 7c/8a climbs for the strong. On the L hand end (trad), there are some Severes and a few mid grade extremes. The hard routes take the obvious challenge of the main wall which becomes quite steep at the top. Also stays in the shade in the hot summer afternoons.
G10g,h; Map: 119 (Landranger) 167 726

⑬ MOAT BUTTRESS

A very impressive buttress with about 20 routes in the HIGH grades. Rock can be appalling on this cliff so a good reccomendation for trad climbers would be to give it a big miss. N facing and a bitchilly on winters days, especially for the second belaying next to water, good duvets essential. If the routes proove too hard take punishment on the BLACK BUTTRESS to the L of the crag, easy extreme climbing with no merit at all.
G10g,h; Map: 119 (Landranger) 169 728

⑭ RUBICON WALL *

Another weird oddity of Water Cum Jolly. A lovely piece of rock with some superb hard routes that all tend to be one move wonders. The climbing is genuinely good and varied. Bolting is usually verging on the appalling. In need of a complete equip. Quite a good bouldering venue with a superb stamina traverse. (Lime)
G10g,h; Map: 119 (Landranger) 172 729

⑮ RAVENSDALE

A 50m limestone crag where the view and situation far exceed the actual climbing. There are about 70 routes of which 30 are worth doing. These however are very good though somewhat loose in places. A very good crag for the VS to E1 leader. There are easy routes as well, but only a few hard routes. A scenic spot.
G10g,h; Map: 119 (Landranger) 173 737

INDESCENT EXPOSURE s-7b+, Raven Tor; Dominic Lee

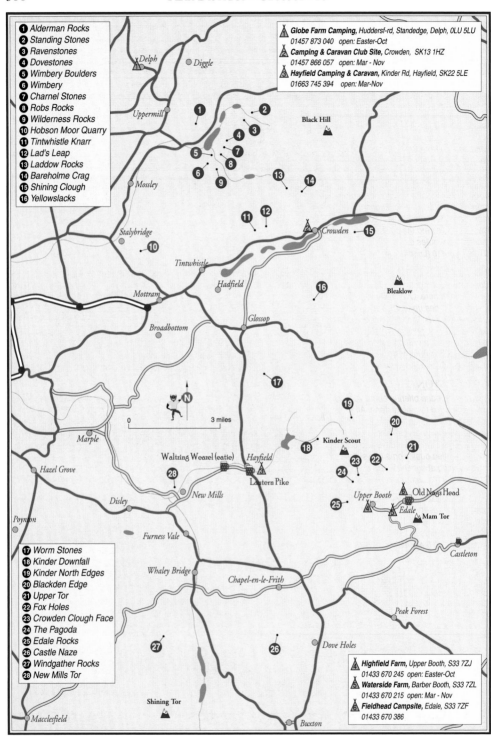

1. Alderman Rocks
2. Standing Stones
3. Ravenstones
4. Dovestones
5. Wimbery Boulders
6. Wimbery
7. Charnel Stones
8. Robs Rocks
9. Wilderness Rocks
10. Hobson Moor Quarry
11. Tintwhistle Knarr
12. Lad's Leap
13. Laddow Rocks
14. Bareholme Crag
15. Shining Clough
16. Yellowslacks

17. Worm Stones
18. Kinder Downfall
19. Kinder North Edges
20. Blackden Edge
21. Upper Tor
22. Fox Holes
23. Crowden Clough Face
24. The Pagoda
25. Edale Rocks
26. Castle Naze
27. Windgather Rocks
28. New Mills Tor

Globe Farm Camping, Huddersf-rd, Standedge, Delph, 0LU 5LU
01457 873 040   open: Easter-Oct
Camping & Caravan Club Site, Crowden, SK13 1HZ
01457 866 057   open: Mar - Nov
Hayfield Camping & Caravan, Kinder Rd, Hayfield, SK22 5LE
01663 745 394   open: Mar-Nov

Highfield Farm, Upper Booth, S33 7ZJ
01433 670 245   open: Easter-Oct
Waterside Farm, Barber Booth, S33 7ZL
01433 670 215   open: Mar - Nov
Fieldhead Campsite, Edale, S33 7ZF
01433 670 386

0   3 miles

❶ ALDERMAN ROCKS

Some pleasant climbing to be found on this natural gritstone edge. About a dozen or so routes 30-70ft in the lower grades, with a classic VS. Plenty of scrambling around, with a southerly aspect. Good for beginners.
G10b; Map: 110 (Landranger) 015 045

❷ STANDING STONES

A very isolated position but with the wind coming from the N the main road can be clearly heard. Gritstone and mostly around 50ft offering 30 or so routes in the middle grades, Severe upwards. A few diffs but an excellent crag for the Hard Severe leader. SE facing and pleasant but peat soil often washes down onto the crag making many of the routes dirtyish.
G10b; Map: 110 (Landranger) 040 053

❸ RAVENSTONES

Some very good gritstone offers excellent climbing here. Over 100 routes in the lower grades up to VS. Very good for the beginners. Well protected climbs 30-60ft in a nice position. At 1500ft and N facing, worth a visit on a nice summers day. Vile in winter. 40 min walk in.
Map: 110 (Landranger) 036 048

❹ DOVESTONES EDGE*

A very good edge offering about 70 climbs on good rough gritstone. All grades to E2 with lots of Diffs as well as VS's. NW aspect at 1400ft makes this a crag for the better days and can offer unrivalled quality on a late summers evening at sunset. Worth a visit.
G10b; Map: 110 (Landranger) 025 040

❺ WIMBERRY BOULDERS

Down at the reservoir at the back end of the plantation are some good gritstone boulders to look out for.
G10a; Map: 110 (Landranger) 016 024

❻ WIMBERRY ROCKS*

Most probably regarded as the best outcrop in the Chew Valley - Dovestones Reservoir area. About 50 routes in all grades on very good firm gritstone. The best routes are the hard ones but this should not deter the V Diff leader who equally can enjoy this crag. 20-70ft climbs on N facing crag. Best on a fine summers day when the rays are too strong man.
G10b; Map: 110 (Landranger) 016 024

❼ CHARNEL STONES

Some good rocks offering a score of climbs in all grades to HVS. 20-70ft and W facing, at 1500ft. Afternoon spot.
Map: 110 (Landranger) 027 027

❽ ROBINSON'S ROCKS

About 15 climbs in the lower grades with plenty of Diffs, V Diffs. Southerly aspect, 30ft. Worth a visit ,especialy for beginners. Pleasant surrounding. 1500ft.
G10b; Map: 110 (Landranger) 029 019

❾ WILDERNESS ROCKS

A crag with about 30 unpleasant routes worth a visit for the masochistic and ardent gloom doom climber. Route are in the easier grades but are mostly lichen and peat covered. 50ft.
Map: 110 (Landranger) 025 016

❿ HOBSON MOOR QUARRY

A popular quarry for some amusing bouldering and traversing. Good enough to make the peak grit bouldering guide - looks limited though.
G10a,b; Map: ?(Landranger) ?

⓫ TINTWISTLE KNARR

The climbing here though is reported to be very good indeed, especially in the central section. There are some two score routes listed here in the lower grades of VS and HVS. Routes are from 30-80ft on very high quality gritstone. More of a place for the VS climber upwards. Faces S at about 1250ft.
G10b; Map: 110 (Landranger) 043 992

⓬ LAD'S LEAP ROCKS

About a dozen routes on this natural gritstone outcrop. 30-90ft and of the lower grades around Diff-Severe. Sw facing at 1500ft and sheltered from the N winds. A nice relaxing spot.
Map: 110 (Landranger) 052 997

⓭ LADDOW ROCKS*

A great gritstone crag of tradition in a splendid situation and often very quiet. About 70 routes to HVS of which nearly all are worth doing. The climbs in parts reach over 100ft but in most cases 60ft is the usual route length. The cliff faces E and morning is the best time in which to appreciate the climbing Laddow has to offer. At about 1500ft it can get very hostile in the winter months.
G10b; Map: 110 (Landranger) 056 014

⓮ BAREHOLME CRAG

A superb small gritstone crag, ideal for beginners and those who enjoy climbing only to the standard of Severe. About 30 routes 20-40ft in the lower grades around Just Hard Very Difficult Almost. W facing and in a very pleasant situation. One can spy with binoculars the tigers at Laddow romping up the Severes.
Map: 110 (Landranger) 000 000

WESTERN GRIT
Topo guidebook
304 pages - Colour
Photo topos
A5 floppy style
Pub-2003
by Rockfax
(Chris Craggs
Alan James)

A good extensive guidebook to a wide variety of cliffs - Leek-Runcorn-Blackurn - area. Very easy to find the climbs if you are unfamiliar with the cliffs, not every route - but wow - a lot.

G-10b △ Good guide to familiar venues

KINDER
Historic
Route book
? pages -
Pub 1991
BMC guides
In progress

Various books

There is a current edition to the Kinder area, of all the listed and historic routes, however this may be out of date by now.

G-10j △ Area under review (17-28)

CHEW VALLEY
Historic
Route book
? pages -
Pub 1988
BMC guides
In progress

Various books

There is a current edition to the Chew Valley area, of all the listed and historic routes, however this may be out of date by now.

G-10k △ Area under review (1-16)

KENT/SUSSEX
DORSET
CORNWALL
DEVON
BRISTOL
SOUTH-WALES
MID-WALES
NORTH-WALES
LEICSETER
PEAKS
YORK-LANCS
CLEVELAND
KENDAL
LAKES
PENRITH
NEWCASTLE

HERFORD'S ROUTE Hard Severe, The Pagoda; Andrea Wright

⑮ SHINING CLOUGH

The majot outcrop of the Longendale area. A gritstone crag 20-80ft offering about 80 good routes in all grades to the extremes. Extensive and very good climbing to be found here. The crag is in most parts steep. N facing and at 1600ft. Worth a summer visit.
G10b; Map: 110 (Landranger) 098 986

⑯ YELLOWSLACKS

A gritstone outcrop offering about 20 routes 20-40ft. S facing but at 1500ft. Climbs are generally in the lower grades with a few VS's as well.
Map: 110 (Landranger) 075 957

⑰ WORM STONES

For the keen gritstoner. Some small buttresses offering about 20 routes in the lower grades with some more difficult problems for the connesieur. E facing and at about 1000 ft, requireing a warm day.
Map: 110 (Landranger) 042 916

⑱ KINDER DOWNFALL

This area offers plenty of climbing in the lower grades but at 2000ft is predominantly a summer crag. The very nearby Pennine Way, popular walk makes it rather busy with walkers and one should always be aware to the possibility of rocks kicked, or even thrown over the edge.
G10b; Map: 110 (Landranger) 082 889

⑲ KINDER NORTH EDGES

This area is dealt with as one for the purposes of this guide since it represents one continous edge offering very similar climbing. About 3m in total length offering about 200 routes in the lower grades on mostly good gritstone. The cliffs face N in most places and attract a lot of lichen, any bad weather that is going, 2000ft high and always in a cool airstream. Not a lot in favour really. Buy someone the guide for christmas, and you'll get it back next year. The routes though are quite good and if a high settles over the Peak in summer with many nice days a trip up here can be very enjoyable. It is not a crowded area. Climbs are 20-70ft and are on the whole quite strenuous. The well known parts of the edge are called ASHOP EDGE, RH side and CHINESE WALL to the LH end, with MISTY BUTRESSES at the turn in the crag.
G10b; Map: 110 (Landranger) 093 898

⑳ BLACKDEN EDGE

Climbing to be found on a 30ft gritstone pinnacle with a handful of routes around the Severe grade. The buttress is situated just below the rocky escarpment of Blackden Edge. At 2000ft and N facing.
Map: 110 (Landranger) 127 588

㉑ UPPER TOR

A brilliant gritstone crag offering about 30 climbs Diff to Extreme, of 50-70ft. Ther are lots of climbs in the Hard Severe grade, even so most routes are worth doing. At 2000 ft S facing with a nice sheltered aspect and getting and sun thats going makes this the best crag on S Kinder. Worth a visit. To the far LH end of the crag is the cliff known as FAR UPPER TOR with about 10 climbs around the Severe grade but on rock of a lesser merit.
G10b; Map: 110 (Landranger) 113 876

㉒ FOX HOLES

A good score of climbs in the Diff- V Diff grades on very good gritstone. 20-40 ft with just a couple of hard climbs for the VS tigers. About 2000ft up and facing NE, chilly. Worth a visit though on a good day especially for the V Diff leader.
Map: 110 (Landranger) 108 870

㉓ CROWDEN CLOUGH FACE

Some excellent gritstone here offers a dozen routes up to HVS on SE facing cliffs. Up to 80ft and very enjoyable. 2000ft high with superb views. There is also some climbing to be had on CROWDEN TOWER, which is to the L of the crag. About 40ft and a handful of Diffs-Severe climbs. The jump across the top always provides entertainment. Worth a visit.
G10b; Map: 110 (Landranger) 096 873

㉔ THE PAGODA

A fine outcrop of good solid gritstone in a lovely setting offering the best climbing in the immediate area. A handful of 50ft routes Severe to VS take the obvious lines. S facing and delightful. In between this outcrop and Edale Rocks on the W side of the valley is the NOE STOOL, a interesting mushroom shaped rock offering plenty of fun and scrambling. All at about 2000 ft and need a good sunny day. Not to be missed.
G10b; Map: 110 (Landranger) 091 868

㉕ EDALE ROCKS

A couple of outcrops of weathered gritstone rising to about 30ft. A dozen routes mostly in the lower grades around Diff, but there are some more taxing problems for the enthusiastic. SE facing and at 1800ft make this a crag for a fine summers morning. There are also a handful of easy climbs on EDALE CROSS ROCKS which are about 300 yds to the S. These climbs are even shorter though but worth a visit for the lower grade climber.
G10b; Map: 110 (Landranger) 079 867

㉖ CASTLE NAZE

A gritstone outcrop with about 40 routes up to VS. An excellent spot but at about 1500 ft and open to strong W winds. Best on a nice summers day. The crag is on private ground and climbers are asked to act responsibly. Worth a visit especialy for beginners.
G10b; Map: 110 (Landranger) 054 785

㉗ WINDGATHER ROCKS

An excellent outcrop for beginners offering about 30 routes in the lower grades, 20-30ft, excellent natural gritstone and W facing. About 1200 ft up with a very good view.
G10b; Map: 110 (Landranger) 995 784

㉘ NEW MILLS TOR

A small inner city outcrop that has crawled out of the New Mills suburbs. Sandy gritstone and rather gloomy - to say the least. Quoted as a unique experience - wow! 25 routes across the grades on flatish and cracked grit walls.
G10b; Map: ? (Landranger) ?

KENT/SUSSEX DORSET CORNWALL DEVON BRISTOL SOUTH-WALES MID-WALES NORTH-WALES LEICSETER PEAKS YORK-LANCS CLEVELAND KENDAL LAKES PENRITH NEWCASTLE

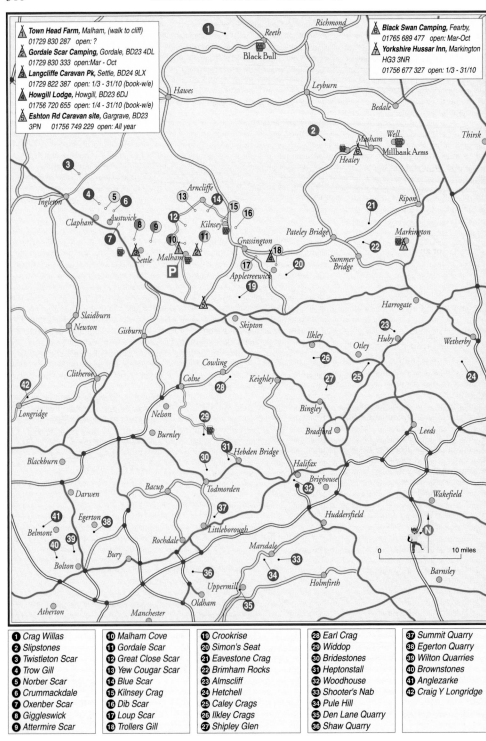

Town Head Farm, Malham, (walk to cliff)
01729 830 287   open: ?
Gordale Scar Camping, Gordale, BD23 4DL
01729 830 333   open:Mar - Oct
Langcliffe Caravan Pk, Settle, BD24 9LX
01729 822 387   open: 1/3 - 31/10 (book-w/e)
Howgill Lodge, Howgill, BD23 6DJ
01756 720 655   open: 1/4 - 31/10 (book-w/e)
Eshton Rd Caravan site, Gargrave, BD23
3PN   01756 749 229   open: All year

Black Swan Camping, Fearby,
01765 689 477   open: Mar-Oct
Yorkshire Hussar Inn, Markington
HG3 3NR
01756 677 327   open: 1/3 - 31/10

❶ Crag Willas	❿ Malham Cove	⓲ Crookrise	㉘ Earl Crag	㊲ Summit Quarry
❷ Slipstones	⓫ Gordale Scar	⓴ Simon's Seat	㉙ Widdop	㊳ Egerton Quarry
❸ Twistleton Scar	⓬ Great Close Scar	㉑ Eavestone Crag	㉚ Bridestones	㊴ Wilton Quarries
❹ Trow Gill	⓭ Yew Cougar Scar	㉒ Brimham Rocks	㉛ Heptonstall	㊵ Brownstones
❺ Norber Scar	⓮ Blue Scar	㉓ Almscliff	㉜ Woodhouse	㊶ Anglezarke
❻ Crummackdale	⓯ Kilnsey Crag	㉔ Caley Crags	㉝ Shooter's Nab	㊷ Craig Y Longridge
❼ Oxenber Scar	⓰ Dib Scar	㉕ Ilkley Crags	㉞ Pule Hill	
❽ Giggleswick	⓱ Loup Scar	㉖ Shipley Glen	㉟ Den Lane Quarry	
❾ Attermire Scar	⓲ Trollers Gill	㉗ Shipley Glen	㊱ Shaw Quarry	

The Pennines form the high moorland ridge of area that includes both Yorkshire and Lancashire. No less than 6 climbing guidebooks are included in this area which underlines the huge amount of climbing available here. There is a complete mixture of limestone and gritstone, which demands very different approaches and styles of climbing. The traditions of climbing have really changed over the past 10 years with huge effect, and we are now seeing the bolting up of a great many crags in the lower grades. Up until the late 1980's, the majority of new routes were climbed with substantial bolt protection. From then until the late 1990's, the bolting up of nearly all the hard 7b and upwards climbs has taken place. Over the past 5 years, middle grade climbers have finally protested at having to risk life and limb every time they go out climbing, and are now bolting up routes all over the place. There will no doubt be countless discussions as to the appropriate merit of this, but the majority of climbers seem to be very content and prefer to stop breaking bones, backs etc. Some of the old traditional lines have not been bolted, and judging from the vegetation on them, they will either get left for obscurity or be bolted up in the future. The gritstone on the other hand is still regarded as sacrosanct rock. You only have to look at the beautiful shapes of the rock at Brimham, Crookrise and Widdop, to see that this rock must be preserved forever, and always be left unblemished. As for the Lancashire quarries, well that is anyones guess but perhaps best left for the ultimate in highball bouldering.

For a lot of people, this area is on their back door step and is somewhere to climb in the summer evenings and weekends for an hour or two. For other climbers around the country, the idea of a weekend or even a holiday here is a pretty good idea. You have to judge the weather correctly, but there is a huge diversity of climbing here that will keep any grade of climber busy for ages. The guidebooks generally split into ridiculous areas such as counties or rock types. Since all the cliffs are in such close vicinity of each other, this overview should give you a quicker and easier perspective of how to tackle the area and get the best out of it. The bouldering is cutting edge, but also incredibly varied. There are the short little quarries and semi urban edges, there are the perfect lines at Caley and Widdop, then there is the high moor of Crookrise that is splendid and tranquil. There are good low grade cracks at a lot of the major outcrops, and anybody into jamming will find no shortage of lovely delights to amuse. The limestone offers some majestically hard climbs, but also can provide good entertainment for a lot of mid grade climbers now. Overall, there is a lot more here than you think, you just have to be prepared to look for it.

YORKSHIRE LIMESTONE

Topo & Text book
496 pages - B&W text & drawings small hardback style Pub-1992 by Yorkshire MC (Team Musgrove)
A good effort to a text route book, with some lovely line drawings of crags, plus excellent high quality photos. Lacks the ease of use with more modern formats.

G-11a △ All Yorkshire limestone routes

YORKSHIRE GRITSTONE

Topo & Text book
688 pages - B&W text & drawings small hardback style Pub-1998 by Yorkshire MC (Musgrove Army)
A good effort to a text route book, with some fun line drawings of grit; photos a touch dubious & misleading. Needs a lot of study to sort the good from bad.

G-11b △ All Yorkshire gritstone routes, err!

YORKSHIRE GRIT BOULDERING

320 pages - B & W Topos & plans A5 floppy style Pub-2000 by Rockfax (Alan Cameron-Duff)
A superb guidebook to the good bouldering all over West Yorkshire. Easy to use, full of info, and a landmark in bouldering publishing. Nice design and some classic photos (p90).

G-11c △ Both urban and wild moors

LANCASHIRE ROCK

677 pages - B & W Text & history Breeze block style Pub-2000 by BMC (Everyone)
It's the biggest book in climbing history. Very dull reference trudge to every lump and quarry dig in Lancashire. For the ticker - a dream. It fails on the inspirational level. Handy for short to stand on - reach holds

G-11c △ Gritstone by the bucket

No shortage of strange drinking folk to be found in the pubs around here

NORTH EAST ENGLAND

G-12a △ North York Moors, plus oddities

NORTHERN LIMESTONE

G-10g △ Peak-York- Lakes cliffs

KENT/SUSSEX · DORSET · CORNWALL · DEVON · BRISTOL · SOUTH-WALES · MID-WALES · NORTH-WALES · LEICESTER · PEAKS · YORK-LANCS · CLEVELAND · KENDAL · LAKES · PENRITH · NEWCASTLE

CRAG WILLAS, fine high-ball routes and problems, with a long hobble back if it goes wrong! Wobbly on cruise control

❶ CRAG WILLAS

| Grit | 20 | 👟 | Alt-600m | 8m | **7.3** |

| | 70 | 50 | HBall | **Q-D** |

A very good small ridge of high moorland gritstone, broken buttresses that give both easy short climbs and hard boulder problems. The rock is granular and a bit frail. The whole strata slopes the wrong way, making all the problems a lot harder than they look. A completely remote spot, lovely and beautiful on a fine day. There are plenty of shooting buts nearby, so watch out and look out for any access notices.
G12a; Map: 92 (Landranger) 975 012

❷ SLIPSTONES*

| Grit | 10 | 👞 | Alt-320m | 6m | **7.1** |

| | 100 | 88 | ☀ | ❄ |

A very good crag with lots to do. High in the bouldering list of places to go, but still quite a lot of easier climbing. A nice postion and is often warmer than you think. Popular but never busy. Walk in is almost dry, until you reach the laden bilberry bushes and get a complete soaking. It doesn't deserve a highball status, but the landings can be really bad, so don't skip on the pads here.
G11b; Map: 99 (Landranger) 138 821

❸ TWISTLETON SCAR

Access - important. The crag is on private land and access to it must first be approved by the farmer at Twistleton House Farm beneath the crag A long rambling crag. SE facing 30-60ft. Of the 150 or so climbs here few are memorable but climbing is nevertheless quite enjoyable. The rock is good in most places and there is easily enough to never warrant treading on poor rock. Most of the climbs are in the Diff to HS catergory. There are a fair few VS and harder climbs but nothing to even slightly tax the forearms. Always worth a visit.
G11a; Map: 98 (Landranger) 711 759

❹ TROW GILL

A slow to dry crag with about 15 routes 20-35m, HVS to E5. In a dry spell worth a visit. Most of the routes are good and are across the E grades.
G11a,10g; Map: 98 (Landranger) 754 717

❺ NORBER SCAR

A slow to dry crag with about 15 routes 20-35m, HVS to E5. In a dry spell worth a visit. Most of the routes are good and are across the E grades.
G11a,10g; Map: 98 (Landranger) 754 717

❻ CRUMMACKDALE

The crag is on private ground, but you don't have to get permission to climb anymore which we are thankful for - also do not park down the private road. The name of this crag is shortened from Crummy Rock Dale. Need I say more, it lives up to expectations in fine style, you are invited to take a hold home with you. About 50 routes 50-150ft in grades VS to E4, S facing. Some nice climbing, but the position and location are the major plus points.
G11a; Map: 98 (Landranger) 782 703

SLIPSTONES, another problem with an iffy landing; Jingo

322

the new **Scarpa Vision**

Visionary **comfort**
Visionary **quality**
Visionary **performance**

0191 296 0212 » www.scarpa.net

MALHAM COVE

Ale Flop 5a-8a (depending upon level of intoxication) Oxenber Quarry

❼ OXENBER SCAR

A short crag 30-55ft offering about 40 climbs in the grades Diff to E2 and quite evenly spread. The crag faces W and dries out quite quickly and in most places is solid. There is some vegetation but this hinders little. The crag is quite sheltered and pleasant. Worth a visit.

G11a; Map: 98 (Landranger) 779 683

❽ GIGGLESWICK

A series of crags running up the side of the A 65 out of Settle to the NW. About 150 routes in total of all grades and with a lot of newly developed sport routes across the grades, look out in the new Northern Limestone guide that will have details.

G11a,10g; Map: 98 (Landranger) 800 658

❾ ATTERMIRE

One of the better areas in Yorkshire to climb. There are over 200 routes here in all grades Diff to E5 with most being in the lower grades Diff to HVS. SW facing and quick to dry, but at 1200ft and quite exposed, not really for the cold winter days. However there is some very good bouldering here to be found for the colder days. Now has the added attraction of some sport climbing in the Victoria cave area, details in the new Northern Limestone guidebook.Worth a visit. (Bit of a hike from the car so bring the walking boots and umbrella)

G11a,10g; Map: 98 (Landranger) 834 642

❿ MALHAM COVE***

The most impressive crag in the whole of Britian without doubt. A wonderful collection of sport routes in the 7b and upwards category, and very popular with hard climbers. All of the hard routes that occupy the central curved area - around 100 are bolted up and are generally in good condition. Outside of this all climbers should be very wary. The rock at the side is very shattered and chunks can easily fall off and fly down. Make sure you have insurance since walkers are below, and will most probably sue if you kill them. The trad routes on each side are very mediocre and feel horrible when you are on them. Some of the old classics are ok, but the stars given to this cliff apply only to routes of 7b and above.

G11a,10g; Map: 98 (Landranger) 897 642

⓫ GORDALE SCAR*

A highly impressive and awe inspiring place to visit. The climbing in the 7c-8a grades is very good, sustained and a perfect combination of technicality, power and sustained endurance. For the other areas, the rock is simply too brittle and fragile to give any sense of enjoyment to the routes. If you are looking for mid E grade, freaky and dodgy routes, maybe it's your forte. Overall, dark, dank, chilly and windy. Great for a heatwave, but don't hold your hopes up.

G11a,10g; Map: 98 (Landranger) 916 641

⓬ GREAT CLOSE SCAR

Bird restriction 1/3 - 31/7 A very good crag offering lots of climbs in the lower grades. A pleasant setting facing SW and with quite good protection and on mostly sound rock. There are about 50 climbs Diff to E1 with a couple of good E3's also. Most of the routes are worth doing. About 80ft high for the most. Dries out quickly, can be cold & windy.

G11a; Map: 98 (Landranger) 901 667

GREAT CLOSE SCAR, set to the NE of Malham Tarn, a barren - yet beautiful landscape

GORDALE SCAR, at the end of yet another scorching hot summer day.

COMEDY s-7c+, Kilnsey; Steve Dunning

⑬ YEW COUGAR SCAR

Previouly dismissed as loose and unworthy of a visit, there have been a lot of new bolted climbs in the top level grades, little interest being in the unbolted lines. A lovely quiet position and gets the afternoon sun late on. A nice stroll down to the cliff, but a hike back up again.

G11a,10g; Map: 98 (Landranger) 918 707

⑭ BLUE SCAR

Bird restriction 1/3 - 31/7. Why this crag needs a restriction though amazes me. This crag deserves to remain thoroughly unpopular. It is loose, devoid of bolts and dries out only occasionally. (some folk complained at this description in the last book, we visited again recently to find whole sections of the cliff having fallen down - we were right so there!) There have been some 50 routes climbed here 60-100ft, about one is worth doing and that is the route back down to the car and off for a curry. Popular with 8a climbers when they want to do a bit of trad; if you don't crank 8a or higher, climbing here is a bit risky.

G11a,10g; Map: 98 (Landranger) 938 708

⑮ KILNSEY *

Lime	②	👟	Alt-205m	40m	7.3

| | | 70 | 20 | 😊 | Pump |

A classic hard climbing cliff in a quiet valley. Facing east it remains chilly and ideal for top level sport climbing in summer. A 2 star cliff but the bolting is in a state, especially in the lower grade routes; not the ideal cliff if you climb below 7c. There are quite a few old fashiond trad routes, but these virtually never get done (I've never ever seen anyone on one!) A good bouldering area at the bottom that stays dry in the rain, just about the only limestone bouldering area in Yorkshire. Please park considerately and do not block any part of the road or gates.

G11a,10g; Map: 98 (Landranger) 974 681

DIB SCAR

⑯ DIB SCAR

A small version of Malham Cove 60-100ft climbs. There are about 15 climbs here VS to E5. Most of these are old trad routes and look like being lost to obscurity. There are some new clip ups on the right hand side in the s-6b grade; but the bolts were placed by an amateur with their heads too proud, so be careful. (please see a proper bolt in the Bristol section). (Lime)

G11a,10g; Map: 98 (Landranger) 990 663

⑰ LOUP SCAR

About a dozen routes in the E2-E5 grade. 40-70ft with access being governed by the state of the river. Very sheltered and S facing, also quite steep, now a clip up crag, see new Northern Limestone guide (Lime)

G11a,10g; Map: 98 (Landranger) 800 658

⑱ TROLLERS GILL

A small crag 30-60ft offering a dozen climbs VS to E5. Most are worth doing with some classics at E4. The gorge allows climbing on both sides and is quite sheltered. Worth a visit, apparently now a clip up venue. (Lime)

G11a,10g; Map: 98 (Landranger) 069 620

⑲ CROOKRISE * *

Grit	㉑	👟	Alt-360m	8m	7.1

| | | 150 | 140 | ☀ | HBall |

🠒 The crag is on private land but access is granted and a good relationship is in existence. Moor is closed for up to 30 days each year 12/8-31/12 but never on Sundays (01756 752 774 to check).

One of the great climbing and bouldering spots of Britain. A bit too highball for many, so a top rope may be helpful. Great views, perfect friction and some iffy landings. Just hope that the wind keeps up, or the midges will eat you whole. Many sectors and a long rambling escarpment, a guidebook here is very helpful to find elusive problems.

G11b,c; Map: 103 (Landrg) 987 558

⑳ SIMON'S SEAT

🠒 A high grit crag to get away from the masses, but you have to be prepared for an uphill slog across the moors. About 60 routes up to 20m high, most are north facing, but a few are SW facing. In good weather it can be a very nice spot. A touch on the esoteric side for most. None of the boulder problems are worn.

G11b; Map: 104 (Landrg) 079 598

KENT/SUSSEX · DORSET · CORNWALL · DEVON · BRISTOL · SOUTH-WALES · MID-WALES · NORTH-WALES · LEICESTER · PEAKS · YORK-LANCS · CLEVELAND · KENDAL · LAKES · PENRITH · NEWCASTLE

THE ALAMO E2 t-5b, Eavestone Rocks; Jonathon Banner

㉑ *EAVESTONE ROCKS*

A crag deep down, deep in deep dingle dell. In summer it is a mosquito ridden swamp and not quite my cup of tea. May suit some. Soft gritstone with friability, but does take nuts and nuts to climb it. Some of the routes are very good, but many others are esoteric. I remain to be convinced, needs clearing of the jungle to make a better appraisal.
G11b; Map: ? (Landranger) 223 680

㉒ *BRIMHAM ROCKS* ***

Grit		Alt-250m	19m	7.0
		350	300	☀ HBall

A simply wonderful place. Owned by the National Trust - (parking). There are about 30 isolated towers that stand up wonderfully any mystically. Wherever you turn there are boulder problems all over the place, only 3 stars compared with Font's 5, but still very good and extensive. You need a guide to the area because of its scale and diversity. Some of the blocks are giant size and give very respectable routes on their own. A very popular spot with families and picnic enthusiasts; also the elderly with a nice wheelchair track around the area. Be prepared to be watched! Down on the lower tiers it is quieter and more laid back. On a crisp winter's day in midweek, it is quiet, calm and at it's best.
G11b,c; Map: 99 (Landranger) 208 647

BRIMHAM ROCKS, Pinnacles Area

CYCLOPS SLAB t-5b, V1, Brimham Rocks; Nick Reyner

㉓ ALMSCLIFF**

Grit	④ ▸	👟	Alt-250m	22m	**7.1**
▦▦▦▦▦■		**120**	**140**	Ouch	**HBall**

A very traditional crag with a great reputation. The crag faces in most directions but generally W. The climbing is very good from strenuous to delicate. Most of the routes however demand a typical yorkshire thuggish blunt approach for the easiest success. The crag is very exposed and dries instantly after rain if even the slightest breeze is blowing. Always worth a visit.
G11b,c; Map: 104 (Landranger) 268 490

㉔ HETCHELL

A small gritstone crag offering about 30 routes 30ft high. The rock here is much softer then most gritstone crags and care should be taken accordingly. A nice selection of routes in all grades Diff to t-6a. Worth a look.
G11b,c; Map: 104 (Landranger) 376 424

FLUTED COLUMNS Highly difficult; Mike Allison

Almscliff

㉕ CALEY BOULDERS**

One of the best bouldering areas in the country. There are 50 or so climbs but most of these are just large boulder problems. A rope here is useful for the unsteady and novice, not for the hard man. Boulders up to 50ft high on the main craggy section with smaller ones scattered around the fern fields. A lot of problems are well polished as with Almscliff, so there is no excuse for even having a hair out of place when cruising a problem. The crag is generally N facing but one can usually find some problems which are in the sun of at least dry.
G11b,c; Map: 104 (Landranger) 231 444

BOB'S BASTARD t-5c, V2, Caley Boulders; John Kirkham

26 ILKLEY*

A popular gritstone areas N of Leeds. There are over 160 climbs here in all grades and none ever seem really easy. There are various areas all within a few minuite from the Cow and Calf Hotel, a serious temptation to a days climbing, especially in winter. There is a natural crag on the moor called the COW AND CALF, which is the home to some hard and powerful boulder problems. There is a quarry to the L which is sandstone and offers some very good crack climbs up to 60ft high. Going .5m to the W are ROCKY VALLEY CRAGS, which are 6 buttresses and about 45ft high.
G11b,c; Map: 104 (Landranger) 125 465

ILKLEY COW AND CALF

27 SHIPLEY GLEN

A very pleasant bouldering area with plenty of fun for all. The crag is a series of small buttresses which offer about 5 problems each. Over 100 routes in all but none over 20ft. Generally regarded as a very good bouldering area. A rope can be useful also since the landings are not always comfortable and the finishes leave you in awkward positions.
G11b,c; Map: 104 (Landranger) 131 389

28 EARL CRAG*

Approach by footpath from the top of the crag in the centre, behind the cliff at the monument. A crag of many buttrese offering about 90 routes in all grades. N facing at 1000ft. Can be cold in winter. Very good on a summers day with plenty of bouldering, about 300 listed problems. Landings can be steep and iffy in places, excellent friction on the rock though. (Photo overleaf)
G11b,c; Map: 103 (Landranger) 988 429

28 WIDDOP*

A good outcrop on the moor overlooking Widdop Reservoir at 1100 ft. Not the place for a bleak winters day. Some very good rock offers about 50 climbs when in condition, N facing. All grades up to E10 with some harder problems. 10-20m. Down by the reservoir and a far easier walk, are Widdop boulders. These are immaculate and almost warrant an inclusion on their own, with over 100 problems. Individual and technical masterpieces, and wonderfully pure lines. Excellent landings. The boulders are in the lee of the hill and get full protection from westerly winds, so even in gales it can be calm. The crag can stay green because of this, and the boulders can get swarmed on by midges. At least there is a pub if it gets too bad. Plenty more bouldering around the local area.
G11b,c; Map: 103 (Landranger) 935 326

30 BRIDESTONES*

One of the best bouldering areas to be found. Problems at all grades in a very peaceful setting. Best on a good summers evening. Quite exposed and quick drying. 15ft.
G11b,c; Map: 103 (Landranger) 928 269

31 HEPTONSTALL QUARRY

A fine quarry with about 50 routes in all grades. The central quarry wall has very few easy routes including the classic Forked Lightning Crack, 5c. The main quarry is of a hard sandstone and the outcrops to the L and R are of gritstone and offer the easier routes. The crag offers plenty of hard climbing to amuse. 80-120ft climbs in general.
G11b; Map: 103 (Landranger) 985 277

32 WOODHOUSE

A small gritstone crag offering about 60 climbs in all grades to E4. The crag has a habit of becoming green and unclimbable. Most routes are around 30ft. Some very good bouldering to be found here also, with over 200 listed problems in the Yorkshire bouldering guide. Worth a visit after some dry weather.
G11b,c; Map: 104 (Landranger) 082 235

33 SHOOTERS NAB

A very large quarry on the N edge of Binn Moor. The gritstone edge is about 1000yds long and offers a good 70 routes in all grades to E4. N facing and at 1300ft, in parts quite impressive. 20-60ft routes. Worth a visit. A few classic HVS's.
G11d; Map: 110 (Landranger) 065 109

WIDDOP CRAG AND BOULDERS

EARL BUTTRESS E2 t-5b, Earl Crag; Steve Horne

㉞ PULE HILL

This gritstone area consists of an Edge and a Quarry, both referred to by the title. A good area with about 100 routes covering all grades well to E1, 20-60ft. The crag is W facing and one of the most popular in the area.
G11d; Map: 110 (Landranger) 032 105

㉟ DEN LANE QUARRY

Quite a large gritstone quarry but a bit mouldy. About 100 routes Diffs to mid Extremes. 30-50ft. Some routes are good, others not so.
G11d,10b; Map: 109 (Landranger) 994 059

㊱ SHAW QUARRY

A good gritstone quarry offering about 50 routes in grades VS to E4. 20-50ft. Well worth a visit and bringing a top rope along for some of, or even all of the routes. There is a lot around 5b to occupy the 5b,5c climber who enjoys the saftey of a top rope.
G11d; Map: 109 (Landranger) 952 102

㊲ SUMMIT QUARRY

A very good gritstone quarry offering about 70 routes in all grades, but even so there is an abudance of VS routes. 30-40ft. Well worth a visit.
G11d; Map: 109 (Landranger) 948 196

㊳ EGERTON QUARRY

Quite a large are of climbing with about 100 routes in all grades up to 50ft. Some climbs are better than others and should be seeked out, others should be avoided at all costs. Fairly predictable gritstone.
G11d; Map: 109 (Landranger) 719 143

㊴ WILTON QUARRIES*

Quarries 1 and 4, no restrictions. Quarries 2 and 3; local shooting club use the quarries on wed, fri, sun & boxing day. Do not enter even if there is no shooting. Look for local signs.
There are four quarries here and are numbered 1-4. The largest is Wilton One with over 200 routes in it. There are over 400 routes in the Quarries altogether and enough to keep any standard of climber busy for quite a time. The routes vary quite a lot in length but generally are around 30-60ft with some bigger and smaller. The walls face many aspects and it is easy to find climbs in or out of the sun as desired. They are generally sheltered and dry out very quickly. There is very good bouldering to be had by all.
G11d,10b; Map: 109 (Landranger) 700 133

㊵ BROWNSTONES

A very good bouldering area with around 130 short routes up to 20ft. Good gritstone that dries out quite quickly. Worth a visit, good on cold winters days when all the other crags are too cold
G11d,10b; Map: 108 (Landranger) 681 125

㊶ ANGLEZARKE

Although the rock is called flagstone it is for the purposes of most, gritstone in character. A very good crag with some very good routes. About 130 in total up to 70ft, plenty of problems as well There are climbs here to suit everyone. The rock is good but does deteriorate towards the top rather too often.
G11d; Map: 109 (Landranger) 621 162

㊷ CRAIG-Y-LONGRIDGE

An excellent crag offering superb bouldering on good to poor gritstone. The rock deteriorates towards the top and it is usual not to complete the routes. The crag is quite steep and offers zilch below t-5a. Nice setting.
G11d; Map: 103 (Landranger) 619 384

DAWN HVS t-5a Wilton Two Quarry; Gary MxCandlish (top)   CRAIG-Y-LONGRIDGE, traverse bouldering wall

KENT/SUSSEX | DORSET | CORNWALL | DEVON | BRISTOL | SOUTH-WALES | MID-WALES | NORTH-WALES | LEICESTER | PEAKS | YORK-LANCS | CLEVELAND | KENDAL | LAKES | PENRITH | NEWCASTLE

KENT/SUSSEX | DORSET | CORNWALL | DEVON | BRISTOL | SOUTH-WALES | MID-WALES | NORTH-WALES | LEICESTER | PEAKS | YORK-LANCS | CLEVELAND | KENDAL | LAKES | PENRITH | NEWCASTLE

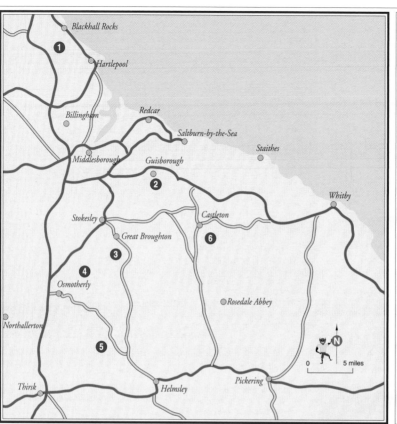

1. Castle Eden Dene
2. Highcliffe Nab
3. Hasty Bank
4. Scugdale
5. Peak Scar
6. Clemitt's Crag

An area that we don't know that well, having only visited a couple of times. We also have to rely on a lot of comments made to us over the years from other climbers who have visited this area. Not great comments unfortunately, and that is the exceptionally polite version! So what do we do - in or out? We say "in" - and have listed the 6 major climbing sites, if you search on the web using these names, you will find all the topos and information and get out climbing and have a great time. There is a 'new' guidebook that the locals are keeping quiet about (and hiding all copies away eek!), so there must be something in the wind.

NORTH EAST ENGLAND - Guidebook
A secret new guidebook
G-12a ⚠ North York moors & obsucra

❶ *CASTLE EDEN DENE*

Some esoteric crags in the woods. There are quite a few crags giving about 50 routes 30-50ft of all grades Severe thorugh to Extreme. The area will not appeal to all but to some but the setting is peaceful and the limestone is reasonably steep in places.
G12a; Map: 93 (Land) 429 392

❷ *HIGHCLIFFE NAB*

A very good sandstone crag offering some very fine climbing. N facing and best in the summer months, in fact a delight. About 80 climbs in all grades Diff to E5. The harder routes can often be quite bold, and those wishing to top rope will find a 30ft length of rope for the belay very useful since the top does not lend itself to many natural belays. 30-70ft. The crag has a fine view and is exposed, drying quickly and also getting cold quickly. Worth a visit.
G12a; Map: 94 (Land) 610 138

❸ *HASTY BANK*

One of the best outcrops in the area. The crag is sandstone and generally green in appearance. It is N facing and takes a few days to dry after rain, not sounding good. In summer during a dry spell however the crag dries out and gives superb routes in all the grades up to 6b. About 60 routes 30-60ft with the best routes perhaps being in the harder grades. Worth a visit.
G12a; Map: 93 (Land) 566 037

❹ SCUGDALE

An area of sandstone crags streatching along the hillside for about 1m and offering over 100 climbs in all grades, The crags face SW and are often dry. This makes them very popular. The area has been compared to Fontainbleau but given the choice I wouldn't think twice. Rarely does the rock exceed 20ft in height, but the interesting moves make up for this. A great spot for everyone. Individual areas are known as STONEY WICKS, to the R; BARKER'S CRAGS in the middle; SCOT CRAGS to the L; and SNOTTERDALE around in the valley to the L, 10 min walk.
G12a; Map: 93 (Land) 520 004

❺ PEAK SCAR

The North York Moors have never been famous for Limestone crags. This crag saves the day in many ways. Most of the climbs are around 100ft and in the Lower grades. About 70 routes in total. There is vegetation at either end and the crag is in general need of more traffic. For the VS climber the crag is very popular, also surprisingly solid. N facing. Worth a visit.
G12a; Map: 100 (Land) 527 884

❻ CLEMITT'S CRAG

Some good solid sandstone which for the most part is clean and very worthwhile. SE facing 25-40ft. About 30 routes spread over the grades Diff to E2. Worth a visit for most.
G12a; Map: 94 (Land) 709 037

MAGIC IN THE WIND t-6b, Highcliff Nab; Nick Dixon

KENT/SUSSEX · DORSET · CORNWALL · DEVON · BRISTOL · SOUTH-WALES · MID-WALES · NORTH-WALES · LEICSETER · PEAKS · YORK-LANCS · CLEVELAND · KENDAL · LAKES · PENRITH · NEWCASTLE

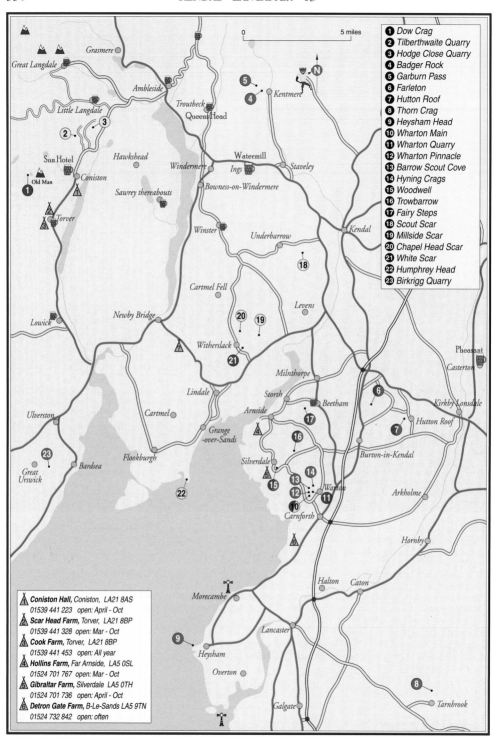

Map legend:

1. Dow Crag
2. Tilberthwaite Quarry
3. Hodge Close Quarry
4. Badger Rock
5. Garburn Pass
6. Farleton
7. Hutton Roof
8. Thorn Crag
9. Heysham Head
10. Wharton Main
11. Wharton Quarry
12. Wharton Pinnacle
13. Barrow Scout Cove
14. Hyning Crags
15. Woodwell
16. Trowbarrow
17. Fairy Steps
18. Scout Scar
19. Millside Scar
20. Chapel Head Scar
21. White Scar
22. Humphrey Head
23. Birkrigg Quarry

Campsites:

Coniston Hall, Coniston, LA21 8AS
01539 441 223 open: April - Oct

Scar Head Farm, Torver, LA21 8BP
01539 441 328 open: Mar - Oct

Cook Farm, Torver, LA21 8BP
01539 441 453 open: All year

Hollins Farm, Far Arnside, LA5 0SL
01524 701 767 open: Mar - Oct

Gibraltar Farm, Silverdale LA5 0TH
01524 701 736 open: April - Oct

Detron Gate Farm, B-Le-Sands LA5 9TN
01524 732 842 open: often

0   5 miles

Page side tabs: KENT/SUSSEX, DORSET, CORNWALL, DEVON, BRISTOL, SOUTH-WALES, MID-WALES, NORTH-WALES, LEICSTER, PEAKS, YORK-LANCS, CLEVELAND, KENDAL, LAKES, PENRITH, NEWCASTLE

Most of the cliffs in this area wouldn't even register in other areas, so don't get your hopes up if you are planning a months vacation here. Alternatively, there are some good small bouldering spots that have gained maturity over the past few years, and it would be silly of course to forget the classic crags of Trowbarrow and Chapel Head Scar. Places like Hodge Close are now very much regarded as loopy territory and we hardy saw anyone there climbing in 2003, not to mention that the bolts are old and rusty. It is a wonderful climbing location but has fallen victim to half hearted bolting, and that the trad style on this fragile and loose slate, seems too dangerous for most peoples liking. The main emphasis has been on Chapel Head Scar with some top end sport climbs, and with bouldering in and around the woods of Arnside and Silverdale. This area in particular, is often very quiet and a hidden gem. If you are into hardcore bouldering, then it should be on your agenda.

The area of Arnside &Silverside consists of a lot of Natural Trust wildlife sites, and is a real treat to visit. It also benefits from much better weather than the Lake District; View from Warton Pinnacle cliffs, Beetham village (next to good pub), Woodwell - simply tranquil & midgy.

THE LAKES
Topo guidebook
192pages - B &W
Line topos
A5 floppy style
Pub-1994
by Rockfax
(Andy Hyslop &
Paul Cornforth)

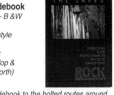

An old guidebook to the bolted routes around the lakes, plus trad routes on the same cliffs. A lot of esoteric locations. An easy guide to use, but now out of date with new N-Limestone.

G-13a /\ Lakes sporty routes

NORTHERN
LIMESTONE
Topo guidebook
276 pages - Colour
Photo topos
A5 floppy style
Pub-Due 2004
by Rockfax
(Alan James, Chris
Craggs, Mark Glaister)

A practical guidebook to all the best limestone cliffs in the three areas, including all the latest bolted clip ups. A substantial book that will keep you ticking for a while.

G-10g /\ Peak, Yorks and South Lakes

LANCASHIRE
ROCK
677 pages - B &W
Text & history
Breeze block style
Pub-2000
by BMC
(Everyone)

It's the biggest book in climbing history. Very dull reference trudge to every lump and quarry dig in Lancashire. For the ticker - a dream. It fails on the inspirational level. Handy for short to stand on - reach holds

G-11c /\ Gritstone by the bucket

KENT/SUSSEX DORSET CORNWALL DEVON BRISTOL SOUTH-WALES MID-WALES NORTH-WALES LEICESTER PEAKS YORK-LANCS CLEVELAND KENDAL LAKES PENRITH NEWCASTLE

❶ DOW CRAG***

See Lakes section

❷ TILBERTHWAITE QUARRY

A series of two quarries that are set in the hillside and offer about 40 routes. Some are well bolted, and others are invariably top roped. Also some easier slabs for kids. 10 mins from the car up a steep incline. Surprisingly open for a quarry, and with a nice view to the Langdales
G13a; Map ref: 305 008

❸ HODGE CLOSE QUARRY

Most people regard this as a place to definitly avoid at all costs. It catches the afternoon sun, dries out instantly and is very sheltered, 25 seconds from the

HODGE CLOSE QUARRY

car. The protection in general is terrible, and if you're squeamish, don't be a second. Sticky boots essential plus a towel and a 40ft piece of rope to make top roping easy. There are about 40 routes E1 to E6, and about 30 routes on the outlying smaller quarries all of a similar nature. 150 - 200ft. Car break-in's have been a problem in the past, so take precautions.
G13a; Map ref: 316 016

❹ BADGER ROCK

An excellent single block on the upper edge of a field, set in a remote valley. A mixture of all different styles, but mainly in the lower bouldering grades. Dries out quite quickly and with am-sun.
Map ref: 450 042   *(no dogs please)*

TILBERTHWAITE QUARRY

❺ FONT & GARBURN PASS

Just across and up the hill from Badger Rock is an area called little Font. Nasty with midges in the summer, but at other times you can find lots of good and short problems. Another 20 mins up the Garburn Pass takes you to the Garburn Pass boulder with about 15 excellent problems. Also in this area is the harder style bouldering to be found in Valley of the Kings. The whole area is worth checking out on the web to get the latest and up to date topos. Park and access as for Badger Rock

Try:
www.lakesbloc.co.uk
www.nwbouldering.co.uk

BADGER ROCK

WARTON MAIN

❻ FARLETON

Some excellent rock up to 60ft however nearly all of the 50 or so climbs are only 30ft high. The routes are from Diff to HVS with a lot at VS. Worth a visit for the VS climber. Faces SW and very quick to dry.
G11d; Map ref: 539 796

❼ HUTTON ROOF CRAGS

Lots of small limestone crags to explore at will. 20-30ft high and offering plenty of scope in the lower grades. Set in the woods and with some good overhanging boulder problems, recent popularity.
G11d; Map ref: 554 781

❽ THORN CRAG

Bird restriction 1/4-15/7; Private land; a good access agreement. Keep a quiet profile and please ring 01524 791 339 to let them know you are intending to climb. An excellent gritstone bouldering venue that is small, and in a nice location. A few longer climbs up to 10m high. (no dogs please)
G11d; Map ref: 596 571

❾ HEYSHAM HEAD

A coarse sandstone outcrop. One part of the bouldering is in the woods, and the other is out in the open. Good all round fun. (Do not climb if the rock is wet, since it becomes soft and breaks)

❿ WARTON MAIN

Bird restriction: Peregrines sometimes nest here, so please respect any signs for this. A large and jumbled quarry that for most part is best left to the birds. On the right hand end there is a good wall with a few clip up routes. The quarry will no doubt become a more important venue as loose rock is cleared and routes get properly bolted up, and belays put at the top. About 10 sport routes at present.
G11d; Map ref: 492 144

⓫ WARTON QUARRY

A small quarry with about 30 trad climbs up to 25 ft. The rock here is limestone and is formed into horizontal beds. It has got very polished over the years and consequently your feet can fly off at any moment, may well get bolted up in the future, simply for safety. Gets full shade in summer and still sunny in winter, a popular little venue.
G11d; Map ref: 498 724

⓬ WARTON PINNACLE CRAG

On the top of the hill at Warton are a series of small buttresses, set in the trees and of exceptional quality limestone, as good as in France. Some nice boulder problems but the landings need crash pads for sure. A lovely out of the way spot to boulder, can be difficult to find in leaf filled summer.
G11d; Map ref: 491 727

⓭ BARROW SCOUT COVE

A short and steep crag set up in the trees that gives a handful of hard John Gaskins problems. Faces south and gets winter sunshine. Check it out.

⓮ HYNING CRAGS

Some small limestone crags that are set in the woods. A scenic setting with some limited but hard bouldering. Looks like undercut roofs and sitting starts, so get on down there.
Map ref: 503 735

BOREAL

WARTON QUARRY

⑮ WOODWELL

A couple of small limestone escarpments set in lovely woodland. Cool in summer and dries out in winter. Good hardcore bouldering and mini routes that can be top roped very easily. 18ft high and around 50 routes.
G11d; Map ref: 465 743

⑯ *TROWBARROW*

A pretty awful quarry that reminds me of a lunar landscape, maybe this is where NASA shot the landing eh! One good face of rock, that is still pretty crumbly and is going to fall down sometime. The rest of the quarry doesn't bear thinking about, rambling tottle. A very good boulder to play on at the bottom though. You are best off climbing here in dark glasses.
G11d; Map ref: 481 758

MAX POUNCY slappin at Woodwell

⑰ *FAIRY STEPS*

I managed to find a guidebook to here with 150 routes on a crag, I couldn't find a cliff but found the fairy steps and around 150 boulder problems on lots of small bulging lumps of rock. A short top rope would be great for beginners to enjoy the climbs, but face up to it, leading short routes - you hit the ground before the runner holds anyway. This is an exemplary bouldering crag with literally hundreds of crimpy problems all over the place. Have fun, bring a pad.
G11d; Map ref: 487 789

⑱ *SCOUT SCAR*

A limestone clip up venue, see new Northern Limestone guidebook

⑲ *MILLSIDE SCAR*

A limestone clip up venue, see new Northern Limestone guidebook

⑳ CHAPEL HEAD SCAR

Bird restriction 1/3-30/7. A limestone clip up venue, hard routes generally.
G10g, 11d; Map ref: 443 862

㉑ WHITE SCAR   SAND

Loose generally.

㉒ HUMPRHEY HEAD

Some clip up routes here, about 25 on limestone up to 25m high, check the latest in the new guidebook.
G10g, 11d; Map ref: 390 740

㉓ *BIRKRIGG QUARRY*

Good and vertical bouldering, slippy
G11d; Map ref: 281 746

Side tabs: KENT/SUSSEX | DORSET | CORNWALL | DEVON | BRISTOL | SOUTH-WALES | MID-WALES | NORTH-WALES | LEICESTER | PEAKS | YORK-LANCS | CLEVELAND | KENDAL | LAKES | PENRITH | NEWCASTLE

MAJOR TOM E2 t-5c, Trowbarrow Quarry; Charlie Hill

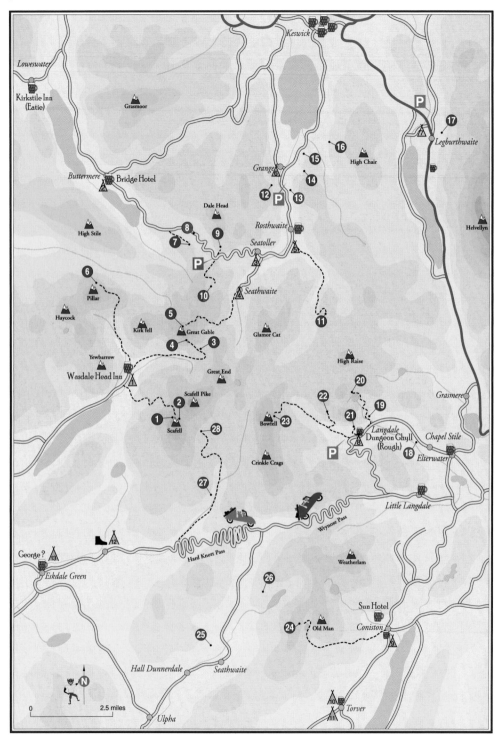

Loweswater

Kirkstile Inn
(Eatie)

Grasmoor

Keswick

Buttermere

Bridge Hotel

Grange

High Chair

High Stile

Dale Head

Rosthwaite

Seatoller

Helvellyn

Legburthwaite

Pillar

Haycock

Kirk fell

Great Gable

Seathwaite

Glamor Cat

High Raise

Yewbarrow

Great End

Wasdale Head Inn

Scafell Pike

Bowfell

Grasmere

Scafell

Langdale
Dungeon Ghyll
(Rough)

Chapel Stile

Elterwater

Crinkle Crags

Little Langdale

Wrynose Pass

George ?

Hard Knott Pass

Weatherlam

Eskdale Green

Sun Hotel

Coniston

Hall Dunnerdale

Seathwaite

Old Man

N

0   2.5 miles

Ulpha

Torver

I always enjoy climbing in the Lake District, who couldn't? But you do need to know what it's all about up here, and how to go about it. There a lovely balance between taking a nice walk and enjoying the countryside, having plenty of time on your hands to go at a snails pace, loving the glorious sunshine and fresh breeze; and wandering up some rocky route with stunning views. These are the central elements to climbing in the Lake District, and are hardly related to any climbing wall or bouldering activity. You can mix modern climbing with the lakes, but you have to be careful and fully appreciative of what you are getting involved with. We have included 28 cliffs as a selection of the finest, enjoyable and relatively safe cliffs. There are many others that come with a health warning, so investigate locally. The Lakes are split into several climbing areas that are very well covered by traditional climbing guidebooks. (You never get tired on a route here, because you spend so much time resting, and trying to fit the guidebook description to the route you are on!) The easiest to get to and most popular areas being Borrowdale and Langdale. Both of these areas have good cliffs with plenty of good climbs in the diff up to HVS grades, but you will find that the easier routes do get incredibly busy, so an early start is always a sensible move. Tiny mountaineering is how the majority of climbers who trip to the lakes - view it! An average classic climb in the lakes will have 4-5 pitches and can take the majority of climbers, a good 3-4 hours to get up it. The norm on most easier mountain routes, is to carry a little sac with your trekking boots, flask and sandwiches, and make a full day tour. Even on the harder climbs, the descent down from the top of the cliff can take a good 20 mins and you definitely should always carry a pair of descending shoes with you. The lakes are very much a trad climbing domain, where woolly trousers and helmets are still the in fashion. You can't mock, because this is driven partly out of necessity since it is often so darn cold, and the place is full of beginners who come to the 'Mountains,' and end up knocking bits of rock off, all over the place - so watch out. Placing protection here is an art and a skill, not something that you learn in the gym, and not something to be taken lightly. Many nut placements are poor or marginal, and you have to take advantage of any crack or crevice, hence double ropes are essential for parallel placed runners. Also remember that runners will always fail more easily on big shock loading, so ditch those locking belay devices and use a soft-breaking style. Warning - the high fells and are a big hike up to. Any city dweller, should add a good extra amount of time to the walk in estimates given in the local guidebooks, plus you are going to need a very good map, good waterproof boots to wade through bogs, and a cagoule in case the weather turns nasty, it can easily be a couple of hours back to the car. Parking is an issue with the many (unattended) pay and display car parks; make you car look obviously empty. If you join the NT at present, you get free parking.

1 Scafell Crag	
2 Scafell East Buttress	
3 Kern Knotts	
4 The Napes	
5 Gable Crag	
6 Pillar Rock	
7 High Crag	
8 Honister Boulders	
9 Buckstone How	
10 Gillercombe	
11 Sergeant Crag	
12 Goat Crag	
13 Bowderstone	
14 Black Crag	
15 Shepherd's Crag	
16 Reecastle Crag	
17 Castle Rock	
18 Langdale Boulders	
19 White Ghyll	
20 Pavey Ark	
21 Raven Crag	
22 Gimmer Crag	
23 Bowfell Buttress	
24 Dow Crag	
25 Wallowbarrow	
26 Burnt Crag	
27 Heron Crag	
28 Esk Buttress	

Wasdale NT, Wasdale, CA20 1EX
01946 726 220   open: All year
Dalegarth, Buttermere, CA13 9XA
01768 770 233   open: April-Oct
Seatoller Farm, Borrowdale, CA12 5XN
01768 777 232   open: All year
Seathwaite Farm, Borrowdale ?
01768 777 394   open: ?
Stonethwaite Farm, Borrowdale, CA12 5XG
01768 777 234   open: All year
Hollows Farm, Grange-in-B, CA12 5UQ
01768 777 298   open: All year
Bridge End Farm, Thirlmere, CA12 4TG
01768 772 166   open: ?
Great Langdale NT, LA22 9JU
01539 437 668   open: All year
Coniston Hall, Coniston, LA21 8AS
01539 441 223   open: April - Oct
Scar Head Farm, Torver, LA21 8BP
01539 441 328   open: Mar - Oct
Cook Farm, Torver, LA21 8BP
01539 441 453   open: All year
Hollins Farm, Boot, CA19 1TH
01946 723 253   open: All year
Fisherground Farm, Eskdale CA19 1TF
01946 723 349   open: 1/3 - 15/11
Camping notes:

LAKE DISTRICT ROCK
Topo & Text guidebook
512 pages - Colour
Heavyweight big pocket style
Pub-2003 (Selected climbs)
by Fell & Rock Climbing Club
(Team Zing along with Steve Reid)
A practical guidebook to a superb
selection of cliffs and routes all
over the Lake District. Very well
illustrated indeed, with (very small)
diagrams. Plenty of colour photos
- illustrating routes with a very high
feel good factor, an eye opener.

G-14a (500 Best tunes)

LAKE DISTRICT - Text; route book series
Around 400 pages - B&W with colour photos
Heavyweight pocket style; Pub by Fell & Rock Climbing Club
G-14b - Scafell - 1996
G-14c - Gable and Pillar - 1991
G-14d - Borrowdale - 2000
G-14e - Eastern & Buttermere - 1992
G-14f - Langdale - 1999
G-14g - Dow, Duddon - 1993

The originals started as tiny pocket books; now approaching
half a kilo each! Advantage; they contain all the known routes,
(no 'Q's on routes outside selected guide) Disadvantages;
layout is text printout, diagrams very small & highly difficult to
understand, having to carry shed loads of E route details!

KENT/SUSSEX · DORSET · CORNWALL · DEVON · BRISTOL · SOUTH-WALES · MID-WALES · NORTH-WALES · LEICSETER · PEAKS · YORK-LANCS · CLEVELAND · KENDAL · LAKES · PENRITH · NEWCASTLE

KENT/SUSSEX | DORSET | CORNWALL | DEVON | BRISTOL | SOUTH-WALES | MID-WALES | NORTH-WALES | LEICSTER | PEAKS | YORK-LANCS | CLEVELAND | KENDAL | LAKES | PENRITH | NEWCASTLE

❶ SCAFELL CRAG*

Vol	80	👢	Alt-791m	120m	7.4

| | 70 | -- | 🢀 | Zzz |

A very highly regarded crag in the Lakes with traditionalists. Steep and uncompromising. The cliff comprises of a big main cliff with a few classic lines, especially in the VS-E2 grades and offers little below the severe grade. There are quite a lot of other routes on the buttresses to either side, but you have to be prepared for dampness and high chill factor. Worth a trip only in very good weather. Walk up is a bit grim.
G14a, b; Map ref: 209 068

❷ EAST BUTTRESS***

Vol	80	👢	Alt-750m	70m	7.3

| | 50 | -- | 🧗 | 🢀 |

A stupendous high cliff and very prone to wind whistling around it and being a bit cooler than you had anticipated. The cliff leans out at you and can be amazingly blank in sections, for both gear and holds. Rock quality is very good, but really does need an extended dry spell as there is a green tinge to just about everything. Lovely and sunny in the morning, cool shade in the afternoon. The best crag in the lakes during a heatwave, just no easy routes on it. Approach from Wasdale.
G14a, b; Map ref: 215 067

❸ KERN KNOTTS*

Vol	70	👟	Alt-520m	9m	7.3

| | 25 | -- | ❄ | 🢀 |

In my humble opinion this is the best small crag in the Lakes. A grand position and fantastic rock, it was a pity when half of the crag fell down! The LH part offers half a dozen climbs 120ft around VS, that catch the sun all day. On the E face there are classics VS to E3 70-150ft. A very attractive crag since the Napes is yet more of a slog uphill just when you don't need it. A must for the VS climber. You can see the crag from the car park, but you do need a telescope, it's a long way away.
G14a, c; Map ref: 216 095

EAST BUTTRESS Scafell

❹ NAPES CRAGS*

Vol	90	👟	Alt-700m	75m	7.6

| | 60 | -- | ❄ | 🏃 |

The SE side of Great Gable has a series of crags that offer a few very good climbs, and a series of broken ridge routes in the lower grades, with only a handful of classic routes. There is of course Napes Needle, a classic piece of rock in itself and should be on everyone's tick list. A good area for a mountain day out and making a trip to the top of Great Gable and beyond.
G14a, c; Map ref: 211 099

❺ GABLE CRAG*

Vol	120	👢	Alt-800m	65m	7.6

| | 40 | -- | 🐾 | Zzz |

A fair crag with some high quality routes around the E3-4 grade. The crag is quite steep and is hardly to be reccomended for most climbers. It is an ideal place to get away from it all and be in complete isolation. It can stay damp for a long time after rain, only bother in a really dry period and to catch the late evening sun - perhaps.
G14a, c; Map ref: 213 105

NAPES NEEDLE

APPIAN WAY Severe, Pillar Rock; Dave Kirby

6 PILLAR ROCK**

Vol	135 +	⬛	Alt-600m	100m	7.5

| ⬛⬛⬛⬛⬛ | 80 | -- | ⬅ | Zzz |

Most people are impressed by this huge piece of rock so
long as there visit is on a good sunny day. After Napes
Needle it must have more history attached to it than the
whole of the Lake District put together. The climbing is quite
good in most places, indeed some of the routes are quite
exceptional, but the main reason for such stature attached
to the rock itself can be more attributed to the fine setting it
commands over Ennerdale. The best routes are in the lower+
grades around V Diff and it is this climber who will most
probably benifit most from a visit. Catches the afternoon sun.
There are many other crags in the area of a broken smaller
nature offering endless Diffs and Severes.
G14a, c; Map ref: 172 123

7 HIGH CRAG*

A cliff that comes by high recomnedation from a variety of
sources. At 450m and NE facing, there are a good selection
of medium 1-2 pitch routes of exceptional high quality. A fine
looking piece of rock. Good also in a heatwave since it goes
nicely into shade.
G14a, e; Map ref: 183 145 (55 mins)

I know your watching but I just ain't doing another sit start

8 HONISTER BOULDERS

A couple of superb, high quality boulders by the road in the
middle of the pass. Lots of problems, and a lovely picnic spot
Map ref: 217 144

KENT/SUSSEX · DORSET · CORNWALL · DEVON · BRISTOL · SOUTH-WALES · MID-WALES · NORTH-WALES · LEICSETER · PEAKS · YORK-LANCS · CLEVELAND · KENDAL · LAKES · PENRITH · NEWCASTLE

❾ BUCKSTONE HOW

| Vol | 14 | 👟 | Alt-403m | 55m | **7.6** |

| 18 | -- | |

A large and steep crag with some interesting climbing on. The rock is most parts is of dubious nature and should be treated accordingly, an absorbing cliff for a VS climber trying to break into the HVS category. The cliff has a habit of throwing out awkward moves. Coins needed for pay & display car park.
G14a, e; Map ref: 223 143

❿ GILLERCOMBE *

| Vol | 70 | 🥾 | Alt-480m | 180m | **7.4** |

| 12 | 15 | |

A cliff with about 11 routes and an all time classic, Gillercombe Buttress - Severe. Worth walking all the way up for just that route. The other routes are quite broken and ramble around. There could be more easy classics all over the crag, but everyone seems to just follow the same old route. Down below are some boulders in a lovely location. Nothing wonderful but still nice to play on; t-4a up to t-6b
G14a, d; Map ref: 223 124

KENT/SUSSEX
DORSET
CORNWALL
DEVON
BRISTOL
SOUTH-WALES
MID-WALES
NORTH-WALES
LEICESTER
PEAKS
YORK-LANCS
CLEVELAND
KENDAL
LAKES
PENRITH
NEWCASTLE

⑪ SERGEANT CRAG SLABS *

| Vol | 55 | | Alt-400m | 45m | 7.3 |
| | 20 | | -- | ☀ | 🏃 |

A very fine set of slabs high up on the fell with some excellent routes in the VS category and harder. The majority of the hard climbing moves are in the t-5a/b standard and it is only the protection that is either there or not. Some climbers take an abseil rope to the crag and make life a lot easier for the day out for everyone to easily descend.
G14a, d; Map ref: 271 113

In the area is Sergeant Crag with a gully climb of severe standard; more like severe load of s......

⑫ GOAT CRAG

| Vol | 35 | | Alt-350m | 100m | 7.5 |
| | 160 | | -- | 🌿 | ∞ |

The only crag of real significance on the W side of the Borrowdale valley. To be kept for those real scorching summer days! The main crag some 300ft high is very imposing when you are actually on it, about 20 middle grade Extremes. Some of the harder routes are clean and sometimes in a fair condition, but I've often found the vegetation to be rampant. A cliff that struggles with its own charisma.
G14a, d; Map ref: 245 165

⑬ BOWDERSTONE AREA *

There is the Bowderstone for a start, a wonderful piece of rock that is one of the finest boulders in the whole of England, if not - the finest. It takes a while to get sucked into the addiction of the bouldering here, and you have to be able to crank good t-6a V3, to even get onto any of the worthwhile problems. The landings are impeccable, and the shady location is fantastic. If you can crank really hard, then it really gets good. Nothing else in the bouldering around here though. There are some small cliffs in the area with a few really hard trad classics E6 upwards. Certainly the area for a pumped up and eager gorilla.
G14a; Map ref: 254 164
(quite a lot of info in the best tunes)
Dir: follow signs to the Bowderstone from the NT pay and display car park.

THE BOWDERSTONE; Caleb 'Cal' Reid, cranking away

KENT/SUSSEX · DORSET · CORNWALL · DEVON · BRISTOL · SOUTH-WALES · MID-WALES · NORTH-WALES · LEICSETER · PEAKS · YORK-LANCS · CLEVELAND · KENDAL · LAKES · PENRITH · NEWCASTLE

TROUTDALE PINNACLE, Black Crag, Borrowdale; Wobbly solo

CASTLE ROCK, Thirlmere

DERWENT WATER, almost from Reecastle Crag

⑭ BLACK CRAG*

| Vol | 20 | 👟 | Alt-260m | 100m | 7.5 |

| | | 47 | -- | ❄ | |

A good crag with plenty of good routes in the VS and HVS category. The classic of the crag is Troutdale Pinnacle and has about 20 ascents each day of the year, deservedly so. A lot of the crag suffers from vegetation as the routes are not very popular. Rock in places has a nice texture, but in other areas is very suspect and smooth, so bring cams with a soft - rather than an expansive mechanism. The top of the crag is particularly quiet and beautiful, one of the finest views in the Lake district.
G14a, d; Map ref: 263 172

⑮ SHEPHERDS CRAG**

| Vol | 25 | 👟 | Alt-140m | 26m | 7.4 |

| | | 100 | -- | Fun | Q-D |

The crag is only a short distance from the road, but you have to park a long way away which is a bit naff

unfortunately. The rock is really flat and of very high quality, perfect for good old fashioned trad climbing. A huge variety of climbs from easy slabs, to big exposed walls with jugs on, and eventually overhanging grooves - without jugs on. If you can't enjoy a day climbing here, give up outdoor routing. The only disadvantage is that it does get busy as it is the first crag to dry out in the area. It also can be protected from the wind and on damp mornings is a mosquito and midge dense habitat. Other spots can be a wiser choice.
G14a, d; Map ref: 263 185

⑯ REECASTLE CRAG

| Vol | 8 | 👟 | Alt-300m | 9m | 7.4 |

| | | 32 | -- | ❄ | 👾 |

If you climb hard and fancy yourself as a top end E grade climber, then this is your crag. Not that steep - for the grade, just quite necky and nerve demanding. A crag that most people enjoy top roping the routes at s-7a/7c
G14a, d; Map ref: 273 176

⑰ CASTLE ROCK*

| Vol | 11 | 👟 | Alt-270m | 85m | 7.5 |

| | | 160 | -- | ❄ | 👾 |

A crag that should definitely come with a health warning. The rock is surprisingly good, but it doesn't take much gear, and the falls are very nasty. I have backed off plenty of routes here in the interest of self preservation, you have been warned! The climbing is very good and split into 2 parts; a nice easy section with lovely open walls and pleasant routes - rock is a bit weird in places. Then the main rock part, which is more somber but impressively steep. Many classics - Overhanging Bastion at VS being high in the grade is a classic nasty testpiece - just how awkward to these little buggers get! Not an ideal crag to make the transition from wall climbing to trad.
G14a, e; Map ref: 322 197

KENT/SUSSEX | DORSET | CORNWALL | DEVON | BRISTOL | SOUTH-WALES | MID-WALES | NORTH-WALES | LEICESTER | PEAKS | YORK-LANCS | CLEVELAND | KENDAL | LAKES | PENRITH | NEWCASTLE

⑱ *LANGDALE BOULDERS*

Some small boulders of the utmost quality and in the strangest of positions, forming part of a farmers wall. Please be exceptionally careful not to damage anything and keep the area spotless. Some fun problems and a nice setting. No climbing on the face just south of the stile - English heritage
G14a; Map ref: 314 058
(handy info in best tunes)
Dir: Leave Chapel Stile on the main road, soon as the road goes downhill, a footpath & gate is seen on the L, this leads to the boulders in 1 min.

Hotel Entrance
Hikers Bar

⑲ WHITE GHYLL *

One of the most impressive crags in the Lakes. Being tucked up high in a gully keeps the crag away from the touroids having heart attacks wandering up to langdale tarn, and shelters the crag from most of the cold winds in autumn, spring and even summer! The cliff is in two sections, a lower and upper crag. Both are very good, the lower crag offers the easier climbing, even so there are VS routes which weave there way through the overhangs on the upper crag. The best routes are to be found on the Upper Crag and of the 30 or so routes VS to E4, all are worth doing. A great crag. In total about 60 routes, all grades Diff upwards 150-250ft. W facing.
G14a, f; Map ref: 297 071

⑳ *PAVEY ARK* *

A very good summer crag but quite a walk up from the valley bottom, a good hour. SE facing and large. There are about 80 routes here and an abundance of Extremes, E1 to E6 but mostly around E2,E3. The climbing on the hard routes is continous and often with sustained interest. The easier routes are quite rambling. 100-300 ft routes. Alt 570m.
G14a, f; Map ref: 286 080

㉑ *RAVEN CRAG* *

The most accessible crag in the Langdale valley. Plenty of climbing in all grades. The rock here is suspect and soloing cannot be reccomended. Some of the routes are also quite pokey. A great crag though nevertheless offering some 70 routes in all grades Diff to E5. 100-200ft. S facing.
G14a, f; Map ref: 285 064

㉒ GIMMER CRAG * * *

This cliff is a sheer delight to climb upon. The climbs are not difficult, which is preferable since the situation high on the side of the Langdale Pikes in the evening sun, is there to be enjoyed in a relaxed frame of mind. There are about 60 routes mainly up to VS with half a dozen Extremes E1 to E3. W facing at 1600ft.
G14a, f; Map ref: 277 070

㉓ *BOWFELL BUTTRESS* *

The classic crag of the area. A very impressive High Mountain crag which needs good weather. NE facing with a dozen routes around Diff to Severe. The odd Extreme in this really Diff territory. 200-350ft routes all worth doing. A must in any ones climbing years.
G14a, f; Map ref: 245 069

㉔ *DOW CRAG* * * *

One of the finest crags in the Lake District. E facing and best in the morning. To climb all day here needs a very warm afternoon indeed. There are 5 large buttresses with almost 100 routes in all grades, 250-350ft. The best climbs are to the L of the crag and it is they that keep the sun the longest. A crag not to be missed. A good 80 min walk-in; 610m alt; 7.4 rock.
G14a, g; Map ref: 264 977

LEPOARD'S CRAWL, HVS t-5a, Dow Crag; Al Phizacklea - solo

KENT/SUSSEX | DORSET | CORNWALL | DEVON | BRISTOL | SOUTH-WALES | MID-WALES | NORTH-WALES | LEICSETER | PEAKS | YORK-LANCS | CLEVELAND | KENDAL | LAKES | PENRITH | NEWCASTLE

25 WALLOWBARROW CRAG

Not one of the greatest crags in the world, but the best cliff in the area, and what a beautiful valley it is; don't tell anyone about it - ok, sshhh! Nice climbing, especially in the lower grades, SW facing and only a 15-20min hike up to it. A low altitude crag at 150m, about 15 routes Severe-E1.
G14a, g; Map ref: 264 977

26 BURNT CRAG*

Another small crag but one for the stronger climbers to head for.
G14a, g; Map ref: 263 991

27 HERON CRAG

Quite a good crag offering many climbs of quality for which its appearance undermines. Not unduly steep but offers nothing to the Severe leader. All of the 20 or so routes here are between VS and E3. SE facing and very tempting if you know how far Esk Buttress actualy is. 200ft routes. Worth a visit. Further up the valley on the same side in about half a mile is Round Scar. This crag offers very good rock and plenty to accomodate the Severe leader.
G14a, b; Map ref: 222 030

28 ESK BUTTRESS**

An excellent crag with the finest position in the Lake District. The climbing is good but does not match the position except for the harder routes E3 upwards. The two classics Humdrum E3 and The Cumbrian E4 take the centre of the two obvious walls. It is the most remote crag in the Lakes, so much that nobody ever goes there except on a superb day. Expect to find it very busy. About 30 routes H Severe to E5, 250ft. S facing.
G14a, b; Map ref: 223 065

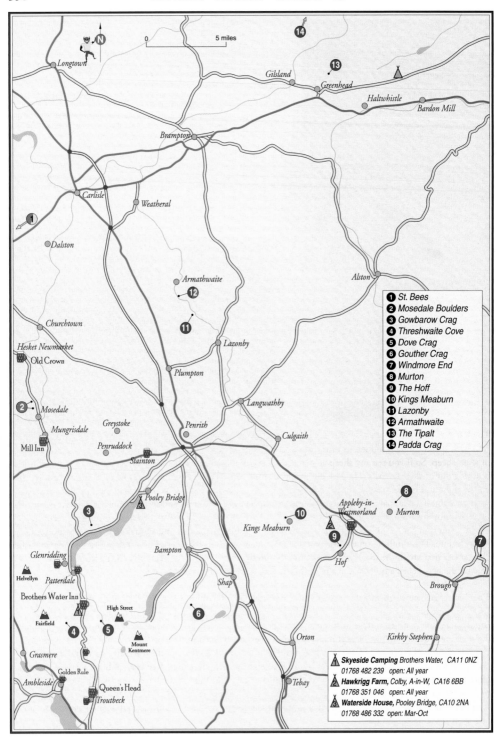

1 St. Bees
2 Mosedale Boulders
3 Gowbarow Crag
4 Threshwaite Cove
5 Dove Crag
6 Gouther Crag
7 Windmore End
8 Murton
9 The Hoff
10 Kings Meaburn
11 Lazonby
12 Armathwaite
13 The Tipalt
14 Padda Crag

Skyeside Camping Brothers Water, CA11 0NZ
01768 482 239 open: All year
Hawkrigg Farm, Colby, A-in-W, CA16 6BB
01768 351 046 open: All year
Waterside House, Pooley Bridge, CA10 2NA
01768 486 332 open: Mar-Oct

N

0   5 miles

The fast way into Borrowdale is generally from the M6 via Penrith, but be careful since the police patrol the main A66 with speed cameras hidden in vans - word about thinks that they would even resort to a speed camera hidden inside a sheep. So if you see any sheep anywhere looking highly suspicious, don't get caught out by the radar beaming out of their nostrils! The first hill that you come to before approaching Keswick, is Carrock Fell, set back on the right and home to some superb bouldering down at ground level, plus some good local pubs in the area. After this you have to make the choice of coping with the tourist coaches and seething masses of Borrowdale, or maybe opting for something different - for a change. This area around Ullswater though stunningly beautiful, is hardly a top spot for rock climbing, but does have a few hidden gems that you should seek out at least once in your lifetime. The climbing on the very good crags is quite hard, in the E2 and upwards category. There are other cliffs about that are in the local guidebooks and should be seeked out. Gouther crag in Swindale will most probably be the best bet of a quiet adventure for most, with some excellent climbing in the medium grades.

There are also areas further afield that will most probably only be of interest to local climbers that get fed up with the same old hike up to the fells. We include the sandstone and weird crags of the Eden Valley. Here the countryside is very quiet and beautiful, nice enough in itself. There is fun bouldering that can spice up a winter's day walk, and other outcrops of soft rock that will serve a purpose to some of us - who simply have to seek out a climbing venue in every part of Britain. The secret gem to visit is St. Bees sandstone cliffs and boulders over on the coast. It's not on this map since there is no climbing anywhere near there (see back of book map for location). Here there are giant soft cliffs with stainless steel bolts, sporty climbing in the harder grades. The boulders on the rock platform are the best fun, and give a host of problems with especially good landings for most of the time. It is somewhere completely different. An area to remember when you have ticked the routes you want to do, and just want some peace and quiet.

MOSEDALE BOULDERS, off Carrock Fell; Eddie Wright

① ST. BEES HEAD *

San	(15)		Alt-05m	30m	8.3
		35	120	☀	Zzz

A wonderful situation down by the sea. The routes generally go from a non tidal platform, and the bouldering is mixed between tidal and non tidal areas. Good stainless bolt, but still be careful since the rock itself is not over strong. Getting down the cliff requires a scramble and holding in-situ ropes- not the place for a pram.
G13a,14a Map ref: 939 145

② MOSEDALE BOULDERS *

Some wonderful volcanic boulders on the lower slopes of Carrock Fell. Good and rough texture for lovely mid grade problems, a few soggy landings and you want a few pads. Boots to walk around in. Very quick drying.
Map ref: 357 330

③ GOWBARROW CRAG

A crag on three terraces; low down are single pitch easy climbs for beginners; then the top areas are great and in a fabulous position and great feel good factor. Diff-E1. Top pitches need bolts like the routes lower down, perhaps!
G14a, 14e; Map ref: 414 205

ST. BEES BOULDERING, Stephen Murphy

GOWBARROW t-5b, Wobbly solo

TOP GEAR E4 t-6a, Threshwaite Cove; George Smith

❹ THRESHWAITE COVE *

Bird restriction, sometimes peregrines nest here so be prepared for a restr. 1/3-30/7. A very good crag completely away from the toroids. Not much here though around Diff, or even below E4. About 15 routes E2 to E6. Don't expect loads of protection here, but nevertheless the climbing is very good, bold but safe, just, well maybe not! SE facing and ideal on a good sunny morning. Go for it. 200ft. Yet another cliff called Raven Crag in the guide (1 of 13!)
G14a, 14e; Map ref: 420 112

❺ DOVE CRAG *

A crag for the super spurter super cruiser. NE facing, 100-250 ft routes of testing overhanging adrenalin driving exhilarating rock romping. Its cool aspect though demands a good dry spell, if it rains you're not going to get wet here. About 20 routes E2 to E6, but half of which are E4 and above. Long walk in, uphill.
G14a, 14e; Map ref: 375 110

❻ GOUTER CRAG *

One of the more secluded areas of the Lake District. A NW facing crag of good sound rock. Climbs 60-180ft in all grades Diff to E4, about 50 in total on different buttresses. Worth a visit especially if you feel that it is in the rain shadow of a light front.
G14a, 14e; Map ref: 515 127

KENT/SUSSEX · DORSET · CORNWALL · DEVON · BRISTOL · SOUTH-WALES · MID-WALES · NORTH-WALES · LEICESTER · PEAKS · YORK-LANCS · CLEVELAND · KENDAL · LAKES · PENRITH · NEWCASTLE

7 WINDMORE END

A quarried limestone edge that is 6-10 metres high, and has 100 small routes listed in an old guidebook. Most seem around Severe to VS and may prove a nice excursion.
Map ref: 822 169

8 MURTON

The crag is on an Army firing range, keep out if the red flag is flying. A limestone crag which starts off solid at the bottom and becomes interesting towards the top. About 10 routes 40-60ft in the Severe to HVS grades. SW facing with a fine view.
Map ref: 743 228

9 THE HOFF

A small 20ft crag of conglomerate limestone. The rock is pocketed and quite rough though unfortunatly is not reliable! It does face SW and dries very quickly. Not a bad crag in winter for a bit of amusement. About 20 routes in and around the Severe grades.
Map ref: 677 180

10 KINGS MEABURN

A different crag this one. A 30-40ft limestone crag resting on a bed of sandstone. The rock overhangs at the start with interest and then goes to limestone which cannot be regareded as totaly solid! About 50 climbs across the grades.
Map ref: 618 213

11 LAZONBY

Climbing is currently banned. A large escarpment of sandstone running along the W side of the river Eden. 100-130ft high buttresses offering about 50 routes in all grades. The rock is quite soft here and although one can lead one is wiser to top rope routes. Quite a spectacular crag.
Map ref: 527 423

12 ARMATHWAITE

One of the great bouldering areas in the N of England. The crag has some 100 routes in all grades Diff to E6 but the harder routes are done either as top rope problems or solo's. 10-50ft sandstone cliffs and boulders situated in pleasant woodland. SW facing and good at all time of the year, midges get a bit hungry in summer months though. Use a long sling to avoid rope grooves.
Map ref: 505 453

Bouldering at ARMATHWAITE, Bill Birkett

13 THE TIPALT

Permission to climb here must be sought from the farm over the road, and is freely given. Climbing is to be found here on sandstone, walls, roofs and everything to keep one amused for several hours, except the finishes, beware. NW facing but still manages to stay quite dry for most of the time. About 20 routes 20-40ft Diff to VS and countless harder problems. Worth a visit.
Map ref: 673 671

14 PADDA CRAG

Some excellent sandstone of the Northumberland variety. There are some 40 routes here Diff to 5c and countless of problems. 20 -30ft and S facing at 1100ft. A bit cold and damp in winter but gets the sunshine. A very remote crag, don't get caught here without an umbrella. Worth a visit.
Map ref: 650 788

KENT/SUSSEX | DORSET | CORNWALL | DEVON | BRISTOL | SOUTH-WALES | MID-WALES | NORTH-WALES | LEICSETER | PEAKS | YORK-LANCS | CLEVELAND | KENDAL | LAKES | PENRITH | NEWCASTLE

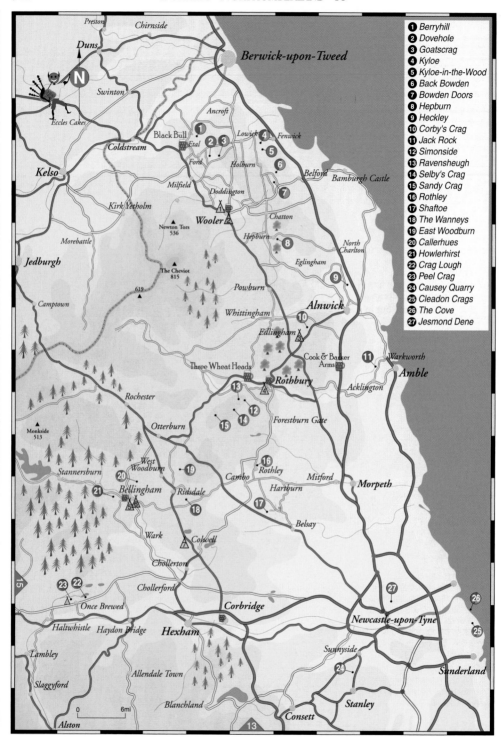

1. Berryhill
2. Dovehole
3. Goatscrag
4. Kyloe
5. Kyloe-in-the-Wood
6. Back Bowden
7. Bowden Doors
8. Hepburn
9. Heckley
10. Corby's Crag
11. Jack Rock
12. Simonside
13. Ravensheugh
14. Selby's Crag
15. Sandy Crag
16. Rothley
17. Shaftoe
18. The Wanneys
19. East Woodburn
20. Callerhues
21. Howlerhirst
22. Crag Lough
23. Peel Crag
24. Causey Quarry
25. Cleadon Crags
26. The Cove
27. Jesmond Dene

Northumberland is one of those places that seems to be a long way from anywhere. Nicely so, it's just like that when you get up here. Gone are the endless traffic jams, gone are the giant supermarkets, gone are the short summer evenings of the South. The whole landscape is beautiful; no giant mountains or alpine glaciers, but moorlands that seem to roll on forever in search of Scotland. The people speak with a lovely twang that often finishes on an up note, a real sign of optimism and good humour – well, for most of the time. The whole area is well criss-crossed, with amazingly straight roman roads that go up and down like a roller coaster ride; get your open top sports car up here and enjoy the summer months. The architecture is timeless, a wonderful mixture of stone built small hamlets, castles and even Holy Island. The two larger towns of Rothbury and Wooler, offer great venues for a quiet few days away climbing, enjoying the never ending spell of good weather.

Rothbury giant superstore   *Heavy traffic jams in Wooler*

For the climber it is a complete delight. Sandstone is the predominant rock here and comes in many different forms – from very soft, to exceptional gritstone. It has always been a popular area to climb, but in reality it is always quiet, busy climbing periods here signify that you actually might meet someone else at the crag. The most famous outcrops are Bowden and Kyloe in the North. They are climbing of very different contrasts and are deservedly famous. However,

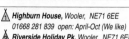
Pub at Etal

one should really look at all the other outcrops that there are to fully appreciate the depth of the quality in the climbing here. There are high level crags such as Simonside, to catch a breeze when it is sweltering hot in summer. Even Kyloe-in-the-Wood gets some glimmering sunshine in summer, rays that reflect off the golden pine needles of the forest floor. Then there is the ridiculously tiny humps of Shaftoe, not worth stopping to boulder on – until you do, and get hooked. It is an area of great diversity and interest, somewhere that offers more than you think.

⌂ **Highburn House,** Wooler, NE71 6EE
  01668 281 839 open: April-Oct (We like)
⌂ **Riverside Holiday Pk,** Wooler, NE71 6EE
  01668 281 447 open: Mar-Nov
⌂ **Cherry Tree Farm,** Edingham, NE66 2BL
  01665 574 635 open: Easter-Oct
⌂ **Cocquetdale Caravan.Pk,** Whitton, NE65 7RU
  01669 620 549 open: April-Oct(Nice camp area)
⌂ **Demesne Farm,** Bellingham, NE48 2BS
  01434 220 107 open: Mar-Oct
⌂ **Brown Rigg Cara-Pk,** Bellingham, NE48 2JY
  01434 220 175 open: Apr-Oct
⌂ **Elwood,** Barrassford, Hexham, NE48 4AN
  01434 681 421 open: All year

NORTHUMBERLAND BOULDERING
Guidebook

234pages - B & W
Sketches & Text,
A few colour photos
A5 paperback
Pub-2000
by John Earl & NMC

A very welcome bouldering guide that shows lots of areas and problems. A taster to the huge amount of bouldering here. Grades vary wildly, but at least it gets you climbing, thanks.

G-16a ⛰ 1-10,12,13,16,17,27 + a few more

NORTHUMBERLAND
Text - route book

336 pages - B & W
Text, some diags.
A few colour photos
pocket size
plastic cover
Pub-1989
by John Earl & NMC

A classic old style book, with just the written route descriptions. An update is planned! This still is a good book to the area, difficult to find a copy though.

G-16b ⛰ 1-23 plus a few others

KENT/SUSSEX | DORSET | CORNWALL | DEVON | BRISTOL | SOUTH-WALES | MID-WALES | NORTH-WALES | LEICESTER | PEAKS | YORK-LANCS | CLEVELAND | KENDAL | LAKES | PENRITH | NEWCASTLE

❶ BERRYHILL *

San ⏦ 🥾 ⛰ | Alt-75m | 15m | **8.1**
30 | 35 | ☀ | 👻

There is space on the right to park before the farm; also ask permission at the farm before climbing. It is a pleasant crag in a very quiet setting. The sandstone is soft, grainy and brittle. A mixture of cracks and slabs, be very careful if soloing. Some nice looking roofs, but holds come off on these. An extra rope for a top belay is useful. Good bouldering in the low-med grades, mainly south facing.

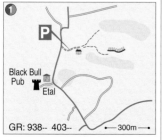

Black Bull Pub
Etal

GR: 938-- 403--   ← 300m →

❷ DOVEHOLE BOULDERS *

San ⑦ 🥾 ⛰ | Alt-155m | 6m | **8.3**
-- | 55 | ☀ | Zzz

Please drive up beyond the obvious boulders and ask permission to climb at the farm, this is at the end of the track - Fordwood Ho. These boulders are in a lovely quiet and picturesque setting. They are set in a nice grassy area, surrounded by pine trees. Can be a bit bad for midges on occoasions. The rock is very soft, so please be careful. Do not try to work any of the problems, as this will wear them out instantly. Use your feet carefully. The Bouldering is really only mediocre, but with

Lowick
Ford
❷
❸
P   P
Kimmerston   Fordwood Ho.
GR: 967-- 368--   ← 1 mile →

Scallywag's Wall 4b, Berryhill; Wobbly

❸ GOATS CRAG *

San ⑩ 🥾 ⛰ | Alt-155m | 12m | **8.2**
45 | 53 | 🐾 | Zzz

It is essential to ask for permission before climbing here. (Private Land) The crag is nice and high above the trees so it dries quickly. The rock here is a lot rougher and more solid than Dovehole boulders. Quite steep sections for good pumpy traverses. Many different variations on all the different problems.
G16a; Map ref: 976 371

NELLIE t-5c, Doveholes; Jingo

❹ KYLOE CRAG **

San ⑤ 🥾 ⛰ | Alt-108m | 16m | **8.1**
90 | 40 | ☀ | 👻

A very good crag indeed, with some lovely sandstone of varying styles and quality. Big nice slabs that can get a bit airy, then giant overhangs to really scare you; some fragile walls with delicate holds too. Leader placed cams in the cracks do not always hold falls, so climb with care. Dries out quickly and is almost an all year round venue. There are a lot of good boulder problems on the

PARITY Hard Severe t-4c, Kyloe Crag; Jingo solo

❺ *KYLOE-IN-THE-WOOD* *

| San | 19 | | Alt-154m | 12m | 8.0 |

102   90

This outcrop is one of the great hidden gems of the North East. It lurks, deep inside a thick plantation forest, and is neither easy to find, or easy to get up. It is very heavily shaded by trees. This

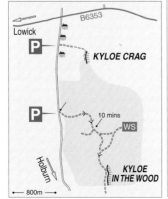

Kyloe-in-the-Wood; Jingo finding more difficulty understanding the guidebook; than the 6b.

leads to a sombre feeling, but completely enchanted at the same time. There are a lot of routes, but these are rarely climbed since the finishes are very overgrown. Hard, cutting edge bouldering is the

real attraction here because the rock overhangs almost everywhere. The texture is sharp and hard-finegrained - similar to parts of Fontainebleau. Expect a full workout here, but come fit enough

KENT/SUSSEX · DORSET · CORNWALL · DEVON · BRISTOL · SOUTH-WALES · MID-WALES · NORTH-WALES · LEICESTER · PEAKS · YORK-LANCS · CLEVELAND · KENDAL · LAKES · PENRITH · NEWCASTLE

BOWDEN DOORS

⑥ *BACK BOWDEN* * *

San	10	👟	Alt-170m	14m	8.1
	70	75	❄	🌙

Parking: You must not block the gate to any field at any time, this is a serious issue here. A very good crag and a lot more sheltered than its neighbour. Feels very high in places reaching a full 50ft. Very good climbing in all grades but quite strenuous. Some very good roof problems here. Always worth a visit. (May be a restriction on evening climbing - check on the web first)
G16a, b; Map ref: 065 336

⑦ *BOWDEN DOORS* * * *

San	5	👟	Alt-160m	15m	8.2
			--	--	❄	Zzz

The most famous cliff in Northumberland and deservedly so. A sandstone bulging cliff with invariably difficult starts and very popular for bouldering.

There are many bigger routes that go to the top of the wave and over the lip, but they are quite scary, and finding a belay at the top isn't straightforward either. The rock is quite soft in a lot of parts and erosion is a big issue. Please think before you overcrank on delicate holds, or place runners that will simply snap the rock in a fall. The view and position is wonderful, perhaps best at sunset with a slight wind to keep away the midges. Check latest access and parking issues.
G16a, b; Map ref: 070 326

⑧ *HEPBURN*

A small bouldering location with a great view and some proper highball problems. Rock is pretty good quality and gets the advantage of being high up to dry quickly, west facing, lovely and sunny location. Very easy parking in a proper car park and access is not a problem generally. About 60 problems on scattered boulders.
G16a; Map ref: 073 247

⑨ *HECKLEY*

A very small crag of overhanging sandstone with a handful of routes on it. Handy if passing through to relieve that desperate climbing urge when bored stiff driving up the A1. About 25 boulder problems, including traverses, faces NE and can stay dry in the rain.
G16a, b; Map ref: 187 165

GR: 073-- 247--   ◄—— 3/4 mi ——►

MAIN ARETE t-5a, Hepburn; Jingo solo

KENT/SUSSEX | DORSET | CORNWALL | DEVON | BRISTOL | SOUTH-WALES | MID-WALES | NORTH-WALES | LEICESTER | PEAKS | YORK-LANCS | CLEVELAND | KENDAL | LAKES | PENRITH | NEWCASTLE

CAIRN SLAB, Severe, Simonside; Jingo solo

⑩ CORBY'S CRAG*

A very good crag with about 60 climbs in all grades and some very good bouldering also. Quite steep 30-50ft and facing NW. Quite sheltered but best in the late afternoon. Very handy for those who dislike walking. Limited bouldering on quite soft rock (8.2)
G16a, b; Map ref: 127 101

⑪ JACK ROCK

A sandstone crag offering about 30 climbs 40ft, grades Severe upwards. The crag is quite steep and does not lend itself to easy routes, or even routes easily climbed. Worth a look.
G16a, b; Map ref: 235 044

⑫ SIMONSIDE*

An excellent crag with lots of climbing in all grades. 1300ft up with about 80 routes, 20-50 ft. N facing and not the place to go in winter except on a walk to Selby's Cove. The rock is very good here and I would classify it as gritstone (7.3) There is bouldering all over the moors on isolated boulders that is great when you want something different and out of the way. Wherever you climb, it's a long walk in - 40 mins, but a beautiful walk at that.
G16a, b; Map ref: 025 988

⑬ RAVENSHEUGH*

Good compact sandstone/gritstone cliffs at 1300ft, N facing. A summer spot. There are about 100 climbs here in all grades easy to very hard. A fantastic view and well worth the walk on a fine day, at any time of year. Worth a visit, especially if you combine it with Simonside. Walking boots are handy for both crags since you have to sometimes leave the main, well drained track.
G16a, b; Map ref: 025 988

⑭ SELBY'S COVE

A small and compact crag up to 13m high. Set in a beautiful position and a bit of a sun trap, there are around 25 routes here across most of the grades. Worth remembering about.
G16a, b; Map ref: 023 976

⑮ SANDY CRAG

Access issue: This is a grouse moor 1/ 3-31/7. So check for up to date restrictions on web. There are about 30 routes here of mixed quality and difficulty. The bouldering however is very good indeed, some of the best in the county. 20-70ft. Worth a visit.
G16a, b; Map ref: 968 972

⑯ ROTHLEY*

There are about 15 routes here, but the venue is far better known as an excellent bouldering venue, with over 100 problems - just about all variations on slopers, really mean and nasty, Also some excellent aretes, and a few mean high balls. (Mean midges hang out here - we had to bail out eventually)
G16a, b; Map ref: 043 887

Wobbly at Wotherly

⑰ SHAFTOE*

An area with around 300 different problems. When you first arrive, you are not impressed - that I can promise you. When you look at most of the problems, you are not impressed either. When you start climbing, it just gets better and better, and you finally get into the groove of the short and difficult problems. A spot - only for a true boulderer

who can appreciate sitting starts and eliminate lines. Rock quality varies from superb to soft; spongy grass underneath that could easilly be very boggy, 10-15 min walk in - and prey you have a wind to keep the midges at bay. When you drive up the private track to the parking, keep your speed right down.
G16a; Map ref: 054 824

⑱ GREAT WANNEY
A very good area offering the nearest really good climbing to Newcastle. 60-70 climbs in all grades Diff to 6c. Quite exposed at 1000ft and steep offering easy routes to those with big biceps. 30-50ft. Always worth a visit. Excellent for bouldering.
G16b; Map ref: 935 835

⑲ EAST WOODBURN
Some small crags that offer around 12-15 routes. Some nice climbs away from it all and with a very nice and open setting, SW facing. Please close all the gates, and don't swing on them! Park off the road too.
G16b; Map ref: 917 873

⑳ CALLERHUES
One of the great crags in the area. About 60 routes and lots of very fine bouldering. SW facing at 1000 ft. There is not a lot here for the low grade climber but one can always struggle up the 5a climbs on a top rope. The crag is about 10m high and with quite good landings! Worth a visit, beautiful spot.
G16b; Map ref: 854 862

㉑ HOWLERHIRST
A good 40ft sandstone outcrop with about 10 routes on it in the middle grades VS to 6a. W facing and excellent for bouldering in the afternoon. Worth a glance.
G16b; Map ref: 787 830

㉒ CRAG LOUGH
A well established crag of quartz dolerite of up to 80ft in height. About 100 routes in all grades Diff upwards. Something for everyone here. N facing over a lake. Bad in the summer months for midges. Worth a visit. Quite popular.
G16b; Map ref: 765 679

㉓ PEEL CRAG
Generally the same as Crag Lough but more broken and vegetated. N facing with about 80 routes, half of which are in the lower grades around Severe.
G16b; Map ref: 755 677

CORBY'S CRAG

㉔ CAUSEY QUARRY
A quarry of mixed opinion. Mostly soft rubbish but with a top rope plenty of good climbing can be found here. It is requested though that you use a long sling at the top to prevent undue wear. Sandstone up to 60ft with about 40 routes and endless variations. Worth a trip if stuck in Newcastle.
G12a; Map ref: 204 560

㉕ CLEADON CRAGS
Some climbing in some old limestone quarries, and some overhanging buttresses. Maybe worth an investigation. About 80 short routes and problems.
G12a; Map ref: 391 630

㉖ THE COVE
Bouldering on a 7m limestone overhanging cove, investigate this one.
G12a; Landranger 88 - Map ref: 394 662

㉗ JESMOND DENE
An urban sandstone bouldering spot with around 40-50 problems. A bit woody and can be humid and damp, better at Aut-spring without leaves.
G16a; Map ref: 254 672

❓ CALLER BOULDERS [SAND]
Some completely duff boulders not to be confused with Callerhues.

SHAFTOE; Ryan Thompson & Mark Todd

ABC; Association of British climbing walls;
Alpine Club & Mountain Library; *55 Charlotte Road, London EC2A 3QT*
Tel: 020 7613 0755
AMI - Association of Mountain Instructors; *Tel: 01690 720 314*
Austrian Alpine Club-UK; *2 Church Road, Welwyn Garden City, Herts, AL8 6PT*
Tel: 01707 386 740
BMC; British Mountaineering Council; *177-179 Burton Road, Manchester, M20 2BB*
Tel: 0870 010 4878
BMG; British Mountain Guides; *Address at MLTUK.*
Tel: 01690 720 386
CWMA; Climbing Wall Manufacturers Association;
www.cwma.co.uk
MCS; Mountaineering Council of Scotland; *The Old Granary, West Mill St, Perth PH1 5QP*
Tel: 01738 638 227
MLTUK; *Mountain leader training UK; Siabod Cottage, Capel Curig, Conwy, LL24 0ET*
Tel: 01690 720 272
MLT-England; *Tel: 01690 720 314*
MLT-Wales; *Tel: 01690 720 361*
MLT-Scotland (Glenmore Lodge); *Tel: 01479 861 248*
MEF; Mount Everest Foundation; *Gowrie, Cardwell Close, Preston, PR4 1SH*
Tel: 01772 635 346
Mountain Rescue Council for E&W; *69 Werneth Rd, Simmondley, Glossoop SK13 6NF*
Tel: 01457 869 506
Plas-Y-Brenin; National Mountain Centre; *Capel Curig, LL24 0ET*
Tel: 01690 720 214
Ramblers Association; *Camelford House, 87-90 Albert Embankment, London SE1 7TW*
Tel: 20 7339 8500
Royal Geographic Society; *1 Kensington Gore, London SW7 2AR*
Tel: 20 7591 3000
Sport Industries Federation; *Fed House, N.A.C. Stoneleigh Park, Warwicshire, CV8 3RF*
Tel: 02476 414 999
Ski Club of GB; *57-63 Church Road, Wimbledon, SW19 5SB*
Tel: 0845 458 0780
UIAA; Union Internationale des Associations d'Alpinisme; *Postfach CH-3000 Bern 23, Suisse*
Tel: 00 41 31 3701 828
YHA-Youth Hostels Association; *PO Box 6028, Matlock, DE4 3XB*
Tel: 01629 592 710

CLIMBING EQUIPMENT CONTACTS:

Allcord; *Ilford Road, Newcastle-Upon-Tyne NE2 3NX*
Tel: 0191 284 8444
AMG Outdoor Ltd; *2 Kelburn Bus.Pk. Port Glasgow, Scotland, PA14 6TD*
Tel: 01475 746 000
Arc'teryx; *distributor - Big Stone*
Asolo; *distributor - Lowe Alpine*
Barbour; *Simonside, South Shields, Tyne and Wear, NE34 9PD*
Tel: 0191 455 4444
Berghaus; *12 Colima Ave, Sunderland Bus-Pk, Sunderland, SSR5 3XB*
Tel: 0191 516 5700   Fax: 0191 516 5601

Beta Climbing designs;
Tel: 114 221 8332
Beyond Hope; Saddleworth Buis-Ctr, Delph, Oldham, OL3 5DF
Tel: 01457 877 081
Big Stone; Clifton Works, John St, Sheffield, S2 4QU
Tel: 0114 263 4261
Black Diamond; distributor - First Ascent
Boreal UK; 2nd Floor, The Portergate, 257 Ecclesall Rd, Sheffield S11 8NK
Tel: 0114 209 6220   Fax: 0114 209 6001
Burton McCall; 163 Parker Drive, Leicester, LE4 0JP
Tel: 0116 234 4611
Camp; distributor - Allcord
Campingaz; Gordano Gate, Portishead, Bristol, BS20 7GG
Tel: 01275 845 024
Cassin; distributor - D.B. Outdoor Systems
Charlet Moser; distributor - Lyon Equipment
Cicerone Outdoor Books; 2 Police Square, Milnthorpe, LA7 7PY
Tel: 01539 562 069
Coleman UK; See Campingaz
Cordee Maps & Books; 3a De Montfort St, Leicester, LE1 7HD
Tel: 0116 254 3579
Dark Peak Marketing; 73 Sunfield Lane, Diggle, Oldham, OL3 5PT
Tel: 01457 875 168
D.B.Outdoor Systems; Parkside Bus-Pk, Kendal, Cumbria, LA9 7EN
Tel: 01539 733 842
Deuter; distributor - D.B. Outdoor Systems
DMM International; Y Glyn, Llanberis, LL55 4EL
Tel: 01286 872 222
E9; distributor Beta climbing designs
Edelrid; distributor - D.B. Outdoor Systems
Edelweiss; distributor High Places
Equip Outdoor Tech; Wimsey Way, Somercoates, Alfreton, Derbs, DE55 4LS
Tel: 1773 601 870
First Ascent; Units 2-7, Limetree Buis-Pk, Matlock, Derbs DE4 3EJ
Tel: 01629 580 484
First Choice Expedition Foods; High Raindale, Stape, Pickering, YO18 8HX
Tel: 01751 473 330
Five Ten; distributor Dark Peak Marketing
Garmin Europe; Unit 5, The Quadrangle, Abbey Park Indus-Est, Romsey, SO51 9AQ
Tel: 0870 850 1242
Gore; Simpson Parkway, Kirkton Campus, Livingston, EH54 7BH
Tel: 01506 460 123
Grivel; distributor - Mountain Boot Co.
Haglofs Scandanavia; The Bridge, Langford Rd, Lower Langford, N.Somerset, BS40 5HU
Tel: 01934 863 561
Harvey Maps; 12-22 Main Street, Doune, FK16 6BJ
Tel: 01786 841 202
HB Climbing; 24 Llandegai Indus-Est, Bangor, Gwynedd, LL57 4YH
Tel: 01248 370 813

Helly Hansen; *Regent House, Clinton Ave, Nottingham, NG5 1AZ*
Tel: 0115 960 8797
High Places; *Unit 34, Stroud Buis-Ctr, Stonedale Rd, Oldends Lane, Stonehouse, GL10 3SA*
Tel: 01453 822 840
Jack Wolfskin; *3 Tynedale Mews, Market Place, Corbridge, Northumberland, NE45 5AW*
Tel: 01434 633 900
Kayland; *distributor Allcord*
Kong; *distributor High Places*
Lost Arrow; *distributor Big Stone*
Lowe Alpine; *Ann St, Kendal, LA9 6AA*
Tel: 01539 740 840   info@lowealpine.co.uk
Lucky; *distributor High Places*
Lyon Equipment; *Rise Hill Mill, Dent, Sedbergh, LA10 5QL*
Tel: 01539 625 493
MacPac; *11 Moncur Place, Christchurch 8002, New Zealand*
Tel: 00 64 3338 1106
Mad Rock; *distributor DB outdoor systems*
Marmmut; *distributor - DMM*
Marmot; *distributor - Mountain Works Ltd.*
Megagrip; *47 Oldham Road, Delph, Oldham, OL3 5EB*
Tel: 0145 787 8875
Merrell Europe; *GCS Centre, Vale Lane, Bedminster, Bristol, BS3 5RU*
Tel: 0117 963 5263
Metolius; *distributor Beyond Hope*
Millet Ropes; *distributor - Allcord*
Montane; *Unit 21, North Seaton Ind-Est, Ashington, Northumberland, NE63 0YB*
Tel: 01670 522 300
Moon; *www.benmoon.co.uk*
Tel: 01539 739 314
Mountain Boot Company; *Unit 5, New York Way, New York Ind-Est, Wallsend, NE27 0QF*
Tel: 0191 296 0212
Mountain Equipment; *Redfern House, Dawsern St, Hyde, Cheshire, SK14 1RD*
Tel: 0161 366 5020
Mountain Hardwear; *16 Mill St, Oakham, Rutland, LE15 6EA*
Tel: 01572 771 133
Mountain Technology; *Old Ferry Road, Onich, Fort William, PH33 6SA*
Tel: 01855 821 222
Mountain Works; *Parkside Buis-Pk, Parkside Road, Kendal, LA9 7EN*
Tel: 01539 739 314
Nikwax; *Unit F, Durgates Ind-Est, Wadhurst, East Sussex, TN5 6DF*
Tel: 01892 786 400
North Cape; *Velos House, Froxmer St, Manchester, M18 8EF*
Tel: 0161 230 8333
North Face; *Aynam Mills, Little Aynam, Kendal, LA9 7AH*
Tel: 01539 738 882
Ordnance Survey; *Romsey Road, Soton, Hants, SO16 4GU*
Tel: 023 8030 5030
Petzl; *distributor - Lyon Equipment*
Prana; *distributor - Beyond Hope*

Rab Carrington (Manufacture); *32 Edward St, Sheffield, S3 7GB*
Tel: 0114 275 7544
Rab Downware; *distributor Equip*
Red Chilli; *distributor - Wild Country*
Rock Empire Harness etc; *distributor Equip*
Roca Ropes; *distributor Equip*
Rock Pillars; *distributor Equip*
Rock Technologies; *Holmlea, Shaw Hall Bank Road, Greenfield, Oldham OL3 7LD*
Tel: 01457 871 801
Rohan; *30 Maryland Road, Tongwell, Milton Keynes, MK15 8HN*
Tel: 01908 517 900
Rosker; *Unit 13, Quay Lane Ind-Est, Gosport, Hants, PO12 4LJ*
Tel: 02392 528 711
Royal Robbins UK; *see Mountain Hardwear*
Salewa UK; *Unit 13, Blencathra Buis-Ctr, Threlkeld Quarry, Keswick, CA12 4TR*
Tel: 01768 779 877
Saloman GB; *Jays Close, Viables Buis-Pk, Basingstoke, RG22 4BS*
Tel: 01256 479 555
Scarpa; *distributor - Mountain Boot Co.*
Sigg; *distributor Burton McCall*
Silva; *Fleming Rd, Kirkton Campus, Livingston, West Lothian, EH54 7BN*
Tel: 01506 406 277
Sportiva; *distributor Big Stone*
Sprayway;
Tel: 0800 605 050
Terra Nova Tents; *Ecclesbourne Park, Alfreton, Derbs, DE55 4RF*
Tel: 01773 833 300
Teva; *distributor AMG*
Thermos; *BHL, Parkside Ind-Est, Middleton Grove, Leeds, LS11 5BX*
Tel: 0113 276 3456
Tilley International; *30/32 High St, Frimley, Surrey, GU16 7JD*
Tel: 01276 691 996
Tomen Altimeters; *distributor High Places*
Trangia; *distributor AMG*
Troll; *distributor HB*
Ultrapods; *distributor High Places*
Vango; *distributor AMG*
Victorinax; *distributor Burton McCall*
Weird Fish; *distributor Freedom Sailboards Limited*
Wild Country Ltd; *Meverill Road, Tideswell, Buxton, Derbs SK17 8PV*
Tel: 01298 871 010
Zamberlan; *Buis-Pk 8, Barnett Wood Lane, Leatherhead, Surrey, KT22 7DG*
Tel: 01372 377 713

CLIMBING WALL MANUFACTURERS:
Bendcrete; Aqueduct Mill, Tame St, Stalybridge, Cheshire, SK15 1ST
Tel: 0161 338 3046
DR Climbing Walls; 39 Steps, Leeds Road, Old Pool Bank, Otley, W. Yorks LS21 3BR
Tel: 0113 284 2369
Entreprises (UK) Ltd; Eden Works, Kelbrook, Lancs, BB18 6SH
Tel: 01282 444 800   Fax: 01282 444 801   info@ep-uk.com
King Kong Climbing Walls; Unit 1C, Aspatria Buis-Pk, Aspatria, Cumbria, CA7 3DP
Tel: 01697 323 444
Rockworks; Ouseburn Workshops, 36 Lime St, Newcastle-Upon-Tyne, NE1 2PN
Tel: 0191 230 3793

CLIMBING WALL HOLDS:
Beacon Holds; Beacon Climbing Wall, North Wales
Holdz; 01924 265 222
Metolius; See Beyond Hope Equipment
Wagerholds; 76 Victoria Park Grove, Bramley, Leeds, LS13 2RD
Tel: 0161 338 304

INSURANCE:
BMC; British Mountaineering Council; Freepost NAT 11244, Manchester M20 7ZA
Tel: 0870 010 4878
Sportscover direct;
Tel: 0117 922 6222

SHOE RESOLING:
Cheshire Shoe Repairs; 64 London Road, Stockton Heath, Warrington WA4 6HR
Tel: 01925 269 777
Feet First; Unit 4-5, Foundry Street Ind-Est, Chesterfield, S41 9AU
Tel: 01246 260 795

ASSOCIATED CONTACTS:
Brand Events; 1st floor, Earls Court Exhibition Ctr, Warwick Rd, London SW5 9TA
Tel: 020 7471 1080
Ernest Press;
Tel: 0141 637 5492
Go Outdoors; Outdoor Industries Association, Morritt House, 58 Station Approach, Ruislip HA4 6SA
Tel: 020 8842 1111
Greenshires Publishing; Telford Way Indus-Est, Kettering, Northants, NN16 8UN
Tel: 01536 382 500
Warners Group Publishing; West St, Bourne, PE10 9PH
Tel: 01778 391 181

FILMING & LOCATION SPECIALISTS:
Jingo Wobbly Climbing; Holmwood House, 52 Roxborough Park, Harrow, London HA1 3AY
Tel: 020 8423 6056
Mountain Experience; Pike View Barn, Whitehough Head, Chinley, Stockport, SK12 6BX
Tel: 01663 750 160

Mountain Leader Training UK (MLTUK) is the umbrella organisation that administers the three higher "national governing body" awards in mountaineering in the UK:

The Mountaineering Instructor Certificate (MIC)
Mountaineering Instructor Award (MIA)
European Mountain Leader Award (EML)

Supporting these awards, and providing a direct route towards gaining them are the summer & winter Mountain Leader (ML) awards, the Walking Group Leaders Award (WGL) and the Single Pitch Award (SPA). The home nation Boards in England, Wales, Northern Ireland and Scotland (MLTE, MLTW, MLTNI and MLTS) work in close cooperation with MLTUK, the BMC, and course providers to ensure that the very best level of training and instruction are available.

WGL   The Walking Group Leader Award is the award for leaders of hill walking groups not venturing into mountainous terrain, but into country known as upland, moor, bog, fell, hill or down. As such it should not be possible to stray onto terrain where movement on steep or rocky ground is required. This relatively new scheme is designed to complement the long established ML Award.

ML   If you want to improve your hill walking and navigation skills, a mountain leader (ML) will be able to help. ML award holders are qualified to lead groups in remote mountain terrain. Summer ML is for mountain walking in non winter conditions which can occur at all times of year. The Winter ML is specifically for leadership of hillwalking parties in winter conditions.

EML   The European Mountain Leader Award enables the holder to lead walking parties within the European Community. EML holders are walking guides not climbing guides and are specialists in the mountain areas below permanent snow and glaciers. They have a passion for the mountains and an environmental knowledge that will enhance any mountain journey.

SPA   A Single Pitch Award holder is able to lead and supervise groups on single pitch crags and indoor walls. SPA holders run rock climbing taster sessions and can teach belaying skills and abseiling, but they are not qualified to teach lead climbing. To complete an SPA the holder will have been climbing for 18 months or more and have been assessed by an MIA (see below).

MIA   If you would like to improve your climbing skills, go multi pitch climbing, scramble along an exposed ridge or hill walk in any conditions (other than winter) a Mountaineering Instructor Award (MIA) holder will give you a good day out. The scheme trains and assesses people in the skills required for instruction of mountaineering including all aspects of rock climbing.

MIC   The Mountain Instructors Cerificate covers the same remit as MIA but also includes snow and ice climbing. An MIC is therefore qualified to instruct all aspects of hillwalking rockclimbing and mountaineering in summer and winter conditions. The Association Mountaineering Instructors (AMI) is the representative body of professionally qualified mountaineering instructors in the British Isles. As such it represents all MIA's and MIC's

GUIDE   British Mountain Guides hold the international professional qualification to instruct and guide all climbing and mountaineering activities including ski mountaineering. Qualified guides operate world-wide and have considerable experience. They offer all types of training and lead tailored ascents in Britain and the Alps. Some guides lead expeditions to remote and high-altitude peaks.

AALA   Not a mountaineering award at all but the Adventure Activities Licensing Authority. If you are looking for a commercial course at an outdoor activity centre for anyone under the age of 18 the centre must hold an Adventure Activities Licence. This means that their safety and risk assessment procedures have been inspected. It is reasonable to ask a centre which activities they are licensed for and to see a copy of the licence.

International bouldering grades		Sport grades	Technical grades		
Font(F)	V	Sport(S)	GB(T)	D	USA
1-2	-	1-3	1-3	1-3	5.5
3	Vb-	4	4a	4	5.7
4a	Vb	5	4c	5	5.8
4b	V0-	6a	5a	6	5.9
4c	V0	6b	5b	7	5.10b
5a	V1	6c	5c	7+	5.11a
5b	V2	6c	5c	8-	5.11b
5c	V3	7a	6a	8	5.11d
6a	V4	7a+	6a	8+	5.12a
6b	V5	7b	6b	8+	5.12b
6c	V6	7b+	6b	9-	5.12c
7a	V7	7b+	6c	9-	5.12c
7a+	V8	7c	6c	9	5.12d
7b	V8	8a	6c	9+	5.13b
7c	V9	8a+	7a	10-	5.13c
7c+	V10	8b	7a	10	5.13d
8a	V11	8b+	7a	10+	5.14a
8a+	V12	8c	7a	11-	5.14b
8b	V13	8c+	7b	11-	5.14c
8b+	V14	9a	7b	11	5.14d
8c	V15	9a+	7b	11+	5.15a

Grades: We always use a prefix to our grades because of the common use of Font, Sport, Trad and V grades. This also allows an E grade extreme route, to even have a V grade or sport grade, which may be helpful.